THE COLUMNIST

THE COLUMNIST

LEAKS, LIES, AND LIBEL IN DREW PEARSON'S WASHINGTON

DONALD A. RITCHIE

OXFORD
UNIVERSITY PRESS

OXFORD

UNIVERSITY PRESS

Oxford University Press is a department of the University of Oxford. It furthers
the University's objective of excellence in research, scholarship, and education
by publishing worldwide. Oxford is a registered trade mark of Oxford University
Press in the UK and certain other countries.

Published in the United States of America by Oxford University Press
198 Madison Avenue, New York, NY 10016, United States of America.

© Oxford University Press 2021

Library of Congress Cataloging-in-Publication Data
Names: Ritchie, Donald A., 1945– author.
Title: The columnist : leaks, lies, and libel in Drew Pearson's Washington / Donald A. Ritchie.
Description: New York : Oxford University Press, 2021. | Includes bibliographical references and index.
Identifiers: LCCN 2020057180 (print) | LCCN 2020057181 (ebook) |
ISBN 9780190067588 (hardback) | ISBN 9780190067601 (epub)
Subjects: LCSH: Pearson, Drew, 1897–1969. | Journalists—United States—Biography. |
United States—Politics and government—20th century.
Classification: LCC PN4874.P38 R58 2021 (print) | LCC PN4874.P38 (ebook) |
DDC 070.092 [B]—dc23
LC record available at https://lccn.loc.gov/2020057180
LC ebook record available at https://lccn.loc.gov/2020057181

DOI: 10.1093/oso/9780190067588.001.0001

1 3 5 7 9 8 6 4 2

Printed by LSC Communications, United States of America

Frontispiece: The fedora became Drew Pearson's trademark once Lee
Hats and later Adam Hats became his radio sponsors. *Lyndon B. Johnson
Presidential Library, B-8526-12*

For Jeff, Jack, and Boone

"Democracies die behind closed doors. . . .
When the government begins closing doors,
it selectively controls information rightly belonging to the people.
Selective information is misinformation."

—Judge Damon J. Keith
Detroit Free Press v. Ashcroft, Sixth Circuit, 2002

CONTENTS

ACKNOWLEDGMENTS

———❖———

I FIRST BECAME AWARE OF the "Washington Merry-Go-Rosund" column when I attended graduate school at the University of Maryland in 1967 and began reading the *Washington Post*. None of the papers I grew up reading in New York City had carried it. I followed the column during Drew Pearson's last two years, until I was drafted—unexpectedly into the marine corps—three months before he died. When I returned to graduate school in 1971, Jack Anderson had charge of the column, which I followed compulsively throughout Watergate.

During the 1970s while writing my first book about James Landis, who served in the government from the New Deal to the New Frontier, I interviewed many of the political figures about whom Drew Pearson wrote and who also appear in this book. In 1976 I joined the staff of the Senate Historical Office, where I interviewed others and was in turn interviewed by news reporters in search of historical information. My curiosity about how they gathered news, and the accuracy of reporting, led to three other books: *Press Gallery: Congress and the Washington Correspondents* (1991); *American Journalists: Getting the Story* (1997); and *Reporting from Washington: The History of the Washington Press Corps* (2005). By chance, Drew Pearson appeared in all three.

Full credit for inspiring this book belongs to Tyler Abell. I met Bess and Tyler Abell through mutual friends, and Bess and my wife, Anne, served together on the national advisory board of the University of Kentucky Libraries. We enjoyed their gracious hospitality at Merry-Go-Round Farm with its panoramic views of the Potomac River from their terrace. When I retired as Senate Historian, Tyler approached me—several times—to suggest that I explore Drew Pearson's career, which he feared was fading into the recesses of historical memory. He offered complete access to Pearson's papers, diaries, and family oral histories, taking me up into the hayloft of his barn to uncover file cabinets filled with records destined to go to the Lyndon B. Johnson Presidential Library, with the rest of Pearson's papers. Tyler also extended ready advice but made no effort to shape my interpretation of these records. His assistant, Christy Thrailkill, also helped to provide material for the book.

Tyler and Bess hired Brien Williams, a skilled oral historian, to interview members of Pearson's family and his staff. This project proved especially fortuitous when Kay Raley Watkins arrived for her interview with two large archival boxes filled with correspondence that Drew Pearson had personally culled from his massive manuscript collection to write his never-completed memoir. These were the items Pearson thought best represented his life. They served as a map to guide me through the immense amount of correspondence he produced throughout his life, on top of forty years of daily newspaper columns, which astonishingly are all available online in their original format through American University's Digital Research Archives.

Historians depend upon archivists, and I had great assistance from Martha Murphy and Richard Hunt at the National Archives; Claudia Anderson and Brian McNerney at the Johnson Library; Leslie Nellis and Austin Arminio at American University's special collections library; Jay Wyatt and Jody Brumage at the Robert C. Byrd Center for Congressional History and Legislation, at Shepherd University; and the staff of George Washington University's special collections and the Library of Congress's manuscripts division.

Chris Banks at the LBJ Library, Jeff Shlosberg at the National Press Club Archives, and Heather Moore at the Senate Historical Office were especially helpful in locating photographs.

I owe special thanks to the always supportive staff of the Senate Library, especially to Meghan Dunn, Zoe Davis, and Nancy Kerwin, who over the years gave me access to their rich collection of books on American politics and government and ordered additional material from the Library of Congress. As Senate Historian I depended enormously on the Senate

Library, and I greatly appreciate their extending those same courtesies and cooperation to an emeritus.

Texas Humanities director Mike Gillette invited me to participate in a teachers' workshop in Austin, which offered the opportunity to research at the Lyndon B. Johnson Library. Other friends read and commented on various chapters in the manuscript, including Carl Ashley, Tracy Campbell, Rodney Joseph, Keith Olson, Jim Sayler, Sam Walker, and Matt Wasniewski. Judi Jennings provided insights from her research on Quakers. David Hollinger alerted me to the American missionaries' role in leaking secrets about British rule in India; and Michael Hopkins provided a telling document about British attitudes toward Pearson. Michael Devine, former director of the Truman Library, shared his expertise on that era. Irv Gellman offered advice on Richard Nixon, Larry Tye on Joe McCarthy, and Harvey Klehr on David Karr. Tim Chambless gave me access to interviews he conducted with Jack Anderson. Felicia Cameron provided information about her grandfather Drew Pearson's role with the Friendship Train. And Ken Rudin introduced me to the Committee to Horsewhip Drew Pearson.

Michael Birkner shared his research into the Sherman Adams saga. Long before I began pursuing Drew Pearson, Michael invited me to speak at the annual Eisenhower seminar at Gettysburg College. There I participated in a panel discussion with three veteran reporters who covered Eisenhower and worked closely with Jim Hagerty: Bob Clark, Sid Davis, and Al Spivak. Their vivid recollections shaped my understanding of the Eisenhower-Hagerty relationship for this book.

Nancy Toff has been my longtime editor, friend, and fellow conference goer. I learned long ago to trust her judgment and follow her advice, implicitly.

My wife, Anne, deserves profuse thanks for her love, encouragement, and understanding. She has cheered me up and kept me going over the years, as well as providing her own insights as an archivist and oral historian. I dedicated previous books to the women in my family; this one is for the men: my son-in-law, Jeff, and grandsons, Jack and Boone Reid.

Because this is a book about a newspaper columnist, quotations from the "Washington Merry-Go-Round" are included in each chapter, identified by the image of a newspaper, known to printers as a "dingbat." The passages following each dingbat give a sense of the column's variety and flavor.

Introduction

The Man Who Broke Secrets

HE WAS NOT AT ALL what they had expected. Four young whistleblowers sat face to face with the nation's most famous newspaper columnist, Drew Pearson, on a Saturday evening in April 1966, at his farm in Maryland. They had not met him before but knew him through his daily newspaper column, the "Washington Merry-Go-Round," which had made him a household name. Pearson had a reputation for investigative reporting that had sent members of Congress to jail, caused the resignation of high-level officials, and provoked presidents to apoplexy.

The four had caught their boss, Connecticut Senator Thomas Dodd, pocketing campaign contributions for his personal use. Appalled and angry, they slipped into his Senate office over several weekends and looted his files, removing, copying, and replacing a mass of incriminating evidence. They handed these documents to Pearson's right-hand man, Jack Anderson, who churned out a stream of columns exposing the senator's misconduct—until Drew Pearson put a halt to the series. Editors who carried the syndicated column had complained to Pearson about the fixation on Dodd. They worried that such a prolonged attack on one person might be considered malicious intent and open them to libel suits. The Justice Department was also looking into whether he and Anderson had stolen the senator's files. All of that prompted his caution.

Protesting that Pearson had let them down, the four staffers nervously made their case. The famed columnist listened quietly, projecting what one described as "an undeniable presence, almost a forbidding one." He occasionally pulled at his mustache or cleared his throat with a harrumph, but never changed his deadpan expression. He waited until after they finished to say that he agreed with them and would resume the Dodd columns the next week. He had never let the threat of a lawsuit stop him before, and in fact was proud of having been sued for libel more than any other journalist and of having won his cases by proving the accuracy of his accusations. He worried that if politicians flouted the system, the American public could become disillusioned with their government. Now convinced that the column should push the case to a just conclusion, he asked: "What do you have in mind?"

With that, the atmosphere changed. Pearson's reserve vanished, and the four informants found him easy to talk with. "There was in this feared and notorious muckraker, a kindliness, a gentleness, a sensitivity that we had not expected," observed James Boyd, the chief whistleblower. "The battles, feuds, intrigues, and libel trials of forty turbulent years seemed not to have marked his personality. He seemed a shy man, actually." Pearson spoke with a wry, self-effacing humor and showed no cynicism. He intended to publish the facts, no matter how they acquired them, and used the column to defend their tactics:[1]

> If it is a crime for newsmen to seek evidence documenting charges of corruption against a United States Senator, then the press must give up one of its important functions and Senators will remain a sacrosanct body, able to expose others . . . but immune from exposure themselves. For it is almost impossible to prove indictable facts regarding a Senator, or for that matter any official, without using evidence obtained from the inside.[2]

Who was Drew Pearson? For four decades, he produced a daily newspaper column that made news by breaking secrets. At its peak, his "Washington Merry-Go-Round" appeared on the pages of more than six hundred newspapers in the United States and abroad. From the Great Depression through World War II, the Cold War, the civil rights movement, and war in Vietnam, the columnist revealed major policy disputes and petty political spats, accomplishments and blunders, hypocrisy and malfeasance. He attacked bigotry and promoted social justice. He pumped up some political careers while destroying others. For revealing hidden news, he caused angst within seven presidential administrations and ruined countless days for members of Congress. He undermined demagogues, forced the resignation of a powerful White House chief of staff, and may have driven a cabinet secretary to suicide. He attracted eager readers and fierce detractors.

Jacqueline Kennedy told Pearson that he seemed more benign in person than in print. Others similarly puzzled over the contrast between his public and private persona. Lady Bird Johnson compared him to "a sophisticated Britisher with his sort of aristocratic face and bristly mustache." British intelligence agents, who kept a close eye on Pearson during World War II, described him as "a tall, tight-lipped individual, who looks uncomfortably like a horse, a likeness which is increased by his habit of snorting as he speaks." An English visitor to Washington exclaimed, "What kind of a capital is this where a scandal columnist looks like a country squire?"[3]

Pearson's disarming personality and tweedy wardrobe camouflaged what *Time* magazine called "a tough, diamond-hard core." In a cover story, *Time* celebrated Pearson's "brand of ruthless, theatrical, crusading, high-voltage, hypodermic journalism" that made him the most feared and hated man in Washington: "It is the kind of journalistic vigilance that keeps small men honest, and forces bigger men to work in an atmosphere of caution that frequently cramps their style." He combined Quaker morality with a driving ambition to prevail professionally, attract attention, influence policy, shape politics, and better the world.[4]

A man on a mission, Drew Pearson called public officials to account and forced them to confront the facts. As a self-professed keyhole peeper, he dismissed much of the news coming out of Washington as so much propaganda—the government's version of the truth—and devoted his career to determining what officials were doing behind closed doors. He broke secrets, revealed classified information, and passed along rumors and conjectures based on sources high and low within the government. Going against the official line meant presenting charges as forcefully as possible without exposing himself to government prosecution or successful libel suits. Fellow journalists claimed that he knew more dirt about more people in Washington than even the FBI. Those who worked for him later compared his efforts to Daniel Ellsberg and the Pentagon Papers or Edward Snowden and WikiLeaks, except that he did it daily for decades.[5]

How did Pearson defy authority for so long? He owed much of his success to an instinct for news that his staff rated nearly infallible. "I won't say he was always right," Jack Anderson explained. "But he was usually right. He had an uncanny ability to see the real rascals up here—and to see their flaws." Pearson made his share of mistakes, but his errors resulted from haste or misunderstanding rather than ill will. Although his targets invariably charged him with lying, he denied intentionally publishing anything he thought untrue, and successfully defended his accusations in court. "Why do people call me a liar?" he responded to that often-asked question. "Well, for one reason, when you hit the truth, sometimes it hurts most." He asserted that truth was his best defense in winning libel suits and keeping his column in print.[6]

Pearson's admirers dubbed him a true prophet of his times. Daily, he went on record expressing opinions about people and events from the presidency of Herbert Hoover through that of Richard Nixon—two fellow Quakers whom he liked the least and tormented the most. Liberal and humanitarian views led him to defend the New Deal's efforts to overcome the Great Depression, to oppose fascism, and to promote military preparedness before World War II. He sought to reduce East-West tensions during the Cold War, opposed the Red Scare, and stood up to Senator Joseph McCarthy. He endorsed the Great Society while harboring serious doubts about America's intervention in Vietnam. Believing that the public had a right to know what their government was doing, he fought secrecy and censorship, lifted the cloak of national security, and advocated transparency. Tackling corruption from statehouses to the Capitol, Pearson's reporting revealed a populist streak. He believed that powerful elements in society already had "plenty of money to defend themselves, plenty of press agents, and plenty of ways of getting their story across to the public," and he prided himself in defending "the little guy."[7]

Detractors sneered that Pearson was often in error but never in doubt. "Being human, I make mistakes," he accepted. "But I endeavor, when I do make them, to correct them." He took tips from those trying to peddle stories, often with ulterior motives, but did his best to verify their accusations. Most of all, he relied on his sense of smell: "If something smells wrong, I go to work." He expounded on this trait when instructing his staff on how to operate during his absences: "It is your job as newspapermen to spur the lazy, watch the weak, expose the corrupt. You must be the eyes, ears and nose of the American people. Yes, the nose, too, is important. For no matter what stench you may be exposed to, never lose your sense of smell."[8]

Unwilling to limit himself to reporting the news, Pearson injected himself into many of his stories. He generated ideas, recruited members of Congress for support, testified before their committees, drafted their speeches, extolled their efforts, and appealed to his readers. His columns created what the like-minded reformer Ralph Nader called "an atmosphere of inevitability" for legislation he favored, beating the drum to attract public attention and keep the issue in legislators' minds. His impulse to shape national politics led to suspicion that he slanted stories to promote his aims. Indeed, his firm belief in the virtue of the sides that he took countenanced the tactics that he adopted and the conclusions that he reached. A skeptical nature led him to pursue any hint of dishonesty, whether bribery, kickbacks, misuse of public funds, influence peddling, or tax cheating. "Though no one knew more about the seamy side of government or expected less from public officials," the historian Arthur Schlesinger Jr. marveled, Drew Pearson "was continuously and freshly outraged—no doubt because of his Quaker conscience—by each new case of malfeasance."[9]

Pearson's targets accused him of taking cheap shots and called him a smear artist and a rumormonger. "I have them squirming on their seats," he responded, "and they hate me!" But after engaging in political combat, he tried to balance his ruthless image with a tradition on his birthday, just before Christmas, of telephoning those with whom he had fought to make peace. He helped find jobs for some of the reprobates he sent to jail when they got out. He confessed at times a yearning "to be more loved by my fellow men," but could not step out of character. "If you have made your name by being the Boris Karloff of journalism, there is no use trying to be a Marlon Brando."[10]

The journalist Patrick Anderson compared Drew Pearson to Lyndon Johnson, the president with whom he developed the closest relationship. The two shared many personality traits, both being "flamboyant, vainglorious, emotional, ruthless, maudlin, shrewd, corny, power-obsessed, effective, durable." It took equally oversized ambition and self-confidence for Pearson to achieve his status as a columnist as it took Johnson to reach the political pinnacle. Both advanced themselves at times at the expense of others, sure that their accomplishments excused their excesses.[11]

What set Pearson apart? In a crowded field of syndicated political columns, his "Washington Merry-Go-Round" stood out from all others. Rather than offering the usual informed interpretation of news that others had reported, his column generated its own news, well ahead of the pack of Washington reporters. Breaking news hiked the column's popularity among readers but made it risky for subscribing papers. Editors placed the "Merry-Go-Round" everywhere from the front pages to the editorial pages to the comics pages. Nervous over his accusations, fearing libel, or unhappy with its disagreements with their own editorial positions, they might drop a column entirely or trim out its most worrisome passages.

Opinion columns were still relatively new to American newspapers when Drew Pearson and his partner Robert Allen broke into the field in December 1932. A decade earlier, the *New York World* had swept everything off the page opposite its editorials to create an "op-ed" page reserved for so-cial and political commentary, and many other papers followed suit. While news sections attempted to report the news objectively, columns permitted selected journalists to speak their minds and take sides. A few Washington-oriented columns got underway in the 1920s, although surveys showed that only 3 percent of newspaper readers at that time paid much attention to happenings in the national capital. Americans far more enjoyed reading about Babe Ruth, Charles Lindbergh, and Al Capone. Then came the Great Depression and the New Deal's efforts to restore and reform the economy, which thrust the federal government into the public's consciousness and daily life. Scrambling for ways to explain fast-moving developments to their readers, editors across the country found syndicated columns an attractive solution, and Washington columns proliferated during the 1930s. Some syndicates priced columns according to a newspaper's circulation, so that small weekly papers as well as major metropolitan dailies could afford them. A paper unable to hire its own correspondent in Washington could add the insights of a columnist based there, while diversifying opinion on its edito-rial pages.[12]

During World War II, a British government agent in Washington, eager to improve Britain's image in American public opinion, advised officials in London that the United States had no national newspapers because the country was too large. Even the *New York Times* was read only within "a widish radius" around that city. But the syndicated columnists appeared in hundreds of papers and constituted an important opinion forming el-ement, "e.g. Walter Lippmann to take the best and Drew Pearson to take the worst!" The erudite, Harvard-educated Walter Lippmann sought to place unfolding events into perspective, drawn from his own philosophy of life. In 1931, Lippmann launched a syndicated column, "Today and Tomorrow"—known in the trade as TNT—based at the New York *Herald Tribune*. Although he analyzed Washington, he lived in Manhattan until 1938, when he moved to the capital with considerable fanfare. He expressed reservations about socializing with those about whom he wrote, but no one had better sources at the highest levels of government. Distrustful of public opinion in shaping public policy, Lippmann addressed himself primarily to the nation's power elite and foreign embassies, less concerned with others who might be reading him. Wise but not always right—he underestimated presidential candidate Franklin Roosevelt as an "amiable boy scout" and supported the internment of Japanese Americans during World War II—Lippmann remained skeptical of unrealistic goals in foreign and domestic policy. Neither the best paid nor the most widely circulated Washington columnist (distinctions that belonged to Drew Pearson), Lippmann led the pack in prestige.[13]

Other Washington columnists presented an array of opinions. NANA, the North American Newspaper Alliance, recruited Joseph Alsop and Robert Kintner to imitate Pearson and Allen as "specialists in a kind of urgently personalized political gossip." Alsop and Kintner published a "Capital Parade" column before both enlisted for military service during World War II. Alsop returned to launch "Matter of Fact" with his brother Stewart. Supremely confident, Joe Alsop claimed to write his columns as a reporter, but his views often ran contrary to the evidence he collected. Alsop derived much of his credibility from personal ties to the top people at the Central Intelligence Agency. This made his exposure of government secrets resemble strategic leaks rather than challenges to national security. Yet Alsop caused consternation among official ranks because he insisted on interpreting the news rather than simply repeating what his sources fed him.[14]

Among the rest, the modest Midwesterner Raymond Clapper offered neutral, unadorned news without "gossip and chitchat" in his "Watching the World Go By" column. Frank Kent's syndicated "The Great Game of Politics" appeared on the front page of his home paper, the *Baltimore Sun*, even when his caustic conservatism ran contrary to its editorials. David Lawrence expressed more tempered conservative views. Mark Sullivan embraced all things Republican. Ernest K. Lindley advocated Franklin Roosevelt's New Deal. Paul Mallon mixed straight reporting with an explosive Irish temper. Arthur Krock also ranked high among them, but unlike his syndicated competitors' columns, his "In the Nation" appeared exclusively in the *New York Times*.[15]

By the 1940s, Washington columnists had achieved higher prominence and influence than most of the editors and publishers whose papers carried them. Their public images established them not only as interpreters of news but as forces in their own right. Substantial incomes allowed the more

widely circulated columnists to buy stately homes in the capital's most fashionable neighborhoods. They were "sought after, wined and dined by officialdom and in turn, entertained officialdom themselves," a lesser colleague
chronicled enviously. "Invitations to their homes are considered 'musts' by
all who expect to get along in the Washington swim." Social connections
enabled the columnists to gain insights and test their opinions. Alternating
as sounding boards and critics of official thinking, they exercised influence
over the rest of Washington reporting through their prominently published
opinions.[16]

Drew Pearson combined many of his competitors' qualities while managing to stand apart. Pearson devoted his columns to uncovering inside information, mixed with close-hand observations, strong opinions, and moral
indignation. The "Washington Merry-Go-Round" grabbed readers' attention by taking them off the well-worn track and covering news that others
ignored. Rather than rework press releases it revealed what their issuers
held back. Producing a column that ran every day of the year—including
weekends and holidays—and featured original news as well as opinion required help. Pearson functioned as the editor-in-chief of his own news organization. He hired a squad of reporters, known as his leg men, to patrol the
halls of government and bring back leads. They proved adept at gathering
news through ingenuity, persuasion, guile, and intimidation, and served
Pearson as a "kind of private FBI," marveled Charles Fisher in a survey of
American newspaper columnists.[17]

Pearson himself made allies among those at the highest levels of government and gathered news and chatter from a circle of politically savvy
friends. He pursued tips from low-level whistleblowers, civil servants, and
anonymous informants. His columns blended gossip with breaking news in
a style that resembled the society columns of the era, peppered with brief
items on the affairs of the rich and famous, except that he focused on affairs
of government and politics. Not everyone regarded political gossip as superficial. The columnist Peter Edson contended that gossip gave color to the
news by revealing the character of the people being gossiped about: "And
it is important to understand the personality of the people who make the
news if you would understand the news itself." Before social media allowed
people to introduce themselves and their accomplishments, columnists like
Pearson did it for them.[18]

It helped that Washington, DC, was what Pearson called "the gossip
center of the U.S.A." Word traveled fast and little remained hidden for long
at the capital. For every official with a reason to keep something secret there

was usually an opponent who saw the advantage in getting the news out. A reporter once asked Senator Allen Ellender if he and his colleagues could protect classified documents. "You can't mumble something to a mirror in this town without it getting around in a few hours," the senator replied. Pearson picked up well-informed rumors from a close circle of Washington friends who played deck tennis and badminton in his Georgetown backyard, swam at his Maryland farm, and frequented his dining table. Many of them were attorneys who had served in the government before going into private practice, men like Thurman Arnold, Randolph Paul, Marvin Braverman, and Ernest Cuneo. The odd thing about lawyers, Pearson found, was that they discussed their clients with each other. "The lawyer to whom they talk is not bound by any confidence" and would then make disclosures to him.[19]

Pearson's knack for breaking secrets made him powerful enemies. Herbert Hoover tried to have him fired. Franklin Roosevelt called him a chronic liar. Harry Truman sent the FBI to investigate him. Dwight Eisenhower ostensibly ignored him while having his press secretary trash him. John Kennedy griped that the powers of the presidency gave him no influence over the columnist. Lyndon Johnson did his best to coopt him. Richard Nixon put him at the top of his enemies list. Presidents of both parties fumed over his ability to reveal their decisions prematurely or air their dirty laundry. Pearson simply shrugged off presidential criticism, holding himself responsible for keeping the public informed.

"Drew Pearson was a muckraker," declared Jack Anderson. "Of all the names he was called during four decades as Washington's top investigative reporter, muckraker was the one he liked best." That honorific began as a pejorative. At the start of the twentieth century, reform-minded writers for the new mass-circulation magazines made a splash by exposing political corruption and confirming readers' worst suspicions about those in power. Newspaper reporters had heard the same rumors but shied away from them. Working on daily deadlines required Washington correspondents to cultivate high-placed sources who could provide reliable news, but also constrained the press corps from offending their sources. The magazine writers who operated mostly out of New York could breeze into Washington, collect sordid stories, publish exposés, and leave without succumbing to a "Washington point of view." Tensions between the two groups surfaced at an off-the-record Gridiron Club dinner in 1906, when President Theodore Roosevelt won cheers from the club's members—all Washington newspaper correspondents—by delivering a vigorous attack on "The Man with the Muck-Rake." TR denounced the magazine writers as hysterical sensationalists. Reporters in the audience urged the president to go public with his attack on their magazine rivals, which he did in a toned-down version (to preserve his progressive credentials) a month later while laying the cornerstone of the House Office Building. TR's speech popularized "muckraker" as a label for journalists who specialized in digging up the dirt.[20]

The muckrakers faded as the Progressive Era ended, but they set the pattern for later investigative reporting. During the 1920s, Paul Y. Anderson, Washington correspondent for the *St. Louis Post-Dispatch*, kept the practice alive and won a Pulitzer Prize for exposing the Teapot Dome scandal, when oil company executives bribed members of Warren G. Harding's administration to exploit naval oil reserves. Anderson disdained the "journalistic statesmen" who overlooked the sordid side of the Harding, Coolidge, and Hoover era. Pearson and Allen hailed Anderson as a "crusading journalist, hard-boiled and pugnacious," and cited him as inspiration for their column.[21]

Readers wondered how the column got away with printing so many shocking stories they had not read on the front pages. Pearson's muckraking fed on tips from inside and outside the government, and he spent much of the time trying to turn small leads into big stories. Specializing in news that the rest of the Washington press corps hesitated to print meant avoiding off-the-record press briefings and instead quizzing the correspondents who had attended and agreed not to publish what they had heard. Other Washington reporters slipped him stories they could not get past their own bureau chiefs. Or they goaded their chiefs into running a touchy story by warning, "If you don't use it, Pearson will."[22]

"It's the exposés that sell the column," Pearson readily admitted. "I plead guilty to being a showman." A sense of showmanship and self-dramatization infused his journalism and promoted his causes and ideals. In his youth, Pearson organized parades to attract crowds to his father's traveling tent shows. Later in life he used a carnival huckster's gimmicks to intrigue his lecture audience with hints of previously undisclosed information, and his radio listeners with predictions of things to come, promising to take them behind closed doors and let them in on confidential conversations. Hollywood even arranged for him to play himself as a broadcaster announcing the landing of a flying saucer on the Mall, in the science fiction classic *The Day the Earth Stood Still*.[23]

While the "Washington Merry-Go-Round" concentrated on the national government, Pearson remained attentive to political corruption elsewhere. He augmented his capital sources with a nationwide network of friends.

An Alabaman admired the columnist's "time-consuming and patience-trying" efforts to maintain contact by telephone with a coast-to-coast circle of contacts who could tell him what was going on. "This reviewer knew a few of the Pearson tipsters in Alabama and while he did not always feel that Pearson chose them wisely or that they necessarily reported faithfully, yet the net effect of the whole was to keep Pearson in touch with happenings all over America," wrote Carl Elliott in the Jasper *Daily Mountain Eagle*. "Pearson could write a column that touched on happenings in a remote community in, say, North Dakota, and make it sound like he was standing on its main street."[24]

Polls confirmed that Drew Pearson was the nation's best-known columnist, and his syndicate touted the "Merry-Go-Round" as the best column from Washington "by advertising, promotion and selling." In 1944, the Washington press corps begrudgingly voted him the Washington correspondent who exerted the greatest influence on the nation, giving him twice the votes of Walter Lippmann. Even his most outspoken critics credited him for being virtually a government within a government, with his own corps of agents.[25]

The hundreds of newspapers that carried the "Merry-Go-Round," with their collective readership, gave him political clout. A board game about presidential politics included a "crisis card" that read: "Drew Pearson just exposed you. Go take a vacation in Maine." His influence intimidated politicians, bureaucrats, and military chiefs. Pearson claimed that he hated to antagonize these officials "because I respected them even when I disagreed with them," but he found that he could use their animosity to his advantage. He relished it whenever prominent people lost their tempers and called him names and made sure to reprint those attacks in the column. Quarrels helped, he assured his staff. "If you write a column like ours, you've got to be controversial. People will read you even if they hate you."[26]

The column was "read by everybody, particularly the politicians," attested a Senate aide who had felt its sting. While the government's inner circles kept a wary eye on the "Merry-Go-Round," Pearson addressed the column to the much vaster audience outside of Washington. To hold general readers' interest, he emphasized the personal side of public life, recording who was up and who was down, their accomplishments and embarrassments, and any amusing anecdotes about them. "I think it's helped make my broader points about clean government more effective," Pearson explained, "and it doesn't put people to sleep as fast as some of my thumb-sucking colleagues." Getting that kind of news was mostly knowing the right people, and he claimed that he and his staff knew "three fourths of the Senate, half of the House, and everyone in the Cabinet."[27]

At its best, the "Merry-Go-Round" exhibited a vivid writing style, packed with direct quotes and firsthand impressions of the leading political characters of the day. At its worst, a critic likened its prose to "jottings on an envelope in a lurching taxicab." Ragged writing was part of its appeal, suggesting that digging out hidden facts mattered more to its author than polished prose. The columnist adopted a breezy informality, labeling powerful politicians "bigwigs," military officers "brass hats," and congressional investigators "gumshoes." He reproduced dialogue provided by those who overheard it. Rather than describe a confidential document, he published portions verbatim. When news was slow, he resorted to what other reporters called the "Pearson Treatment": taking known facts and instilling them with urgency.[28]

Readers never knew what to expect. One day the column might concentrate on a single issue, and the next day it might mingle an assortment of topics. It veered from news to opinion, slashing exposés to calls for civic action. Some columns took the form of personal letters to his family, offering observations on recent trends, signed affectionately "from the old man." Some speculated on upcoming appointments, provided brief biographies of the newest players, and eventually predicted their removal and replacement. Columns might begin, "It didn't leak out at the time, but . . ." or "The inside story can now be told . . ." or "It wasn't shouted from the rooftop, but . . . ," promising to reveal secret strategies, and draw attention to actions officials were trying to do on the sly. On any day, the "Merry-Go-Round" might unmask a charlatan, blast pork-barrel politics, expose political rivalries, or reveal a vice president's high-stakes winnings at the poker table. If the column broke a major news story, editors might condense the report into a front-page box and direct readers to see the op-ed page for details. Pearson sometimes hammered home his accusations in column after column until a reluctant federal agency finally took up the investigation against his target. He disclaimed getting pleasure out of bringing public figures down, however, no matter how much they deserved it, and insisted that far greater satisfaction came from using the column to arouse public interest for charitable purposes, from rebuilding a dynamited school in the South to sponsoring a Friendship Train to send food and supplies to war-torn Europe.[29]

Unlike a newspaper reporter, who ran a risk of exhausting the publisher's patience and budget, Pearson appeared in so many papers, from metropolitan dailies to rural weeklies, that no single editor or publisher could curtail him. "Editors get tired of difficult stories and difficult reporters," the investigative reporter Seymour Hersh affirmed from personal experience. Pearson's editors did express skepticism about some stories. When he revealed an ominous new development in government eavesdropping, editors at the *Washington Post* confessed that they had waited for a denial of the story, "something to show that Mr. Pearson had exaggerated or had been misinformed." When no official protest came, they reluctantly concluded that the story was true. The column's liberal leanings discomforted conservative subscribers who suspected that Pearson's information might contain half-truths and distortions due to ideological bias. William Randolph Hearst's *New York Mirror* ran a disclaimer: "The author of this column is given the widest latitude. His views do not necessarily reflect those of *The Mirror*." The *Meridian Star* in Mississippi proclaimed that because it believed in representing all sides of issues, "we have published the column of Drew Pearson, whose views on most matters are completely at variance with the editorial policy of this paper" (the *Star* eventually dropped the column over its stance on civil rights). Sometimes his syndicate deemed a story too hot to circulate and withheld the column. Pearson would then mail the unexpurgated text directly to his subscribers, letting them decide whether to publish it.[30]

Surveys showed the "Washington Merry-Go-Round" a consistent favorite among readers. The daily mail bags of fan letters and irate protests tracked how closely people followed it. The publisher of the Mobile, Alabama, *Register* complained that every time Pearson's column included something that his readers did not like, they jumped on him, and when he left it out, they jumped on him again, so he published it with an editorial disclaimer.[31]

Pearson took his editors seriously. When he traveled on the lecture circuit, he made a point of visiting the offices of local newspapers to create personal bonds with their editors and overcome any lingering ill feelings. He would puff them up by calling them "boss." After Ben Bradlee became editor of the *Washington Post* and Pearson called him boss, Bradlee confessed, "I was ridiculously proud & amused at myself. I suspect no one was his boss & therein lay his greatest strength." The column often included a "mail bag" of random observations from editors and readers around the country. Pearson respected even the hostile mail he received. "To live here in Washington is to be daily impressed by the power of public opinion, expressed not so much through the newspapers as through correspondence which floods, with expressions of emphatic opinion, practically every executive desk in the Capital," he answered one critical reader. "It is in this way that democracy finds its proper expression."[32]

Over the four decades of his career, the news business changed dramatically. Evening television news programs drained advertising revenue away from once profitable afternoon papers, and mergers eliminated competition in cities across the nation. Operating long before the Internet became a factor, Pearson lamented that the shrinking media posed a risk of his kind of disagreeable news being omitted, buried, or minimized. He took up radio broadcasting in 1935 and television in 1952, partly as a means of getting out news that his syndicate would not carry. These ventures inflated his audiences and his income but forced him to alter his presentations to fit each medium. When a niece asked him to give a reading at her wedding, he asked in Quaker style: "Does thee wish me to read it with my staccato radio delivery? Or should I read it with the more solemn delivery I use on television? Should I read it with a more dulcet tone I use with my wife and family?" His most successful efforts were the live fifteen-minute national radio broadcasts he delivered on Sunday evenings. He would spend each Sunday writing, editing, and rehearsing his scripts before heading to the studio. Afterwards, he eagerly quizzed his family: "How did I do?"[33]

Other Washington reporters resented Pearson's determination to elbow his way to the front on every story. Some dismissed his columns as "factually shaky." A group having lunch at the National Press Club was rehashing these complaints when one of them interrupted, "Let's face it, not one of us here would have the nerve to write what Pearson does, or hope to get it printed!" The others agreed that they read his column because they could never tell when it was going to carry the day's best story out of Washington. A Detroit reporter added: "While other newsmen scoffed at him in Washington, the folks out in the hinterlands viewed him as their man in the capital, a fearless fighter uncovering the ways in which their tax dollars were being squandered or their congressmen improperly influenced." At times, his exposés met with indifference from the rest of the media, but some of his scoops caught everyone's attention and encouraged the rest of the pack to join in the pursuit.[34]

Drew Pearson knew that his more sedate colleagues in the Washington press corps did not always approve of him. Their need to cultivate knowledgeable sources too often led them to swallow the official line and suppress the embarrassing stories that he relished exposing. "They sometimes refer to me as a Barnum-and-Bailey type of journalist," he acknowledged. "Perhaps they are right." But he doubted that he could write the news as honestly as he wanted and still be loved. When he investigated someone, he rarely bothered to get the target's side of the story, reasoning that tipping his hand in advance only allowed them to prepare their defenses. He preferred to catch them by surprise. "What if we're wrong?" Jack Anderson protested, but Pearson would push ahead, trusting his instincts whenever his sense of smell detected the odor of corruption. The *Washington Post*, which published his column with some trepidation for three decades, described his technique as scattershot, sometimes right on target and at other times missing altogether. "It almost seemed as if this was a conscious strategy," the *Post* editors reflected, "this readiness to risk being wrong now and again as the necessary price for being, more often, right."[35]

Though Pearson aimed for the truth, the pressure of daily deadlines meant sometimes settling for less than the whole truth. When challenged, he occasionally found he could not substantiate a claim because a key source had reneged, and he had to print a retraction. Some scoops never made it into the column. James Scheuer, who worked for Pearson before his election to Congress, assured colleagues that the "Merry-Go-Round" regularly withheld criticism of members who were retiring, resigning, or dying, reasoning that it would serve no useful purpose to shatter a career about to end. Representative Scheuer described Pearson as "simply a news-behind-the-news professional who determinedly trod the news trail where the evidence lay." Nevertheless, Pearson built a reputation for telling readers what those in power did not want them to know.[36]

After Franklin Roosevelt labeled Pearson a chronic liar, Winston Churchill broadened that slur to "the champion liar of the United States." Both leaders were trying to deflect the damage his embarrassing revelations could do. Breaking secrets was the heartbeat of Pearson's column, even in wartime. His staff scoured the subterranean world of national security and often returned with documents stamped secret. He concluded that rather than protect national security, much of what got classified protected officials by hiding actions that were either embarrassing or illegal. Pearson's ability to reveal classified information motivated foreign and domestic intelligence agencies to hunt for his sources. He played cat and mouse with the investigators who shadowed him, tapped his phone, read his mail, rifled his files, and planted agents among his friends. They never got any help from him about who was feeding him the classified information. The FBI found it so fruitless to track down leaks that it advised agencies just to do a better job of keeping their files secret.[37]

During the Cold War, the Soviet embassy staff in Washington read the "Merry-Go-Round" and marveled at its candid criticism of FBI Director

J. Edgar Hoover. A correspondent for the Soviet newspaper *Pravda* informed Pearson that the embassy's staff had asked him, "What kind of a guy is this man—how does he dare write these things about Hoover? How can he stay in business?" Pearson appreciated that he would have had no chance to buck the secret police in Moscow if he had been a Russian. For many years, he did his best to remain in Hoover's good graces and turned to the bureau to verify some of the tips he received. The two men eventually fell out during the 1950s when they took different sides in the Red Scare. They carried their mutual hostility to the grave.[38]

Recognizing his controversial image, Pearson could poke fun at himself in the column, letting readers in on some of the criticism:

> My wife, whom people credit with having a better nose for news than yours truly, has been giving me advice on what I ought to write about.
>
> "Get folks away from this idea that you're a keyhole peeper," she says. "Quit looking under people's beds. Why don't you be a statesman like Walter Lippmann?"
>
> "But editors pay me to write that backstage stuff," I remonstrate. "They don't want me to suck a column out of my thumb."[39]

By "backstage stuff," he meant paying attention to how officials behaved privately, rather than what they did publicly. He devoted himself to exposing falsehoods and misconduct, and made his column an outlet for those who could not speak out themselves. The consequences to Pearson were irate denunciations, expensive libel suits, and an occasional punch, which he accepted as the penalty for performing as a national watchdog and public protector. He needed political certitude, moral indignation, a zest for combat, and a thick hide to sustain his long ride on the "Washington Merry-Go-Round."

I

Launching the Column

BEFORE THE COLUMN, FIRST CAME the blockbuster book. The Great Depression offered an inauspicious time for a book launch, and books on American politics had rarely sold well until one titled *Washington Merry-Go-Round* raced through 150,000 copies and multiple printings in 1931. So popular was the spicy political exposé that Columbia Pictures bought the rights to the title—and turned it into a movie that had little to do with the book. Publisher Horace Liveright touted it as "first really successful book of factual reporting about Washington that the country had known." Although published anonymously, its two authors had proved themselves, Liveright insisted, "in no sense superficial, in spite of the jocularity and breeziness of their writing." The capital buzzed with speculation about who might have written it, and part of the market appeal was guessing their identities.[1]

The authors slyly hid themselves within the book, cloaked in the third person. They identified Robert S. Allen as Washington's youngest bureau chief, whose newspaper experience at home and abroad had been held down "by the conservative views and many prohibitions" of his employer, the *Christian Science Monitor*. Even more effusive was their description of Drew Pearson, the *Baltimore Sun*'s foreign affairs correspondent, who had "the reputation of knowing more about the State Department than most of the people who run it." Pearson cut a dapper figure among the diplomats, although "few people realize he was once a sailor, circus hand and vagabond journalist working his way around odd corners of the world."[2]

Robert Sharon Allen started writing this tell-all book out of frustration over working for a newspaper that shied away from his style of aggressive truth-telling. Born in Kentucky in 1900, Allen stood five-foot-four and compensated for his slight stature with a pugnacious personality. As a teenager, he lied about his age to join the cavalry. He served on the Mexican border and later in France during World War I, rising from private to first lieutenant. Enrolled in journalism classes at the University of Wisconsin, Allen won notice for his undercover reporting on the Ku Klux Klan. To get that story, he joined the local Klan, attended meetings, published a list of its members, and risked being lynched. He went on to study at the University of Munich, where he managed to cover Hitler's Beer Hall putsch for the United Press. Allen then settled in Washington as bureau chief of the *Christian Science Monitor*. At the Senate press gallery he met Ruth Finney, a reporter for the *Sacramento Star* whose unflinching reporting had won her the nickname "Poison Ivy." They courted while covering Herbert Hoover's presidential campaign in 1928 and married the following year.[3]

During his off-hours, Bob Allen wrote candid profiles of politicians for H. L. Mencken's irreverent *American Mercury* magazine. Since the *Christian Science Monitor* disapproved of its staff writing for anyone else, his articles appeared anonymously. Mencken admired their iconoclasm and encouraged him to expand them into a book. Taking his advice, Allen submitted samples to Horace Liveright and Company, where they caught the attention of editor-in-chief Thomas R. "Tommy" Smith, a cherubic man said to combine the looks of a Baptist minister and the tastes of a devil, being a renowned collector of erotica. Tommy Smith relished Allen's ability to puncture Washington's pretensions and uncover its foibles, but he felt the sketches lacked the kind of social gossip that could make the book more sellable. He urged him to find a collaborator. Smith also changed Allen's title from *Washington Carousel* to the more American-sounding *Washington Merry-Go-Round*.[4]

For a partner, Bob Allen turned to a reporter he had met at the State Department, the tall, debonair diplomatic correspondent of the *Baltimore Sun*, Drew Pearson. It seemed an unlikely pairing. Allen's press colleagues regarded him as "brusque and direct," while Pearson was "urbane and elegant." Still, the two men hit it off from the start. "The first time I met Bob Allen he was fighting," Pearson recalled. It was at a press conference at the State Department where the "red-headed, belligerent" Allen peppered Secretary of State Frank B. Kellogg with questions about why he had sent the marines to Nicaragua. Pearson relished the image of him berating the secretary for "picking on little nations." He admired Allen's willingness to side with the underdog: "No cause was too hopeless for Bob to champion—if it was just." Sharing Allen's disdain for pompous politicians and deferential reporters, Pearson accepted the chance to put those views into a book. But the offer came just before he left to cover the London Naval Disarmament conference of 1930. By the time Pearson returned, Allen had completed the largest share of the manuscript. In later years, it bothered Allen that his partner received so much credit for the book and the column they launched together. "Well, let me interrupt here," he cut off an interviewer who had identified him as its "co-author." "I originated and conceived the idea of the *Washington Merry-Go-Round* book from which the column grew, and I conceived that idea, too. . . . I wrote about 60–65 percent of the first book."[5]

Yet it was Drew Pearson's droll chapter on the "boiled bosoms" of Washington society that opened the book and set its tone, leading into Bob Allen's hard-nosed political reporting. ("One of the most charming things about Washington is that it is almost never without a social, diplomatic or matrimonial war," read Pearson's setup of the power elite, "and as in all one-industry villages these feuds are waged so earnestly that before they are over they line up on one side or the other almost everyone in town.") Allen spent most of his days at the Capitol, interviewing members and their staffs, and disdained Washington's social scene. Pearson operated out of the ornate State and War Department Building, beside the White House. Like Allen, he stood up to those in power. When Hoover's secretary of state, Henry Stimson, barred foreign reporters from attending his press conferences, Drew Pearson led a revolt that created the State Department Correspondents Association, through which the diplomatic correspondents themselves took charge of issuing press credentials. Pearson also gained easy access to Washington's high society by marrying the daughter of Eleanor "Cissy" Patterson, the city's wealthiest woman. That union made him part of the smart set and got him invited to the most fashionable events, where he had no trouble gathering news and gossip.[6]

Pearson and Allen shared a belief that the newspapers of their era were too timid to show how Washington really worked. They intended to present an uninhibited view of the political scene, revealing secrets and naming names. *Washington Merry-Go-Round* trashed President Herbert Hoover, painting him as a failed chief executive who presided over a lackluster cabinet, and a man whose campaign promises of unlimited prosperity had dissolved into Depression. ("Every possible trick, every new device, known or capable of being invented by skilled publicity agents, had been invoked to make Hoover the Superman, the Great Executive," the book alleged, "and a reputation thus made was all the more easily washed away.") Irate and thin-skinned, President Hoover ordered the Bureau of Investigation (not yet the FBI) to uncover his critics' identities. He sent word to the *Christian Science Monitor* that Robert Allen would no longer be welcome at the White House. Quizzed by the *Monitor*'s management, Allen admitted his authorship. They promptly fired him—by mail. "It was typical of those sanctimonious people," he growled. Allen suspected that his editors had been glad to rid themselves of his squabbling.[7]

The Depression forced Allen to patch together some freelance reporting jobs. He even sold news to a Soviet agent, who was likely posing as a reporter for the Soviet news agency TASS. The KGB archives contain a report from the agent, informing Moscow that he had recruited Allen as a "valuable contact" who would operate under the cover name George Parker. The agent paid Allen $100 a month to provide news, but the record of this arrangement lasted for only two months and provided the kind of information anyone could have read in the papers a day later. Perhaps the relationship ended so quickly once the Soviet handler realized that the most famous George Parker of the day was a conman who made his living selling the Brooklyn Bridge to gullible customers. Allen needed the money and would sell news to anyone who paid. He also gathered up the items left over from his various assignments and cobbled together a weekly column for William Randolph Hearst's International News Service (INS), filling the column with the sort of colorful anecdotes that appealed to Hearst's readers. Allen went too far, however, in another essay for the *American Mercury*. He portrayed President Hoover's slovenly secretary of labor William K. Doak as "Greasy Bill" because "you could tell from his vest what he'd had for breakfast the last week or so." Secretary Doak prevailed on his friend Hearst to fire Allen once again.[8]

Editors at the liberal *Baltimore Sun* were bemused to learn that one of their reporters had written *Washington Merry-Go-Round*. Baltimore journalists did not mind that the book skewered Washingtonians, so Drew Pearson kept his job despite President Hoover's protests. The next year Pearson and Allen attempted to build on their success with a sequel, *More Merry-Go-Round*. "It is filled with revelations that . . . are served up with a new flip and a flair," cheered one reviewer. Still anonymous on the book jacket, the identities of the two reporters by then had become known—and they were reputed to have gotten additional help from George Abell, a gossip columnist for the

Washington News. Rather than repeat their original success, however, the sequel flopped. The Depression had devastated book sales, Liveright went bankrupt, and their royalties evaporated.[9]

The failed book had costly repercussions. At a white-tie-and-tails dinner party in honor of General Douglas MacArthur, Pearson encountered Hoover's secretary of war, Patrick Hurley, "in full regalia, medals and all." Hurley cornered Pearson and berated him for having belittled him as a "cotillion leader." After calling him every expletive he could summon, Hurley took his complaint to Pearson's bosses, intimating that his political enemies had paid for Pearson's poison pen. Pearson indignantly denied that charge. "Anyone who knows us down here, knows that space in the Merry-Go-Rounds or in anything else we write is not for sale," he insisted. But his editor summoned him to Baltimore and proclaimed that the *Sun* was "not a keyhole paper." Offered the choice of resigning or being fired, Pearson reasoned that being sacked would generate the most publicity.[10]

"The *Baltimore Sun* fired me for my connection with the new book," Pearson informed his former wife. "It appeared to be a combination of the fact that they thought I made enemies by the book and the fact that Secretary of War Hurley protested vigorously regarding the chapter on him. I did not mind being fired by the *Sun*, because on the whole I think it will do me good. I have already got some orders for important magazine articles and have got a bunch of telegrams from places as far west as Omaha wanting me to speak." What irritated him was that Secretary Hurley, having been criticized for getting the reporter fired, was issuing denials that made him look like a terrible liar. Still, Pearson found the whole affair stimulating. "I seem to be such a turbulent person," he mused, "always getting into stormy political and personal situations."[11]

Turbulence seemed out of character for someone raised on the Quaker principles of spiritual equality, peace, simplicity, and hard work. Andrew Russell Pearson was born in Evanston, Illinois, on December 13, 1897. William McKinley occupied the White House at the time, and Pearson's life would span thirteen presidencies, seven of which he would vex. Even his name had a political connection. A great-great-grandfather, James Cameron, had fought under General Andrew Jackson at the Battle of New Orleans. He named his son Andrew Jackson Cameron. The family passed that name down until it reached Andrew Cameron Pearson, called Drew. His nephew, Drew Pearson, was named for him, "nickname and all."[12]

Drew's father was born Pearl Martin Pearson but as an adult took the name Paul. Possessed of a mellifluous voice, he was studying speech at the

Methodist-affiliated Baker University in Kansas when he met Edna Rachel Wolfe, whom he married in 1896. By then he had moved to Northwestern University in Evanston, Illinois. There he earned a master's degree and became an instructor of elocution, and their sons Drew and Leon were born. In 1901 he took a year's leave of absence to pursue graduate studies at Harvard, and then through the Fisk Teachers Agency negotiated a job at Swarthmore College, as a professor of public speaking for $1,200 a year and four weeks off for "platform work"—paid speaking engagements. Having relished the cosmopolitan atmosphere of Northwestern and Harvard, Edna Pearson felt apprehensive about settling into a Quaker community, but her husband assured her: "I think you are wrong about there being little opportunity for social affairs at Swarthmore . . . there are many faculty who are not Quakers, and Prof. Sanford assures me that the unorthodoxy Quakers are quite sociable."[13]

Others on the faculty used "the plain language," and advised the newcomers to "drop into it gradually." The whole family joined the Society of Friends and within their household adopted the Quakers' "thee," "thy," and "thine." The children—by then including daughters Barbara and Ellen— grew up in the ideal atmosphere of a college campus, albeit on the salary of an underpaid teacher. In 1908 their father took the title "Dr. Pearson" after Baker University awarded him an honorary Doctor of Letters.[14]

The family lived in what Drew Pearson called a "picturesque mausoleum, no electricity, uncertain water supply, antique toilets, ancient hot air furnace." Habitually pressed for funds, Paul Pearson expected his sons to work to help the family. In nearby Philadelphia he established a small publishing house that produced magazines for public speakers. He used Drew and Leon to stuff envelopes. The boys also earned pocket money by trapping skunks in the nearby woods. They sold magazines to commuters at the railroad station and hauled milk and groceries from the express company to neighbors. As a boy, Drew Pearson was so shy that he took his younger brother with him when he went from door to door selling eggs. Drew would ring the bell and then let his brother make the sale, sometimes while sitting on his shoulders. That arrangement ended on the day that Leon nervously wet his pants. Drew also started a neighborhood journal, the *Crum Creek Monthly*, and as a teenager he freelanced for the *Philadelphia Bulletin*, covering baseball and track meets at Swarthmore.[15]

For weeks each year, Paul Pearson traveled as a public speaker, leaving Edna behind to raise the children and run the household. Ten miscarriages weakened her, and Paul Pearson encouraged his oldest son to be "a little gentleman" and "be sure to be good to Mother while Father is away." Young Drew assumed more responsibilities around the home, and later recalled nostalgically: "It is true that my father had to travel a lot and that Mother missed him and we all missed him, but I could always be certain that he would be back, bubbling over with enthusiasm and with stories about his trip."[16]

During the summer, the Pearsons sometimes rented out their house and sent the boys to their grandparents' farm in Kansas, while Paul gave lectures and read poetry at Chautauqua tent meetings. Begun as a Methodist camp meeting on the shores of Chautauqua Lake in upstate New York, the popular summer events expanded into traveling shows that served rural communities. Pitching tents in small towns, Chautauqua meetings provided speakers and entertainers for adult education and moral uplift. With his combination of idealism and personal charm, Paul Pearson persuaded a dozen Quaker friends to contribute funds to launch the Swarthmore Chautauqua Association in 1912. Its shows traveled among hundreds of small towns along the Atlantic seaboard, from Canada to South Carolina. He purchased tents and folding chairs and hired lecturers, actors, singers, and instrumentalists to perform during the annual summer circuit. Fourteen-year-old Drew Pearson became a tent boy, part of the three-man crew that erected the tents in pastures, school yards, and courthouse squares, kept them clean, punched tickets, supplied water to the speakers and musicians, and then took down the tents at the end of the week. Later promoted to crew captain and advance man, he organized parades and other attractions to draw in the crowds. Chautauqua developed the promotional skills that would serve him handily as a columnist and broadcaster.[17]

Drew Pearson often reminisced about the life lessons he gained from those experiences. He recalled that when he lost his temper as head of the wrecking crew, he could not get the others to do as he wanted. When he muted his anger, he achieved more. Late-night schedules also trained him to sleep "anywhere and at any time," a knack that facilitated his peripatetic life. As soon as they heard the last notes of the final act, his crew would start dismantling the tents. They rarely finished their work before four in the morning, grabbing a few hours of sleep in the baggage car before the train left at eight. Railroad engineers usually let them have a bucket of hot water from the train boiler for washing up. At Reidsville, North Carolina, during the summer of 1914, there was no water available at the train site, so Drew and another worker found a spigot at a tobacco factory near the tracks. "It was just beginning to be dawn, which did not faze us because the area was rather deserted," Pearson later recollected. "But as dawn came, a Negro pedaled by on a bicycle, whom we later learned had turned us in to the police. At any rate, we were arrested an hour later while asleep in the baggage car." A judge ruled them not guilty of obscene exposure on the grounds that it was everyone's duty to be clean. Insignificant at the time, the incident later became grist for Pearson's opponents, who salaciously distorted it.[18]

Pearson attended the private Swarthmore Preparatory School, which his cash-strapped father paid for by giving poetry recitals there each year. In 1914 he convinced his parents to send him to a "big league prep," the prestigious Phillips Exeter Academy. On his way to the academy, the teenage Pearson informed his father that he planned to "stop off about half a day each in New York and Boston to see about newspaper work," to help pay his way. He received a scholarship that required him to keep his grades high enough to maintain it. Reporting that Exeter was "a tough grind," Pearson managed to graduate cum laude, and credited the school's hard regimen with helping him through later life. Exeter's curriculum also introduced him to foreign policy and sparked a lifelong, unfulfilled dream of becoming a diplomat.[19]

He returned home to attend Swarthmore College, which he sailed through with comparative ease after the rigors of Exeter. Pearson joined a fraternity, took the lead in student plays, edited the college newspaper, and made Phi Beta Kappa. As a sophomore in 1917, he went to Washington to witness Woodrow Wilson's second inauguration, and eagerly followed the news as the United States entered World War I. Despite attending a Quaker college, some Swarthmore students promptly enlisted in the army—his dorm roommate died in action in France. Paul Pearson, who employed Chautauqua shows to entertain and educate American troops, had a mixed mind about military service, but Edna Pearson ardently opposed the war and dissuaded her son from volunteering. "To think of my enlisting made her sick," he recalled. "We could not even discuss it." Instead he joined the Students Army Training Corps, which enabled him to delay the draft.[20]

Swarthmore students drilled with brooms rather than rifles because pacifists on the board of managers refused to allow firearms on campus. As editor of the student newspaper, Drew Pearson fought the policy but lost. The war ended before he graduated in 1919, cutting off his student training and any chance of seeing combat. He won the state oratorical championship that year with a tribute to his fallen classmates, "Our Debt to Humanity": "The work of every hour, if well and faithfully done will be preparing us to render a higher and better service to the liberated world, so that the sacrifice of those who have toiled and suffered and died in our stead shall not have been in vain." After graduation, he sought to carry out those ideals by enlisting in Herbert Hoover's food mission in Europe but found that humanitarian effort already glutted with volunteers. Then he heard that the American Friends Service Committee planned to send a small unit to help rebuild villages in war-torn Serbia. After checking an encyclopedia to determine the difference between Serbia and Siberia, he signed up and became director of the mission.[21]

On August 15, 1919, Pearson's small band of Quaker volunteers sailed from New York. Just twenty-one, he grew his signature mustache on the trip to appear more mature. His team built houses in the Balkans, and the inhabitants of one Serbian town renamed it Pearsonovatz in gratitude. After two years of benevolent labor—much of it involving deskwork, writing reports, and answering mail—he returned to New York in steerage, eager for new adventures in distant lands. Back home, however, he detected a change in the national attitude, realizing that most of his friends had "quit worrying about the rest of the world."[22]

Drawing on his Serbian experiences, Pearson lectured at Chautauqua, which raised family hopes that he might assume charge of the whole program. Instead, he took a job as an instructor of industrial geography at the Wharton School of Business and Finance, replacing his brother Leon on the teaching staff. This interlude served only to convince him that he wanted no career as a teacher. He aspired to become a diplomat but learned that the American foreign service depended on independently wealthy men who could afford to live and entertain from their own money. "It was impossible to succeed in this rarefied profession without a private income and I had no such income," Pearson concluded. He settled on becoming a journalist, anticipating that a reporter could travel the world while building his financial resources. "Little did I understand at the time," he later reflected, "how poorly newspapermen were paid."[23]

Taking odd jobs for Philadelphia newspapers, Pearson hoped to break into big-time journalism. Over the Christmas holidays in 1921, he persuaded Swarthmore's student newspaper, *The Phoenix*, to send him to the Washington naval disarmament conference. A student newspaper correspondent was not likely to gain entry to such a prestigious event, but a reporter for the *Philadelphia Public Ledger* had charge of issuing press credentials and took pity on him. After attending a few sessions, Pearson determined to quit academia and go abroad again. This time he would pay his way around the world as a freelance correspondent. He assured his disappointed family that there was nothing he would rather do than "settle down, marry and help Father with Chautauqua. But I have my own life to live and my own ideas to work out—and after trying them, I shall come back and do what I have long wanted to do."[24]

Armed with an imposing prospectus, he set out to persuade editors to subscribe to his one-man syndication. Traveling by train across the country, he got off at various cities along the way. By the time he reached Seattle, he had contracts with thirty-five newspapers willing to pay for his "learned reports on the Far East." To cross the Pacific, he signed on as a seaman, and for authenticity got his chest tattooed before sailing. Other sailors easily spotted the fresh tattoo as a sign of his inexperience. In later years, however, the star and crescent tattoo (the insignia of his college fraternity) benefited his visits to Muslim countries.[25]

From Tokyo, Pearson headed to New Zealand and Australia to deliver lectures and find more papers willing to pay for his columns. He dashed out a few columns but counted on Asia to furnish more colorful and substantive news. His father, always ready with advice, urged him to "Write and re-write your articles; sift your material; make this series give you a reputation." Traveling through China, Pearson made his way north to Siberia and west to London, later recounting that he had slept "on the tops of freight cars, and in Turkish inns, and in the baggage racks of Hindu third class carriages, and behind the smoke stacks to keep warm in a Siberian boat." An Australian contract to interview Europe's twelve greatest men gave him license to call on dignitaries from Mahatma Gandhi to Benito Mussolini. All those articles earned enough for him to travel first class across the Atlantic. "I had come around the world in a year and a half, starting with $700 and arriving in New York with $730," he boasted. "I had seen a lot of the world, but more important I had learned a lot about the affairs of the world and concluded that it was not going to be too easy to make the world safe for democracy." But the trip did not lead to the full-time reporting job he wanted, and he reluctantly returned to academe, this time teaching economic geography at Columbia University. (One of his Columbia students, Ernest Cuneo, be-came a lifelong friend, adviser, and news source.)[26]

By the spring of 1924, Pearson was hawking features for the United Publishers Corporation News Service, a small operation run by his uncle Drew that produced such trade journals as *Hardware Age*. The assignment gave him 60 percent of the sales but no salary or travel expenses. Still, he earned $100 a week on a trip to the West Coast and back. Along the route he conducted interviews with some famous figures, from auto manufacturer

Henry Ford in Michigan to the botanist Luther Burbank in California, to sell through the syndicate.[27]

In search of more stable employment, Pearson went to Washington one weekend in 1924 to gather advice from his father's friend, the veteran newspaper reporter William Hard. The journalist was ill, and his wife, Anne, invited Pearson to accompany her to a dinner party hosted by Eleanor "Cissy" Patterson at her imposing mansion on Dupont Circle. An imperious socialite whose grandfather had owned the *Chicago Tribune*, Cissy Patterson was then writing for her brother's *New York Daily News* and the Hearst newspapers in Washington. Pearson described her as "one of the most gifted women in Washington but who has dissipated her gifts, for the most part on trivialities." Eyeing her unexpected guest, Cissy Patterson rushed upstairs and persuaded her eighteen-year-old daughter, Felicia Gizycka, to join them for dinner. She seated the young people next to each other. Pearson was immediately smitten with the blue-eyed blonde. She regarded her twenty-six-year-old dinner partner as "older than God," but when he described himself as a writer, she confided her own literary ambitions, and went nightclubbing with him after dinner.[28]

"Into the lap of this fast-moving, hard-boiled family I landed," Pearson marveled, "a naive, unsophisticated young Quaker from Philadelphia." The object of his affection, Countess Felicia Gizycka, was the daughter of a Polish count. Her father had kidnapped her as a child to use as a bargaining chip while divorcing his wealthy wife. Felicia grew up under the gaze of a distant and disapproving mother, who made her feel unlovable despite her beauty. In an interview she later commented that a transient life could cause a lack of stability that "can destroy a person." After their first encounter, Drew Pearson found multiple excuses to visit Washington, but Felicia did not want to be tied down and resisted her would-be suitor.[29]

To encourage the relationship, that summer Cissy Patterson invited Pearson to her ranch at Jackson Hole, Wyoming. Her unexpected overture reached him by telegram in Columbus, Ohio, where he was peddling syndicated features to local newspapers. He sold a woman's feature to the *Columbus Dispatch*, got an advance on the commission, and caught the next train to Wyoming. The reunion could not have gone worse. Felicia ignored him and fought constantly with her mother. Finally, she fled on horseback, with Pearson riding after. He caught up with her at the train station, and rode with her to Salt Lake City, mostly in silence. "You bore me," she told him bluntly, "and the more I see of you, the more bored I get."[30]

Rebellious Felicia sought independence by working as a waitress in San Diego. After a while, she contacted Pearson to ask if he would review her writing. Their relationship gradually warmed until she began to see marriage as another path for escaping her dominating mother. "You're nineteen now," Pearson reasoned. "Marry me until you're twenty-one and I'll let you go then if you want to go." He felt sure he could make the marriage succeed, telling a friend that it would work because he knew the Poles pretty well from his world tour. "Yes," said the friend, "but do you know the Pattersons?" He would be marrying into the capital's most vituperative family.[31]

In 1925, with her mother's blessing, Felicia Gizycka married Drew Pearson in California. Years later he looked back with wonder that a "gawky newspaperman" drawing an account from United Publishers on sales commissions rather than a salary was able to make a living and support a new wife, "but I did." Leaving Felicia in San Diego, he traveled to San Francisco, Portland, Seattle, Santa Fe, and Denver selling columns. He finally abandoned this arduous assignment by wangling an expedition to the Far East as a reporter. His syndicate's financial backer—a banker friend of his uncle's—agreed to underwrite the trip, which enabled Pearson to sail back across the Pacific first class this time. For the next year and a half, the newlyweds journeyed from Japan into China, Russia, and Europe. His biggest story confirmed rumors that the Bolsheviks were shipping arms into China to stir political unrest, but his syndicate could only manage to persuade a single newspaper— William Randolph Hearst's *New York American*—to carry his reports.[32]

The couple settled in New York City, where Pearson sold features for United Publishers and again taught at Columbia. He weighed a few business opportunities, but his syndicate warned that he would be making a serious mistake if he gave up a future in journalism. At least he earned enough to turn down Cissy Patterson's offer of an allowance. "From now on Drew and I will accept *no* money and I will ask for no clothes or presents," Felicia informed her mother. "I am, after all, grown up and married and your responsibility has (fortunately for us both) ceased. There will not be any discussions about our plans. Drew and I will do very well on whatever salary he makes plus my present from Gram's trust fund." She assured her mother that many young couples got along fine on half of her husband's salary. They adopted a more unconventional style of life, taking pleasure in drinking and dining in places her mother would abhor.[33]

At last in 1926, Drew Pearson landed the kind of job he had been seeking, as foreign editor for David Lawrence's new Washington-based *United States Daily* (later *US News & World Report*). Neither he nor his wife realized that her mother had secretly brokered the offer. Since his new position carried a more impressive title than salary, Pearson supplemented his income by freelancing for the *Christian Science Monitor* and the *Baltimore Sun*, and by signing on as the American agent for the Irish Hospitals' Sweepstakes. Lotteries were illegal in the United States at the time, a detail he willingly overlooked since the job paid handsomely and provided a chauffeur-driven limousine. For almost a year they lived in his mother-in-law's Washington mansion, which impressed his visiting father as "beautifully furnished, elaborate, grand, elegant, expensive." Then they moved to a Georgetown townhouse, where Felicia entertained and Drew cultivated news sources. Attending one of his son's "soirées," Paul Pearson marveled at the distinguished guests who "discussed various problems in the frankest way, as it is understood that no person is to be quoted or the things that are said are never to be mentioned in public."[34]

The birth of their daughter, Ellen, revived Felicia's feelings of constraint in marriage. After rebuking her husband for being self-centered and complaining that they could not communicate, she exercised the option that he had proposed, to let her go when she turned twenty-one if she was unhappy. Felicia expressed no bitterness toward her husband; she just wanted to live on her own, write, and earn enough not to depend on her mother. Pearson believed that his young wife had not tried hard enough to make the marriage work, but he agreed not to contest the divorce. The breakup made him feel like a terrible failure. "I suppose it is chiefly a blow to my self-conceit," he admitted. "I am a self-opinionated person and have always prided myself that I could succeed at anything. So probably it is a good thing for me to come off my high-horse." Since they shared a child, he promised to remain friends even after the marriage ended. He fully expected her to remarry, telling her that "people like yourself don't stay single very long."[35]

Six weeks after Felicia moved to Reno, Nevada, in 1927, Pearson read a newspaper article announcing the divorce decree that ended their brief marriage. His close friend George Abell was a gossip columnist with entrée into the liveliest social events of Jazz Age Washington. Abell introduced the new bachelor to a hedonistic lifestyle. In private notes Pearson wrote that once he had no wife of his own, he "did not hesitate to make love to all kinds and sorts and sizes of wives," including his ex-mother-in-law. Cissy Patterson blamed the divorce on her daughter and remained fond of her ex-son-in-law. In 1930, when she became editor of William Randolph Hearst's morning paper, the *Washington Herald*, she tapped Pearson to write unsigned editorials and a gossip column—under the pseudonym Peter Carter. When rumors attributed the column to Cissy herself, she chided him: "You hid behind my skirts long enough. You let me take all the blame for your articles which I tried my best and unsuccessfully to control. If you were any kind of a man you would have come out long ago and told the world the truth about Peter Carter."[36]

As Drew Pearson ascended, his father fell on hard times. Paul Pearson had resigned as head of the public speaking department at Swarthmore to devote himself to Chautauqua programs in the United States and abroad. But radio and motion pictures caused tent show audiences to dwindle, until the Depression permanently extinguished the Swarthmore Chautauqua Association in 1930. Having taken out mortgages on his home and borrowed money from friends to pay the association's debts, Pearson had to file for personal bankruptcy. Fortunately, the director of the US Bureau of Efficiency, Herbert Brown, was seeking someone to become the first civilian governor of the Virgin Islands. A Quaker himself, Brown consulted friends at Swarthmore, who assured him that Dr. Pearson possessed the necessary qualities. Further endorsements came from Paul's brother Drew, who had worked for Herbert Hoover during World War I and contributed financially to the Republican Party, and from Cissy Patterson, who felt indebted to her former son-in-law and exerted her influence to help his father.[37]

The United States acquired the Virgin Islands from Denmark during World War I, to keep them from falling under German control. The US Navy took charge but sought to be freed from the burden after the islands' economy collapsed. Prohibition had ruined the rum industry, turning the Virgin Islands, in President Herbert Hoover's tactless phrase, into "an effective poorhouse." Hoover assigned control to the Interior Department and appointed Paul Pearson as governor. Tasked with finding ways to boost the economy, Pearson built a hotel to encourage tourism, reestablished rum production, and created agricultural and trade cooperatives to lift the largely black population from devastating poverty. His efforts won praise from progressives but raised protests from the islands' powerful landowners and their allies in Congress.[38]

The last thing Governor Pearson needed was for his son to publish a book criticizing the Hoover administration. Other than having appointed his father, Drew Pearson dismissed Hoover as a dismal failure, stubbornly unable to lead the nation through the Depression. Family members chided him for writing *Washington Merry-Go-Round*, which would "reflect on Uncle Paul." They reminded him of "how many damn rotten breaks" his father had gotten and begged him to be more discreet. But that was not his style of journalism, as he explained: "I have won the reputation of being unsparing, even with my friends, even with my family." For his part, Paul Pearson urged his son not to change his convictions "to give support to thy father's position." He calculated that since President Hoover faced a tough reelection, he would want to avoid bad publicity. "It would make a lovely story to give the press that the Gov. had been recalled because his son was a Democrat and an anti-Hoover man."[39]

But by then, the public had soured on Herbert Hoover. The authors of *Washington Merry-Go-Round* reminded voters that he had campaigned for president on promises of bold action but in office had vacillated. They cited his administration as conspicuous for "abysmal incompetence, do-nothingness and reactionary stultification." That Hoover received any favorable press coverage, the authors blamed on the nation's predominantly Republican newspaper publishers and the "trained seals" they hired as Washington correspondents. Reporters who covered Hoover witnessed his pettiness and bad temper, and measured his failures, but "no matter how damning the facts, the correspondents of these papers must suppress or distort them where the President and his administration is concerned." Having been subjected to Hoover's vindictiveness themselves, Pearson and Allen felt they had nothing else to lose by reporting the news that others dodged.[40]

Bob Allen came up with the idea of their writing a "Daily Washington Merry-Go-Round" newspaper column. For Paul Pearson, the prospect of his son entering into partnership with the rough-hewn and profane Allen was deeply disturbing. From the Virgin Islands, Governor Pearson wrote that he was proud of Drew for "being so gentle, kindly, genuine, and *unprofessional*," meaning that he avoided the "cynical, hard, superior air" of so many newspaper reporters. "When I urge thee to be thyself I am only anxious that thee guard carefully against the Bob Allen influence," he made clear. "He is such a dominating person, demanding for himself the center of the gravy and is so intolerant of others whom he dislikes—and he dislikes nearly everybody, and he is so bitter in his denunciations, that one must avoid him or pull hard against him in order not to take on his complexion. . . . Thee is his opposite in every way." As much as Drew Pearson revered his father, he did not follow this advice.[41]

Pearson and Allen peddled the idea of a daily column to carry on the mission of the *Merry-Go-Round* books, telling the Washington stories that newspapers dare not print. Their column would combine serious reporting with a light touch, promising "the same wit and gaiety, the same passion for truth, the same sound judgment and fair appraisal" that had made the books so notable. They approached several syndicates but got no offers until United Features Syndicate—a subsidiary of the Scripps-Howard newspaper chain—invited the pair to New York to discuss their proposal. Since Allen was away covering the presidential campaign, he authorized Pearson to seal the deal. When he saw the final contract, however, he was surprised to find that his brainchild would have the byline "Drew Pearson and Robert S. Allen."[42]

United Features advertised "The Merry-Go-Round Cocktail," a mix of important news, amusing events, brisk style, realistic reporting, and crusading spirit: "Shake well with vigorous advance publicity for best results." Yet after a month of promotion, they had gotten only one definite order to subscribe—from the *Richmond News Leader*. Even the Scripps-Howard newspapers viewed the samples unenthusiastically. Editors expressed skepticism about a news column and preferred something more interpretive. They belittled Pearson and Allen's samples for containing more gossip than analysis. The last year of the Hoover administration had seen further erosion of public interest in news from Washington. Still, United Features held out hope that if Franklin D. Roosevelt won the election that fall "there will be a gorgeous opportunity to start the Merry-Go-Round whirling and we would like to supply the calliope effects."[43]

That wish came true. Heightened public demand for news about the coming Roosevelt administration encouraged papers to expand their Washington coverage. Over the next decade, the number of correspondents in the congressional press galleries doubled. Papers that could not afford a Washington bureau found it cost effective to subscribe to the "Washington Merry-Go-Round." Still, when the column officially debuted on Monday, December 12, 1932, it had only six subscribers, including Cissy Patterson's *Washington Herald*. That first column led with some unexpected news:

Washington—Capitol Hill is abuzz with reliable White House information that President Hoover seriously considers himself a 1936 contender. When the report first reached Republican congressional leaders they brushed it off as idle rumors. Some of them differ on the causes of the party's defeat. But all were agreed that the President was through as a political figure. Developments in the last week, however, authoritatively confirm the report regarding the President's attitude.[44]

Their premier allegation was not as far-fetched as it seemed. Despite his landslide defeat, Hoover was already angling for renomination in 1936, blindly unaware of what a political liability he had become for his party. Despite getting that story right, the column's slow acceptance convinced both columnists to take day jobs. Pearson doubled as Washington correspondent for the French news agency Havas and Allen as Washington bureau chief for the *Philadelphia Record*. By the end of their first year, however, more than two hundred papers had subscribed. Although Allen continued straight news reporting for the *Record*, Pearson now concentrated his efforts on the column.[45]

Before long, the "Merry-Go-Round" had more subscribers than all syndicated columns except for Walter Winchell's celebrity gossip column "On Broadway." Where Winchell sprinkled a dash of politics into his society reporting, Pearson and Allen injected occasional social items into a primarily political column. While they included colorful sidelights drawn from capital chatter, they wanted the column to be more than just a rumor mill. It would dissect policies, cast judgment on political decisions, and provide backroom scuttlebutt to bureaucratic infighting, military maneuvering, and political stupidity.[46]

The columnists drew only one boundary on their reporting. The straight-news Bob Allen had no taste for exposing politicians' personal indiscretions, and Drew Pearson's personal history made him shy of reporting sex scandals. "Like all prying journalists, he treasured his privacy," the novelist Gore Vidal archly observed. In 1936 Pearson's private life spilled into the headlines when he married Luvie Moore Abell, the ex-wife of his best friend, George Abell. Described as a tall, "streamlined, art moderne beauty," Luvie was a social creature with a wide circle of friends in Washington. She shared Pearson's liberal politics and outlook on life and was a "soft velvet glove" of tact and diplomacy, who could soothe feelings that her controversial husband offended.[47]

George Abell's drinking and extramarital affairs had destroyed his marriage and driven his wife to seek refuge with Pearson. Abell could neither reconcile himself to the divorce nor forgive his former friend. He uttered such violent threats at the National Press Club bar that Pearson felt compelled to hire a bodyguard for protection. Abell then violated court orders by spiriting his five-year-old son, Tyler, out of the country, secretly taking the boy to the Channel Island of Sark. With help from Scotland Yard, Drew and Luvie Pearson tracked them down, and made international headlines by retrieving the boy. That tumultuous experience encouraged Pearson to steer

the "Merry-Go-Round" away from accounts of adultery and divorce—
although if an exceptionally juicy story came his way, he would slip it to
Walter Winchell. "Frankly, we are not particularly interested in the private
life of Secretary Ickes," Pearson wrote to one tipster eager to blow the whistle
on FDR's Interior Secretary, "and if it is true that a young lady is seen going
into his house late in the evening, doubtless it is his secretary."[48]

"What a columnist may write in his column may not always be news,"
his ex-mother-in-law's paper noted. "But when a columnist elopes with another columnist's wife—even though the lady has been duly divorced—that
IS news." Cissy Patterson remained so close to her former son-in-law that
she hired his new wife to review movies for her papers. Having remained
friends also worked to Pearson's advantage when Patterson bought the
Washington Herald along with Hearst's afternoon *Washington Times* and
merged them into the *Washington Times-Herald* in 1939. As publisher, she
turned the *Times-Herald* into a lively, colorful, and widely popular newspaper. She relied on Drew Pearson as a trusted adviser, and her paper carried
his column.[49]

As columnists, Pearson and Allen practiced the teamwork they had
worked so well with their books. Allen regarded his own "somewhat exuberant" writing style as better than Pearson's, but Pearson edited the final
copy, polishing its prose and adding sparkle before sending their joint text
to the syndicate. Each contributed his own area of expertise. Pearson concentrated on the State Department, leaving Congress almost entirely to
Allen. One senator commented, "I do not see Drew much. Drew must
edit the stuff Bob writes, because Drew never comes around here, and Bob
is always here." On one of Pearson's rare visits to the Senate press gallery
for a debate on South American policy, he stunned Allen by being unable to recognize anyone. "Who is that?" he asked. "That's [Idaho Senator
William] Borah." Allen exclaimed. "Don't you know Borah? Everybody
knows Borah." His partner had not yet made it his business to know many
senators. "His whole orientation," said Allen, "his whole interest was society and diplomatic."[50]

Unabashedly provocative, the partners rarely hesitated to jump into a
dispute or disclose damaging information. They promised stories that the
newspapers had not printed, either because they did not have it, or had
suppressed it. Publishing unauthorized information was as old as the federal
government, but Pearson and Allen drummed the word "leaks" into eve-
ryday vocabularies by touting theirs. Revealing items that others had kept
off the record brought them under fire but further piqued their readers'

interest. Paul Pearson encountered that phenomenon while speaking in Illinois. A white-haired lady inquired if he was Drew Pearson's father, and then told him: "Well you tell Drew that what we in Petersburg want to know is how he finds out so many things that nobody else in Washington finds out."[51]

2

Nothing to Fear

THE NEW DEAL PROVIDED A bonanza for the "Washington Merry-Go-Round." President Franklin D. Roosevelt and his cabinet members showered the columnists with strategic leaks, usually to test the waters for public and congressional reactions before making official announcements. This enabled Pearson and Allen to scoop the rest of the press corps on pending appointments and become the first to report that the United States would give diplomatic recognition to the Soviet Union. Although they appreciated being the beneficiaries of presidential largesse, the columnists resisted playing propagandists. Criticizing the implementation of some of Roosevelt's programs, and poking fun at some of his appointees, they managed to ruffle the president despite their overall support for the New Deal. The column also irked Roosevelt by revealing items he was not yet ready to release or did not want known at all. "Roosevelt got sore at me over many things I wrote," Pearson noted. "I praised him when I thought he was right and panned him when I thought he was wrong."[1]

Critics accused Drew Pearson of having been called more names by more presidents of the United States than any other journalist in history. His friends claimed that he enjoyed having presidents call him names. But it hurt when FDR, the president whom Pearson most admired, blasted him as a chronic liar. That stinging rebuke marked the worst moment of their uneven relations. Roosevelt's invective confirmed to Pearson that his reporting was bound to irritate those in power. At least the insults kept his name in the news.[2]

Although Pearson identified with New Deal liberalism, the "Washington Merry-Go-Round" appeared in papers of all ideological hues. To avoid

alienating readers and editors, he portrayed himself as politically bal-
anced: his father was a Republican, his mother a Democrat, and when he
lived with his family in Pennsylvania he had registered as a Republican. As
his politics shifted, he did not bother changing his affiliation since as a resident of Washington, DC, he could not vote. Not until after a constitutional
amendment in 1961 gave District citizens a ballot in presidential elections
did he register as a Democrat. Meanwhile, the "Merry-Go-Round" managed to irritate presidents from both parties.[3]

FDR aimed for friendlier relations with the Washington press corps
than his prickly predecessor, Herbert Hoover, had. Reporters appreciated
his administration's more open atmosphere, although they understood that
Roosevelt was using them to sell his programs to the public. No matter how
artfully the president courted the correspondents, he could not control the
news they reported. In 1934, FDR complained to *New York Times* reporter
Charles Hurd that he often read news reports of what was in his mind before he had reached a decision. There was too much interpretive reporting,
he groused, especially in the "inside dope" columns being syndicated from
Washington—singling out the "Washington Merry-Go-Round" as an of-
fender. When Hurd asked what type of reporting he thought more appropriate, Roosevelt replied that "retaining of the facts as announced would be
sufficient," adding that the public had enough intelligence to make its own
interpretation. In common with most presidents, he wanted the press to accept his official pronouncements and stop second-guessing them.[4]

Roosevelt lifted the nation's spirits with a bold inaugural address, assuring
Americans they had nothing to fear except fear itself. In hearty agreement,
Pearson and Allen cheered passage of the Emergency Banking Act during
the new president's first week in office:

> Not for a dozen years has there been any real control over banks.
> Politics played too big a part, prevented strict inspection. . . . Aiding
> and abetting [the bankers] were various members of the House Banking
> and Currency Committee, scrap-heap for all the financial cranks in
> Congress. Personal jealousy dictated their action. If they could not
> get glory out of sponsoring a bill, they would not pass it out of com-
> mittee, regardless of the need of the country. . . . Roosevelt was told
> all this and more. He decided that the flattering of the House Banking
> Committee, the lobbying of the bankers, the cries of "Radicalism"
> from Big Business, all could be overcome in one week because of the
> need of the hour.[5]

The "Merry-Go-Round" introduced the New Dealers and explained their intentions at a time when Americans were eager to learn what was underway in Washington. Beyond the headlines, the columnists promised to tell the "untold story" of the New Deal. Their inside sources enabled them to reproduce private conversations nearly verbatim, giving readers a sense of listening in on public officials. They also profited from the many rivalries and power struggles within the Roosevelt administration, recording the bickering of cabinet secretaries and bureau chiefs who jockeyed for presidential approval. One side or another would leak information to bolster its own position or undermine its opponent's. FDR encouraged rivalries, calculating that they produced imaginative proposals and creative compromises. But Roosevelt also liked to keep people guessing. He did not mind the column's reports on his advisers' squabbles so much as he resented having his own hand revealed.[6]

Roosevelt's secretary of state, Cordell Hull, once opened a staff meeting by asking, "Are we talking for this room or for Pearson?" What leaked into the column from State proved so accurate that the editors of the *Kansas City Journal-Post* identified predictions in the "Merry-Go-Round" as "tantamount to a State Department announcement." Officials in other agencies also learned the impossibility of making government leak-proof. Even Roosevelt floated trial balloons he could deny if necessary. Angry over an embarrassing leak, FDR once threatened his staff with dire consequences unless they stanched the flow. But he conceded that an occasional, well-timed leak could help, and offered as an example an item that they might leak to Drew Pearson in order to assess the congressional reaction. "Prichard, couldn't you manage to do that?" Roosevelt asked his aide Edward F. Prichard Jr. "I already have," Prichard replied.[7]

Mirroring the Democratic Party, the New Deal yoked Northern urban liberals together with Southern rural conservatives. The "Merry-Go-Round" aimed its fire at the most conservative members of the cabinet, notably Commerce Secretary Jesse Jones, tapping information that his liberal colleagues leaked about him. Jones owned a string of newspapers in Texas and had an instinct to fight back against bad publicity. Editors who published the "Merry-Go-Round" regularly received his protests over items in the column, demanding that they print retractions. "Of course, Jesse is very smart," Pearson commented. "He also knows that editors hate to waste white paper and also hate to print retractions. He knows that retractions damage a column like mine." Pearson never backed off covering Jones, citing his national economic influence in providing government loans. Anyone who held "life and death over a large percentage of American business," he wrote, should not be immune from scrutiny.[8]

Pearson played the State Department's sternest analyst, considering it out of step with the rest of the New Deal. He portrayed Secretary of State Hull as jealously guarding his position against ambitious subordinates aiming to replace him. Although Hull professed never to read the "Merry-Go-Round," he periodically erupted with fury over its charges. Such feisty public officials as Cordell Hull and Jesse Jones fought back against every criticism, while others took the column's negative appraisals in stride, without protest. Male chauvinism likely led the columnists to belittle the liberal Labor Secretary Frances Perkins, the first woman ever to serve in the cabinet, but she refrained from responding, suffering through the bad press while retaining her post throughout the Roosevelt presidency.[9]

The agency that garnered the column's most favorable coverage was the Federal Bureau of Investigation (as the old Bureau of Investigation had been renamed in 1935). Attorney General Homer Cummings consulted with Pearson and Allen about how to boost the FBI's public image. Recent publicity bestowed on the crime sprees of John Dillinger and Baby Face Nelson made Cummings fret that the press was romanticizing gangsters. Pearson and Allen advised him "to build up the FBI"—not in numbers of agents but in its public standing—and recommended that FBI Director J. Edgar Hoover hire public relations specialists. Thereafter, their columns and radio broadcasts inflated Hoover's reputation, referring to him as "Super-G-Man J. Edgar Hoover," and "Boss Man J. Edgar Hoover, who seldom slips up." Not until years later would Pearson conclude that he had "helped create a monster."[10]

Good relations worked both ways. Anxious to retain the friendship of opinion shapers, Director Hoover instructed his aides to make sure the columnists got copies of all the FBI's news releases "and interesting material which we have sent out from time to time." When Pearson's stepson was kidnapped and spirited off to Great Britain, Hoover introduced Pearson to the Scotland Yard officials who helped him find the boy. Yet Hoover gritted his teeth whenever the muckraking journalists uncovered some wrongdoing ahead of the FBI or published the slightest criticism of the bureau. In 1938, for instance, the "Merry-Go-Round" outraged Hoover by quoting a Guatemalan diplomat who expressed surprise that Hoover wore "a distinctive and conspicuous perfume." Hoover declared it a lie and tried to get the diplomat fired.[11]

Once when Pearson and Allen took a vacation, they invited J. Edgar Hoover to be a guest columnist, offering this as a gesture of apology for any "whacks and jibes" they might have taken at him. They sometimes showed items to Hoover in advance of publication, allowing him to review them for accuracy. Whenever Pearson felt that something might have gotten Hoover's dander up, he would drop by the director's office to apologize. Theirs was always a tenuous relationship, but it paid the columnists significantly to have the bureau verify their reports.[12]

At the start of the New Deal, even the most conservative Washington columnists of the day—Frank Kent, David Lawrence, and Mark Sullivan—backed FDR. Regardless of ideology, Mark Sullivan reasoned that for them to make things difficult for the new president as he struggled to lift the nation out of the Depression would have been "almost unpatriotic." Within months, however, they had reverted to form and condemned the New Deal's tendencies toward centralization and regimentation. With the Republican Party decimated and demoralized during Roosevelt's first term, these critical columnists took the lead in opposing his policies. By contrast, Pearson and Allen reveled in the New Deal's liberal experiments. No matter how favorable their treatment, however, Roosevelt was never satisfied. He frequently vented steam against the "Merry-Go-Round," telling one group of newspaper editors that he could not see why any of them printed the column.[13]

The "Merry-Go-Round" floated so many trial balloons for the administration that Roosevelt's opponents called it a White House pet. One reader contrasted the column's favorable treatment of Arthurdale, a New Deal planned community in West Virginia, with the *Saturday Evening Post's* scathing critique of that project's inefficiency. Pearson responded that the *Post* had been conducting a prejudiced campaign against the Roosevelt administration, while his column had highlighted both the New Deal's virtues and faults. The conservative Abilene, Kansas, *Reflector* agreed, advising its readers: "Their inside stories which the administration is trying to keep quiet are causing much anguish among the faithful."[14]

Among the stories that irritated Roosevelt was the column's exposure of his plans to use public works money to rebuild the navy, packaging military rearmament as job-creating programs. Their revelation sparked a rebellion among isolationists in Congress, killing the program and marking the first legislative resistance the president encountered. Later in the 1930s, when America's military unpreparedness became more evident, Pearson came to regret his part in hindering Roosevelt's early efforts at rearmament.[15]

Simmering resentment prompted FDR to try to put the column out of business. At a cabinet meeting in 1934, Roosevelt boasted that he had persuaded General Douglas MacArthur to file a libel suit against Pearson and Allen. MacArthur's tour of duty as army chief of staff was coming to an end and he craved an unprecedented second term. The president advised the general that he could not reappoint him while the "Merry-Go-Round" was making serious accusations against him but might reconsider if MacArthur acted to clear his name. Taking his cue, General MacArthur sued the columnists for $1.75 million, charging that they held him up to ridicule and accused him of conduct unbecoming an officer. Not only was the demand staggeringly high, but it carried the threat that he might also sue each of the 270 newspapers that ran the column at the time. Pearson worried so much about this suit that he transferred the deed to his Georgetown home to his mother to keep it from being levied against any court order. When he remarried in 1936, she passed the ownership to his bride.[16]

The "Merry-Go-Round" belittled MacArthur as the "hero of the Bonus Battle." In 1932, when unemployed veterans of World War I encamped in Washington to lobby for early payment of their promised bonus, MacArthur had led the army in driving the Bonus Marchers from the capital with bayonets and burning their shacks. The column also pictured him pushing through a throng of notables in order to stand next to Roosevelt to watch the inaugural parade the next year. But what most galled MacArthur was the column's claim that he had pulled strings to advance his career. Pearson and Allen revealed that MacArthur had persuaded his father-in-law, a generous contributor to the Republican Party, to intervene with the secretary of war to win MacArthur's promotion to major general over more senior officers. Pearson had gotten that story personally from MacArthur's ex-wife, Louise Cromwell. When the general filed his suit, however, she refused to confirm in public what she had divulged at the dinner table.[17]

Urged by their lawyer to settle the potentially ruinous lawsuit, Pearson and Allen instead searched for more dirt on the general. A Mississippi congressman mentioned that MacArthur paid frequent visits to the rooms of a Eurasian woman at the Washington hotel where he stayed. That tip led the columnists to Isabel "Belle" Rosario Cooper, who candidly admitted she had been the general's mistress in the Philippines. At eighteen, she accompanied him to Washington, but instead of being welcomed into his home and introduced to his mother, she found herself installed in a hotel. When they fell out, he cut her off financially and rebuffed her every effort to contact him. But the young woman had kept a diary and saved the general's love letters, written in purple prose and signed "Doug" and "Daddy." She lent the letters to Pearson and Allen and authorized their lawyer to put them up for sale. Pearson advised his syndicate that she also confirmed MacArthur's obsession with being reappointed as army chief of staff, and his intention "to jail Bob and me, and various other threats to get our jobs."[18]

When General MacArthur learned what was happening, he dispatched his aide, Major Dwight Eisenhower, to track down Belle Cooper. But Pearson's brother Leon had hidden the young woman in a Baltimore hotel. "We had so much evidence on the old boy, that it was almost a little pathetic," Pearson chuckled. "In the end, the old boy came through completely, surrendering his sword in gallant form. We gave no retractions, no apologies, and no payment." MacArthur paid for the love letters. He was unmarried at the time and might well have won his case, despite the embarrassing evidence, but other military officers surmised that "He didn't want his mother to learn about that Eurasian girl!"[19]

The MacArthur case made Pearson lose confidence in lawyers. Whenever he was sued, he rejected lawyers' advice to settle out of court and preferred to let a jury decide his fate. He was not averse to using other means to avoid court cases, however. In 1937, Judge Albert Levitt threatened to sue in every city where the column was published, after the "Merry-Go-Round" reported that he had been reassigned to a Justice Department office long known as "a dumping ground for political misfits." Pearson insisted there was nothing libelous in the story since they could back it up fully, but he was not anxious to face another suit so soon after General MacArthur's. Rather than go to court, Pearson telephoned Judge Levitt and offered acceptable corrections.[20]

After prodding MacArthur to sue, FDR continued to veer between consulting Pearson and condemning him. He grew especially irate over the "Merry-Go-Round"'s invasion of his family's privacy. Regarding the president's children as "spoiled brats," the column exposed their efforts to capitalize on their father's position. It also followed Eleanor Roosevelt's peripatetic projects. At a press conference, restricted to women journalists, a reporter asked the first lady about one of her activities that Pearson and Allen had revealed. "How on earth did they find out about that?" she laughed. "I'm astonished at your astonishment," the reporter replied. "Does anything happen in Washington without someone finding out about it?" Finding herself in the swirl of so much publicity, the first lady lamented, "Sometimes I think I am the Washington 'Merry-Go-Round'!"[21]

"Presidents, I have found, can be upset by the most unexpected trivia," Pearson reflected. A brief mention in the column of the breakfast pastries that had accumulated at the White House during his absence infuriated Franklin Roosevelt:[22]

> 📰 When the President departed for Warm Springs last week, he left behind a surplus supply of Danish twisted buns. This is the President's favorite breakfast brand, and the White House has a standing order with Taylor's bakery in Washington for the daily delivery of twisted buns. But when the President left the other day, someone forgot to cancel the order, and there were Danish buns to spare.[23]

Roosevelt insisted that the story was false, and various cabinet secretaries backed him up. "The President is mad as hell," Postmaster General Jim Farley advised Pearson. "He doesn't like Danish pastry." Pearson followed with a second column, explaining that his sister-in-law had gotten the story while shopping at a Georgetown bakery whose truck was regularly parked outside the White House kitchen. Rather than denying the account, Pearson conceded that he should have identified the pastries simply as breakfast rolls. The columnists further irked Roosevelt by identifying "Home on the Range" as his favorite song (it was the favorite of his appointment secretary, Marvin McIntyre). Afterwards, bands everywhere played the tune for the president, who grew to detest it.[24]

Presidential peevishness surfaced again in 1936, when *New York Times* Washington correspondent Arthur Krock urged that FDR might defuse tensions in Europe by meeting foreign statesmen secretly at sea. Roosevelt waved off the idea. As soon as his ship dropped anchor, he was sure he would find Pearson and Allen appearing with "pencils in hand, from the mouth of a sea-going whale!"[25]

During the 1936 election, the popular magazine *The Literary Digest* conducted a postcard survey that showed Republican presidential candidate Alf Landon trouncing Roosevelt. On their radio program, Pearson and Allen asked listeners to rate the president's chances of reelection. The 20,000 responses they received in the first two weeks ran two to one in favor of Roosevelt. "Some people have difficulty in believing this, and I was rather surprised at it myself," Pearson told his father, speculating that their listeners were "more the ordinary class of people" than those surveyed by *The Literary Digest* (whose reliance on telephone books and car registrations for addresses favored those better off during the Depression). To further test public opinion, Bob Allen set out on a tour of the pivotal states, while Pearson called his many contacts to poll sentiments in their areas. On October 19, the "Merry-Go-Round" flatly predicted "it's in the bag for Roosevelt." Pearson slipped an advance copy of the column to the publicity director for the Democratic National Committee, "for whatever distribution you care to make of it." In November, the president's landslide reelection confirmed their forecasting, attracted more papers as subscribers, and put *The Literary Digest* out of business.[26]

That election year, Pearson and Allen produced another bestselling book, *The Nine Old Men*, detailing how the Supreme Court had undermined New Deal reforms. The book and columns popularized the notion that crusty septuagenarians opposed to innovation dominated the court. When Justice Owen Roberts began calling himself "just one of the Nine Old Men," his wife lamented that columnists had persuaded everyone to use the phrase. A young entrepreneur tried to sell copies of *The Nine Old Men* on the Supreme Court's steps until an indignant Chief Justice Charles Evans Hughes had him arrested. The book put Pearson and Allen back in Roosevelt's good graces and won them another exclusive. They were the first to report that the president would ask Congress for power to curb the Supreme Court's power, a week before he publicly proposed his ill-fated plan to "pack" the court with six additional justices.[27]

The "Merry-Go-Round"'s defense of the court packing plan incensed the conservative papers that carried it. When editors raised objections, Pearson insisted that they tried hard to build a reputation for impartiality. Reminding them that the column had received complaints from readers who were both anti–New Deal and pro–New Deal, he added, "I don't want to be taking this criticism too lightly, but as long as we get criticism from both sides I am not tremendously worried."[28]

Compensating for the president's periodic coolness, Pearson made friends with the liberal members of the cabinet, particularly Interior Secretary Harold Ickes and Agriculture Secretary Henry Wallace. These were not clandestine relations, as he often dined with them in public, usually for lunch at Washington's Mayflower Hotel. FDR informed Ickes that the conservative Commerce Secretary Jesse Jones had accused him of leaking a story to the columnist. Ickes assured the president that he had nothing to do with it. "And I can prove it by the fact that my name was mentioned in the story," he persisted. "If I had been the source, Pearson would not have mentioned my name. He always protects his sources."[29]

Pearson similarly courted the politically ambitious Attorney General Frank Murphy, a former governor of Michigan. It was Murphy who provided him with a list of those cabinet members who opposed an embargo on shipping arms to Spain during its civil war. Pearson backed the left-wing Spanish Republican government against a right-wing military rebellion led by General Francisco Franco. The column denounced the US embargo for denying aid to the Loyalists who backed the Spanish government while Nazi Germany and Fascist Italy were arming Franco. Murphy's list had included his own name, but the Catholic Church's conservative hierarchy reacted so negatively when the column appeared that Murphy denied opposing the embargo. Pearson never revealed Murphy as the leaker. He accepted the retraction as an act of political expediency. The "Merry-Go-Round"'s persistent attacks on Franco created a lingering feud between the columnist and the Catholic Church. The Quaker Pearson accused American Catholic leaders of lobbying for Franco. He disdained the Church's hierarchy but denied any religious prejudice, praising progressive members of the clergy. Pearson saw the Spanish civil war entirely through an anti-fascist prism. Only years later did he realize how much the Loyalist government's efforts to abolish parochial schools had offended church leaders.[30]

More focused on Washington politics, Bob Allen did not consider the Spanish civil war a fit subject for the "Washington Merry-Go-Round," but he tolerated his partner's passionate support for the Spanish Loyalists. Pearson took his crusade a step further by appealing to the antiwar Senator Gerald P. Nye to introduce a resolution making an exception to neutrality laws and permitting the sale of munitions to the Spanish government. He twice lobbied President Roosevelt to support the munitions sale. The president "always appeared on the side with me," he recorded, "but had always done the opposite."[31]

Overcoming their strained relations, Pearson teamed with President Roosevelt in 1938 in a failed attempt to unseat Maryland Senator Millard Tydings. In Congress, a coalition of conservative Republicans and Southern Democrats was obstructing New Deal programs, inspiring Roosevelt to purge his Democratic opponents, Tydings among them, by campaigning against them in party primaries. Pearson had his own reasons for opposing Tydings's reelection: the Maryland senator had cost Paul Pearson his post as governor of the Virgin Islands. Trying to pull the islands out of an economic slump, Governor Pearson's government had bought sugar mills and leased them to a nonprofit corporation, earmarking the revenue for better housing and education. FDR hailed these programs as a testing ground for New Deal experimentation, but congressional conservatives denounced them as socialist. Southerners also grew alarmed over Pearson's racial policies. When Eleanor Roosevelt visited in 1934, Governor Pearson hosted the Virgin Islands' first "mixed color reception." The event delighted the First Lady but stirred congressional fear of integration.[32]

Paul Pearson further managed to offend Senator Tydings, the chair of the Senate Committee on Territories, by having his patronage appointee fired as government attorney for the islands. In 1935, Tydings responded with an investigation into the collected charges against the governor. The governor's former administrative assistant, Paul Yates, was scheduled to testify but as he approached the hearing room Yates encountered Robert Allen in the hallway. The scrappy Allen, who had recommended Yates (a fellow Washington correspondent) for the job, now regarded him as a turncoat. Interior Secretary Harold Ickes reported that "Allen called Yates a double-crosser and Yates called Allen a son of a bitch, whereupon Allen, who is a little fellow but husky, proceeded to beat Yates up. He knocked him down once or twice, closing one eye and cutting his lip." Instead of testifying that day, Yates went to the hospital.[33]

Secretary Ickes accused the senator of whitewashing Governor Pearson's opponents, and Senator Tydings told the interior secretary to stop "intruding your unwelcome person into purely legislative matters." The Virgin Islands squabble grew so testy that President Roosevelt intervened to preserve party harmony. He summoned Ickes and Tydings for private consultations, after which Senator Tydings abruptly ended the hearings in the middle of Paul Yates's belated testimony. FDR solved the problem by finding the governor a new job, putting him in charge of a public housing program, promising that post would give him "a chance to assist in the social rehabilitation of those underprivileged fellow citizens of ours who, on account of economic conditions, have been forced to live in slum conditions." Paul Pearson accepted the transfer but told the president that while he might appear calm, he was bleeding inwardly.[34]

After the contentious hearings, Senator Tydings reported to the FBI that Drew Pearson had approached him to ask that he cause his father as little trouble as possible. When the senator refused to agree, the columnist grew "quite unpleasant in his remarks." Tydings's staff recalled Pearson saying: "All right Millard, up to now I've been your friend, but I know a lot of things I could write about you which would make juicy reading in Maryland." When Paul Pearson died of a stroke in 1938, his son sought vengeance by defeating Tydings. In that year's Democratic primary, Pearson served as behind-the-scenes campaign manager for Tydings's opponent, wrote his speeches, raised campaign funds, and drafted FDR's endorsement of the challenger. He also launched a separate "Maryland Merry-Go-Round" for the state's newspapers, using it to accuse Tydings of everything from incompetency to graft.[35]

In one of their radio broadcasts, the columnists engaged in a pointed dialogue:

ALLEN: Don't forget Senator Tydings of Maryland, Drew.
PEARSON: That's right, Bob. Senator Tydings has promised us a poke in the eye. I'd forgotten.
ANNOUNCER: Well, what's the Senator sore about?
PEARSON: Well, we suddenly became interested in checking up on Government works and discovered that the Senator had put through a very interesting little deal. Just to help keep the WPA workers busy, he had them build a road and yacht basin on his private estate.

Senator Tydings denied that federal money had improved anything on his property. The FBI investigated and found that while Tydings had benefited from various public works projects—a WPA-built road stopped outside his property and a marina was situated near his house—he had not diverted any funds. The radio network issued a public apology for the charges, and Pearson later claimed neither to have written that radio script nor seen it until just before going on the air. "The whole thing was just a technical error, anyway," he shrugged.[36]

Along with nearly everyone else whom Roosevelt sought to defeat in 1938, Millard Tydings won reelection. The senator then demanded that the Justice Department prosecute Pearson and Allen for malicious libel. Attorney General Murphy declined to intervene, advising that "The high regard in which freedom of speech and press is held in this country has made the action of criminal libel a rarity." Tydings contemplated bringing a civil suit on his own, but Pearson settled the matter peacefully. "I know that father does not believe in revenge and would not have me go after Tydings for his sake," he wrote his mother, conceding "perhaps because I am not as broad and forgiving a man as father."[37]

Using the "Merry-Go-Round" for personal revenge cast a shadow on the column. Bob Allen regretted having indulged his partner's vendetta. "You had a long and just personal grievance against the bastard," he observed; "I was for fighting him because he is pure unadulterated rat." But he wanted Pearson to cut it out. "I don't want to be used as a whipping boy in any personal grudge fights. Further, I don't think they have any place in the Merry-Go-Round, unless what you have to say is legitimate news."[38]

In 1939, the column carried on a more legitimate political campaign by exposing corruption within Louisiana's WPA relief program. Former Governor Jimmy Noe traveled to Pearson's Georgetown home with evidence documenting graft that ran from WPA Director George Carpenter up to Governor Richard Leche, all of whom had made personal use of government funds. Pearson presented the evidence to Attorney General Murphy but found him skittish about prosecuting President Roosevelt's political allies. Nothing happened until the "Merry-Go-Round" revealed the scandal publicly. To reduce fears of libel suits, United Features Syndicate sent out the column along with an affidavit affirming the graft charges. Even so, only one Louisiana paper, the *Shreveport Journal*, published the charges (and saw its sales surge). Other papers in the state waited until after the "Merry-Go-Round" had been reprinted in the *Congressional Record*, making the charges libel-proof. In June and July 1939, Pearson and Allen wrote column after column on the scandal until their revelations prodded the Justice Department to act. WPA Director Carpenter and Governor Leche went to prison, as did the president of Louisiana State University. Although United Features nominated their columns for a Pulitzer Prize, the award went instead to rival columnist Westbrook Pegler for exposing corruption in organized labor.[39]

Despite his misgivings, Franklin Roosevelt enlisted Pearson and Allen to back his effort to overcome the isolationists and prepare America militarily on the eve of World War II. Militarism in Germany and Japan stimulated a national debate between isolationists and internationalists. The columnists stood with the president but still managed to displease him by prematurely reporting his deal with the British to exchange overaged destroyers for bases in the Western Hemisphere. They gained that knowledge from access to both the FBI and British intelligence.[40]

The rumble of FDR's complaints unnerved Bob Allen. He begged Pearson to kill a critical item about Roosevelt right after the Munich crisis. "We can't prove the piece," he complained. "Under present conditions it may be picked up by the antis and made an issue. FDR would deny it, leaving us holding the bag. You've got so many other grand stories, this one won't be missed." Reinforcing that concern, Harold Ickes met with Roosevelt and found him in a foul mood. Angry with a piece in the "Merry-Go-Round," Roosevelt accused Ickes of leaking it. "I stopped the President's tirade by remarking that the only thing to do about the columnists was to make me co-ordinator of them. This brought a laugh."[41]

Pearson predicted that international events would persuade FDR to run for an unprecedented third term. Before Roosevelt made up his mind, Vice President John Nance Garner jumped into the campaign for the Democratic nomination. At that time, the Daughters of the American Revolution had denied their concert hall to the African American contralto Marian Anderson, and Interior Secretary Ickes had arranged for her to sing at the Lincoln Memorial instead. The "Merry-Go-Round" reported that Ickes got no response to his invitation to the vice president. Garner complained that he had never received one, but Ickes confirmed that he sent two telegrams. Ickes recorded in his diary that "the President proceeded to outline what I ought to tell Drew Pearson or Bob Allen in order to nail down the story. He wanted me to be very sure, however, that nothing could be traced to him. There was no doubt that he enjoyed the tight hole in which the Vice President found himself. Here he is, a vigorous candidate for President, putting himself in a position of offending the Negro vote everywhere." After the item appeared, Garner stormed into Roosevelt's office and loudly challenged the columnists' account, while Roosevelt nodded sympathetically and smiled.[42]

During the 1940 presidential campaign, Republicans protested that the "Merry-Go-Round" propagandized for the New Deal to the detriment of their candidate, Wendell Willkie. "I suppose that in interpreting some of the things the New Deal is doing we left ourselves open to this charge," Pearson replied. Writing to the publisher of Iowa's *Newton News*, he argued that if he looked back over the column carefully, he would see that they had also exposed "an awful lot of iniquities" inside the New Deal. They had exposed the State Department's ineptness, administration friction within the War Department, political bickering in the navy, and squabbles within the Democratic Party.[43]

Pearson felt both ambiguous about Roosevelt's third-term ambitions and attracted to his Republican challenger, which kept the column neutral during the campaign. The Bridgeport, Connecticut, *Times-Star* commended the columnists for giving the race a "fair and unpoisoned appraisal." The "Merry-Go-Round" also won accolades by calling the election results even more accurately than the Gallup Poll. What no one knew was that Pearson sat on a story that could have seriously damaged Willkie. He had learned that the candidate and his wife had been living apart while Willkie carried on an affair with Irita Van Doren, the book review editor for the *New York Herald Tribune*. When the dark horse Willkie surprised everyone by winning the Republican nomination, party operatives rushed Edith Willkie to the convention so she could be photographed alongside her husband. Pearson suppressed the story to avoid being accused of smearing the candidate before the election and waited until Roosevelt had won before describing Willkie's dubious marriage in a column. Even then, United Features chose not to distribute it. In 1945, a thinly disguised version of the story became a Pulitzer Prize–winning Broadway play, and later a motion picture, titled *State of the Union*.[44]

After the 1940 election, the "Merry-Go-Round" identified another rising political star:

> To the boys on the Democratic side of the House of Representatives, many of them still nervously mopping their brows over narrow escapes, the hero of the hair-raising campaign was no big-shot party figure. The big names got all the publicity, but in the House all the praise is for a youngster whose name was scarcely mentioned. But he left his mark on the battles—as the GOP campaign managers will ruefully attend. Their nemesis and the Democrats' hero was Representative Lyndon Baines Johnson, a rangy, 32-year-old, black-haired, handsome Texan who has been in Congress only three years but who has political magic at his fingertips, and a way with him that is irresistible in action.[45]

The "Merry-Go-Round" awarded its brass ring to Lyndon Johnson for heading the House Democratic Campaign Committee and turning what had been expected to be a Republican rout into a Democratic triumph. Rather than winning the House, Republicans lost seven seats, thanks largely to the campaign funds Johnson raised from Texas oil and gas producers. The day after the column appeared, Johnson carried a copy to the White House to show to the president. "Before I got it out of my pocket," he later recalled, "President Roosevelt gave me a lecture about people who got their names in the papers. 'I had a young fellow helping me named Tom Corcoran,' FDR said, 'but he kept getting his name in the columns. It looked as if he deserved the credit for all the things that were done around the White House. I had to let him go.' President Roosevelt looked at me hard," continued Johnson, "and I just snuck out without taking that clipping out of my pocket."[46]

The dissimilarity between the "Merry-Go-Round"'s co-authors continued to amuse the rest of the press corps. "Here is Bob Allen, red-headed, thick-set, muscular, never wears a vest, clothes somewhat untidy, feels best when he needs a shave," described Harold Horan, Washington correspondent of the London *Daily Express*. "And here is Drew Pearson, long, lean, lithe, wears an English guardsman's moustache, sports beautifully tailored clothes." At press conferences, Pearson raised questions in a soft, silky voice, while Allen roared his with a mixture of "sarcasm, grunts, and profane asides." They might be opposites, but they made a formidable combination, Horan judged. "It doubles the punch while halving the responsibility."[47]

The partners worked independently, Pearson out of his Georgetown home and Allen in an office at the National Press Club. They could go for days without seeing each other, but even at a distance their contrary temperaments sparked friction. Beginning in 1935, they added to their workload with weekly fifteen-minute radio broadcasts. Like the column, the show leapt from theme to theme, occasionally focusing on a single "meaty" story. Pearson convinced Allen that they could use the radio program to air some of the stories that United Features censored from their columns because they threatened the syndicate's business dealings. It did not take the short-fused Allen long to start griping about the time it took to rehearse the programs. Pearson reminded him how much time he had spent selling the programs to sponsors and keeping those sponsors contented. "We may expect other people to sell it for us, but usually it doesn't happen that way," he snapped. Pearson added that he wrote most of the radio scripts and had to wait when his partner's copy arrived belatedly.[48]

Bob Allen felt uncomfortable with Pearson's showmanship, which had manifested itself in such spin-offs from the column as a "Merry-Go-Round" board game and a "Hap Hopper" newspaper comic strip about a Pearson-like investigative reporter. Allen bickered so much that Pearson called it "god-damn boring, to say the least. I have got so I have no particular desire to call you on the phone any more, and as a result many news stories which otherwise might develop are not discussed, and many points in the column which should be clarified in editing, are not."[49]

In any argument, Allen was quick to remind his partner that the column carried two bylines, "yours and mine." Allen spent his days on the move, collecting items for the column and straight news for the *Philadelphia Record*. Returning exhausted from pounding government corridors, he sent his copy to Pearson and went to bed. Pearson worked late into the night, drafting his own segments, merging them with Allen's, polishing the final copy, and telegraphing it to the syndicate. Consequently, Allen rarely saw the finished column before he received the mimeographed copy that the syndicate distributed to their papers. Only then would he discover if Pearson had rewritten his text or added something critical of one of his sources. "Here we are engaged in the toughest fight of our joint careers," he wrote during one of their libel suits, "and yet you breezily indulge yourself in the luxury of taking socks at guys who can be of great help to us, several of them as you know voluntarily offered to help us, and for no other reason as far as I can see other than to vent your personal spleen." Allen protested a snide story about Oregon Senator Charles McNary, his best contact on Capitol Hill, and potshots taken at Tommy Corcoran, who had been such a good friend to them. Both items could have been easily eliminated, he insisted, since neither story amounted to much. Allen called their share of the reporting 50-50, but on the editorial side it was 99 to 1. He proposed that they start sending their copy separately to the syndicate and let someone in New York edit the column.[50]

Pearson defended the formula that made them so successful. If they let the syndicate decide what went into the column, the result might reveal their conflicting opinions, "instead of being a homogenous product today, so that few people can tell who writes what." Nor did he think it necessary to sugarcoat those who provided information to the column. "They don't respect you for it," he argued with his partner. "They figure you will always be with them, and they step on you. You have to give them the straight-arm occasionally." He agreed that the column should not go out of its way to offend its friends, but "it's a small-time friend who gets sore over one item in a long row that have been down his alley. After all, Bob, our only reason for existing is keeping a degree of objectivity."[51]

Yet Allen steamed whenever Pearson added opinion to his straight reporting, calling them editorial ruminations and "breakfast table annoyances." He thought they should concentrate on domestic issues, while Pearson wanted to inject more foreign news. Each man produced enough copy to fill the column by himself. The resulting backlogs meant that some of Allen's material sat on Pearson's desk for days until he found room for it in a column. "The chief editing I do is for space purposes," Pearson justified. "It is no easy job to squeeze everything in that we both want, and every word that can justifiably be cut is important."[52]

Despite their bickering, the partnership still offered some advantages. If the gritty Bob Allen stormed out of someone's office, the suave Drew Pearson could mollify the injured party. If the column offended one of their sources, Allen could blame Pearson. Reporter Charles Fisher, who observed the two closely, noted that for all of Bob Allen's hard-boiled manner, he was really "a gentlemanly, if not genteel, soul in all his relationships," while contrary to Drew Pearson's country gentleman appearance, he was tougher in his handling of news. Allen himself described producing the column as "a job of delicate personal relations." He visited his sources regularly and heard their complaints. He admitted sometimes writing stories more to please his sources than to enlighten his readers, but in order to move beyond press conferences, handouts, and public debates, he had to build the trust of those willing to talk. "Being objective is very swell, Drew, and I'm all for it—but it has a lot of edges," Allen wrote in one of his angry letters. Taking potshots at those who were in their camp made no sense to him. The column needed "to lay off personal vendettas and to hit only on real issues."[53]

Following their periodic outbursts, the partners would back off, cool down, apologize, and return to work. "We have been comrades-in-arms together for nearly ten years," Allen wrote in a letter to Pearson; "we have come through much and it is my most fervent wish and hope to have the privilege of battling side by side with you for many more years to come. You are a man's fighting man and no one knows better than I how patient and tolerant you have been toward me and my eruptions. Your skill, your ingenuity, your tirelessness, your generosity, have certainly been the keystone of the column. No one knows that better than I do. The column wouldn't be what it is today without you. You have sold it, you have led it, you have starred it." If he had hurt Pearson's feelings, he had felt the same way himself. "You know how often I have made a nuisance of myself by crabbing about revision of my copy. And the point I always sought to make in those protests, though apparently I failed to get it over, was not the revision itself but that frequently the revision injected inaccuracies in the copy, tampered with the context of the story."[54]

The partnership had already begun unraveling by the time the Japanese attack on Pearl Harbor finally ended it. Once the United States entered the war, Bob Allen rejoined the army and abandoned reporting for the war's duration. He planned to leave for training camp in April 1942. During the four-month interregnum, the partners negotiated terms of their separation. A sticking point was whether Pearson would retain Allen's assistants, who had been critical of him. "They have never caused you any loss or trouble and if you and I are to continue together, as far as I am concerned, it's got to be without nagging or strictures from you," Allen fumed. "You are not my boss or the boss of the column." Pearson snapped back: "Bob, if you feel that way, anytime you want to split its OK by me." "I didn't say anything about splitting," Allen retreated. "I just asked to be let alone and to run my own affairs. If you are thinking in terms of splitting, that is entirely agreeable to me. I haven't the time to do anything about it now, but as soon as I return we'll act on the matter."[55]

Allen's name would remain in the byline even though Pearson would be left as a one-man operation. Financial questions remained unresolved. Between the column and the radio broadcasts, the two men were each earning $75,000 a year (members of Congress then earned $10,000). They also collected payments for their comic strip, magazine articles, and book royalties. Pearson initially offered to pay Allen a flat 10 percent of the gross receipts during his absence, but he soon calculated that he could not afford it. On the day that Allen boarded the train for army camp, at Washington's Union Station, Pearson stunned his partner by backpedaling on their agreement. He would need to deduct from Allen's share expenses for legal fees as well as salaries for additional assistants to fill the void.[56]

Although taken by surprise, Allen accepted his reasoning. He let the United Features Syndicate know that while he retained a half-share of the "Merry-Go-Round," they should pay all its income to Pearson until he got out of the army. It would require his share of the royalties for Pearson to run the column adequately. "It is only fair that Drew should be adequately compensated for his extra labor," Allen acknowledged to the syndicate's manager. "I don't have to tell you that Drew has a man-sized job on his hands running the column alone. Together we had our hands full and the past ten years took plenty out of us. It's only proper that Drew should get more money for his greatly increased responsibilities for work." He wanted to eliminate any quibbling over taking a percentage or otherwise reserving money for him. "I will get along very well on my Army pay, especially when I get foreign service," Allen wrote. "Drew is entitled to the full authors' share."[57]

Both Allen and his wife, reporter Ruth Finney, planned to provide items for the column. Sensitive to his role in the army, however, he wanted to make sure that Pearson never attributed anything to him. When he sent anything, he wanted it to appear as if Pearson had acquired it from others.[58]

Pearson honored the request but immediately angered Allen by writing a column in the form of a letter commending his army service. Allen had agreed that the column's byline would read "Maj. Robert S. Allen on Active Duty" but had not expected being mentioned in its content. He demanded that Pearson no longer refer to him without prior approval. "To say that I was shocked by this last 'letter' is to put it mildly," Allen huffed. "If you insist on dragging in personal stuff that has no place in the column and isn't

[of] the slightest interest to Merry-Go-Round readers, or editorializing or using the column for pot-shoting in personal feuds, then I must insist that you do it on your own score. Please do not drag me into that kind of stuff."[59]

The partnership suffered a fatal blow in 1943, when Pearson broke an embarrassing story about General George S. Patton, whom Allen idolized. Visiting army hospitals in Sicily, the mercurial general had slapped two shell-shocked soldiers. All the war correspondents in Europe picked up the story, but General Dwight D. Eisenhower implored them not to publish it, lest Patton lose his command. Back in Washington, Pearson learned of the incidents from his friend Ernest Cuneo, then working in the Office of Strategic Services. President Roosevelt had just called Pearson a chronic liar over the column's revelation of anti-Russian sentiments inside the State Department. The column had been accurate, but FDR denied it to avoid jeopardizing the wartime alliance with the Soviet Union. Cuneo persuaded Pearson that he needed to break a big story to restore his reputation. Since United Features refused to let him use the Patton story in the column, he delivered it instead on the radio. On Sunday evening, November 21, 1943, Pearson predicted that the general nicknamed "Blood and Guts" would no longer hold a command in Europe because "He was a bit too bloody for the morale of the army," and then told his radio audience how the general had slapped the hospitalized soldiers. A storm of criticism erupted for his daring to impugn the popular general.[60]

As required during wartime, Pearson had submitted his radio script to the censors for review. Nervous network executives counted on the censors to suppress it, but they could find nothing in their code that barred the story's release. They advised Pearson to use his own judgment, and he went ahead with it. Breaking the story damaged General Patton's image but did not remove him from battle command for long. Nor did the story undermine its narrator. "I have been subjected to being called a chronic liar again. However, I knew that my facts were right," Pearson reassured his daughter. "And this morning press associations and radio broadcasters from Algiers have been telling the real story which bears me out 100%." For his part, General Patton never doubted that he had been justified in treating the soldiers as shirkers. In his diary, Patton summed up the experience immodestly: "If the fate of the only successful general in the war depends on the statements of a discredited writer like Drew Pearson, we are in a bad fix."[61]

The following year, United Features terminated Pearson's contract and the "Washington Merry-Go-Round" shifted to the smaller Bell Syndicate. Pearson explained that he made the change because Roy Howard, head of the Scripps-Howard newspapers and United Features, censored the column frequently—both for political disagreements and for revealing news that his own reporters had failed to uncover. The FBI, which regularly monitored the column, reached a different conclusion. Its agents attributed the break to two of Pearson's harshest detractors: Secretary Hull and General Patton. In the spring of 1944, Hugh Baillie, the head of United Press, which controlled United Features, conferred with the secretary of state on extending the United Press's news coverage internationally. "Secretary Hull told Baile [*sic*] that while the State Department would help them in every possible way, the time might come when Drew Pearson might prove to be very embarrassing to United Features in view of his methods of operation," FBI agents reported. Then Baillie traveled to Europe and met with George Patton. "General Patton also stated that he was amazed and could not understand the United Press and United Features sponsoring Drew Pearson, when the UP is so conservative always in its reporting." Baillie made up his mind not to renew Pearson's contract when it expired.[62]

Given the "Merry-Go-Round"'s popularity, Pearson had no trouble finding another outlet. The directors of Bell offered him a hefty raise in salary and provided direct telegraph service from his home, eliminating the need for messengers. When Pearson outlined the deal to Allen's wife, Ruth, however, she demanded official accounting and expressed dissatisfaction with not having been compensated. Her response surprised Pearson, since he had a copy of Allen's letter specifying that he receive no financial return from the column while in uniform.[63]

Lt. Col. Robert S. Allen served in the Third Army's G-2 intelligence unit under the command of General Patton. Irate that Pearson had reported the slapping incidents, Allen dashed off a handwritten note declaring their partnership had ended and that Pearson could keep the column. Then on April 7, 1945, weeks before the end of the war in Europe, Allen's jeep ran into a German roadblock. Wounded and taken prisoner, he had his right forearm amputated at a German field hospital that lacked antiseptics and bandages. Four days later, American troops rescued him. General Patton awarded him a Purple Heart and arranged for him to stay on his staff despite his injury. At the war's end, Allen returned to Washington to spend a year undergoing treatment at Walter Reed General Hospital. After learning to type with his left hand, he wrote a book on Patton's Third Army. When Pearson visited the hospital, he assured his recuperating partner that he regarded his resignation as impetuous and would not hold him to it. That peace offering restored their friendship, but Allen declined his offer to return to the

"Merry-Go-Round." Instead, he agreed to sell his half of its trademark for a series of annual payments. At the same time, Allen sued the *Philadelphia Record* for refusing to rehire him after he left the army.[64]

In January 1946, the column carried a tribute to its co-founder. "Bob Allen is back now," Pearson trumpeted, "a little older, a little thinner, a full-fledged colonel, several rows of battle ribbons across his chest, and an empty right sleeve—mute testimony of what he gave for his country." That October the syndicate officially dropped Robert S. Allen from the byline he had created. In later years, he occasionally stepped in as a guest columnist for the "Merry-Go-Round" and a substitute on Pearson's radio broadcasts. He also published an article on "My Pal, Drew Pearson," but went his own way. Allen would eventually start a new column, for which he promised "straight, impersonal reporting with no hoopla."[65]

3

Breaking Secrets in Wartime

THROUGHOUT THE 1930S THE "Washington Merry-Go-Round" blasted the US Navy for its woeful lack of preparedness. The column revealed glaring defects observed during naval maneuvers, inadequacies in new warship designs, and rivalries rampant among high-ranking naval officers. Most of all it lamented the rigidity of mind that caused admirals to fail to recognize new means of warfare, "which is responsible for the fact that the fleet today is not adequately armed against airplane attacks." The admirals protested when Pearson and Allen published that assertion in June 1940, and the navy tried to plug the leaks that had furnished such stories. But after the surprise Japanese air attack decimated the US Pacific Fleet at Pearl Harbor, on December 7, 1941, United Features Syndicate touted that the column's reports had stood up consistently.[1]

Once his partner left for the army, Drew Pearson devoted more of the column to foreign and military affairs. The "Merry-Go-Round" had reached a saturation point among subscribers, he reasoned, and needed to broaden its appeal. With the United States at war, Pearson expected his readers to want more international news, so long as the column did not neglect the Washington angle that had been its hallmark. One critic rebutted that the wire services already covered foreign news and questioned his ability to cover the world the way he did the capital. "If the reader or radio listener, in a thirst for 'inside' information or in search of entertainment, turns to Drew Pearson," scoffed William P. Carney, who had covered the Spanish Civil War for the *New York Times*, "he has only himself to blame if he is taken for an occasional ride. After all, it is Pearson himself who calls his column a 'Merry-Go-Round.'" Such animosity hardly dissuaded the columnist.

Carney's unabashedly pro-Franco reporting was one reason Pearson felt a need to report more on world events. He would keep focusing on what governments twisted or hid—even in wartime.[2]

A willingness to publish the stories that others held back helped explain Drew Pearson's contradictory standing among his peers. In a 1944 poll, the Washington press corps rated Pearson the columnist who exerted the greatest influence over national opinion, giving him twice as many votes as Walter Lippmann. In the category of exerting the greatest influence on Washington, Pearson ranked second, behind the *New York Times* bureau chief and columnist Arthur Krock but still ahead of Lippmann. Yet Pearson received only two votes out of the 165 that were cast for "reliability, fairness, ability to analyze the news."[3]

A better measure of his influence was the anguish that his columns caused inside the White House, State Department, Pentagon, and even the British cabinet. During World War II, the FBI tapped his phones, naval intelligence officers tailed him, and foreign operatives spied on him. British embassy personnel were shocked to read their own government's classified documents in the "Merry-Go-Round." British intelligence agents in the United States asserted that in Britain, they would have prosecuted the columnist for violating the Official Secrets Act. But in the United States they lamented that the First Amendment made him immune, "provided that he did not publish information which might have caused the loss of American lives."[4]

The combination of a daily newspaper column and weekly radio program gave Pearson immense influence over American public opinion, which made government officials skittish about challenging him. Despite wartime censorship, he went about business as usual. Pearson even benefited from wartime secrecy. For security reasons, officials could not always deny his reports of what went on behind closed doors, making his accusations harder to disprove. A skeptical profile of the columnist in the *Saturday Evening Post* identified Pearson's formula for success as "aggressive indiscretion." He had a knack for making enemies, preferably those with big names, who kept him at the center of public controversies. He could also invest trivial matters with urgency and present gossip as established fact.[5]

Pearson's columns attracted readers at the highest levels of government, as attested by their many complaints. Franklin Roosevelt kept up with it, as did his wartime vice president, Henry Wallace, who followed its clues about his own political fate. Members of Congress read it to find out what was happening within an administration that consulted them less and less during the war. Ambassadors forwarded it to their governments as forecasts of American actions. "The people who call Pearson or write him anonymous letters about situations that begin to smell of fish are legion," said rival columnist Peter Edson. "On top of this, Pearson is an aggressive reporter and he never seems to be happy unless he is up to his Adam's apple in trouble." He made mistakes, but his rate of accuracy made the rest of Washington pay attention to his breaking news.[6]

The war years marked the peak of Pearson's success, when his column made news of global significance. The rest of the media often reported his exposés, providing him with additional publicity. But he deemed the war years his most frustrating, forcing him to "buck a lot of recalcitrant officials in Washington who are intent on hushing up the news or denying it afterwards." He also had to deal with "reactionary editors" and his own syndicate, "at least those who control it." The most formidable of these obstacles was an unforgiving ex-mother-in-law.[7]

As carefully as Pearson tended to his relations with Cissy Patterson, he drifted away from her side during the national debate between isolationists and internationalists. The "Merry-Go-Round" had from its inception assailed pro-Nazi, antisemitic sentiments in the United States. As war in Europe approached, the column beat up on isolationists in Congress. President Roosevelt enlisted its support by instructing the FBI to provide Pearson and Allen with information on any connections between the isolationists and Nazi Germany.[8]

In Washington, the "Merry-Go-Round" appeared in the pages of Cissy Patterson's fervently isolationist *Washington Times-Herald*. Pearson considered the woman he still called "Mom" a faithful customer who had been one of the first subscribers to the column. In January 1941 when United Features began trimming more from their copy, Pearson threatened the syndicate that he might abandon the column altogether and accept one of Cissy's offers to join her in publishing and editing the *Washington Times-Herald*. In such ways he could work their relationship to his advantage, but as the sole publisher of his column in the capital, she held the upper hand.[9]

▤ SPECIAL FOR ALL PAPERS FOR RELEASE ON RECEIPT: Some of the most important conversations ever to take place with Great Britain in 150 years have been transpiring behind the scenes recently. They concern the desperate position which England now faces, plus possible help for her by the United States. . . . If the United States will supply Britain with destroyers and small motor-torpedo boats, then the British will transfer to the United States any island possessions it desires any place in the Western hemisphere, and will also permit the United States the use of land, air and naval bases on any territory which it controls.[10]

When the "Merry-Go-Round" broke the news that the administration planned to swap American naval destroyers for British bases in the Caribbean, the White House denied the story and Cissy Patterson chided the columnists in print for their supposed blunder. Three weeks later, to her dismay, the government belatedly confirmed their report. When her friend Ernest Lundeen, the outspokenly isolationist senator from Minnesota, died in a plane crash in 1940, the "Merry-Go-Round" revealed that he had been on his way to deliver a pro-Nazi speech written by an American Nazi sympathizer, George Sylvester Viereck. Patterson's isolationist allies in Congress roundly denounced Pearson and Allen for this accusation, and appropriated funds to investigate them. Viereck's later arrest and trial proved that he had indeed been a German agent and confirmed that he wrote Lundeen's speeches. Being right only worsened the columnists' relations with their Washington publisher. She began cutting out more of the columns or omitting them entirely when they contradicted her fixed opinions.[11]

Cissy Patterson was hardly alone in trimming the "Merry-Go-Round," just more rigorous than other editors. "Those who publish my column often hack it up and twist it around," Pearson complained. But since a typical "Merry-Go-Round" column consisted of many loosely linked items, editors found it simpler to prune other columnists' denser thought-pieces. "Hell, one editor said he likes my columns better than Lippmann's," he grumbled, "because mine are easier to cut."[12]

Bob Allen considered Patterson's incisions intolerable. She was censoring the column in the paper where most federal officials would likely read it. Shortly before he left for the army, Allen had a chance encounter with Eugene Meyer, owner-publisher of the *Washington Post*, and impulsively proposed that the "Merry-Go-Round" switch its Washington outlet. Allen advised that the *Times-Herald*'s contract would soon expire and urged the *Post* to make a bid for it. Since the *Post* lagged far behind the *Times-Herald* in circulation, Meyer jumped at snatching away the popular column. He offered to pay $100 a week—compared to the $35 Patterson was paying. When this meeting occurred, Drew Pearson was attending a diplomatic conference in Rio de Janeiro. On his return, Allen presented him with the plan to extract the column from his mother-in-law's blue-penciling. Dropping a newspaper as a customer was almost unprecedented for the syndicate, and Pearson knew how much Cissy Patterson would resent it, but Allen remained adamant and Meyer was persuasive. For the rest of his life, Pearson rued having agreed to the decision. Along with everyone else who read the *Times-Herald*, he had enjoyed its publisher's vitriolic public feuds with prominent Washingtonians. "Little did I dream that the acid that dripped from my mother-in-law's pen would fall on me," he lamented.[13]

The *Times-Herald* received a six-month notice of the cancellation in February 1942. Cissy could forgive the columnist for getting divorced from her daughter but not for deserting her paper. Even though she had been shredding the column in print, she regarded its switch to a rival paper as a betrayal. Patterson immediately dropped the "Merry-Go-Round" from her pages and refused to let the *Post* publish it until her exclusive contract expired that summer. Having effectively blacked it out of Washington during the first months of the war, she then launched an editorial war against "The Headache Boys," claiming that she had canceled their column for being unreliable, irresponsible, and reprehensible. Pearson and Allen prepared a rebuttal, explaining in an advertisement that they had voluntarily left the *Times-Herald*, but no Washington newspaper would run the ad and risk offending the malevolent publisher. Only the *Washington News* printed their rebuttal as a news story. (Published by Scripps-Howard, which ran the United Features Syndicate, the *News* could not carry the "Merry-Go-Round" column because of Patterson's exclusive right to it in the capital.) "Cissy's attacks came so thick and fast that we didn't have time to answer," Pearson recounted.[14]

Her paper threw every possible insult at her ex-son-in-law. She called him a "a phony Quaker who thee'd and thou'd his way out of World War I," and compared him to a cockroach. She sank to antisemitism by accusing Pearson of being the "big mouthpiece for the Anti-Defamation League, a powerful Jewish organization which, seized by war hysteria, sought by hook or by crook to force quite a number of free Americans to change their way of thinking." She claimed that the League "put in his pocket money beyond his wildest dreams." Patterson encouraged her friends in Congress to reprint her attacks on Pearson in the *Congressional Record*. She even stopped publishing broadcast listings for the local radio station WMAL because they included Drew Pearson's weekly program. For good measure, Cissy fired Pearson's brother Leon as her Latin American reporter and Luvie Pearson as her movie critic. She hired Luvie's ex-husband to write a gossip column, eventually called "Ready, Willing and George Abell."[15]

Drew Pearson's daughter Ellen was Cissy Patterson's granddaughter, but that which had once tied them together now drove them further apart. In 1930 her grandmother bought a large tract of land along the Potomac River in rural Maryland, just north of the District of Columbia. She deeded this land to Ellen as a tenth birthday present, assigning Drew Pearson as trustee. Pearson fell in love with the property and bought it from his daughter in order to build a hillside house there as a rustic weekend getaway. During World War II, he felt it patriotic to turn the land into a working farm. He planted a victory garden and established a dairy, producing among other commodities sacks of "Drew Pearson's Manure, All Cow, No Bull, Better Than the Column." His irate former mother-in-law accused him of stealing the land from her granddaughter and took him to court to recover it. She lost the case.[16]

Despite her relentless abuse, when Cissy Patterson died in 1948 Pearson attended the funeral at her spacious Dupont Circle mansion. A gasp went up when he appeared. "Now I know she's dead," Walter Trohan, Washington correspondent for the *Chicago Tribune*, whispered to his wife, adding that he would not have been surprised if Cissy had risen from her coffin and ordered her ex-son-in-law out. Pearson devoted a "Merry-Go-Round" column to her, under the heading " 'Headache Boy' Lauds Great Lady." Her method of running a newspaper had been "brilliant, sometimes vitriolic, always personal," he reported, and he still felt its sting. "Not only did she play up every speech attacking me on the Senate floor," he wrote, "but she kept a file and at times a ghost-writer to help senators write those speeches." Friends asked him why he had not sued Cissy for libel. "I didn't partly because she and I had been through a lot together," he explained, "partly because I have come to the conclusion that the American public is the best judge of these things and will eventually decide that a man is what he is, not what someone else says he is."[17]

On August 12, 1942, six months after Cissy Patterson had received her notice, the "Washington Merry-Go-Round" column finally appeared in the *Washington Post*, which would remain Pearson's capital outlet. Before long, however, Eugene Meyer grew uncomfortable with Pearson's muckraking and the complaints it raised. The *Post* continued carrying the column because it boosted circulation—reader surveys regularly listed it among the paper's favorite attractions. Eugene and Agnes Meyer and their daughter Katharine Graham also enjoyed close friendships with Luvie Pearson, which helped tie the column to their paper. Yet Meyer showed his dismay by moving the "Merry-Go-Round" further and further back until it landed among the comics. Pearson professed not to take it as a slight, calculating that more readers turned to the comics than to the editorials.[18]

On their radio program just a week before Pearl Harbor, Pearson and Allen had delivered an ominous report that the Japanese fleet had steamed out to sea to an unknown destination. That tip Pearson had collected from his close friend Under Secretary of State Sumner Welles. High-level inside information enabled him to score memorable scoops, often clothed as predictions. Pearson's book *The American Diplomatic Game*, published in 1935, had concluded that war would come to Europe within five years, and "when it does come to Europe it will come also to the Far East." Despite that bold prediction, the book did not sell as well as he had hoped. "Apparently it did not contain enough juicy stuff," he regretted. When he began weekly radio broadcasts that year, he expanded his forecasting, ending each program with "predictions of things to come." These predictions served as a gimmick for holding listeners' attention, and while sometimes wide of the mark, he boasted an overall accuracy of 82 percent, making sure to remind everyone whenever something came true. On the night of the Pearl Harbor attack, Pearson and Allen recalled that just two weeks earlier they had forecast that the United States would be at war with Japan before the year was up. "That prediction today was fulfilled," they asserted.[19]

Two army generals contacted officials of the National Broadcasting Company (NBC) after that broadcast and demanded that they remove the columnists from the air. The network declined their request, and Pearson wondered "just how J. Edgar Hoover found out about the meeting of the two generals with NBC," as he jotted in his diary. "He called me on the telephone and read to me the brief transcript of what happened at the meeting." Hoover would call back five days after Pearl Harbor, when he got word that Pearson and Allen had prepared a column outlining the extent of American naval losses:[20]

Now in regard to the current disaster in Honolulu, we are purposely withholding much of the information we know, in deference to the President's request. But we believe that just as the British have been given immediate, cold, sometimes sickening facts, such as the loss of the Republic and Prince of Wales, so the American public must face the facts, unpleasant as they may be. For the debacle at Honolulu was the worst naval defeat in the nation's entire history, and it will take the combined effort of every American citizen to pull this nation out on top again.[21]

The columnists accused President Roosevelt of having minimized the damage to the fleet, even though "every military attache in Washington had cabled the real facts back to his government and the Japanese knew exactly what had happened." They blamed the naval disaster on a mixture of "cock-sureness and sleepiness," and warned that Americans should not assume that their navy was in hot pursuit of the Japanese. The public needed to know "that 90 percent of our ships at Hawaii were wiped out."[22]

United Features recognized that the account was news of the first magnitude but declined to distribute it, preferring to wait for release of the official inquiries—which took another year. Whenever the syndicate suppressed a column, Pearson and Allen mimeographed the text as a special release and sent it to subscribers on their own. This time the columnists promised: "When it is in the national interest, we shall be glad to forego an occasional news beat. On all occasions, we shall scrupulously avoid publication of anything which might aid the enemy. But we also feel that we have a responsibility to our readers to continue pointing to inefficiency, stupidity and corruption."[23]

As soon as the publisher of the *Orlando Morning Sentinel* received the Pearl Harbor column, he telegraphed the president's press secretary, Stephen Early, to report that he did not want to print the column but that he knew his competitors would. Early immediately alerted FBI Director J. Edgar Hoover to the column's "inaccurate and unpatriotic" charges. Hoover at the time had wartime censorship duties, pending creation of a censorship agency. The director warned Bob Allen that if they printed their claims "the Government would be compelled to appeal to their subscribers direct and to bar them from all privileges that go with the relationships between the press and the Government." Faced with a threat that could put them out of business, Allen agreed to telegraph all their papers asking them to suppress that column.[24]

Hoover next tracked down Pearson in Quantico, Virginia, where he was dining with the commandant of the marine corps. After receiving his warning, the columnist asked if the army and navy could deny the information in the column. If the story was inaccurate, they did not want to print it. But if it was correct, the government had no right to bar them from their press privileges. "Drew Pearson took the attitude that he was not going to be treated by any threats to what he should and can print," Hoover informed his staff. "I told the Attorney General that I cut Pearson short when he assumed this attitude by telling him that I did not care to argue the question, and that he would wait until a permanent censor is appointed if he wanted to know definitely what newspaper men will be allowed to write."

Hoover later reported that Pearson had called him back to concede "that perhaps he should have talked to me before he had prepared the article."[25]

There was no question about the story's accuracy, and Pearson could never understand why the US government would deny information that the enemy already knew. Suppressing such information from the American public might bolster morale in the short run but would undermine confidence in the federal government once the truth came out. Cover-ups fanned rumors and distrust, and he reasoned that "loss of public confidence can be more serious than losing battleships."[26]

Pearson believed the government was simply trying to quash reports of a military blunder, but his partner proved more receptive to the censors' demands. "We've got to watch our step—this is war," Allen implored Pearson. Their readers wanted patriotism, hope, cheerfulness, and were not keen on having wartime blunders exposed. "That may wear off later, but right now people are touchy and sensitive about their country, its armed forces and its leaders." The two columnists notified subscribing papers that they were withdrawing the offending column due to certain matters "put before us by the highest authority," although they continued to vouch for its accuracy. "The issue was solely one of timeliness," they told their editors. "As men who have served in our country's armed forces once, and may do so again, we naturally responded to an appeal predicated on patriotism." It remained a question whether they should suppress bad news "or attempt to tell the truth in such a way that the Administration would be sure to clean up inefficiently." They promised to praise or criticize government leadership during the war the same way they had in peacetime.[27]

Pearl Harbor frayed nerves at the United Features Syndicate. General Manager George Carlin—whom the columnists called their "midwife, patron saint and godfather"—had consistently defended the columnists until he read their Pearl Harbor reporting. A veteran of World War I, Carlin had no desire to provoke military protests. "You both seem to have developed a genius for convincing yourselves that you are right even when, as in this case, you are admittedly wrong to fact," he lectured them after an army officer complained about a column. Pearson replied that they would go ahead with a column only when they were sure of the facts, even if that meant contradicting the highest officials. "If we get public statements from diplomats, senators, etc., about various stories which involve them," he insisted, "we would have the column chucked full of equivocations and diplomatic denials. I hardly know more than a handful of diplomats, senators, etc., in Washington who will not lie when they are up against it."[28]

Freedom of the press grew precarious in wartime. Government censors scrutinized reports, and newspapers and news syndicates conducted their own self-protective self-censorship. United Features trimmed more material from the column before distributing it, despite the columnists' protests. "We are doing our damnedest, but would appreciate a little support from guys like you," Pearson told one editor. He conceded that a few papers had canceled the column. "However, we intend to keep battling."[29]

FBI agents monitored Pearson's broadcasts and his columns, and he suspected they had recruited informants inside his syndicate. "I wonder if there isn't a possible leak in your office," Pearson asked George Carlin. "This afternoon I got a telephone call from one of J. Edgar Hoover's assistants saying they understood we were writing a story about Mr. Hoover's attempts to stop Japanese espionage activities in Hawaii. You will recall that the story was in your hands at the time of the telephone call, having been sent up last night." Pearson said he had already talked the story over with Hoover. "But frankly, I don't like the idea of someone in your office snooping around any more than I guess you do."[30]

J. Edgar Hoover had threatened the columnists with the possibility of imprisonment if they let the Pearl Harbor column be published. "I told Edgar that he was nuts, and that there was no law by which he could put me in jail," Pearson asserted. Since Hoover was still courting favorable publicity from the columnist, he excused himself by saying he had only acted in his "official capacity as temporary coordinating of censorship arrangements." Soon afterwards, an executive order transferred those responsibilities to a new Office of Censorship. Pearson called it a "moron censorship outfit," but did his best to comply with its edicts for the rest of the war.[31]

Editors who carried the "Merry-Go-Round" encouraged the columnists to get in step with the war effort. "I know that both Pearson and Allen are fervent and sincere patriots, and, like all of us, want to do everything possible to help win the war," George Carlin assured subscribers. "But wars are not won by a democracy in suppression of bitter truths or distortions for propaganda purposes." As journalists they stood on their inalienable right to report what was going on, so long as their revelations did not conflict with the wartime newspaper code, which barred publication of any information of potential value to the nation's enemies. They promised to live up to the regulations, but also to make sure the public was fully informed, "even when the facts hurt."[32]

A squad of censors questioned items large and small, creating hurdles for the entire Washington press corps, especially for dedicated secret breakers. During the summer of 1942, Pearson disclosed the amount of influence British Prime Minister Winston Churchill exerted on President Roosevelt's decisions. When the Office of Censorship refused to approve the story, he wrote a column criticizing the censors, and then got annoyed when his syndicate toned the piece down. "We have the right to comment on inefficiencies in government bureaus," he snorted. "The Censorship Office is not immune from this—and as a matter of fact doesn't claim to be." By rewriting the column, the syndicate had made it "inane and innocuous." He worried that editors might think that now that he was producing the "Merry-Go-Round" by himself that it had somehow slipped. Pearson also felt sure he understood public opinion better than the syndicate or the censors did. "I am in touch with scores of editors every week, by mail, telephone and through personal visits to Washington; in addition to several hundred letters every week from readers all over the country," he told the syndicate chiefs. "I think I am in a better position to know the pulse of editors and the country than you."[33]

Almost daily, Pearson received mail from soldiers and sailors complaining about the shoddy equipment the military issued. He reported about American paratroopers being shot down by friendly fire, and about officers who indulged themselves, such as the admiral who flew a cow to the Aleutian Islands to provide fresh milk. He grumbled that United Features axed his reporting on deficiencies in submarine warfare before the rest of the press picked up the same charges. "Belatedly, and in part due to this criticism, the Navy is getting on the ball—after thousands of lives and hundreds of thousands of tons of ships have been lost," he protested to the syndicate. "If our story had been published last March, when written, it might have contributed to a betterment of the situation." Members of the Maritime Commission and the navy had been anxious to have the story published, and the Office of Censorship had approved it. "Yet it was killed. I regret to make these complaints, but the column has got to stay ahead of the ball."[34]

In 1942, two FBI agents appeared on Pearson's Georgetown doorstep and accused him of having violated the Espionage Act by revealing military secrets. They cited an after-dinner speech he gave in New York, one of the many paid speaking engagements the columnist accepted each year to supplement his income. Addressing the National Association of Insurance Agents, Pearson had advised his audience that they would hear things he could not include in his column or radio program. He implored them to make sure that nothing left the room that might aid the enemy. At the back of the hall, *New York Times* reporter Russell Porter took notes. "He told a lot of secret information, which the newspapers and radio are not permitted to publish," Porter informed his editors. The *Times*, which did not carry the "Merry-Go-Round," saw no need to shield the columnist and forwarded the report to the Office of Censorship. The censors passed it to the attorney general, who dispatched the FBI.[35]

Waving aside the complaint, Pearson assured the agents that nearly everything he said that night had already appeared in his columns and radio broadcasts. Telling an audience that they would hear things he could not print was just a little showmanship to arouse their interest. The agents took the matter more seriously. Although the Justice Department declined to prosecute Pearson, the attorney general ordered the censors to review all his radio commentary prior to going on the air, a procedure that lasted throughout the war and covered 145 scripts, making Pearson the only broadcaster so singled out. Each Sunday night, a designated FBI agent also monitored his radio broadcasts to note anything said about the FBI and prepare a rebuttal for the director's attention on Monday morning. Bureau staff similarly clipped copies of his newspaper columns.[36]

Pearson so often challenged the censors that he practically memorized their codes. One of the censors confirmed that the columnist "could rattle off the fine print in our rule book faster than we could." Censorship rules required journalists to find authoritative sources to approve any story dealing with military or foreign policy. Reporters had to name names and could no longer cite anonymous sources unless they shared their identities confidentially with the censors. Pearson had to adjust his style. To avoid revealing whom he had talked with, he offered more stories as speculation, or found some cooperative politician in Congress or military officer to verify publicly the stories he had acquired from more reticent sources. Once he could name an "authoritative source," he could reveal secrets that others had been sitting on.[37]

The censors ran Pearson in circles, sometimes ordering him to suppress material that was already publicly known. In one instance in 1942, the Office of Censorship demanded he delete a line critical of Romania, Hungary, and Bulgaria from his radio script. "Those countries have declared war on us," he exclaimed. Inconsistent and contradictory rulings frustrated him. Competitors sometimes scooped the column with information that he had agreed to hold back. His syndicate instructed him to resubmit one column to the censor for further review, the substance of which turned out to have already appeared on the front page of a Florida newspaper, with a note saying it had already been passed by the censors. If two censors differed over a news item, Pearson protested to the head of the Office of Censorship, "they will never agree, and there will be nothing left of it."[38]

When General Jimmy Doolittle led a squadron of planes on a daring mission to bomb Tokyo in 1942, Pearson identified the USS *Hornet* as the carrier that had launched the raid. That information came from Assistant Secretary of War John McCloy, but McCloy's office later retracted the report and labeled the identification of the *Hornet* combat zone material, not to be exposed. Pearson protested that one of his reporters had reviewed the story, line by line, with the head of the army's Bureau of Public Relations, who had deleted anything he considered problematic, but left in the name of the carrier. When the Office of Censorship cut this fact out, Pearson asked why this news should be held back from the American public since Japanese radio broadcasts had already linked the *Hornet* with the Doolittle raid. Despite his complaints, the censors withheld their permission until American military authorities finally confirmed it officially in 1943, after the aircraft carrier had sunk in combat.[39]

The issue was not simply that the public had a right to know, Pearson maintained, but they needed to be excited and entertained to become better informed. He regretted that all the rewriting required to meet the censors' demands took "most of the spice out of the story."[40]

To attract and hold readers and listeners, Pearson packed his columns and broadcasts with scuttlebutt about misguided policies, leaked by dissident civil servants and military officers. On the eve of World War II, a group of younger officers alerted Pearson that the fate of four senior generals depended on their performances during upcoming field maneuvers. The army's chief of staff, General George C. Marshall, telegraphed the generals: "I hear rumor that a syndicated article is about to issue to the effect that three of four Army Commanders are to be relieved. This is merely to notify you that the foregoing is news to me." Pearson's prediction proved partially correct. One of the four aging generals, Hugh Drum, managed to get captured during the tactical exercises. General Walter Krueger drew more favorable notice, mostly for having selected Colonel Dwight D. Eisenhower as his chief of staff. The "Merry-Go-Round" credited Eisenhower, who planned the strategy that routed General Drum's forces, with having "a steel trap mind plus unusual vigor." That Eisenhower also served as Krueger's press officer may also have contributed to the glowing notices he received. General

Marshall was indeed evaluating how the four generals handled the exercises and would shunt those who failed into non-combat roles. But Marshall worried that columnists like Pearson were deliberately forcing the army to deny leaks. "It is news to them to keep the pot boiling, and it is very difficult for us to determine just when to intervene and how to go about it."[41]

The "Merry-Go-Round" also derailed General Marshall's own personal ambition to become Supreme Commander of US Forces in Europe. Winston Churchill had lobbied to bring Marshall to Europe, and FDR appeared to agree. But younger army officers at the Pentagon feared that Marshall's replacement would disrupt the army's leadership and delay their own promotions. They advised Pearson that the chiefs of staff regarded General Marshall as indispensable in Washington. General Marshall's biographer later attributed this " 'inside' misinformation" to Roosevelt's change of mind. The Supreme Command went instead to Marshall's protégé, Dwight Eisenhower. Although disappointed, General Marshall graciously praised Pearson as "one of the best inspectors general," for revealing army problems that needed repair.[42]

Rivalries between the military services helped Pearson verify rumors. Whatever he needed to know about the army, naval officers were ready to tell him, and vice versa. His pipelines throughout the Pentagon benefited from new tipsters. Other reporters observed that for every official the column targeted there would be at least one ambitious subordinate ready to volunteer the information Pearson sought.[43]

Further insight came from the haggling within the government over the wartime alliance with the Soviet Union. Whether to trust Russia as an ally or suspect it as a potential rival created divisions within military and diplomatic circles, prompting more leaking. Some military officers cited the need to side with the Soviet Union against Nazi Germany, while others warned Roosevelt that Stalin would turn against the Allies as soon as it served his purpose. At the State Department, most officials distrusted the Soviet Union's postwar ambitions, while some shared Roosevelt's hope of peaceful coexistence after the war, being more offended by British colonialism than Soviet communism. Bureaucratic infighting encouraged leaks. The British *Sunday Pictorial* reported that squabbling factions in the US State Department were passing international secrets to Drew Pearson. "But we in Britain do not want our secrets to be used as weapons by feuding groups of diplomatists."[44]

The leftist politics of some of Pearson's wartime staff helped them develop sources among officials who tilted towards the Soviet Union. They found an ever-ready font of information in Alger Hiss, director of the State Department's Office of Special Political Affairs. Indeed, when Hiss's colleagues worried about his leaking, it was not to the Soviet Union but to Drew Pearson. Some of Pearson's columns clearly originated in classified US military studies of British actions. Several departments received copies of these reports, and Hiss's was one of them. Alger Hiss denied being the source, but investigators observed that Pearson's reporters regularly visited his office.[45]

Pearson's own previous experience in covering the State Department helped him tap multiple sources. His greatest asset was his close friendship with the department's second-highest officer, Under Secretary of State Sumner Welles. Welles alerted him to pending events and could verify the authenticity of information provided by others at the department. Their friendship promoted both of their careers. Both tall, mustached, and patrician in bearing, they shared similar worldviews. They had met in 1925, when Pearson covered the State Department and Welles was assistant secretary of state for Latin American affairs (until Calvin Coolidge fired him for carrying on an affair with a Republican senator's wife, whom he married after her divorce). At the Democratic convention in 1932, Welles and Pearson jointly drafted a Good Neighbor Policy plank for the platform. Welles returned to the State Department during the presidency of Franklin Roosevelt—whom he had known since childhood. As a boy, Welles spent summers on Campobello Island where Roosevelt vacationed, and he served as a page at his wedding.[46]

Although personally close to the president, Sumner Welles could never establish such intimacy with Secretary of State Cordell Hull. The former Tennessee representative and senator was a leader in the conservative wing of Roosevelt's political coalition, and the president valued the high esteem with which Congress held Hull. Publicly, Hull projected an avuncular and conciliatory image, but in private he could be vain, suspicious, and painfully sensitive. Pearson regarded him as a "jittery old woman when it comes to criticism." His aloofness encouraged the columnist to needle him, catching Sumner Welles in the crossfire.[47]

When several candidates vied for the post of under secretary of state in 1936, Pearson injected his column into the contest by praising Welles and belittling his opponents. Once Welles got the appointment, the "Merry-Go-Round" gushed about his talents: Welles proved an abler administrator than Hull, having less trouble making up his mind or imposing order on the faction-ridden State Department, which he ran during the secretary's frequent absences. Those same qualities explained why Franklin Roosevelt turned to Welles for advice rather than to Hull. Pearson credited Welles with trying to head off the Japanese conquest of China, opposing the Hitler-Mussolini dictatorships in Europe, and laying the foundation for the United Nations.[48]

Intelligence officers informed Secretary Hull that Sumner Welles frequently visited Drew Pearson's home, planting suspicions that Welles leaked stories to undermine him and claim his job. But the State Department was a hotbed of gossip and rumor, and Pearson did not need to rely on Welles alone. Foreign Service officers routinely cultivated friendships abroad to gather private information about local affairs, and they continued to do so back in Washington. They whispered information that advanced and derailed careers within the department, and they handled state secrets casually. "The mentality of the State Department was rather provincial in those days," recalled Noel Field, a foreign service officer whose spying for the Soviet Union benefited from the department's careless records management. "The most secret documents, sometimes in multiple copies, circulated from hand to hand."[49]

From his years of political campaigning, Cordell Hull read newspapers "as no one else in the Department," one aide attested. Despite becoming so upset over Pearson's columns, he could not resist reading them. Secretary Hull had exploded in 1938 when the "Merry-Go-Round" reported that pro-Nazi "career boys" inside his department had approved the sale of helium for German dirigibles that violated various treaties and the US Neutrality Act. The sale had been held up at the Interior Department, headed by Pearson's close friend and reliable source, Harold Ickes. State Department records released a generation later verified the column, but Hull devoted a full hour at his next press conference denying and denouncing Pearson's accusations. "Mr. Hull was pleasant and smiling," the New York Times reported, "although not entirely concealing his intense feeling." As it happened, Drew Pearson sat among the reporters present at that press conference and sparred with Hull over the charges. Pearson and Allen refused to back down, advising subscribing papers that they remained convinced that Hull was breaking the law. They considered hiring a lawyer to file an injunction that would stop all arms sales to Germany—but ultimately took no legal action.[50]

In 1940, the column again revealed that the "career boys" had planned to make a hundred-million-dollar loan to Fascist Spain, until Under Secretary Welles met with President Roosevelt and persuaded him to block the action. Hull called this report "wholly inaccurate" and "a complete misrepresentation." Privately, however, the secretary knew it was true and accused Welles of leaking classified information. Denying that he had informed Pearson, Welles issued a public statement calling his friend a liar. In a subsequent column, Pearson retracted the allegation that Welles had appealed to the president over Hull's head but reiterated his accusations about the proposed loan to Spain. Admiral William Leahy, chair of the Joint Army and Navy Board, noted at one meeting that Hull was boiling with indignation over the story. "I felt that the Secretary was personally irritated by Pearson," Admiral Leahy observed, "which was probably exactly what the columnist wanted to accomplish." Whenever Hull suspected that Sumner Welles was feeding information to Pearson, the "Merry-Go-Round" would find something to rebuke Welles about mildly. Then Pearson and Welles would be seen dining together, which counteracted their protestations of innocence.[51]

Pearson assured his editors that he had discussed the column on Spain "with some of highest officials of the State Department—not one, but several of them, including Mr. Welles." A top-level official had read over his account in advance and confirmed it as "absolutely accurate." The day after the story ran, Sumner Welles had come to see him and said that he had never been in such a tough spot in his life. Welles reported that "the old man had cursed like a Tennessee mountaineer," and almost asked for his resignation.[52]

Recurring bouts with tuberculosis kept Secretary Hull away from his department for long stretches, and Pearson informed his readers that for all practical purposes Sumner Welles was Secretary of State. Rather than relinquish his position, however, Hull grew determined to force Welles from office, assuring associates that he was a great believer in giving people enough rope to hang themselves. In 1943, Hull seized on a damaging report describing how an intoxicated Welles had sexually propositioned several male sleeping car porters on an overnight train. Rumors of the incident spread across Washington, but reporters refused to print them on the then-honored grounds that a public official's private life should remain off limits to the press unless it affected his public duties. Pearson had heard the rumors but dismissed them since he regarded Welles as a ladies' man.[53]

Brandishing these charges, Hull attained Welles's resignation. Drew Pearson regretted that "stories of divorce, domestic infelicity and sex rumors have been spread regarding certain progressive members of the State Department whom it is out to purge. Once these stories circulate to enough people through the gossip underground, the target of the gossip is told by his superiors that his usefulness is over and he must resign." In his weekly radio broadcast, Pearson decried Secretary Hull's determination to remove "one of the few liberals" in the State Department. While Welles had been working to maintain US-Soviet relations during the war, Hull's secret hope was to see Russia "bled white" by the Germans. That inflammatory charge of being anti-Russian prompted the secretary of state to demand that the Justice Department prosecute Pearson. Once again, the attorney general declined to intervene.[54]

Within the Soviet Union, Pearson's accusations received full press coverage, fanning Stalin's suspicions of his allies. The Kremlin knew of Sumner Welles's friendship with Pearson and had no reason to doubt his charges. For those same reasons, the highest American officials rushed to denounce his account. At a press conference, Cordell Hull in icy tones declared Pearson's accusations "monstrous and diabolical." Privately, he alerted the US ambassador to the Soviet Union that the column contained "deliberately false statements." Nor did President Roosevelt want to jeopardize the US-Soviet alliance with the impression that the columnist's portrayal of State Department attitudes had come from Welles. At his own press conference, a red-faced Franklin Roosevelt denounced Drew Pearson as a chronic liar who had unfairly and inaccurately accused the State Department of anti-Soviet sentiments.[55]

Pearson felt sure that the Russians were aware of Hull's anti-Russian attitude. "It didn't take me to tell them about it," he said in his defense. "However, if the President needed a scapegoat, I am glad if anything I have said now assists the Administration to make it clear in words what certainly was not clear before in deeds." Contrary to the self-confidence that his statements expressed, Luvie Pearson could see that Roosevelt's outburst had upset her husband terribly. "I kept telling him it was good publicity, that it built him up," she recalled. Reviving his sense of showmanship, he had his syndicate print large placards with his portrait over the caption: "The Man the President Called a Liar."[56]

Pearson addressed a column to "the many who have wired, written, and telephoned" regarding the incident. Regardless of its publicity value, however, the United Features Syndicate decided that the feud had gone on long enough, and it squelched his attempt to respond. Editors who carried the column kept asking when he planned to offer a "bill of particulars" on his charges against the State Department's stand on Russia, "but I am not permitted to open my mouth," he stated. "Of course, I can use this material on the air, but I don't like to stint the column in favor of the radio."[57]

His efforts had produced the opposite of what he intended. Setting out to promote Sumner Welles, Pearson had undermined his career. "I realize that I was the source of some of the friction, and that was why I have stayed away from you so consistently in the last two years," Pearson apologized to Welles. "But I did not realize that Mr. Hull blamed everything I wrote on you." He regarded the results as a tragedy. "Sumner has plenty of faults and is a difficult man to get along with," Pearson admitted to his diary, "but he has a perspective far beyond anybody else I have known in the State Department." Welles, by contrast, accepted his fate as a political liability. The president needed to play for higher stakes than personal friendship, regarding Cordell Hull as essential for getting the postwar peace treaties and membership in the United Nations through Congress. Welles left government service permanently to write a newspaper column, reduced, as another columnist noted, to telling "three times a week what he would do if he were secretary."[58]

Most of the Washington press corps sided with Pearson in his brawl with the State Department. Correspondents who wrote about foreign affairs could attest to the department's penchant for secrecy and deception, which complicated their efforts to check facts and required more reliance on speculation. An editorial in the *Washington Post*, which did not always agree with the "Merry-Go-Round," praised Pearson's "fearless and necessary work" in revealing the State Department's inner workings. "What Mr. Pearson and other like-minded journalists wish to see is an initiative in the conduct of our foreign policy which would weld all of the Allies together," wrote the *Post*. "So far there has been no sign of it."[59]

In wartime, democratic regimes may resort to totalitarian means to preserve their security, making secret-breakers prime candidates for surveillance. When Pearson began publishing reports of tensions between the American and British governments, both of their intelligence agencies scrambled to discover how he had gotten hold of their top-secret documents. They shadowed him, tapped his phone, and planted a spy among his friends.[60]

Neighbors in Georgetown alerted the FBI about the mysterious cars that kept circulating through their streets. FBI agents determined that the vehicles belonged to the Office of Naval Intelligence (ONI), which was conducting surveillance. Six ONI investigators inexpertly shadowed Pearson everywhere, trying to learn his sources and dry them up. Aware of his tail, he made sure they discovered nothing. When a Philadelphia newspaper revealed the domestic espionage, Pearson assured reporters: "My operations are an open book." Although he avoided revealing military secrets, he had apparently triggered this surveillance by exposing military waste and inefficiency.[61]

The British Security Coordination (BSC) had operated covertly within the United States since 1940 to shape public opinion in favor of Britain's war effort. The BSC planted stories in the American newspapers and radio broadcasts and dispatched agents to develop relationships with American journalists, both to collect inside information and to shape their reporting. The British targeted Walter Winchell and Drew Pearson because their columns and broadcasts reached enormous audiences. Both Winchell and Pearson thrived on "hot news," so the British expected them to be susceptible to manipulation in return for some titillating stories.[62]

Winchell swallowed BSC bait whole, printing some of their news stories exactly as the British wrote them. Not so Pearson, who dismayed the propagandists by putting his own interpretation on whatever they gave him. The BSC did not consider Pearson anti-British, but attributed his hostility to his anti-colonialism. Desperate to stop his access to confidential information, British agents traced his sources to the highest levels within the Roosevelt administration, including Assistant Secretary of War John McCloy. McCoy had alerted Pearson that Britain was dragging its feet on a proposed cross-Channel invasion of France, to open a second front and relieve pressure on the Soviet army.[63]

After Pearson revealed an embarrassing British naval blunder—the loss of fifty-nine out of sixty ships carrying supplies to Murmansk—the BSC planted a spy on him. For this task they selected an injured Royal Air Force pilot who had been stationed at the British embassy in Washington. Wing Commander Roald Dahl, later famous as the author of *Charlie and the Chocolate Factory* and other children's books, moved suavely through Washington society, equally popular at dinner tables and in bedrooms. Dahl visited Pearson's home so frequently that he became one of the family. Tasked with uncovering Pearson's sources, Dahl also tried to dissuade him from publishing anything detrimental to Britain. Once Pearson grew wise to Dahl's agenda, he cooperated with him. He showed Dahl his British-related stories in advance, and Dahl kept him supplied with news for his columns. "We became very good friends and we exchanged information openly," Dahl later recalled. "He wanted it for his column, and he knew I wanted it for other reasons."[64]

Despite Dahl's best efforts, Pearson persisted in irritating the British. The "Merry-Go-Round" broke the news that US Ambassador to India William

Phillips had sent a confidential report to President Roosevelt, warning that Indian resentment against British colonial rule was hampering the war effort:

> Each time the President has discussed India with Winston Churchill, he has received a blunt, cold shoulder. Once, last year, when United States Ambassador William Phillips, after his return to this country from India, talked to the Prime Minister at FDR's request, Churchill banged the table and said: "I have always been right about Hitler and everyone else in Europe. I'm also right about Indian policy. Any change in Indian policy now will mean a blood bath." At about the time Phillips talked to Churchill, he also submitted a report to President Roosevelt, which will be the basis for any new United States proposals to Britain. In this report, Ambassador Phillips, generally considered pro-British, made some critical forthright statements about British policy.[65]

Ambassador Phillips judged India more anti-British than anti-Japanese and predicted that the Indian army would be worthless to the war unless India achieved a promise of independence. "It is not right for the British to say, 'this is none of your business,'" he wrote, when the United States had taken the lead in fighting Japan, with only "token assistance" from the British. The British embassy protested to Secretary Hull that the report would "create an extremely bad impression in London and in India." Hull professed that he never read Pearson's column and was unaware that it had quoted Phillips's letter; but true to form he felt sure that Sumner Welles had leaked it. While State Department officials expressed regret for the leak, they declined to disavow Phillips's views, as the British demanded. In fact, Secretary Hull agreed with Phillips.[66]

The Foreign Ministry instructed British consuls in America to contact newspapers that had published the column and request that they denounce it. The British ambassador himself called Eugene Meyer to suggest that the *Washington Post* run an editorial contradicting the column. Meyer declined, saying this would only add more fuel to the fire and they should "let sleeping dogs lie." In London, Prime Minister Churchill and Foreign Minister Anthony Eden made things uncomfortable for Phillips, who at the time was working out of General Eisenhower's headquarters. When Phillips refused to revise his views, the British leaders finally declared him *persona non grata.* Pearson broke that story as well. Secretary Hull swore that he would discover who had leaked this information, while at the same time other members of Roosevelt's cabinet privately congratulated Pearson for performing a public service. In later years, Phillips's son confided that his father had been glad that Pearson published his report, believing that it had expedited Indian independence.[67]

The columnist heard that Secretary Hull demanded that the FBI take every possible step to find his source. Assuming that his telephones had been tapped, he wrote to his wife from the lecture circuit, alerting her that a trustworthy friend advised him that their house had been wired for sound, "in other words, dictaphones." He carried the most revealing of his documents with him in his briefcase. "The funny part of it is," Pearson added, the British "wouldn't believe the source of this story if I told them."[68]

When questioned, Pearson would say only that he had gotten Phillips's letter from "an Indian." A cynic in the press corps felt sure that he meant "the Great White Father of the Indian tribes in the United States," Franklin Roosevelt. In fact, the letter came from an Indian nationalist, after taking a circuitous path. Robert Crane, a low-level staff member at the India Desk in the State Department's Division of Cultural Relations, had received a copy of Phillips's letter to file. The son of Protestant missionaries, Crane had grown up in Asia and despised colonialism. He had friends in the India lobby that operated within the Indian High Commission in Washington, advocating American support for Indian independence. Crane showed the letter to Kersasp Naoroji, who had his secretary retype it and then passed it along to the commission's press officer, Obaidur Rahman, a nationalist who slipped the document to one of Pearson's staff, David Karr. When the letter appeared in Pearson's column a few weeks later, Robert Crane said he "damn near fainted!" Grilled by State Department investigators, he admitted having shown the document to a friend but denied knowing how it reached Pearson. Things turned chilly for Crane, and he resigned from the State Department to pursue an academic career.[69]

British intelligence officers identified the wrong Indian as Pearson's source. Major Altaf Quadir, third secretary of the Indian High Commissioner's Office, found himself abruptly transferred to combat in Italy. In its postwar *Secret History of British Intelligence in the Americas*, the BSC still did not realize its error, and celebrated that Pearson had lost an excellent source, though they conceded that he had many others.[70]

Pearson indeed had more sources to nettle the British. He soon broke the story of how Chinese troops and the US Air Transport Command had helped block a Japanese invasion of India. Aiming to boost Chinese morale, he reported that British and Indian troops had been "powerless to stop" a Japanese advance until the American air command had flown several thousand Chinese soldiers over "the Hump"—the Himalayas. Since Pearson could not quote the colonel who tipped him off, he sought an "appropriate authority" to satisfy censorship restrictions. The commander of the Air Transport Command had no objection to the story, expressing pride in what his men were doing, but he declined to endorse it since the British had objected to any stories that implied their soldiers were not pulling their weight in the war. Pearson moved up the chain of command to General Henry H. "Hap" Arnold, the top army air force general. But General Arnold would not go over the head of Lord Louis Mountbatten, who headed the Southeast Asian Command, so the story sat on Pearson's desk for weeks until he found someone with enough authority to satisfy the Office of Censorship. The day after its publication, the British embassy confirmed the use of Chinese troops.[71]

Fuming over the repeated leaks, Winston Churchill branded Pearson an enemy of British interests. This seemed strange since Pearson had so strongly supported them before the war, but after D-Day he considered the war in Europe practically over and concentrated instead on postwar issues. American public opinion might be united behind the British war effort, but not in favor of its colonial system, which created barriers for US trade. Pearson knew that President Roosevelt had privately appealed to the British to improve conditions in India, and that Churchill, a convinced imperialist, had replied that India was none of his business. "I, for one, cannot agree with this," Pearson asserted. With India as a base of operations against Japan, the United States ought to have something to say about anything there that hampered an end to the war. "Perhaps the pressure of American public opinion will have more weight with Mr. Churchill than Mr. Roosevelt," he concluded. "This is the only motive I have in disclosing these matters."[72]

Pearson once again stunned British intelligence, this time revealing a top-secret message from Churchill to the British commander in Greece, Sir John Scobie. The columnist had been raising questions about whether the British used news censorship in the Middle East for military or political purposes. He interpreted Churchill's actions as designed to preserve British influence in the region. On December 12, 1944, the "Merry-Go-Round" published a telegram from the American ambassador to Italy to the State Department, quoting Churchill as giving orders to a British general in Greece to suppress public protests in Athens, not to hesitate to open fire on demonstrators, and to "act as if he were in a conquered city." Pearson's columns generally reached his syndicate three days before they appeared in the newspapers. Someone alerted the Justice Department, which tried to kill the column in advance. But when J. Edgar Hoover called Pearson, the columnist said it was too late, that the syndicate had already distributed it and would not call it back.[73]

At the British embassy in Washington, the political theorist Isaiah Berlin, who summarized the weekly news for officials in London, branded Drew Pearson "one of the most malicious and irresponsible political muckrakers in the United States." Churchill repeatedly pressed American officials for an inquiry into the leakage, warning Roosevelt that all their communications were at risk. At first, suspicion fell on the anti-colonial Sumner Welles, but by then Welles no longer held office. Fingers also pointed at the State Department's Near Eastern Division. Officials considered appointing its director an ambassador to get him out of town and prevent further leaks. Pearson reported all this in the column, taunting that they were "not even warm."[74]

As it turned out, Churchill himself bore responsibility for the leak. He had dictated his cable to General Scobie so late at night that his exhausted secretary marked it "TOP SECRET" but neglected to add "GUARD," the signal that the Americans should not see the information. Consequently, the cable went out through US military and diplomatic channels. American officials, offended by the notion that the British might use Lend Lease tanks against Greek civilians, leaked the information to the columnist. Pearson was pressing Roosevelt not to concede the Mediterranean as a British sphere of influence. He also came to believe that the shooting down of Greek women and children in Athens by Greek police under British command provoked the Communist-inspired civil war there.[75]

As a parting gift, Roald Dahl handed his friend a major scoop. Dahl mentioned that he had been transferred to Canada on a highly secret assignment. Curious about this tip, Pearson sought to learn the nature of the assignment from his contacts within the FBI and other intelligence agencies. On a radio broadcast in February 1946, Pearson announced that "the biggest story of espionage and intrigue is about to break." He revealed that a Soviet espionage ring had been operating in Canada and was spying on the development of the atom bomb: "The Canadians have taken over a Russian agent, who has given the names of about 1,700 Russian agents; and has put the finger on certain officials inside the American and Canadian governments cooperating with the Soviets." Although the number of agents turned out to be inflated, the threat was real.[76]

Igor Gouzenko, a cipher clerk at the Soviet embassy in Ottawa, faced recall to Moscow over an infraction and sought to shield himself by turning over secret documents to the *Ottawa Journal*. The paper passed copies to the US Department of Justice. Concerned over tense relations with the Soviet Union, neither the US nor Canadian governments acted until Pearson's revelations prompted a Canadian Royal Commission investigation into Soviet espionage. The Canadians suspected J. Edgar Hoover of having leaked the information to Pearson to force the issue, and FBI records show that Pearson talked to Hoover and assistant director Louis Nichols on the day of his news-making broadcast. His revelation pleased the FBI, which had been seeking a way to publicize the espionage story.[77]

Frustrated with Pearson's ability to break the Canadian case, a rival syndicated columnist, Marquis Childs, called the FBI's Nichols to complain. Childs charged that "Drew Pearson and the director have been friends for over ten years and that Pearson had a by-pass from the Bureau." Nichols refuted the assertion, insisting that "Mr. Hoover did not play favorites," and there was no truth to "the whole bugaboo of columnists being given special treatment." That might be so, said Childs, except that everybody believed Pearson had gotten that information from the director.[78]

Readers on the left met Pearson's accusations of Soviet spying with skepticism and accused him of warmongering. One magazine writer described Pearson as being "daily waited upon by importuning Left-wingers seeking to convince him that he was mistaken." Pearson's leg man David Karr tried to mollify his sources in labor and progressive organizations by telling them that "J. Edgar Hoover asked Drew to use the story, and how could he turn him down? After all, the business works both ways." Suspicions ebbed when the Canadian government belatedly confirmed his charges. Pearson also interviewed a hooded Gouzenko on his new television program.[79]

Decades later, declassified British intelligence documents indicated that Roald Dahl might have been more devious than indiscreet in tipping off Pearson. The Canadian government had been trying to handle the Gouzenko affair quietly, without publicity, to avoid disrupting postwar UN negotiations with the Soviet Union. British intelligence, abashed to learn that a top British nuclear scientist had been a Soviet mole, and intent on exposing Soviet perfidy, aimed to bypass Canada and deflect attention away from itself by selecting an American journalist to break the story. The FBI, eager to alert American citizens to the dangers of Communist espionage and expand its own surveillance powers, willingly verified the news. As is so often the case with leaks, covert motives operated behind them. The Gouzenko story became one of Pearson's biggest coups, but the resulting revelations contributed to sparking a Red Scare in the United States that he wound up opposing.[80]

In order to break wartime secrets, Drew Pearson had to outmaneuver censors, diplomats, military brass, and spies. He raised presidential blood pressure, stirred the bureaucracy, and humbled a powerful army general. After the war, when he was accused of revealing classified information, Pearson sued for libel on the grounds that the charge made him appear unpatriotic. At the trial, he testified that the word "classified" had become an extraordinarily broad term, which the government used "to cover a multitude of sins or a multitude of things they don't want the public to know about." A diligent reporter had to determine for himself whether something marked classified should be published. "When you have been operating in Washington a long time and you have been operating through a war, when you learn the rules of censorship and try to live up to them," Pearson told the court, "why, naturally you have to make some judgments of your own."[81]

Each week on his Sunday night radio programs, Pearson wrapped up the program with predictions of things to come. Prophesizing was a risky high-wire act since fast-moving events could quickly prove him wrong. He veered off course occasionally but called enough correctly to establish an image as a seer. To make his predictions, he relied on inside tips, took some educated guesses, and bent a few rules. Rivals in the press corps detected that Pearson was breaking the White House's release dates by broadcasting embargoed news in advance in the form of a prediction. Since Roosevelt's press secretary wanted Pearson's support, he looked the other way. Reporters finally complained to the president, and Pearson dropped any mention of the White House from his "sure-fire predictions" over the radio.[82]

Predictions also helped him evade the government censors. If he knew something for sure but could not source it as a fact, he could make it sound speculative. So, on a broadcast in November 1943, he reported that "rumors have shot around the world" of an Allied meeting between Roosevelt and Churchill. "My own prediction is that they will go to an African town," he said, knowing full well they would meet in Casablanca.[83]

Occasionally, the censors aided him. They were opening mail sent between the United States and foreign lands and culling anything of a suspicious nature for distribution to the State and War Departments, the FBI, and the Office of Strategic Services (OSS)—all agencies that fed Pearson's pipeline. Paying close attention to mail to Portugal and Argentina, both hubs of Nazi spying, censors intercepted the letters from Connecticut industrialist Vivien Kellems to her German lover in Argentina, Count Frederick Karl von Zedlitz. British intelligence had identified Zedlitz as a German operative. Kellems had run unsuccessfully for Congress in 1942 and had spoken out against federal withholding taxes, Lend-Lease to the Soviet Union, and "evil internationalism."[84]

On his radio program, Pearson read excerpts from Kellems's letters and called Zedlitz "an alleged Nazi agent." He encouraged the Justice Department to investigate her "strange love affair" with a man she believed was "destined to become a leader of Germany after the war." Returning to the story on several programs, he ignored pleas from the censors to stop airing private mail. A Democratic congressman read excerpts from the same letters in the House chamber.[85]

Insisting that her paramour was no Nazi spy, Vivien Kellem called on the House Un-American Activities Committee to investigate how her private correspondence had fallen "into the hands of a second-rate radio commentator and a popgun congressman." The matter was considered instead by the Senate Post Office Committee, whose chairman, Tennessee Senator Kenneth McKellar, a month earlier had spent an hour on the Senate floor denouncing Drew Pearson as "an infamous, dirty, low down, mean, lying scoundrel and skunk."[86]

Officials of the Office of Censorship testified that they distributed suspicious mail to interested agencies that were supposed to handle it "as strictly confidential communications." The chief censor felt certain that the leaks came from the State Department. Senators expressed indignation but conceded that the law contained no penalty for such a violation. That ended the hunt. Vivien Kellems's romance dissolved, and she devoted the rest of her life to campaigning against federal income taxes.[87]

When Pearson continued to report on intercepted mail, the Justice Department tasked the FBI with investigating. But J. Edgar Hoover reasoned that since Pearson would be the bureau's best source of information, all they could do would be to ask him how he acquired the material. FBI agents concluded that identifying Pearson's sources was an impossible assignment. The bureau also turned down a War Department request to investigate leaks to Pearson, advising them just to do a better job of making sure their memos did not leak in the first place. Pearson praised the FBI for the job it did during the war, and assured agents that he enjoyed the relationship and was proud to call the director his friend. He commended the bureau's stand on not pressing the Censorship Office to clamp down "unless there was a real need for this." In return, J. Edgar Hoover commended the columnist "for the wholehearted cooperation and assistance you have rendered me and representatives of the Federal Bureau of Investigation during the national emergency."[88]

As the war neared its end, Pearson promoted Treasury Secretary Henry Morgenthau's vision for postwar peace, which would preserve the alliance with the Soviet Union by demilitarizing Germany and dismantling its industries. "Morgenthau was almost alone in seeing," Pearson later commented, " . . . that if the two most powerful nations in the world, then allies, were able to continue as allies, they could prevent war in the future. If they fell apart, World War III was inevitable."[89]

Lunching together frequently, Pearson and Morgenthau reinforced each other's views. The columnist learned of the struggle within the Roosevelt administration between an anti-colonial Morgenthau clique and an anti-communist Forrestal clique, the latter centered on Secretary of the Navy James Forrestal. "Each had its newspaper friends," Pearson later noted. "Each leaked secret documents to those friends, some of them classified, all of them pertaining to the war effort." Pearson listed Alger Hiss at the State Department among the Morgenthau clique, noting that in making classified documents available to reporters, he did what many others in government were doing.[90]

Officials at the State and War Departments preferred a "soft peace" that would involve reconciling with Germany, reviving its industries, and turning its allied sectors into a strategic barrier against Soviet expansionism in Europe. Morgenthau instead insisted on a "hard peace" that regarded a renewed Germany as a threat to world peace. In August 1944, Morgenthau and his director of monetary research, Harry Dexter White, developed the Morgenthau Plan to strip Germany of its industrial strength. American military officers in London countered with an alternative plan, compiled in a *Handbook of Military Government in Germany*. Morgenthau showed the handbook to FDR, urging that he block any steps to restore a defeated Germany. Pearson described the president throwing down the handbook indignantly and instructing the War Department to rewrite it.[91]

Close enough to Drew Pearson to contribute a guest column to the "Merry-Go-Round," Secretary Morgenthau was the obvious source of Pearson's column revealing his meeting with FDR. "War and State Department officials are still quaking in their boots after President Roosevelt blew up last month over their failure to achieve any clear plan for civilian administration on Germany," Pearson reported. He suggested that the incident indicated that the president "had some very clear ideas on this policy even though it was not yet fully formulated." But planting the story backfired. Morgenthau's opponents leaked their own version of the disagreements within the cabinet, putting the issue squarely before the public. Prevailing opinion sided with the military, and the government ultimately opted to shelve the Morgenthau Plan.[92]

Despite Pearson's eagerness to break secrets, he suppressed the biggest story of the war: development of the atomic bomb. Months before the United States dropped bombs on Hiroshima and Nagasaki, Pearson learned of the atomic research underway in Oak Ridge, Tennessee, and at the Hanford Engineer Works in Washington. Aware that the columnist had discovered "several secret projects of major security importance," the Office of Censorship appealed to him to "set up a red flag" in his own mind against any references to secret scientific projects, and to check with them before mentioning anything in public. He agreed not to reveal what he knew, giving only a hint, two weeks after the first successful test of the weapon, in the form of a prediction that Japan would develop a desire for peace before the end of 1945. "I can't go beyond that," he told his radio audience, "except to say that when peace with Japan comes it will come just as suddenly and unexpectedly as Pearl Harbor."[93]

4

Drew Pearson's Leg Men

FILLING A DAILY COLUMN THAT mixed breaking news with opinion required more news gathering than one journalist could handle on his own.
Soon after the "Merry-Go-Round" got underway, its growing profitability
allowed Drew Pearson to augment his reporting with leg men. An old newspaper term, "leg men" referred to journalists who expended shoe leather to
go directly to their sources. They might be newspaper reporters themselves
or hirelings for more desk-bound writers. During his four decades as a columnist, Drew Pearson assembled teams of able news hunters. His runners
and researchers may have lacked a byline, but they were compensated by
their association with the nation's most famous muckraking columnist. His
clout gave them stature in Washington, making them respected and feared.[1]

Over time, the office staff fluctuated. Pearson relied on a core of reporters
and secretaries, sometimes expanding the squad by hiring those who had
tipped him off about a big story, or who had lost their jobs because of it.
A robust income from the columns and broadcasts covered staff salaries,
but funds for running the office had to compete with steep legal fees for
all those libel suits. These financial constraints made the columnist a notorious penny pincher. He paid his staff so meagerly that most supplemented
their incomes with outside jobs. They tolerated the low salaries because they
shared his passion for uncovering the news behind the news.

Pearson's leg men ranged from veterans to novices, former government
officials, recent college graduates, sons of friends, and relatives. Some stayed
with him for years; others moved on promptly to different careers: one to

Congress, another as a television news producer, another as a corporate executive. They produced copy, scored scoops, and came under fire occasionally for questionable tactics. They denied allegations of using underhanded techniques to obtain information and poked fun at critics who imagined the worst.[2] In 1941 the "Merry-Go-Round" gleefully passed along an account of the nefarious ways they supposedly got their news:

> Blair Bolles, Washington Star ace reporter, was approached the other day by Yelverton Garnett, an ex-reporter for The Star who said he had been commissioned by the Navy Department to find out where Pearson and Allen got their news about the Navy and what naval officers were responsible for leaks to the Merry-Go-Round column. Bolles, without a flicker of an eyelash, replied: "Don't you know how it's done? It's done by a network of bribery. They bribe messenger boys and stenographers and elevator operators. They bribe everybody. That's how they get the news." "Really!" gasped Garnett, his eyes wide with astonishment, and he ran off to tell the Navy.[3]

The staff operated out of half of Pearson's federal-style, yellow-brick house at 2820 Dumbarton Street. Georgetown had not yet become a fashionable part of town in 1928 when he bought a row of dilapidated, century-old townhouses, tore down the middle building, and constructed a connecting link between the remaining structures to create an impressive home. Jack Anderson observed that one side of his boss's house served as "a proper gentleman's domicile," with a butler and cook. It provided the setting for a stream of cocktail parties and dinner parties—all tax-deductible as business expenses on the grounds that they generated copy for the column. The watchful FBI determined that Pearson "attended and gives many cocktail parties where information can be secured," as well as having three or four people working for him with press credentials who contacted government agencies "like reporters."[4]

The other side of the house functioned as a newsroom, crowded with desks, file cabinets, typewriters, and constantly ringing telephones. Several secretaries kept up with the stack of fan letters and other mail that came in every day. The files contained copies of all the back issues of the column along with research notes, correspondence, and a massive card index that listed every person, place, and issue mentioned in the column, and on what day, enabling them to track how they had handled a subject in the past if it should come up again.[5]

Pearson did the lion's share of his work from home throughout the day and, according to his wife, at "all sorts of queer hours in the middle of the night." On the phone he took tips and trawled for news, building a coast-to-coast network of contacts who kept him informed of goings-on in their locations. In Washington, his leg men assembled pipelines throughout the government, locating someone in every department who could provide the information they sought. Much news came in voluntarily. "People would call Drew and tell him a lot," Luvie Pearson remarked. He did not need to look through keyholes or bribe servants because there were always people "furious with each other and dying to give out the story."[6]

For extra revenue, Pearson rented out some upstairs rooms to tenants. He also invited so many visitors that he began referring to the house as "Dumbarton Inn." As he hired more staff, however, he needed more space. "So, the tenant was shooed out, and the upstairs was rearranged so that people could get upstairs from the downstairs without going out the front door," his stepson Tyler Abell recalled. Even then, the offices were so cramped that the leg men sought more room to write in the Senate and House press galleries, using congressional typewriters and free paper. A fireplace in Pearson's private office gave the room the appearance of a gentleman's study, stacked with papers and books. He worked off a desk piled with file folders, using a phone that offered multiple lines. The bookshelf beside him held reference works from *Who's Who* to the *Encyclopaedia Britannica*. In the 1930s, a bicycle messenger would arrive each evening to whisk the latest column to the telegraph office. Then in 1944, his syndicate installed two teletype machines in the office, one that ran continuously, clattering out wire service reports, and the other he could use to send the column directly to the syndicate in New York. They would check it again before distributing mimeographed copies to all subscribing newspapers.[7]

World War II pumped up the pace of work in Pearson's office and the volume of mail. By 1946 the payroll had grown to ten secretaries and reporters. Some of his leg men showed no political leanings, but Pearson inclined toward those who shared his liberal attitudes. His favorite was an energetic young reporter from New York, David Karr. Born David Katz, he had changed his name to evade antisemitism. A short, round-faced man with what associates called a "pixyish personality," Karr blended idealism with opportunism. He often goaded Pearson to intervene in progressive causes.[8]

The nimble Karr got into reporting as a teenager by covering sports for William Randolph Hearst's conservative New York *Mirror*. He lost that job when Hearst took umbrage over one of his articles, and a colleague on the *Mirror* suggested he talk to the staff of the Communist Party's *Daily Worker*. Karr then freelanced for the *Worker*, writing articles and reviews. Always insisting that the only compensation he received was the books he reviewed, Karr swore that he never joined the Communist Party. He landed a job with the Trans-Radio Press Syndicate but took a leave in 1940 to do press work for the National Committee of Independent-Voters for Roosevelt-Wallace. This stint brought him to the attention of some prominent New Dealers who encouraged Trans-Radio to send him to Washington. When the United States entered the war, Karr's deafness in one ear earned him a military deferment. He instead joined the Office of Facts and Figures, later merged into the Office of War Information, where he collected government news for distribution to foreign-language newspapers (despite having no foreign-language skills).[9]

His government job required a background investigation, and Karr's past association with the *Daily Worker* raised red flags. In 1943, a Civil Service Commission report asserted that he had been a Communist while he wrote for the party's paper and was therefore ineligible for government employment. Karr had once written an article accusing Representative Martin Dies, chairman of the House Un-American Activities Committee (HUAC), of having fascist ties, and Dies now reciprocated by including Karr's name on a list of "radical bureaucrats" whom he accused of smearing members of Congress. Called to testify before HUAC, Karr claimed to have given the FBI tips "on all matters of subversive activity." This self-serving exaggeration irritated the bureau by implying he had been an informant, rather than someone who provided unsolicited information. The controversy made his resignation from the Office of War Information inevitable. Karr briefly reported for the *Washington Post* before joining Pearson's staff in 1944. He had been intrigued with Drew Pearson since the day he saw him in a Bromo-Seltzer ad in the New York City subway, pictured while climbing the Capitol steps. "Then and there I decided you were indeed a most remarkable man," he assured Pearson.[10]

Unsure of Karr's political leanings, Pearson checked with the FBI. Agents demurred that they could not tell him what to do about his employees but recommended that he needed to appear "completely spotless" to maintain his public standing. Pearson carried his inquiry to Attorney General Tom Clark, who showed him the Justice Department's file, from which Clark concluded that Karr was not "Communistic." That enabled the columnist to dismiss any allegations against his leg man. "As for David Karr," Pearson commented, "if he is pro-Communist, the Washington Monument is a hole in the ground."[11]

Some editors blamed Karr for the column's attacks on conservative politicians. When the "Merry-Go-Round" urged San Diego voters to defeat a Republican Representative who was under federal investigation for loaning money from his own building-and-loan association to build a hotel on land sold by his father, Pearson had to reassure the editor of the *San Diego Union* that David Karr had nothing to do with the revelation, and that the tip had come instead from the chairman of the Home Loan Bank Board. As the attacks on Karr mounted, Pearson privately mused that "Dave, like a lot of other youngsters, might have had Communist leanings or even been a party member. But if I am any judge of human nature, he was cured of this long ago."[12]

Nevertheless, FBI agents monitored Karr's behavior. They investigated reports that he had posed as a member of Vice President Henry Wallace's staff in order to obtain a confidential report on Soviet Premier Joseph Stalin for the "Merry-Go-Round." They trailed Karr's meetings with the press attaché at the Soviet embassy, as well as his contacts with other embassies. They recorded his conversations with Treasury official Harry Dexter White—whose phone the FBI had tapped—revealing White to be a key source for the column. Karr explained that White gave him "a lot of stuff on the Far Eastern things that the other guys don't get because of his Treasury connections." In return, White earned praise in the "Merry-Go-Round." On January 1, 1946, White thanked Karr for plugging his efforts on behalf of the Bretton Woods international financial agreement—the day before that column appeared. "Drew loves you," Karr assured his source. But Harry Dexter White was not just leaking to Pearson. Decades later the federal government released the Venona transcripts, intercepted messages from Russian agents in the United States sent to Moscow during World War II. Once decoded they revealed that he also provided back-channel information to the Soviet Union.[13]

The "Merry-Go-Round"'s support for organized labor irked its anti-union publishers. But if a publisher dropped the column, David Karr would call on friends in the labor movement, "asking the boys to protest." He reminded union organizers how tough it was for journalists to tell labor's story fairly against their publishers' prejudices. A little labor pressure usually resulted in getting the paper to resume carrying the column.[14]

"Dave had the faculty of being a salesman," Pearson observed, a handy trait because he had to "persuade people to talk, persuade them to hand over important documents." Karr could charm secretaries who guarded the front offices of government officials. He would tell juicy stories to potential sources and encourage them to share their own. He developed a knack for overhearing conversations and for reading documents upside down on desks. Other reporters called Karr one of the brashest correspondents who ever covered Washington. Indeed, Pearson worried more about the young man's impetuousness than his politics. He hoped that Karr could calm down without losing his crusading zeal. Karr in turn found his association with Pearson profitable, "materially and spiritually." Their relationship grew so close that the leg man named his son Andrew and chose Drew Pearson as his godfather. As much as he excelled in the job, however, Karr struggled to support his family on the salary Pearson paid him.[15]

After the 1948 elections, David Karr quit Pearson's staff and moved to New York to become vice president of the advertising agency that produced Pearson's radio programs. Before leaving, Karr persuaded Pearson to keep a diary, which the columnist faithfully continued for the rest of his life. Despite his departure, Karr came under sustained fire from a vituperative rival columnist, Westbrook Pegler. In some fifty columns over the next five years, Pegler repeatedly dredged up Karr's teenage association with the *Daily Worker*, referred to him as "Katz," and named the ad agency where he worked. When the notoriety eventually cost Karr his job, he convinced Pearson to let him launch a business-oriented newsletter, "Personal from Pearson." They advertised the newsletter as a special service to a "carefully selected" list of subscribers, containing confidential information about federal policy decisions, personnel changes, congressional pressure, and "Drew Pearson's own interpretations and predictions." The weekly newsletter came marked "Confidential—not for publication." Karr ran it for only a short while. "Then he dumped it on me," Pearson complained, "and I have been doing it with my left hand . . . ever since." Long accused of flirting with Communism, Karr then pursued a murky career that mixed capitalism with undercover operations. He became president of the Fairbanks-Whitney Corporation, a defense contractor, dabbled in Hollywood and Broadway productions, claimed to have carried out secret missions for Israel, and traded information to the KGB in return for business opportunities in Moscow. Throughout all this, he retained close ties to Pearson, continuing to provide material for his columns and enjoying the chance to be "a part of history" whenever he did.[16]

It was Karr who alerted Pearson that another of his leg men, Andrew Older, had been seen dining with known Communists. Older confessed to Pearson that he had joined the party in 1940 and that his wife had also been a member of the Communist Youth League while in college. He swore that he had drifted away from the party but could not make a clean break "due to the black-mailing tactics which the party uses against those it seeks to hold"—former comrades were threatening to expose him. Worried about the repercussions, Pearson sought advice from the FBI on how to handle this situation. Yet in spite of the bureau's warnings, he decided that since Older had told the truth about his past, he should keep his job. The columnist told Director Hoover that he knew this would "risk some very strong political reactions, but I have had strong political reactions before. And as long as I am convinced that I am right I am willing to take the risk." Besides, "what goes in the column is written by me, not him. And what I have written about Russia and Communism I have written for all the world to read."[17]

The mounting pressure of Cold War anti-communism proved too strong to overcome, however. With HUAC urging patriotic citizens to purge "un-American agents" from their organizations, and grabbing daily headlines with mudslinging investigations, Pearson reluctantly concluded that he had to let Andy Older go. Even so, they remained on good terms and Older continued to feed information to the column. His politics later surfaced publicly when an FBI informant inside the Communist Party testified before Congress that Older and his wife had been registered members. The informant recalled how the head of the party's Newspaper Club had discussed ways of trying to persuade Older to take a more active part in party affairs. When Older died in 1951, during the Red Scare, Pearson minimized his contributions to the column by calling him a "nice boy" whom he hired during the "manpower shortage [at the] tail end of the war," giving the impression that he had done little work of any consequence. Older's mother chastised the columnist for such disparaging statements, coming from someone whose Quaker ideals her son had respected.[18]

Firing Andy Older created a vacancy that Pearson filled by hiring his most successful leg man and ultimate successor, Jack Anderson. Raised in a devout Mormon family in Utah, Anderson reported for the *Salt Lake Tribune* as a teenager and spent two years as a missionary in the American South during World War II. Not keen on combat, he served briefly in the merchant marine before persuading the *Deseret News* to send him to China as a war correspondent. At the war's end, while he was in Chungking, he was finally drafted into the army and reported for the *Stars and Stripes* newspaper and American Forces Radio. During a bull session with other war correspondents in China, Anderson expressed an ambition to report from Washington, "the news capital of the world." An Associated Press reporter suggested he ought to try to work for Drew Pearson, who knew the backrooms and the back alleys and where the bodies were buried. All that Anderson knew about Pearson came from an unflattering profile he had seen in the *Saturday Evening Post*—he had never read any of his columns.[19]

Jack Anderson wore his army uniform for his April 1947 interview with Pearson, hoping to impress the columnist with his experience—limited as it was—as a war correspondent. What impressed Pearson instead was his assertiveness, and his youth. "He was looking for a young reporter whom he could teach and who would stay with him for a while," Anderson surmised, plus a willingness to work full-time for a half-time salary of $50 a week. Out of a hundred applicants, he got the job. Pearson warned that his busiest day was Sunday because of his national radio broadcast that night. "I can't be here on Sunday," Anderson injected. "I go to church on Sunday." "Can you work late on Saturday?" Pearson asked. "I can work as late as you want me to," he promised, and he never had to break his rule against working on Sundays.[20]

A resentful Andy Older escorted his replacement up to Capitol Hill, introduced him to a few backbenchers, and then abandoned him. Anderson knew so little about Pearson's reputation in Congress that he dared to question Tennessee Senator Kenneth McKellar, not realizing that the senator had once spent an hour on the Senate floor denouncing Drew Pearson as a "low-lived skunk." McKellar chased him out of his office.[21]

Jack Anderson brought with him little knowledge about how Washington operated, and a religious sensibility easily shocked by what he found. His ignorance made him "pretty much a creature of Drew Pearson," he later admitted. "I got a Drew Pearson view of Washington from the very beginning—he was the one who trained me. All I knew about Washington before then was what I'd read in civics books." Anderson realized that his new boss had the best sources and the best access of any journalist in Washington. By identifying himself with Pearson, he could instantly gain the same kind of access. He befriended everyone from clerks to congressmen—finding the clerks more useful. His faith-driven morality also emboldened him to challenge his boss whenever he thought he might be crossing an ethical line.[22]

Pearson liked what the young reporter turned in, decided that he could hold his own, and made him a full-time assistant at $100 a week. Anderson covered the Senate while another leg man, Tom McNamara, concentrated on the House. Between them they split the cabinet departments and agencies, with Anderson patrolling the Pentagon. There he pieced accounts together from fragmentary reports gathered among the competing military services. The Truman administration's plan to unify the military services caused anxiety, and senior officers responded by leaking information detrimental to the rival services. Anderson developed contacts and cajoled them into passing along forbidden stories and classified documents. To encourage candor from his sources, he would take no notes during an interview, rushing outside afterward to write down everything he could remember. When Harry Truman signed an executive order in 1951 vastly expanding the national security classification system, Anderson began alarming his boss by showing up with documents stamped "Secret." Anderson insisted that over-classification protected incompetents and scoundrels in high places. For every legitimate item of national security, he estimated that there were dozens of classified documents covering up unsavory activities. He equated the increased classification with censorship.[23]

At the Capitol, veteran reporter Tom McNamara advised Anderson to pump senators to find out what had gone on behind closed doors in the executive sessions where Senate committees did much of their business. Anderson struggled with the dubious process of reconstructing secret discussions until he discovered that in 1947 Congress had mandated that committees make verbatim transcripts of their executive sessions. Rather than stitch together dialogue drawn from different senators' memories, he could quote their exact words from the transcripts. That some of the transcripts were stamped secret proved little obstacle. Once Anderson got a senator to talk about a closed meeting, he would nonchalantly ask to see the transcript for accuracy's sake. "You've already told me who said what," he would say. "I just want to get the quotes straight." Some turned him down, but others let him read their copies of the transcripts. Senator John F. Kennedy, for instance, shared copies of the Foreign Relations Committee's executive session transcripts, to curry favor with the column. "When verbatim extracts began appearing in the column," Anderson recalled, "howls of anguish and outrage reverberated in the backrooms on Capitol Hill."[24]

Publicity-seeking senators could not resist responding whenever Jack Anderson called them off the Senate floor. "Their curiosity makes them come out," he marveled. "Then you've got to con them a little. Pretend you know all about whatever they're doing, even if you don't. A lot of these guys don't have any news judgment and they don't know what's a story and what's not. So if you just get them talking, they'll sometimes mention things that are of great significance without realizing it. Then you press for all the details. . . . It's the richest vein in town. All you have to do is go up there and mine it."[25]

Anderson operated under a cloak of anonymity since only Pearson's name appeared in the column's byline. He professed to not minding the lack of credit since being faceless allowed him to move about without setting off alarms. His famous boss, by contrast, could not enter a Capitol office without causing a commotion throughout the complex. After a few years, Anderson gained his own name recognition among the movers and shakers. In the 1950s, while he investigated a scandal in the Agriculture Department, he called an assistant secretary, identified himself as Jack Anderson, and was surprised to get a candid account of the problem. When he kept asking questions, the official stopped him and asked, "Is this Jack Anderson at the White House?" "No." "Jack Anderson with Drew Pearson?" "Yes." "Oh, God!" he groaned and hung up. (Jack Z. Anderson was a special assistant to President Eisenhower.)[26]

As much as Pearson depended on his staff, the paltry salaries he paid caused periodic unrest among them. When Bob Allen returned from the army, some of Pearson's leg men offered to work for him if he started a new column. Still recuperating from his war wounds, Allen declined, saying, "I don't want to go back on that treadmill." A recurring concern among the staff was who among them might someday share the byline with Pearson and eventually replace him. Pearson had considered adding his brother Leon to the column's byline, after he quit teaching poetry at Haverford to join the staff. Drew Pearson credited Leon with giving the column "spice and humor and color" to balance his own "acid and vitriol." After Bob Allen departed in 1942, some subscribing papers argued that they were now "buying one reporter, not two," and should pay less. Pearson thought that adding his brother would mollify these editors, and also Leon, who had lost his byline for the *Times-Herald* when Cissy Patterson broke with the family. But the partnership never materialized, and Leon struck out on his own, leaving the column to report from Paris for the International News Service and the National Broadcasting Company. "Many people receive me that wouldn't receive Drew," he told a reporter, exposing some coolness. "But then, I don't have to live on sensational attacks on anything. Drew does."[27]

In 1950 Tristam Coffin joined the staff. A frequent tipster to the "Merry-Go-Round," Coffin had left a government job to write a surprise bestseller about the Truman era, *Missouri Compromise*, and launch his own column. Coffin boasted a gossipy style: "I do have a flair for a type of item the editors and readers seem to like, short, light bits or bits of drama." When he joined Pearson, he agreed to give up his own column and sign an indefinite contract in return for a credit line, "by Drew Pearson, with Tris Coffin." Not yet willing to share the byline, Pearson held out as a lure a promise that Coffin would one day succeed him as the "Merry-Go-Round" columnist.[28]

The promise stayed secret until 1954, when it emerged during a staff revolt over low wages. Leg man Fred Blumenthal rifled through the papers on the boss's desk and found memos indicating that Coffin would inherit the column. Blumenthal passed these to Jack Anderson, who by then had married and was struggling to raise his growing family on his sparse salary. Anderson had been willing to play second fiddle to Drew Pearson, he exploded, "but not to Tris Coffin, whom I judged to be a producer of fluff." Once confronted, Pearson admitted to the secret arrangement. "Fine," said Anderson. "You have my two-weeks' notice." He accepted a job as Washington bureau chief for the national Sunday newspaper supplement, *Parade* magazine, at double the salary Pearson had been paying. Loath to lose someone he considered the best news sleuth in Washington, Pearson admitted his mistake. If Anderson would come back, he could keep his new job and could write columns under his own name whenever Pearson went on vacation. "For Drew, giving me a byline was like giving me a little bit of his blood," Anderson recognized, but he felt that editors and readers needed to know he existed.[29]

Their partnership was just as mismatched as Pearson's had been with Bob Allen. Drew Pearson entertained elegantly at his home in Georgetown and played country squire at his farm in Maryland. He hosted the capital's most powerful officials and most prominent international visitors. Anderson lived modestly in the Maryland suburbs with his wife and nine children, shunning the cocktail circuit and embassy dinner parties. Pearson spent his days on the phone and then worked late into the night shaping the column—often putting in sixteen-hour days. Early the next morning he could begin again by walking from his living quarters to his office. Anderson would arrive hours later, having spent his mornings polishing the results of the previous day's corridor-prowling. As the designated "second banana," Anderson took on the additional burden of producing columns whenever Pearson traveled. He became a close friend to Cartha "Deke" DeLoach, widely regarded as the director's heir apparent at the FBI. The two men lunched together weekly and DeLoach recalled that Anderson "would moan and groan about working for Drew Pearson and I would moan and groan about working for J. Edgar Hoover."[30]

Politically neutral, Anderson defined himself as a fact-driven reporter and his boss as more of a crusader: "He was a lobbyist. He was an activist. He was an adversary. He was an advisor—an advisor to presidents and senators," Anderson elaborated. "He played an active part in bringing about the kind of government that he thought [right], the kind of causes that he believed in, which was generally the liberal, humanitarian causes." Pearson always seemed sincerely disappointed to catch a public official doing something wrong but then made it his mission to uncover the facts. "Not only would he expose the abuse," Anderson observed, "he would hound the tribunal until it investigated, instruct witnesses on their testimony, propagandize the galleries, help draft the remedial legislation, and write a popular history of the affair." Anderson speculated that Pearson's moral certitude sometimes led him to manipulate his source material to fit his interpretation. Not that he intentionally lied, Anderson explained, "but he was capable of serious hyperbole and omissions of the truth when it suited his agenda." The fact that so many of Pearson's stories ended as legitimate blockbusters proved how correct his instincts were. Pearson's secretary Katherine Raley agreed that Anderson was the better reporter because "Jack would write a story about his own wife if it was a story. He didn't care. And Mr. Pearson really cared about moving the country in the right direction.[31]

Drew Pearson compared his style of reporting to the way the FBI compiled its files: "A piece of information comes in from a source, which means nothing. Then something comes in from another source, and perhaps from a third, which taken together means nothing. But put together they begin to tell a story." He sent his staff to scour the government for new leads, urging them to "dramatize wrongs" that would capture public attention. What they brought back, he sought to verify, usually by calling his highly placed acquaintances for confirmation.[32]

His longtime secretary Marian Canty had earlier worked as an FBI stenographer and understood how the bureau kept its records, including wiretap transcripts. Once when Fred Blumenthal wanted background material on some offenders, Canty called the FBI and asked for the types of records she recalled were kept by the Criminal Records Section. Top FBI officials conspired to foil her request: "The easiest way to meet its entire situation, in view of the fact Miss Canty is now talking in terms of IC wiretaps which we do have and which we do make available to newspaper representatives, is to pick out two or three of the IC's that are very short and have very little substance to them and go ahead and give them to Blumenthal."[33]

A presidential adviser once turned down a dubious proposal on the grounds that "Drew Pearson never misses a thing. Somehow, he'll find out." The columnist disdained to accept official handouts and rarely attended press conferences. He ordered his staff to find out what was happening off the record. His edict put his leg men up against closed doors, locked files, and phones slammed down on receivers. To overcome these obstacles, they cultivated the nonpartisan bureaucrats who maintained professional anonymity. Lower-level officials placed their loyalty to the nation ahead of the political appointees who came and went with each administration. They held the information that contradicted press releases coming from the top.[34]

Government press officers regarded investigative reporters as troublemakers likely to inflate picayune matters into earth-shaking issues. If a fieldworker got caught committing some infraction, reporters might cite that instance to question the entire program. Edward Bayley, who handled press relations for the Agency for International Development (AID) during the Kennedy administration, recalled how Jack Anderson came to him with a story about some minor misdoing he had uncovered. Bayley pleaded with him to think twice before publishing the story. He could not see how it would accomplish anything other than destroying the man's life, "and it isn't really a government matter." Anderson agreed that it was a personal issue and dropped the story.[35]

Pearson's leg men understood that investigative reporting was not a perfect news-gathering system. They often found themselves searching for facts to support conclusions their boss had already reached, tracking down anything to substantiate or demolish his assumptions. Sources rarely had all the details, and missing information could not always be found. Sometimes they had to be satisfied with just enough hidden scraps to shed suspicion on a blunder or scandal. As investigators, they had to dig deeper than other reporters to verify their facts, sure that mistakes would cause howls of outrage and legal threats.[36]

Working to their advantage was the diffusion of information within government departments, increasing their odds of finding a leaker. They could also tap agency information officers for background information. Beyond issuing official news releases, press officers served as conduits of unofficial news and were adept at covering their tracks as sources. "I hope you understand our position here in the Department," an information officer in the Agriculture Department told a Pearson leg man, "and please remember you could have obtained this list of leaders who attended the farm conference from almost anyone and looked them up yourself, since most of them live here in Washington or have offices here. So please don't quote me, and I am sorry I can't be of more help."[37]

An oft-used trick to force a response was for the leg men to first reveal what they already knew. Fred Blumenthal once started an interview with an army general by saying that before he asked anything, he wanted to cite some correspondence between the general and the secretary of the army. Blumenthal let him know that on an upcoming Sunday night radio program, Drew Pearson intended to blast the secretary for inaction, unless the general could provide some good explanation for the policy in question. The general felt concerned enough to notify the FBI and the threatened blast fizzled.[38]

On Tuesday mornings, Pearson convened his staff to consider story ideas. He handed out assignments but only occasionally gave instructions on how to find what he was seeking, taking it for granted they would do it. Instead of shouting or pounding on his desk, Pearson subjected staff members to "a calm but encyclopedic interrogatory" about the progress of the stories he had been covering. The leg men would return with one- or two-page pieces, which might go in the next column he was writing or be filed for later use. Nothing appeared in the column without his editing, whether for accuracy or style, except when he traveled. During his absences he let his staff handle the column but would complain whenever they included something that made him skeptical. "When the master is out of town his operatives do not function too accurately," he grumbled.[39]

Pearson replicated these weekly staff sessions on his first regular television program in 1953. He broadcast out of WTOP, CBS's Washington affiliate, and that network had a rule against anyone delivering news on the air except for its own reporters. To get around the word "news," he adopted the format of a weekly conference with a couple of leg men and a secretary. "Tips that have been phoned or mailed in, bits of information picked up around town, conjectures about what 'might be' in back of the big news events, will be the featured material," a TV columnist reported. Like the "Merry-Go-Round," the television show packed in multiple subjects, as many as twenty issues in its fifteen-minute format. By then, Pearson had been on the radio for seventeen years and although his ratings still held high, he sensed that radio listeners were rapidly turning into TV viewers. In preliminary tests for television, he employed the same hard-hitting, staccato delivery that he had been his signature on radio until a CBS producer advised him that he could not snarl as effectively on TV as he did on the radio. "You're really not a snarling fella," he counseled. Pearson adopted a more somber style but looked stilted in front of the cameras. Like other radio news stars, he had trouble adjusting to television's lights, makeup, tight formats, and cumbersome technology. The new medium produced a new, younger generation of news analysts, and few of Pearson's cohorts transitioned successfully.[40]

It took ingenuity to encourage people to say things they did not want to say, but the leg men also had to be skeptical of what they heard. During the Eisenhower administration, Pearson sent a reporter fresh out of college, Matt Mitchell, to interview Peter Strobel, who oversaw public buildings for the General Services Administration. The columnist had picked up rumors that Strobel was not handling government contracts "in a Kosher way."

> It used to be that when a government official received a 12-pound ham it made the front pages. Now, when a government official rewards a friend with a $16,000 contract it doesn't even make the inside pages. Maybe that's because the public can eat and understand ham, or maybe it's because some Washington reporters can smell a ham but they can't smell a contract. At any rate, the trail that Peter Strobel, in charge of Ike's government building contracts, has left behind becomes more interesting every day.[41]

"Ask me anything," Strobel greeted the young reporter. "We're completely open here." Mitchell pressed his questions and Strobel denied everything. Not long afterward, Strobel abruptly resigned, without receiving the customary presidential letter of thanks for his service. The novice reporter winced at his first experience of having an official lie to him: "It was an enormous sense of frustration that I'd been sent to do this important job and completely blew it."[42]

Pearson's leg men covered regular beats, stopping at them daily to establish familiarity and confidence, asking simply: "Have you got anything for us?" At other times, the assignments might be more specific. As a new leg man, Matt Mitchell got sent to interview a State Department official. Pearson prepped him: "Go over and see that guy, and remember me to him, and ask him how his wife is, and how his children are, and how his dog is, and then ask him this question." Then, Pearson said, he should ask why the CIA director had sent a wire from Geneva to the State Department on a specific issue. "Has that been made public?" the official replied when the young reporter questioned him. "He hadn't told me what to say when that happens, so I just said, 'Well, we've got it.' He says, 'Get out of my office!' because he realized that he had just confirmed what Drew was really after."[43]

Each Wednesday, Pearson wrote two extra columns to appear on Saturdays and Sundays. The advance work meant that his staff could take a day off at the end of the week. Otherwise, producing a daily column meant filing constant reports. In slow times, they turned to the reliable agencies, bureaus, and committees they could tap for usable copy. If Congress were in session, something would inevitably churn up, and if not, the columnist might concoct a story, based on his assumptions of what was likely to happen. He felt sure that what he wrote would happen eventually, which it usually did.[44]

As the boss, Pearson often seemed disengaged from their work, giving his staff wide latitude and little guidance. He would call on them to perform seemingly impossible assignments. If they succeeded, he would feign to regard it as mere routine. If they failed to get what he wanted, he rarely complained. Despite Pearson's public image as a battling muckraker, his staff found him quiet in private, more of a listener than a talker. He would leave a junior staff member in charge of the Georgetown home—to guard his files from intrusion—while he spent the summer at his farm in Maryland. When the Pearsons returned they would invite the house-sitter to dinner. "I remember particularly that he was a Quaker," one of them said. "And before dinner, we'd hold hands around the table for a silent Quaker grace." That fit with his sense of being on a mission: "That he really felt that American democracy depended upon somebody calling people to account. Forcing people to tell the truth. Forcing people to make known those things that people ought to know when they're choosing their government, and that it didn't require that he be a fire-breathing guy when he was working." That impression was enough to motivate them all.[45]

Years later, another staff member reminisced about working from his tiny second-floor office. "My God, what a wonderful feeling of about-to-happen *drama* pervaded the place," wrote Lee Kentosh. "Was Mr. Pearson in a good mood or was this *radio* day when . . . we all tiptoed and circled the inner sanctum." Whenever he picked up a phone he expected to hear "the little pause and then the two sniffs and a snort. And the marvelous frozen feeling that followed the snort, and fear blocking out the first two or three words that followed, so that you were never quite sure if you had the instructions correctly. And gulping all the way down to the basement hoping to find the right column." He recalled entering Pearson's office with the column, "trying to look terribly nonchalant about the whole thing, to find him sitting solemnly at his desk, hands dangling between his legs, elbows on knees, face bent over desk and not a word said. For, aside from whether one agreed with his column or boss-like quirks, he could do and did, some mighty fine and big things, and some surprisingly small, compassionate and gentle things, and I always felt that if I ever really needed a friend he would be it."[46]

5

Just Mild about Harry

WHEN HE LEARNED THAT Franklin D. Roosevelt had died on April 12, 1945, Drew Pearson felt that the "Washington Merry-Go-Round" had reached an ominous turning point. For a dozen years the column had grown along with Roosevelt's administration, feeding off tips from presidential intimates. "He was vivid, colorful copy," Pearson eulogized in his column. "And I have probably written more about him than any other man in America." Even though Roosevelt had called him a chronic liar, Pearson remained committed to the New Deal. The shock of the president's death sent Pearson out on a long walk, where he reflected on the past and pondered his need to establish sources within a new administration. Although the "Merry-Go-Round" would generally support Harry Truman's policies, it would not take long for it to sour the new president, and have him scorch the columnist.[1]

"Harry Truman will be known as the man who didn't want to be President," Pearson advised his readers a few days after Truman had landed in the job. Content with being a senator, he had been thrust into higher office against his will. "It's all your fault," Truman had told Pearson at a reception during the 1944 campaign. "You were the first one to suggest I should be Vice President. You got me into this." Truman mentioned Pearson's praise for his Senate investigation of the national defense program and citing him as a possible vice-presidential candidate. "I had forgotten all about it," Pearson admitted.[2]

Privately, Pearson regarded Truman's nomination for vice president as unfortunate. He would much have preferred Henry Wallace as Roosevelt's successor. Wallace had made himself a ready source for the column during his years as agriculture secretary and vice president before Democrats dropped him from their ticket in 1944. "Of course, Mr. Roosevelt goes on the theory that when he is in a tough fight he has to sacrifice those who are not a political asset," Pearson reasoned. "In other words, he has to throw out ballast." By 1944, Pearson's enthusiasm for Roosevelt had ebbed, but he could not bring himself to support the Republican nominee, New York Governor Thomas E. Dewey. Distrustful of the circle of men around Dewey, Pearson helped Roosevelt's bid for a fourth term by not publishing damaging information he knew about the president's failing health.[3]

Harry Truman came to office with a dim view of all newspaper pundits and a special distaste for gossip columnists, a category into which he assigned Pearson. Although the "Merry-Go-Round" had treated Senator Truman fairly, he cringed at its criticism of his friends in the Senate and bristled over Pearson's penchant for making predictions. He once rose in the Senate in response to a prediction that Truman's committee on national defense would urge the president to fire his secretaries of war and navy. "The committee of which I am chairman has no such thing under consideration, has never had any such thing under consideration, and does not expect to go into the conduct of the war," Truman said. "I merely wanted to make it plain that there was absolutely no foundation, in fact, for what Mr. Pearson said last night over the radio."[4]

Less tolerable for Truman were perceived slights to his wife or daughter Margaret. Pearson got on his wrong side by questioning Bess Truman's ability as a hostess, revealing that she had complained that her hand hurt from greeting so many guests at an inaugural reception in 1945. Asked for his reaction to this story, the vice president grew red-faced, pounded his fist on a table, uttered an expletive, and said, "In Missouri we have a four-letter word for those who knowingly make false statements." Word drifted back to a bemused Pearson, who judged that this was the real Truman: tough, cocky, and candid.[5]

West Virginia Senator Harley Kilgore advised Pearson that the new president's staff had taken offense over his assessment of Truman during his first radio broadcast after FDR's death. The senator urged the columnist to "give him a break at the start." But almost immediately, Pearson infuriated the new president again by running a piece about the Truman family's long-time cook, Vietta Garr. From the Potsdam Conference, Truman wrote his wife: "I see Drew Pearson has been taking an interest in Vietta. If that so-and-so ever says anything to your or Margaret's detriment I shall give him a little Western district action that he'll long remember. I don't care what he says about me but I can get hotter than a depot stove when he mentions my family."[6] This item made Truman even unhappier:

> It came as something of a shock to Washington dowagers and socially-minded young naval officers when attractive, dynamic Margaret Truman suddenly was whisked out of Washington at the very height of the gay June season and went back to Independence, Mo. . . . However, a very wise presidential papa wasn't happy about the featured newspaper pictures of his daughter shagging at this party, cocktailing at that, and flitting merrily through Washington society with the war still bitterly contested in the Pacific.[7]

After reading this column, Truman apologized to his daughter. "You evidently are just finding out what a terrible situation the president's daughter is facing," he wrote, explaining that this was why he had never wanted to run for vice president. He dismissed the story and urged her to keep her balance and "go along just as your dad is trying to do."[8]

Then came Pearson's report that Bess and Margaret Truman had traveled back from St. Louis to Washington on a special railroad car, leaving returning soldiers behind at the station. Pearson later discovered that the women had a separate compartment, not a whole car, but his retraction did not mollify the president. The columnist had been hearing from wives and mothers who wanted their soldiers back from overseas after the war. He carried to the White House a petition signed by 30,000 soldiers in the Philippines, asking to come home. Truman surprised his staff by agreeing to see him, but the president had something other than petitions on his mind. As Truman recounted the incident, he told the columnist: "You've been writing some nasty things about my family. I want you to know that down in Missouri we put our women on a pedestal, and my women are on a pedestal, and I'm going to keep them there." Pointing across the room he said, "Over in that desk I've got a gold-plated automatic pistol that was given to me for a present, and you son of a bitch, if you write one more line derogatory about my women, I'm going to take that pistol and use it on you." Pearson called it the bawling out of his life. "I stood in front of his desk like a schoolboy, the bundle of 30,000 signatures under my arm, while he proceeded to tell me what he thought of me."[9]

Conscious of being compared to his popular predecessor, Harry Truman proposed a Fair Deal to expand upon Roosevelt's New Deal. His long list of progressive initiatives contained national health insurance, educational aid, public housing, fair employment practices, and anti-lynching laws—most of which congressional conservatives managed to block. Even so, the transition between the two relatively like-minded administrations was not an easy one. Suspicious that some of the White House staff he had inherited from Roosevelt were leaking to Pearson, Truman authorized the FBI to tap their phones. Consequently, the president could read the columnist's candid assessments of him in the transcripts. In one telephone call, Pearson anticipated that the president's conservative opposition would profit from Truman's "sloppy performance and weakness for hacks." He went on to say: "They had a smart guy" to contend with in the White House before, "but now they've got a dumb cookie."[10]

Pearson used the "Merry-Go-Round" to encourage the new president to retain his favorite cabinet members—and best sources—Interior Secretary Harold Ickes and Commerce Secretary Henry Wallace. He predicted that Truman would not remove Wallace because the two men "became good friends during the presidential campaign when Wallace rolled up his sleeves and fought hard for both Roosevelt and Truman, even though he had been ditched at Chicago." He argued that Truman wanted to keep the strongest men of the Roosevelt cabinet. But against those hopes, Truman fired both men.[11]

According to Margaret Truman, it did not take her father long to notice that "almost everything that was discussed at a Cabinet meeting was paraphrased, after having been dipped in acid, by Drew Pearson on the following day." Suspecting Harold Ickes, the president had his staff plant a story with him that they told no one else. Truman showed a grim smile when he read the item in Pearson's column, and the interior secretary was soon out of office.[12]

Henry Wallace lost his post as commerce secretary after President Truman carelessly approved a speech that Wallace planned to make at Madison Square Garden, failing to recognize that Wallace's appeal for friendship with the Soviet Union contradicted his State Department's Cold War policies. The uproar caused Truman to disavow the speech and fire Wallace. A reporter alerted the president's press secretary that Drew Pearson had gotten hold of Wallace's memo about the president's prior approval for the speech and intended to make a column out of it. Caught in a lie, Truman cynically calculated that he could survive the exposé. If Pearson published the memo in his column, Truman recorded in his diary, "there would be doubt on its authenticity because the former President Mr. Roosevelt had branded him a liar, I had, so had all the Senate and House leaders. Therefore, it would not be looked upon as an authentic document."[13]

Whenever Pearson lost a high-placed source, he sought a replacement. The columnist awarded a brass ring ("good for one free ride on the Washington Merry-Go-Round") to Truman's new attorney general Tom Clark. The flattering profile introduced Clark to a national audience and helped make him a reliable conduit of inside information. FBI agents soon learned that Truman suspected that his attorney general had grown too close to Pearson, and that rather than investigate the columnist, Clark would simply tip him off about what was being done. Despite Truman's aversion to Pearson, several of his top cabinet members were longtime friends of the columnist, including Secretary of State Dean Acheson, a friend and Georgetown neighbor for decades, and Secretary of Defense Louis Johnson, who had earlier provided legal assistance at Pearson's libel trials.[14]

A White House military aide who visited Defense Secretary Johnson was surprised to find the columnist in the secretary's private office. The aide reported this to Truman, who instructed him, "I'd like you to go and see Johnson privately and tell him that we were getting a little bit tired of these stories coming out of the Pentagon." The FBI also identified Truman's labor secretary, Lewis Schwellenbach, as the person responsible for a leak to Pearson that the hard-drinking Treasury Secretary John Snyder had been "feeling no pain" at a recent cabinet meeting. Truman could neither plug these leaks nor convincingly deny them. "The sinister part of this matter," one government investigator concluded, "is the fact that Pearson's statements are correct."[15]

Facing an uphill campaign in 1948, President Truman opened one of his press conferences by indignantly denying Pearson's report that he had called Jews disloyal to the country. "I have thought I would not have to add another liar's star to that fellow's crown, but I will have to do it," said the president. "The story is just a lie out of whole cloth." The "Merry-Go-Round" had quoted Truman talking to a New York publisher about Palestine. It described him pounding on his desk and accusing "the New York Jews" of being disloyal. "Would you explain that further, Mr. President?" interrupted the publisher. "When you speak of New York Jews are you referring to such people as Bernard Baruch? Or are you referring to such New York Jews as my wife?" Truman assured his visitor he did not mean to include either Baruch or the publisher's wife, and then abruptly changed the subject. A confidential informant told the FBI that before the column appeared, a lobbyist for the Progressive Citizens of America, which supported US recognition of Israel, had confided that Ted Thackery, editor of the *New York Post* and husband of Dorothy Schiff, the paper's publisher, had met with Truman. The president told him: "The trouble is those New York Jews are putting too much heat on me." The FBI could not determine whether it had been Thackery or the Progressive Citizens who leaked the story to Pearson.[16]

Democrats chose "I'm Just Wild about Harry" as their campaign song in 1948, but Drew Pearson felt just mild about the president. His leg man David Karr went so far as to convince Florida Senator Claude Pepper to challenge Truman for the Democratic presidential nomination from the left—if for no other reason than to stir up some news for the column. That quixotic act eventually cost Pepper his Senate seat when Truman recruited Florida Representative George Smathers to challenge him for the Senate nomination in 1950. "George, I want you to do me a favor," Truman appealed to him. "I want you to beat that son of a bitch Claude Pepper." Pearson assailed Smathers in several columns, and in return the congressman portrayed Pearson as an out-of-state carpetbagger promoting his opponent. "It is a well-known fact that Pearson is friendly to people in Washington who give him information," Smathers declared. "He is fighting me because he knows I will not stoop to give him information." Smathers distributed a booklet linking Pepper to Stalin's Russia, and Pearson noticed that it "even contained references to Dave Karr as a card-carrying Communist and said that Karr and I were responsible for Pepper's short-lived Presidential fling at Philadelphia in 1948." Most Florida newspapers declined to run the "Merry-Go-Round" columns on the race, and Smathers swamped Pepper in the primary.[17]

Pearson watched as Dave Karr rallied for Henry Wallace during the 1948 campaign, but he maintained his own distance, feeling uneasy that the Progressive candidate attracted so many extreme left-wingers. Nor could he support Strom Thurmond's Dixiecrat campaign defending racial segregation. Like everyone else, he anticipated a Republican victory. Pearson cultivated the Republican candidate, Thomas E. Dewey, by offering him advice on whom *not* to pick for a running mate—specifically a congressman with ethical problems. "Don't worry," Dewey assured him. "I've been reading your columns." For much of the campaign Pearson and Dewey "were as thick as thieves," one of the columnist's staff noted, and they too scrambled to befriend Dewey's likely appointees as future sources. As the election neared, Pearson wrote positively about Harry Truman's spunky campaign but still expected him to lose. His vaunted system of contacts around the nation failed him. Along with the pollsters, Drew Pearson got the forecast wrong.[18]

On election night, the early returns stunned Pearson by showing Truman in the lead. At 8:30 that evening he became the first radio broadcaster to predict the president's victory. Pearson broadcast throughout the night until 5 A.M., and then wrote a quick column about the remarkable upset. But he could not retract the post-election "Merry-Go-Round" that the syndicate had already distributed to his hundreds of papers. Having presumed Dewey's election, the column described the Dewey advisers "who will take over the White House eighty-six days from now." His prospective lineup of a Dewey cabinet made readers laugh. A telegram from the *Evening Statesman* in Walla Walla, Washington, advised him: "We are sending you a gallon jug of Bromo Seltzer and a membership in the Gallup Poll. On one of your future columns please tell our readers what happened. An explanation is due and it better be good." A red-faced Pearson admitted that he felt relieved, saying, "I am glad I was wrong." Truman's reelection kept Fair Deal policies—and Pearson's network of inside sources—in place for another four years.[19]

Before the election, Pearson had pledged that if Dewey lost, he would eat his hat. His radio sponsor at the time, Lee Hats, made him a hat out of cereal, which he ate while posing for cameras on the Capitol steps. Despite miscalling the election, Pearson capped the year by appearing on the cover of *Time* magazine, then the ultimate testament to achieving national influence.[20]

The Cold War that dismantled America's wartime alliance with the Soviet Union dominated Truman's presidency. In 1945, Pearson described Russia and the United States as "potentially the greatest rivals and enemies in the world." He turned one column into an open letter to Marshal Stalin, warning him that Americans were "beginning to wonder whether Russia is really sincere about keeping the peace after the war." The columnist held President Truman partly responsible for the deteriorating relations, beginning with the new president's harsh dressing-down of Soviet Foreign Minister Vyacheslav Molotov when he came to pay his respects after FDR's death. But Pearson did not consider the Cold War America's fault. "Stalin faced the problem of keeping his country together, and needed a capitalist bogeyman to do it," he wrote in the "Merry-Go-Round." "So, using the United States as a threat he scrapped in a few months the tremendous reservoir of good-will which Russia, as a wartime ally, had built up among the American people."[21]

In 1946, the "Merry-Go-Round" reported an off-the-record speech that former Prime Minister Winston Churchill delivered at the University Club in Chicago. In it, Churchill raised warnings against the Soviet Union even more dire than his public "Iron Curtain" address in Fulton, Missouri. Pearson picked up this information second-hand, and his version contained a few mistakes, but those who had heard the speech assured him that his overall interpretation had been correct. Writing to reassure directors at the Bell Syndicate, Pearson explained: "Of course, when anyone as important as Churchill makes a speech off-the-record, there are bound to be repercussions. In the first place, suspicions are immediately aroused as to what he is saying along a confidential line which he would not have been willing to say in public. Most public figures in Washington have found, through experience, that it is wisest not to make speeches off-the-record. It is a challenge to newspapermen to find out what actually did happen, and frequently the result is partially erroneous accounts of what they said."[22]

The Cold War forced Pearson to reassess the friends-with-Russia faction within the US government during World War II, realizing now that some of those Soviet sympathizers had also been Soviet agents. When Red hunters later challenged his own patriotism, Pearson asserted that he had been the first journalist to expose the Canadian spy ring at the end of the war; that he had tipped off the State Department concerning Alger Hiss; and that he had warned Treasury Secretary Fred Vinson about Harry Dexter White being "un-American." He also touted his sponsorship of the Friendship Train, a national effort to ship American food supplies to war-torn Europe and "turn the tide against Communism" there. "I used to lay awake nights trying to figure out how I could make the world safer as far as wars are concerned," he told his family.[23]

The Friendship Train emerged from the "Merry-Go-Round" column of October 11, 1947, which called on Americans to donate food and other supplies for distribution in postwar France and Italy. To dramatize and promote the Marshall Plan, then being debated, Pearson proposed running trains through the heart of America to collect food as they traveled. As a measure of how seriously readers took his column, the public embraced the proposal with an outpouring in support. Churches, schools, and other groups organized contributions, and railroads and shipping companies donated their services. The project collected 700 carloads of food and clothing for Europeans. Newsreels recorded the train's progress and the crowds at each stop. "A lot of my editors are probably wondering when I am going to quit collecting food and get back to being a newspaperman," he wrote from the train, which he accompanied throughout the United States and in Europe. Pearson counted the Friendship Train as his proudest accomplishment. California Governor Earl Warren, who rode the length of his state on the train, praised the effort for its lack of hyperbole, exhortation, and jingoism, just a "gentle appeal for real patriotism." The train also provided the sort of news that Pearson "got a lot more kick out of writing about than I do peeking through keyholes in Washington."[24]

During the congressional debate over the Marshall Plan, Senator Arthur Vandenberg, who led the fight, cited the Friendship Train as evidence of how passionately the American people felt about helping Europe. The opposition leader, Senator Robert Taft, countered that food sent through "a real charity, such as the Friendship Train," would produce a better moral effect than funds spent by the US government (the train amounted to only a tiny fraction of the $12 billion in aid that the Marshall Plan provided). Pearson believed that the effort not only saved people from starvation but dissuaded them from voting for Communists out of hopelessness. For his humanitarian efforts, he received the French Legion of Honor, the Order of the Star of Italian Solidarity, and the Knights of Columbus International Gold Medal. He was also one of two Americans nominated for the Nobel Peace Prize in 1949—the other being Eleanor Roosevelt—although that year's prize went to a Scotsman, Sir John Boyd Orr, the first head of the UN's Food and Agriculture Organization.[25]

Success with the Friendship Train inspired Pearson to promote international relations on a "people-to-people" basis rather than diplomat-to-diplomat. He repeated that phrase so often in the column that President Dwight Eisenhower later adopted it for a People-to-People Friendship Committee in 1956. Always a showman, Pearson also organized the release of balloons carrying messages of peace across the borders into Eastern European countries, "trying to see if there wasn't some way we could win friends behind the Iron Curtain and prevent war." Maybe they were "screwy ideas," he admitted. "Certainly, they were just a drop in the bucket. But I used to try."[26]

With his focus on peace, Pearson regarded Secretary of Defense James Forrestal as the most dangerous member of the cabinet, whom he held responsible for pulling Truman into the anti-Russian camp. That animosity dated back to 1929, when Pearson wrote an article for *The Nation* exposing the dubious foreign loan policies of Dillon, Read & Company, the investment house that Forrestal then headed. Dillon, Read forced a retraction from *The Nation* by threatening to sue for libel. Forrestal served as secretary of the navy during World War II and had become an outspoken Cold Warrior by the time Truman made him the first secretary of defense. Pearson objected to conferring so much military power on anyone from Wall Street. Worse, he suspected Forrestal of harboring presidential ambitions. Pearson's long-time confidant, Louis Johnson, had served as Truman's finance chairman in 1948 and coveted Forrestal's job. Johnson divulged that Forrestal secretly contributed to Tom Dewey's campaign against the president. Pearson also identified Forrestal as the leading anti-Zionist in the cabinet, eager to protect military oil supplies from Arab countries by blocking American support for Israel. When Truman failed to drop Forrestal from the cabinet after the election, the columnist grew determined to expel him. So fervently did he proceed that Jack Anderson dubbed it a vendetta.[27]

Beside Louis Johnson, Pearson found another confidential Pentagon source in Stuart Symington, the first secretary of the air force. Symington believed that Forrestal, a former navy secretary, tilted in favor of the navy against the newly created air force and opposed its efforts to expand. Jack Anderson heard rumors that Forrestal was out to purge Symington, from sources who overheard Forrestal at parties, where he tended to talk too much. Warnings drifted back to Symington, who retaliated by leaking negative reports about the defense secretary.[28] In the column, Pearson revealed:

There are definite signs that James V. Forrestal, most powerful member of the Cabinet and the man with the most influence around the White House, is slipping. He has definitely slipped with Congress, and he is also slipping somewhat with President Truman. There was a day when Forrestal could get anything he wanted from Harry Truman. He used the technique of telling Harry what a great man he was, how his policies were absolutely right, that he didn't have to worry about reelection. But now those close to the President say that he has wised up to the fact that the charming Secretary of Defense led him down a blind alley when he got him to reverse the United Nations on Palestine, and that a lot of Forrestal's other advice has had a hollow ring.[29]

Inside sources fed reports to the columnist about Forrestal's agitated behavior at cabinet meetings. Attorney General Tom Clark described the defense secretary as "nervous as a whore in church." Louis Johnson stated that he thought the man was going insane. J. Edgar Hoover became another ally in the campaign after Forrestal proposed a plan to coordinate national security efforts, which would have put the FBI under Pentagon control. Louis Nichols (whom Pearson called a "fast-talking, likeable, public relations lobbyist for J. Edgar Hoover") alerted Jack Anderson to a secret memo that Forrestal had sent to the president and the National Security Council, outlining his proposal. "If this plan is ever carried out and the FBI is brought under subjugation," Nichols warned, "Hoover and his staff will walk out."[30]

Some sources provided dubious hearsay. The cruelest story that Pearson repeated on his broadcasts, and that deeply wounded the defense secretary's pride, recounted how, a decade earlier, Forrestal's wife had been robbed of her jewels at gunpoint, late one night in front of their Manhattan townhouse. Pearson alleged that Forrestal had hidden inside and fled from his house rather than come to his wife's rescue. *New York Times* correspondent Arthur Krock, an old friend of Forrestal's, advised Pearson that Forrestal had slept through the robbery unknowingly. The next morning, with reporters and photographers gathered in front of his house, Forrestal had slipped out back and climbed over a fence to avoid confronting them. Some reporters spotted his flight and jumbled the tale. Pearson neither retracted the accusation nor was able to prove it, which sullied his reputation with Krock and others. "It puts you in a class of gossip columnist where you do not belong," a newspaper colleague chided. "If I had it to do over again I would have left it out," Pearson agreed.[31]

Mindful of the criticism, the columnist told his leg men to do whatever they could to verify the evidence on the Forrestal story. "This is a straight factual report that has been checked and double-checked and documented," one reported back. "All of the evidence needed to support the story in the memorandum is here, except the Justice Department's report dated Jan. 8, 1944. . . . Commercial photographers are afraid to photostat this Justice Department document because there is an order out for them to report to the FBI when any official confidential documents are brought in for photostating. One photographer offered to take the risk for $50.00."[32]

James Forrestal longed to remain in the cabinet, but Truman intended to replace him with Louis Johnson. Unwilling to dismiss his defense secretary under fire, however, Truman proved slow to act. Pearson heard that his broadcasts had made the president boiling mad, but he believed that so long as Forrestal held such a high office the public had a right to know about his mental state. The rest of the press corps buried all reports about Forrestal's instability. Arthur Krock later admitted that for two years his wife—herself a reporter—had "begun to detect inner disturbances in Forrestal that I had not." It was not until Krock listened to Pearson's radio broadcasts that he began to see signs of Forrestal's "irrationality and indecisiveness" that seemed at variance with the man he had admired for so long. After each of Pearson's Sunday broadcasts, Forrestal would telephone Krock "to discuss, but never decide, what to do about them." Krock recorded that "in his mental agony, Forrestal saw Zionist spies and assassins lurking in doorways near his residence bent on revenge for his attitude toward the Palestine partition." The broadcasts may have disturbed Forrestal, but Krock conceded they were only a partial cause for his friend's downfall. He had lost presidential favor for many reasons, primarily his opposition to recognition of Israel and his contacts with the Dewey campaign, where he seemed to be jockeying for a position in a Republican administration.[33]

After Forrestal left the cabinet, his paranoia deepened. His friends begged Pearson to hold his fire, and the columnist agreed that there was "no use applying the whip to someone who is out of office." Yet when Forrestal checked into the Bethesda Naval Hospital for what was described as a routine checkup, Pearson broadcast that the former defense secretary had suffered a mental collapse and attempted suicide. "Drew did not want to be the one to break the taboo" about reporting on someone's mental illness, Jack Anderson recalled, "for it would be attributed to personal malice," but he felt the story needed to be told, given that Forrestal had wielded great power so recently. The ABC network objected strenuously to his radio script and deleted the word "insanity." Pearson got around the ban by ad-libbing "temporary insanity."[34]

On May 22, 1949, James Forrestal plunged to his death from a sixteenth-story window at the naval hospital. In the horrified reaction, much of the blame fell on Pearson. Members of Congress called his attacks on Forrestal unwarranted. Margaret Truman recorded that her father "considered Drew Pearson the murderer of James Forrestal and said so." The trade journal *Editor & Publisher* carried a lead story blaming Pearson and Walter Winchell for their hounding of Forrestal. Pearson's harshest critics sneered that Forrestal's death "confirmed Drew Pearson's status as political big game hunter."[35]

Angry readers threatened to cancel their subscriptions to the *Washington Post* unless the paper dropped his column. "People are repeating the charge that I killed Forrestal to the extent that I am almost beginning to lie awake night wondering whether I did," he recorded in his diary. "Certainly, a lot of people have convinced themselves that it is true." To the *Post's* publisher he added, "I am not thin-skinned on most things, but some of the current criticism seems to me a bit unfair."[36]

The columnist felt compelled to explain himself to his readers: "I have been greatly disturbed that some people seem to believe that my reporting of the illness of the late James Forrestal should have contributed to his death." He accused Forrestal's friends in the media of having contributed to his demise by ignoring his sickness and encouraging him to stay on the job. "His got to be almost an obsession, both on their part and his, until Mr. Truman's final request for his resignation, undoubtedly worsened the illness."[37]

Forrestal's suicide shook Pearson's young assistant, Jack Anderson. They surely had a hand in the tragedy, Anderson believed. "A commentator has the right, even the duty, to campaign for the sacking of an official whose philosophy or conduct he opposes. It was our means that were open to question." Anderson worried that his mentor's weekly broadcasts, with their mix of fresh news with rehashes of old complaints, had "crossed the line that separates propaganda from advocacy, let alone reporting." Over time, Pearson pondered the power over public opinion that broadcasting on a nationwide network gave him and admitted that he was sometimes "not careful in using that power. The more power you have, the more careful you have to be not to exercise it."[38]

History would remember Harry Truman as having the best intentions, Pearson predicted, "and the worst friends." He saw the president as personally honest but too tolerant of the "Missouri Gang" that had followed him to the White House. Hangers-on from Kansas City engaged in influence peddling, gift taking, and graft that would tarnish the administration's reputation and provide fodder for the "Merry-Go-Round."[39]

In 1945, the column had mocked Truman for being the first vice president to need a military aide, and thereafter regularly targeted his blustery sidekick, Brigadier General Harry Vaughn. The two Missourians had met in 1917 at Fort Sill, Oklahoma, on their way to command field artillery batteries in France. Later, Vaughan worked on Truman's campaigns, served on his Senate staff, and became his military aide. As Truman's closest friend in the White House, Vaughn played poker and sipped bourbon with the chief executive to help him unwind. General Vaughan did not measure up to the quality of the rest of Truman's staff, but he boosted the president's morale by making him laugh. Once Vaughn came under fire, Truman rallied to his support. Firing his "court jester" would have been too painful for Truman, even if it might have helped him politically.[40]

In one of many columns on Vaughn, Pearson revealed that Truman had invited Winston Churchill to give his celebrated speech, declaring that an

Iron Curtain had dropped across Europe, at the general's alma mater, tiny Westminster College in Fulton, Missouri:

> All of which highlights an observation sometimes made around the White House that Harry Truman would do anything under the sun for his friend, Harry Vaughn. It also accounts for some of the extraordinary activity of the President's ebullient, irrepressible military aide. In the opinion of seasoned Washington observers, no White House functionary in years has stuck his hand into various branches of the Government with such vigor, and frequently disdain for the public interest, as the blunt-spoken, likable former manufacturers' representative from Missouri who shot from $75 a week to $12,000 a year plus the gold braid, the private limousine, the flunkeys and all the power that goes with sitting at the right hand of the President of the United States.[41]

Having aided Senator Truman's Missouri constituents by making introductions for them at various federal agencies, Harry Vaughn failed to appreciate that such a practice carried a more noxious odor when coming from the White House. In return for pulling strings, Vaughn foolishly accepted gifts. He also associated with dubious characters who could embarrass the administration. While helping one of Pearson's allies get a passport to accompany a presidential fact-finding mission to Greece, Dave Karr encountered the shady fixer John Maragon. A onetime shoeshine boy from Kansas City and railroad ticket seller on Capitol Hill, Maragon had parlayed his connections with Harry Vaughn into becoming a low-level White House staffer and high-level influence peddler. Karr advised Pearson that Maragon frequently rode in the military aide's car and hosted him at his swank hotel suite. Maragon had a White House pass and hung autographed photos of himself with the president to impress his clients. Vaughn and Maragon had their hands in a lot of deals, the "Merry-Go-Round" reported, "and if a congressional committee ever probed deeply enough, it might find some highly interesting things."[42]

Maragon interceded with General Vaughn on behalf of an executive from a perfume company who wanted to fly to Europe on an army plane. The official returned with enough perfume essence to give his company an advantage over its competitors. The grateful company presented Vaughn with seven deep freezers, commodities that were hard to acquire in the postwar economy. General Vaughn sent one freezer to Truman's home in Independence, Missouri, and offered the others to other high-ranking members of the administration. After Pearson's light shone on Maragon, the Senate's Permanent Subcommittee on Investigations (which had begun as the Truman Committee, investigating national defense programs) opened an investigation of the "five percenters," fixers who collected a 5 percent fee for procuring government contracts. On the witness stand, Maragon disclosed the existence of the freezers. They became symbols of outrage for Truman's Republican opponents when they denounced "the mess in Washington."[43]

The investigating subcommittee discovered that Maragon had been making bank deposits many times higher than his White House salary. Those findings led to his conviction for perjury. The day after Maragon got out of jail, he appealed to Pearson for help in finding a job. The columnist decided that his target had been "a little frog way over his head in a big pond," had served his sentence, and deserved a break. Pearson persuaded a compliant congressman to give Maragon a patronage job in the House Folding Room, mailing speeches and booklets to members' constituents.[44]

General Vaughn came in second only to General Douglas MacArthur in the amount of negative column space the "Merry-Go-Round" devoted to him during Truman's presidency. Pearson published evidence that Vaughn had misused his position as coordinator of veterans' affairs to divert scarce building materials, set aside for veterans, to a racetrack developer. He went so far as to testify against Vaughn during a Senate investigation, disclosing that Vaughn had traded access to the White House in exchange for expensive gifts. Since the charges were true, Truman could not rebut them, but he had no doubt that the columnist made them only to embarrass him. He resisted General Vaughn's attempt to quit. "Harry, you and I came in here together and we're going to leave together," another aide recorded Truman saying, "and I don't want to hear any more of this damned foolishness about you wanting to resign."[45]

A Washington printer trying to generate business showed off an ornate engraving to a Pearson staffer in 1949. The document happened to be an invitation to a ceremony for General Vaughn to receive a diamond-studded decoration from the Argentine dictator Juan Perón. Pearson considered the award designed only to help the Argentines obtain a massive loan from the United States. On his radio broadcast, he called on the president to fire his military aide. At a reserve officers' dinner honoring General Vaughn, Truman responded in off-the-cuff remarks, telling the audience: "I want you to distinctly understand that any S.O.B. who thinks he can cause any of those people to be discharged by me, by some smart aleck statement over the air or in the paper, he has got another think coming." No commentator or columnist would determine who served on his staff, Truman declared. "I do the moving—nobody else." The president never mentioned Pearson by name, and the official stenographer changed "S.O.B." to "anyone," but reporters covering the dinner set the record straight.[46]

Truman's salty language took him down a peg in public opinion, and the columnist set about making the most of the publicity. Noting that Truman had launched his tirade during Brotherhood Week, Pearson informed his listeners and readers that he was setting up a "Servants of Brotherhood" club, dedicated to fighting for freedom at home and abroad, and he invited President Truman to join. Truman's insult stuck, however, and a decade later, when Pearson wrote a series of autobiographical articles for the popular *Saturday Evening Post* magazine, he provocatively titled them "Confessions of an S.O.B."[47]

Dave Karr had the idea that Pearson should stake out General Vaughn's awards ceremony at the Argentine embassy. On his radio broadcast, Pearson pledged to stand in front of the embassy and record the names of any American dignitary who attended. Although he soon had second thoughts about the foolish pledge, he felt obliged to go through with it. On the appointed night, Pearson waited in the rain, watching foreign diplomats enter the front door while American officials tried to slip in discreetly through the back door. As Margaret Truman observed, "He stood outside glaring ominously at all those who dared to brave his wrath. . . . Mr. Pearson ran up and down peering into cars like something out of a Marx Brothers movie." Pearson himself admitted, "I made something of an ass out of myself," but he had made his point. Congress forbade the general from keeping the Argentine medal.[48]

The column's barrage against Vaughn lasted throughout Truman's presidency. "A person on the White House staff couldn't sue anybody for libel," Harry Vaughn complained. "I had a score of occasions when I could have sued Pearson for remarks that were absolutely libelous, but it would just make it more newsworthy if I did, so the only thing you can do is ignore it." Instead, Vaughn resorted to having Pearson's phones tapped, proving Pearson's suspicion that Vaughn was J. Edgar Hoover's man inside the White House. When the columnist learned about the latest wiretapping, he joked that his phone calls had so many listeners that he could sell commercials. He was less amused to hear that Vaughn had funneled information from the phone taps to the vitriolic columnist Westbrook Pegler, along with defamatory information about David Karr. General Vaughn also got Karr's wife, Madeline, fired as a reporter for a Greek newspaper, regarding her as Pearson's plant in the White House press corps. Pearson felt sure that Vaughn was behind an Internal Revenue Service audit of his taxes.[49]

Federal income taxes after World War II were graduated up to a top level of 91 percent, which motivated Pearson to claim as many work-related deductions as possible, from his business travels and the office space in his home to all those dinners where he picked up gossip for the column. After an arduous audit, the IRS disallowed only one deduction: a dinner he threw for Chief Justice Fred Vinson. IRS agents determined that since the Chief Justice was not a political news source, the occasion was not a legitimate expense. Pearson paid the government the $25 he had itemized for entertaining Vinson.[50]

Despite his reputation for favoring liberal Democrats, the columnist's willingness to attack corruption and cronyism tarred the Truman administration and gave Republicans a theme they could exploit in the 1952 elections. While the drumbeat of attacks kept his columns and broadcasts fresh, they also bruised egos and angered people to the point of retaliation. Pearson learned this painfully one day when he walked through the lobby of Washington's Mayflower Hotel. A brawny Washington lawyer, Charles Patrick Clark, stepped in front of him and punched him in the eye. Clark had worked for Republican Senator Owen Brewster, a frequent Pearson target, and he also resented Pearson for identifying him on his broadcasts as a lobbyist for Franco's Spain. "I told him I was sick and tired of the misrepresentation and innuendos, he had been putting out in his programs," Clark explained to a reporter. "I told him 'this is for your nefariousness to Forrestal, Vaughn, Brewster, and myself.'"[51]

In June 1950, a Pentagon source tipped off Jack Anderson that President Truman was about to declare war on North Korea for invading South Korea. Since his boss was on a flight and unreachable, Anderson called his radio network and told them to break the story. But ABC would broadcast the news only if it could attribute the report to Drew Pearson, just in case it turned out to be wrong. As soon as Pearson landed, he heard from Anderson: "You just announced that we're going to war." "I did not!" Pearson gasped. "I did it in your name," Anderson explained. "You have just scooped the president." They had beaten the White House's official announcement by an hour.[52]

As a Quaker, Pearson called peace the number-one tenet of his faith, but he supported American intervention in the Korean War to defend an ally.

He wrote a "Washington Merry-Go-Round" column about it in the form of a letter to his draft-age stepson, Tyler. "As you know, I am considered quite a critical newspaperman. I do not hesitate to point out the faults of our Government and our country," he wrote. "But, despite all these faults, I very deeply feel that our country has just about reached the peak of idealism and unselfishness and power for good ever before seen in the world. . . . So perhaps some of us needed Korea. We needed it to keep us from getting too soft, too selfish, too materialistic, etc. But, above all, we needed it to set an example of world unity against an aggressor."[53]

Pearson defended Truman in his confrontations with General Douglas MacArthur, the commander of United Nations forces in Korea. General MacArthur executed a brilliant surprise landing at Inchon that enabled UN troops to reclaim South Korea, and then pressed the conflict into North Korea, aiming to reunite the entire peninsula. US intelligence sources indicated a massive buildup of Chinese Communist troops on the Manchurian border, but MacArthur arrogantly dismissed warnings that ran contrary to his expectations (his chief intelligence officer, Major General Charles Willoughby, also shielded MacArthur from information he knew he would disagree with). MacArthur dismissed Truman's concerns over engaging in a larger conflict with China. The general's willingness to buck official policies prompted sources within the Pentagon to provide Jack Anderson with critical information about the potential for Chinese troops entering the war.[54]

In December 1950, Pearson's columns and radio broadcasts featured exclusive exposés of the general's conduct, "based on secret assessments by the Joint Chiefs, smuggled reports of White House briefings, and classified cables sent to MacArthur or received from him." Senators demanded that the government prosecute Pearson for revealing classified information. The Justice Department and the army once again tapped his phones. "The White House ordered it," J. Edgar Hoover advised Pearson. "You know how Harry is. We have to follow orders and make inquiries." All these efforts failed to prevent additional scoops, including obtaining the secret transcript of President Truman's meeting with General MacArthur on Wake Island. A colonel at the Pentagon slipped the transcript to Jack Anderson and the "Merry-Go-Round" published a condensation in January 1951—four months before the *New York Times'* fuller version won a Pulitzer Prize for its reporting. When Truman finally fired MacArthur for insubordination, the column took Truman's side against a tidal wave of public condemnation.[55]

Predictably furious over leaks that showed how he had ignored intelligence assessments, General MacArthur fired off a cable to the Joint Chiefs demanding that Pearson be indicted for treason, sedition, espionage, or any law they could find to fit the situation. Army intelligence agents went to Pearson's home, not to investigate him, they said, but to advise him that his reporting was undermining public confidence in their ability to protect national security.[56] Unwilling to buy their pretense nor divulge his sources, Pearson said he had held the information for two weeks while he checked with people at the Pentagon. He hinted that the information came from the highest levels, suggesting the secretary of defense or the Joint Chiefs.[57]

In 1952, two FBI agents summoned one of Pearson's regular tipsters, reporter Harry Costello, to their office. During a three-hour interview, with a thick file presumably relating to the columnist on the desk in front of them, they reminded Costello, a former Georgetown University football star, that he was "an American first and an ex-Pearson employee second." As leg man Fred Blumenthal reported: "They told Harry that they were working on a tie-up between Pearson and the commies, and what could he add to their knowledge? They told Harry they were specifically concerned with the 'leak' of one of Gen. MacArthur's cables to the Pentagon last Jan. . . . They had, they said, info leading them to believe that the leak came from a commie." Costello rose to Pearson's defense, calling him one of the greatest Americans he had ever known. By the end of the interview, "the agents admitted that Harry was their last hope in the case and that for the past year they had met 'a brick wall' in their search for the source."[58]

Both the FBI and CIA monitored the daily "Washington Merry-Go-Round," which they received from the syndicate in advance of publication. But the nature of a syndicated column made it difficult for these agencies to suppress. CIA officials once convinced the *Washington Post* to delete some harsh comments concerning the agency from the next morning's edition, before they realized that the full column had gone out to six hundred other papers. Since the fees for telegraphing all those papers would have been exorbitant, the CIA had to let the unwanted criticism appear unchanged across the rest of the nation.[59]

Conservative columnist and radio commentator Fulton Lewis Jr. dismissed Drew Pearson as a "Fair Deal propagandist," but the "Merry-Go-Round" continued to rile the president. Truman blew up again when he received a tip that Pearson planned to write a column about a White House conference with General Omar Bradley, the army chief of staff. "The column had only been on the teletype to New York one hour when I began to hear about it," Pearson reported in a column framed as a letter to his daughter. "The President was really mad. He stormed and raged and said he would throw me in jail. I can't begin to repeat his language, but it was pretty rough. Finally, he told General Bradley to get hold of me and kill the column. However, when General Bradley read the column, he didn't seem to think there was much wrong. He suggested only two changes, which I was glad to make. The column was published on schedule as corrected, no military secrets were revealed, and so far I am still out of jail."[60]

A frustrated Harry Truman ordered the FBI to find out how Pearson had gotten the story, going so far as to have them check whether he had placed a microphone in the cabinet room. FBI agents interviewed thirty witnesses. At first, they assumed that the Bradley column had been pulled, since the *Washington Post* chose not to run it, not realizing it had gone out to other papers around the country. Then they learned that it was not even a scoop—Pearson's old partner Bob Allen had run a similar version of the story in his column two days earlier. That news, Pearson chuckled, "sent the FBI agents off more puzzled than ever." FBI Director Hoover wrote off the investigation as a waste of money and manpower. Pointing out that hundreds of people had access to top secret information, Hoover recommended that rather than trying to track down the leaks, government agencies ought to tighten up the distribution of their most sensitive materials.[61]

Perhaps the biggest secret in Washington was the work of American cryptographers, operating out of Arlington Hall, in Virginia, to decode intercepted messages that Soviet agents in the United States had sent to Moscow during World War II. The American public would not learn about Project Venona, as it was called, until 1995. But in 1951 British intelligence alerted the FBI that Pearson's "runner," Fred Blumenthal, had let slip that the columnist knew that "Arlington Hall has not been able to break a Russian code." Pearson never divulged what he knew about this shadowy project, but his discretion hardly protected that news from the Soviet Union. The FBI had gotten the warning from Kim Philby, who himself was a double agent keeping his Soviet bosses fully informed.[62]

As Venona demonstrated, Pearson chose not to break every secret he uncovered. The volatile nature of the atomic era made him cautious enough to consult military authorities about possible security risks. In one instance, he accepted an air force request to withhold a story about the romantic adventures of US servicemen in Hungary, even though he considered the tale harmless. He also killed an entire column at the request of the chairman of the joint chiefs of staff, who feared it might complicate his relations with the Senate, even though the column had revealed no military or cryptographic secrets. "I have put security ahead of news," he assured the secretary of the army.[63]

Despite such caution, the Cold War strained Drew Pearson's personal relations with J. Edgar Hoover after years of mutually beneficial friendship. In 1948 Hoover nominated Pearson for the American Hebrew Medal, presented by *The American Hebrew* magazine for promoting better understanding between Christians and Jews, citing the years that he had "devoted his talents and every opportunity to focusing the spotlight of public opinion on those forces that breed intolerance." Pearson returned the compliment with a warm tribute to Hoover at a dinner celebrating his twenty-fifth anniversary as director of the FBI. "You were very kind in your remarks," Hoover acknowledged, thanking him for his column's support of the bureau.

But conflicting positions during the Red Scare caused a chill. The break began with a June 1949 "Merry-Go-Round" that featured a protest letter from Dr. Edward Condon, director of the National Bureau of Standards. Condon accused the FBI of having smeared him by questioning his loyalty. (Hoover had erroneously identified him as "nothing more or less than an espionage agent in disguise.") Pearson reprinted Condon's letter as "one of the great human documents." Hoover was astonished that the column would "resort to that kind of viciousness for no good reason," adding, "I thought we had all been pretty decent to Pearson."[64]

J. Edgar Hoover divided the press into "friendlies," whom he could count on for favors, and "unfriendlies," who dared criticize him or the bureau. Pearson now drifted onto the latter list, which came with the caution: "Do Not Contact." As the "Merry-Go-Round" grew increasingly skeptical of the bureau's Red hunting, Hoover came to believe that the Communists had brainwashed the columnist. "What a liar Pearson is!" Hoover penciled in the margins of memos he received whenever Pearson dared to challenge FBI tactics; or "It is obviously a complete fabrication & typical of the pathological liar Pearson is."[65]

Pearson never restored his good relations with J. Edgar Hoover, but he did make peace with Harry Truman. Once his presidency ended, Truman looked better in retrospect, and Pearson found much to praise about the many tough decisions he had made. He invited the former president to give his first televised interview after leaving the White House, and the "Merry-Go-Round" occasionally paid tribute to his character and his achievements. These olive branches softened Truman's attitude, and eventually he agreed to write a note for use whenever Pearson's adversaries cited the former president against him. "He is highly controversial, and while I did not and do not always agree with what he writes or says or does—in my judgment he is by and large a force for the good of the country," Truman affirmed. "He is sincere, fearless, has the courage of his convictions and hammers away at what he believes is right, however unpopular it may be."[66]

6

The Case against Congress

"I ROSE THIS MORNING AND had my breakfast ruined by Drew Pearson," a
Florida congressman lamented on the floor of the House of Representatives.
Reading the "Washington Merry-Go-Round" could make or break the day
for a member of Congress. Favorable mentions boosted political careers;
exposés undermined them. Pearson's leg men found it almost impossible
to walk through the Capitol without picking up news. Eager for publicity,
members and their staffs whispered stories about what had gone on in closed
sessions and dished the dirt on their opponents. Believing that those who
wrote the laws needed to abide by them, Pearson taunted legislators about
their misdeeds and encouraged them to police themselves. He denounced lax
ethics rules that allowed members to accept legal retainers from law clients
who were lobbying Congress. He exposed members who took kickbacks
from staff salaries and chided others for junketing on taxpayers' dollars. He
railed against a seniority system that elevated ancient members, reelected
perpetually from safe districts and one-party states, who blocked more in-
novative legislators from exercising power, and made Congress "overage,
out-of-date, pompous, negative, corrupt, inefficient and, occasionally,
irresponsible."[1]

The columnist took credit for the indictment, imprisonment, censure,
and expulsion of a half dozen members of Congress, and the defeat of many
more. It might not have mattered as much to elected officials if the "Merry-
Go-Round" had appeared exclusively in the *Washington Post,* but its widespread syndication increased the odds that their constituents back home
would also be reading him. Despite their resentment, the column's national

reach encouraged their cooperation. "Take Drew Pearson," a reporter advised a political scientist studying Congress, "I'm sure that many members of the Senate thoroughly despise the man, yet they do business with him. And, at social occasions, I've seen them flock around him. It's a form of self-protection, I suppose."[2]

A senator could talk for hours and get only a few lines of newspaper coverage, while Pearson enjoyed a daily spot in hundreds of papers. Not content simply to write about Congress, he lobbied for legislation, testified before committees, and drafted speeches for friends in the Senate and House. His name appeared often in the *Congressional Record*, inserted by members who praised his columns or cursed him as a liar. During the 1930s, the "Merry-Go-Round"'s liberal leanings led congressional conservatives to complain of becoming targets of "the smear brigade" whenever they questioned New Deal policies. Isolationists and antiwar advocates accused Pearson of portraying them as Hitler's stooges, who harbored pro-German sympathies. The column's relentless attacks on isolationists cost Bob Allen one of his best sources in the Senate, Burton K. Wheeler. The Montana senator grew so enraged over what he read in the column that he demanded—unsuccessfully—that Pearson and Allen be banned from the Senate press gallery.[3]

The "Merry-Go-Round" labeled North Carolina Senator Robert Rice Reynolds the "Tarheel Fuehrer," and claimed that he was allied with the pro-Hitler German American Bund. "Bund members are urged to subscribe to and distribute the *Vindicator*, Fascist weekly recently launched by Senator Reynolds," the column charged, "with mysterious financial backing." Senator Reynolds admitted to reading the "Merry-Go-Round" every day. "We all like to see our pictures in the paper," he said; "we like to see our names in print." But he complained that the columnists had maligned him by labeling him a German agent. An isolationist who headed an organization to keep America neutral, Reynolds delivered a four-hour stemwinder in the Senate denouncing all the journalists who were out to destroy him, beginning with Pearson and Allen. "The only way they will get me to shut my mouth up," he shouted, "is to shoot me." His fate was far less drastic. Facing certain defeat in 1944, Reynolds chose not to seek reelection.[4]

"When Representative Ham Fish was asked whether he rented his New York mansion to the Nazi Consul General, he emitted a loud cry of anguish. 'If you want to make something of it,' he bellowed, 'I'll get you,' the column recounted for its readers. Pearson timed some of his accusations for maximum impact at the polls, revealing just before the election of 1940 that a Nazi official had been renting New York Representative Hamilton

Fish III's Manhattan townhouse at an inflated rate. Pearson got that information from agents from the British Security Coordination, as part of that spy network's efforts to discredit the isolationists. A frequent target of the "Merry-Go-Round" for his far-right politics, Fish predictably denounced Pearson as a New Deal propagandist and smear artist. When he failed to make good on a promise to sue Pearson after the election, British agents encouraged Pearson to sue Fish for libel instead. They hoped to tie Fish up in a lawsuit that would keep the charges before the public. "Personally, I am inclined against it," Pearson demurred. "I have enough to do writing the column, and the less I see of the courts the better." Even without a lawsuit, Fish eventually went down to defeat in 1944.[5]

Libel lawsuits served as an occupational hazard for Drew Pearson, who was sued at least 120 times, sometimes by members of Congress. Yet the columnist paid to settle only one case. He won all the rest or saw them withdrawn. The real penalty of these suits, he professed, was the hours he had to spend on the hard, cushionless benches in so many courthouses. "After a week your bones ache—a week of sitting in court listening to testimony, rebuttal, argument that you are a 'cuttlefish exuding inky filth over everyone,' . . . the jury goes out. You wait, wondering." He made a point of attending every trial, wherever it was held, regardless of the time and cost.[6]

Columnists Westbrook Pegler and Walter Winchell, who were also sued frequently, signed contracts that required their syndicates to pay any libel judgments against them. Pearson refused to enter into such an arrangement. He knew that his syndicate would more likely settle a case than take it to court, and that if it was responsible for costs that would strengthen the syndicate's hand in pre-censoring potentially libelous material or demanding later retractions. This strategy worked deliciously in Pearson's favor when he sued his rival Westbrook Pegler for libeling him (Pegler had blamed him for James Forrestal's death). Since Pegler had just lost another expensive libel suit, the Hearst-owned King Features, which syndicated his column, settled Pearson's suit by agreeing to run the "Washington Merry-Go-Round" in all the Hearst papers—much to Pegler's dismay. While assuring Pearson control, however, independence proved costly. "Lawyers' fees are just about ruining my income," he sighed.[7]

The toughest of all his cases was a chain libel suit brought by Ohio Representative Martin Sweeney in 1938. "He sued in 70 different jurisdictions," Pearson commented, "the biggest chain libel suit in the history of American journalism." Triggering the suit was this accusation of his association with the antisemitic radio broadcaster Father Charles Coughlin:

🔲 A hot behind-the-scenes fight is raging in Democratic Congressional ranks over the effort of Father Coughlin to prevent the appointment of a Jewish judge in Cleveland. The proposed appointee is Emerich Burt Freed, U.S. District Attorney in Cleveland. . . . This has aroused the violent opposition of Representative Martin L. Sweeney, Democrat of Cleveland, known as the chief Congressional spokesman of Father Coughlin. Basis of the Sweeney-Coughlin opposition is the fact that Freed is a Jew, and one not born in the United States. Born in Hungary in 1897, Freed was brought to the United States at the age of 13, was naturalized ten years later.[8]

Despite his public embrace of Father Coughlin, who sympathized with Hitler and preached against Jewish bankers, Sweeney called this a deliberate falsehood and insisted he had no antisemitic feelings. He planned to sue every newspaper that published the column, from coast to coast, in defense of himself, he said, and other maligned members. Sweeney retained a former New York Representative, John J. O'Connor, as his lawyer. A conservative Democrat, O'Connor had lost his seat during FDR's attempted purge of the party in 1938—a purge Pearson had supported. Filing so many suits would be an expensive operation, but Pearson suspected the column's persistent attacks on General Franco during the Spanish Civil War and support for the anticlerical Spanish Republicans had encouraged the American Catholic hierarchy to bankroll Sweeney's effort in retaliation.[9]

Sweeney's actions served as a test case that could subject all syndicated columns to intimidation and potential censorship, if every paper that carried a column could be held liable. A chain of libel suits against all the papers that carried the "Merry-Go-Round" also posed a dilemma in that the United States lacked a uniform standard in libel law, allowing it to vary from state to state. Pearson and Allen needed to hire local attorneys, study local laws, give depositions, and even testify in various state courts. They were determined to fight each of the suits in order to protect their client papers and keep them from dropping the column. The Sweeney case stiffened Pearson's resolve to fight any libel action brought against him by public officials and private individuals who felt maligned by his columns.[10]

Sweeney filed charges against 68 of the 325 newspapers then carrying the "Merry-Go-Round." That included a $250,000 suit against Cissy Patterson's *Washington Times-Herald*, where the congressman had read the offending piece. Courts in the District of Columbia dismissed Sweeney's charges against the *Times-Herald* on the principle that "the protection of the public requires not merely discussion but information"—that people had a right to know the facts before making up their minds. That decision influenced most of the other pending cases.[11]

Courts in jurisdictions with sparse Jewish populations considered an accusation of antisemitism insufficient cause to bring suit. But in New York State, where Sweeney sued the *Schenectady Union Star*, an appeals court ruled in Sweeney's favor, holding that because of the Nazi persecution of Jews anyone falsely accused of antisemitism might gain "the scorn and contempt of the right-thinking in appreciable numbers." The case went to the US Supreme Court, where a 4-4 tie vote (with one justice not participating) automatically upheld the lower court. The Supreme Court did not rule on the truth or falsity of the charges, however, and sent the case back for the lower courts to decide—until Sweeney, as Pearson reported, finally "got tired and quit."[12]

Across the country, Sweeney's multiple suits forced judges to weigh the impact of libel on freedom of the press. On the grounds that the public required information on the conduct of the officials they elected, state courts threw out almost all the cases. The congressman could not even get a favorable verdict in his home state of Ohio. In Texas, a district court judge pointed out the obvious, that "the 'ordinary reader' of defendant *Corpus Christi Caller-Times* probably never heard of Congressman Sweeney before the publication, didn't remember his name five minutes afterward and did not care whether he opposed the appointment of Freed, or on what grounds."[13]

A few newspapers settled with Sweeney for trifling sums, but most resisted taking the easy way out. A Charleston, West Virginia, paper turned down the congressman's offer to settle for five dollars. The only sizeable settlement—for $900—came from the owners of a newspaper in Reading, Pennsylvania, that was up for sale and needed to clean up back liabilities. Faced with disappointing verdicts and mounting court costs, Sweeney's attorney finally capitulated, offering to settle all the suits at once. When the parties reached that agreement on January 12, 1943, Pearson assured his editors that "no apologies or payments of any kind" were involved.[14]

Confirmed as a federal judge in 1941, Emerich Freed held that post for the rest of his life. In 1942, Martin Sweeney lost the Democratic primary for reelection, a not uncommon fate for isolationists after Pearl Harbor. Meanwhile, Pearson filed a $500,000 libel suit on behalf of himself and

Allen against Sweeney and his attorney, John O'Connor, charging that O'Connor held a "violent antagonism" against the column because of what they had written about him while he served in Congress, that he had sent intimidating letters to the newspapers that carried the "Merry-Go-Round," and that he had maliciously induced Sweeney to file the suits. The complaint noted that O'Connor solicited attorneys across the nation to handle the cases with the argument that "these two writers must be brought to a halt someday." The columnists asserted that the multitude of suits had been designed to drive them out of business, but their own suit went nowhere, doing nothing more than make a point.[15]

Outraged targets of the column continued to file libel suits against Pearson, even though the courts usually found in his favor. Significantly, when the US Supreme Court finally handed down a decision in *New York Times Co. v. Sullivan* in 1964, severely limiting the ability of public officials to sue the press for libel, it cited the Sweeney case among its precedents. The Supreme Court determined that the First Amendment required officials to prove that journalists knew the information was false and had published it with actual malice.[16]

Rather than sue Pearson, members of Congress found it easier to vent their spleens by denouncing him on the House or Senate floor, where congressional immunity protected them from being sued in return. The most memorable of these verbal outbursts resulted from an incident that Pearson had witnessed in 1938 but did not report for another half-dozen years. In the Democratic cloakroom, just off the Senate chamber, he had encountered Bennett Champ Clark. The Missouri senator came through the cloakroom's swinging doors and exclaimed, "My God, that fellow McKellar is powerful!" Clark told Pearson how Tennessee Senator Kenneth McKellar had pulled a clasp knife from his pocket and lunged toward New York Senator Royal Copeland during a heated debate. "He started to go for Copeland with a knife in his hand and we had a hard time holding him back," Clark exclaimed. Six years later, Pearson recalled the incident while writing a column about McKellar's ability to place relatives on the Tennessee Valley Authority's payroll. "Most of his colleagues remain in awe of McKellar's lashing tongue, some even in fear," Pearson wrote in the "Merry-Go-Round." "They remember the occasion when McKellar pulled a knife and charged a colleague on the Senate floor until he was disarmed."[17]

Famous for his sharp tongue, McKellar rose in the Senate the next day to howl. "Mr. President, I have a temper," he granted, and if there was ever an opportunity for his temper to be aroused, it was from the "plain lying of this so-called Washington columnist." McKellar described Drew Pearson as "just an ignorant liar, a pusillanimous liar, a peewee liar, and he is a paid liar." He denied ever pulling a knife on another senator. "I say that statement is a willful, deliberate, malicious, dishonest, intensely cowardly, low, degrading filthy lie, out of the whole cloth. I never pulled a knife on any person in my life." Looking at the press gallery, McKellar said he hoped Pearson was up there that day, "because I want him to hear what kind of an infamous, filthy, low-down, mean, lying scoundrel he is, and I think everyone else believes he is."[18]

Although Pearson was not in the press gallery to hear that hour-and-a-half diatribe, he responded by citing Senator Clark as his source for the story. Clark, however, recanted, not eager to tangle with his hot-headed colleague. He told reporters that although he remembered separating the two senators, "Senator McKellar had no knife in his hand." But Pearson checked with Senate press gallery staff, who remembered the knife-wielding incident vividly. For added proof, former Senator James Byrnes recalled that McKellar had yelled: "You make one more move and I'll cut your — heart out, you S.O.B."[19]

Pearson found McKellar's denunciation so amusing that he devoted an entire "Merry-Go-Round" to the speech, reprinting the most vituperative extracts. "I considered it a joke," he grinned. Seeing no humor, Senator McKellar contacted every Tennessee newspaper that carried Pearson's column, demanding that they print his entire speech. The editor of the *Kingston Daily Free Press* advised the senator that he could not comply since the lengthy speech would take up too much space but offered him the opportunity to write a rebuttal. "I do not share your opinion of Mr. Pearson," the editor added. "I know him quite well and I have had more than one occasion to check some of the stories which were denounced as false by those in public life who were criticized and was able to verify them. In fact, there have been few instances, Senator, where Mr. Pearson has not been able to substantiate in the main the revelations that he has made in his columns." For his part, Pearson audaciously drafted a letter for Tennessee editors to use in reply to McKellar. "I do not mind his attacks on me," he assured them. "That is all part of my profession."[20]

Senator McKellar had plenty of company in reviling Drew Pearson. Representative Eugene Cox, a Georgia Democrat, denounced the columnist as "a filthy and cowardly villain, a venomous slanderer, and an insinuating rogue, who makes his living in the blackening of other men's reputations and the practice of blackmail blackguardism." James Morrison, a Democrat from Louisiana, told the House that he had checked into Pearson's record of truth-telling. "I find that United States Senators, Members of Congress, Cabinet members, generals, and even the secretary to the President have in no uncertain terms labeled him as a downright liar and garbage-can collector of filthy, manufactured, synthetic lies."[21]

"Considering all that I have written about members of Congress, you can't really blame them for making speeches against me," Pearson reasoned. But the facts usually proved him correct, no matter how fiercely and profanely his targets howled. To remind readers of the accuracy of his charges, the "Merry-Go-Round" on October 21, 1954, featured a "Liar Scoreboard." It listed the five members he had struck out of office for corruption, despite their insistence that he had lied about them. First up was Ernest Bramblett, whom Pearson accused of padding his congressional payroll:[22]

> Congressman Bramblett of California hurled the liar charge and also sued to the tune of one million dollars when this writer accused him of taking kickbacks. A jury convicted him criminally just the same.[23]

The "Merry-Go-Round" revealed that Ernest Bramblett, a Republican Representative from Pacific Grove, California, had collected kickbacks from his congressional staff and had put his wife on the payroll even though she did not work at the office. The indignant congressman wrapped himself in a cloak of national security. "We know that Communist agents are everywhere around us," Bramblett appealed to his constituents. "They're in place in every strategic place in the nation, particularly so in California." Faced with the threat of subversion, the only person he could trust with the sensitive material in his office was his wife. His explanation failed to convince Pearson, who pointed out that Bramblett served on the House Agriculture Committee and had access to "nothing more top secret than the latest cure for chicken lice."[24]

An FBI investigation confirmed that Bramblett's wife had drawn a government salary but had done no work. The congressman had also doubled his secretary's salary on the condition that she pay him half. Convicted of payroll fraud, Bramblett was sentenced to four months to a year in prison. A judge suspended his prison term, fined him $5,000, and placed him on probation for a year. His appeals failed, as did Bramblett's effort to sue Pearson for damages. Congressman Bramblett did not run for reelection.[25]

Next to strike out was Senator Elmer Thomas, whom the column accused of insider trading:

> 🖾 Sen. Elmer Thomas of Oklahoma called me a liar when I reported that he had been speculating on the cotton market from his privileged position of chairman of the Senate Agriculture Committee. Two years later the Agriculture Department officially confirmed this, and Senator Thomas was defeated by the people of Oklahoma.[26]

The columnist disdained "pocketbook Congressmen" who thought more of their own financial interests than the public interest, and he condemned the club-like attitude of the Senate that kept its members from criticizing their colleagues' behavior, no matter how deplorable. "That explains the notion that no Senator so far has breathed a word regarding two colleagues—Bankhead and Elmer Thomas—who have been trading on the cotton market either directly or through their families at the same time they were making speeches opposing restrictions on cotton speculation." Both Democratic senators served on the Senate Agriculture Committee, where they used insider information to anticipate cotton prices. The column provided a carefully documented report, checking confidential transactions on the commodities market in New York. Pearson later regretted having written it, given that Senator John Bankhead died of a heart attack not long afterwards. "It made me wish I had chosen another profession," he wrote.[27]

Elmer Thomas denied the accusation, called Pearson a liar, and vowed that the only cotton he owned was the shirt on his back. "Senator Thomas was brazen enough to continue speculating on the commodities market," Pearson recorded. "I continued writing about him, and he continued calling me a liar." Then Congress, during an investigation of President Truman's staff, called on the Agriculture Department to report on any speculators who held government positions. Up popped the name of Elmer Thomas, along with his wife and his secretary. Thomas had to admit that he had been speculating in cotton for years. He lost the Democratic primary when he next ran for reelection.[28]

The next man up, Parnell Thomas, flailed at Pearson's charges that he took kickbacks:

🖼 Congressman Parnell Thomas of New Jersey denied kickbacks and called me a liar but went to jail because of those kickbacks.[29]

Pudgy, bald, and florid faced, New Jersey Republican J. Parnell Thomas had an unassuming appearance, but as chairman of the House Un-American Activities Committee he wielded power that could ruin people's careers, most notably during the committee's high-profile investigation into the Hollywood Ten, screenwriters, directors, and actors accused of being Communists in 1947. Thomas posed as a paragon of virtue, Pearson noted, but he had forgotten the old adage about throwing stones in glass houses: "If some of his own personal operations were scrutinized on the witness stand as carefully as he cross-examines witnesses, they would make headlines of a kind the Congressman doesn't like." The column accused Chairman Thomas of padding his office payroll and taking kickbacks from his secretarial staff, which he failed to declare on his income taxes. These were serious charges, but Pearson had gathered evidence from Thomas's secretary and "office wife," Helen Campbell. Jealous of Thomas's attentions to a new clerk-typist in the office, she followed when the boss drove the young woman home. The next morning, Miss Campbell returned and found the congressman's car still parked out in front of the staffer's apartment, its radiator cold. She promptly revealed Thomas's financial misdeeds to Drew Pearson.[30]

Parnell Thomas called Pearson a liar, but an FBI investigation found merit in the columnist's accusations. The indignant congressman responded by charging the Justice Department with "coddling Communist traitors" and subjecting him to a vicious smear. When Thomas appeared before a grand jury, he took the Fifth Amendment—like so many witnesses before HUAC. Although Helen Campbell had provided evidence, the Justice Department indicted her as well for facilitating the kickbacks. Pearson coached her on how to answer questions under cross-examination. At the trial he observed that Thomas no longer resembled the influential committee chairman he had once been, which made him feel "almost sorry that I had brought out all the stuff about his kickbacks." Yet Thomas got a fair trial, unlike the witnesses before his committee whom he had sent to jail, chiefly for not answering his questions. "So perhaps I shouldn't have felt sorry." The trial ended abruptly when Thomas withdrew his not guilty plea. He was convicted, fined, and sentenced to six to eighteen months in prison. His pleading no contest also caused the court to dismiss the conspiracy case against Helen Campbell.[31]

It seemed poetic justice for Congressman Thomas to be sent to Danbury Prison, which also housed some of the Hollywood Ten, who had been convicted of contempt of Congress for failing to answer his questions. President Truman granted Thomas a Christmas Day pardon in 1952, which emboldened Thomas to make one more campaign for Congress in 1954. His loss at the polls that year ended his political career. Helen Campbell, who lost her job for exposing her boss's misdeeds, went to work for Drew Pearson as one of his secretaries, remaining on his payroll for fifteen years until she retired.[32]

Yet another powerful US Representative, Andrew May, waved off Pearson's charges that he took bribes, but still wound up behind bars.

> Congressman Andrew May of Kentucky called me a liar so many times that it got monotonous, in connection with his various under-the-table operations with war contracts. He went to jail.[33]

On his Sunday night radio broadcast, Pearson mentioned that Andrew Jackson May, a Democrat from Kentucky and chairman of the House Military Affairs Committee, opposed pending veterans' legislation. A young reporter for the United Press had written a story related to May that he had been unable to publish and was willing to sell to the columnist. The reporter identified a veteran who claimed that his wife had "some interesting information on Congressman May." Pearson drove to their home, where he found they were raising chinchillas in their basement. "During the course of the evening I became something of a chinchilla expert," he reported. "But I also learned from Mrs. Eleanor Hall that she had once passed an envelope containing, she believed, $1000, to Congressman May on behalf of her then employers," businessmen who lacked any experience in producing munitions but who had obtained profitable government war contracts. "After some days of continuing conversations, she consented to give me an affidavit. This took courage on her part," Pearson attested. "A lot of people will tell you things, but they won't swear to them. But she did swear, and her testimony eventually contributed to the conviction of the congressman—she was the star witness at May's trial."[34]

Representative May characterized Pearson's charges as misleading innuendo and assured his constituents that he was the victim of smears by "reds and pinks." But a Senate investigating committee documented the substantial payments that he had taken as well as the pressure he had exerted on the war department to grant the contracts. May lost his race for reelection, was convicted of accepting bribes, and spent nine months in prison. In a bipartisan gesture, the Democrat Andrew May along with the Republican Parnell Thomas received full pardons from President Truman as he left the White House.[35]

Walter Brehm also swung hard at Pearson's "lies," but his explanations were unconvincing.

🖿 Congressman Brehm of Ohio threatened a libel suit over this column's story that he accepted kickbacks. He was convicted.[36]

On September 26, 1950, the "Merry-Go-Round" assured readers that "Most members of Congress in my opinion are high-type citizens who do not fudge on their payrolls." But Pearson went on to reveal that Representative Walter Brehm, an Ohio Republican, had taken kickbacks from two women on his staff. Predictably, the congressman called Pearson a liar and promised to sue, but other columns followed exposing the exact amounts of money received, and the way the funds had been transmitted.[37]

Congressmen Brehm explained to FBI agents that he had donated the kickback payments to the Ohio Republican campaign committee. Pearson regarded this as an odd defense since such payments violated the Corrupt Practices Act. He also reported that a former employee who had acted as an intermediary, handling the money, had alerted the congressman that the columnist was after a story about him. "If Drew Pearson or his employees contact you," Brehm had responded, "don't talk to them." But Brehm discovered that Jack Anderson had persuaded the intermediary to talk by asserting that the FBI was investigating the allegations of kickbacks. Congressman Brehm "proceeded to berate Anderson for his tactics," according to an FBI report on the incident. When the case went to trial, Brehm was convicted of taking the money, fined, and sentenced to five to fifteen months in prison. The judge gave him a suspended sentence, citing the "exemplary life" he had lived until then. Rather than run for reelection, Brehm returned to his dentistry practice in Ohio.[38]

"I should hate to be remembered only as a jailer of congressmen," Pearson reflected. The hardest job of a journalist was to decide whether a public official was telling the truth. Diplomats lied as part of their profession, and to some politicians, lying just came naturally. Every senator or representative whom he had charged with corruption lied about the facts, the columnist noted. "But the truth convicted them." Exposing members of Congress posed considerable risk. Constitutional immunity allowed them to malign him without fear of libel suits. They could subpoena him to testify, and if he refused to answer questions about his sources, they could jail him for contempt. They could also embarrass him, as did one of his targets, the crusty and cantankerous Michigan Congressman Clare Hoffman, in 1953. The "Merry-Go-Round" accused Hoffman of pressuring the air force to award a contract to two of his constituents, even though their company was too small to handle the job. Pearson had misread the boundary lines, however, and in fact the company lay just outside of Hoffman's district: "In high indignation, Hoffman slapped a subpoena on me and made me squirm before photographers," Pearson winced, "while we went over the geography of Michigan district by district." The columnist apologized for mistakenly identifying the contractors but refused to retract his inference that the congressman had improperly used his committee to get the contract for them.[39]

At another congressional hearing, a senator asked Pearson how he got his information. "I have a file on practically every Member of Congress, including yourself," he replied mischievously. "I try to watch all of your records." Pearson presented himself as a one-man FBI, but like the bureau, he could not trust every bit of evidence he gathered or prove every accusation he made. Jack Anderson credited his boss with being able to detect something wrong even before the facts were in: "He would sniff the air delicately and he would know that there was a scandal. He would with a few whiffs determine that a public official was bad, that a public official was corrupt." That sense of smell led him to Representative Robert F. Jones.[40]

The Jones story began in 1947 when President Harry Truman abruptly withdrew the nomination of a Republican member of the Federal Communications Commission, up for a second seven-year term. The "Merry-Go-Round" determined that the commissioner lost his seat after voting against a radio station application placed by House Speaker Sam Rayburn's nephew. Since the law required that commissioners be drawn from both parties, Truman filled the vacancy by nominating the Ohio Republican Robert Jones. He was likely happy to remove one of his harsher critics from Congress.[41]

News of the appointment sent Pearson back to his files, where he found reports of Jones's "consistent, extreme, isolationist voting record." He telephoned knowledgeable people in Jones's district and came across attorney Francis Durbin, who advised him that Jones had once been a member of the Black Legion—an Ohio offshoot of the Ku Klux Klan. Pearson, in Jack Anderson's opinion, saw in Jones a man with deep and dangerous prejudices, and he wanted to get to the root of them. He accepted the tip about Jones as legitimate because it confirmed everything that he suspected. "One of the things I don't stand for, or rather stand against, is the Ku Klux Klan," he declared in the column. "And when I see a Congressman nominated to high office who comes from a Ku Klux Klan background, I think it's up to me to bring out the facts."[42]

"Drew, where are your facts?" Anderson challenged. "Well, you'll have to go get it," Pearson replied, dispatching Anderson to Ohio. The leg man soon discovered that "Drew's hunch was right." He encountered three former Black Legion members who were willing to sign affidavits about Jones's ugly past and to testify against him. Pearson passed this evidence to a Democratic senator on the committee handling the confirmation. Republican senators wanted to avoid public hearings, but at a closed executive session—which leaked out to Pearson—Democrats insisted on going public. At the open hearing, Pearson testified that Jones's father had been an active recruiter for the Klan, and that he used to introduce his son as the youngest member of the Ku Klux Klan. He promised to produce witnesses who would identify Jones as a member of the Black Legion. "You can forgive a man for the mistakes of his youth. I would not hold that against him," he avowed. "I have done plenty of things, possibly even you have, that we want to forget, in our past." But he insisted that Jones still held highly offensive views.[43]

Jack Anderson escorted his three informants to Washington, and Pearson featured one of them on his Sunday night radio program. The sheriff of Beaver Dam avowed having personally sworn Jones into membership in the Black League. "This is Drew Pearson in Washington," he signed off that night, "reminding Congress that an unbroken mirror placed before the record of Congressman Jones now may save the Nation seven years hard luck later."[44]

Unfortunately for Pearson, veterans of the Black Legion made shabby witnesses. Their characters were far from stellar, he conceded, "otherwise they wouldn't have been Black Legionnaires." The sheriff had spent time in jail and in a mental institution. Another witness admitted to having forged payroll checks. Nor could the commander of the Black Legion recall whether

Jones had been inducted. Pearson admitted that his principal source for the story, Francis Durbin, was one of Jones's political enemies. Congressman Jones rebutted the accusations, denying racial or religious biases, or that he had ever been a Klansman. He asserted that as a prosecuting attorney he had brought suit against members of the Black Legion—including one of Pearson's witnesses. For good measure, he reminded the committee that two presidents of the United States and many of their colleagues in Congress had branded Drew Pearson a liar. Republicans dismissed the charges against Jones as half-truths. They chided Pearson that when he broadcast and published insinuations that turned out to be untrue, there was no way for the public to be re-informed.[45]

Pearson undermined his case further by confessing that he had two personal—"I might say selfish"—motives in testifying. The first he described as idealistic. As a radio commentator, he defended racial minorities and religious faiths from attack, so he opposed putting someone who held opposite views on the Federal Communications Commission. His second motive was more damaging. Pearson and his former partner Robert Allen owned stock in Public Service Radio Broadcasting, which had applied to the FCC to operate Baltimore radio station WBAL. Pearson's attorney had been encouraging him to invest his surplus capital in something related to his news enterprises, such as a radio station, where they could share staff and other resources. Operated by Hearst Radio, WBAL had been under fire for years for providing inadequate public service broadcasting. Given his vigorous attacks on the Ku Klux Klan, Pearson reminded the committee, he doubted that anyone associated with the Klan would give his application a fair hearing.[46]

When Jack Anderson got set to testify, Pearson took him aside. "You've got to raise hell with them," Pearson exhorted. "They're loaded against us. They're unfair. They're prejudiced. Go say so." Anderson followed instructions but lost the battle. Senators mauled him and their three witnesses while treating Congressman Jones politely. The committee unanimously approved the nomination and the Senate confirmed him. Once Jones joined the FCC, the commission denied the Pearson-Allen application and renewed Hearst Radio's license for WBAL. Pearson's enemies seized on the case to claim that he allowed self-interest to dictate his reporting. A *Chicago Tribune* article accused him of smearing Congressman Jones with false accusations to advance his own business interests and noted that the revelation produced a violent reaction in Congress. It made him appear that he was making unsubstantiated assertions for personal gain.[47]

Although the fight against Jones cost the "Merry-Go-Round" seven Ohio newspapers as clients, the incident was more of an embarrassment than an indictment. Pearson had gotten carried away and rushed into print with insufficient evidence to support his charges, and then had produced some tawdry witnesses. Still, his accusations had been in keeping with his stand against political and racial extremism. His battle against Hearst Radio had reflected his concern that big business interests controlled too much of the media, allowing wealthy owners to sway people's thoughts by telling reporters and commentators what to say. What he most resented, his stepson recalled, was that "every time you are in an argument with a publisher, an editor, remember that you have to bow from the waist because they are the ones in control."[48]

For Ohio Senator Robert Taft—known as "Mr. Republican" for his party leadership—the seemingly spurious charges against his political ally Robert Jones confirmed all his suspicions against the columnist. "He brought two or three very shady characters from Lima with criminal records to support his charges, and the Committee was convinced they were wholly untrue," Taft cited. Moreover, he assured the head of the Jewish War Veterans of the United States, "Drew Pearson himself is wholly unreliable, and is an applicant for a radio license before the Commission."[49]

Even though Republicans owned the largest share of American newspapers and regularly endorsed Republican candidates, Taft complained that their Washington correspondents favored liberal Democrats. Journalists were not as impartial as they thought, he insisted. Twenty years of reporting on the Roosevelt and Truman administrations had made the Washington press corps biased against Republicans as a party and Congress as an institution. Taft counted Drew Pearson the worst among them, being "very far on the left," pro–New Deal, and anti-Republican.[50]

Senator Taft especially hated the "Merry-Go-Round"'s practice of citing bits of his conversations, as if the columnist had an ear cocked to his every private encounter. For example:

▦ Despite heated debates on the Senate floor, GOP Leader Bob Taft and the Democrats frequently exchange sympathetic words. Such an exchange occurred during the heat of the debate over confirmation of Joe B. Dooley as United States judge for Texas, an appointment vigorously pushed by Texas' statuesque senior Senator Tom Connally, and just as vigorously opposed by Texas' junior razzle-dazzle Senator Pappy

O'Daniel. Because O'Daniel votes so frequently with the Republicans, he had lined up most GOP Senators against Dooley. But during the debate Taft came over to Senator Connally and whispered: "If you need a vote or two, we can switch them over to you. We wouldn't be for this guy [O'Daniel] except that he has supported us [the Republicans] so much we had to do something."[51]

Taft denied saying anything that remotely resembled that story. In his defense, Pearson explained he had merely used the exchange to demonstrate that despite their opposition in public the Republicans and Democrats could exchange sympathetic words in private. The source was clearly someone on the Senate floor who overheard the conversation. An embarrassed Senator Connally assured Taft that he had never told anybody that the latter had made such a remark. Pearson "did have his so-called spies up here on the Hill," recalled one Senate staffer. "You had to be careful about what you said around people, particularly at luncheons," because there were some senators and staff that Pearson could always call to get the story.[52]

Pearson employed the same surrogate eavesdropping tactic to expose Taft's encouragement of Wisconsin Senator Joe McCarthy's sensational charges about subversion and espionage in the federal government. Oregon Senator Wayne Morse and New Hampshire Senator Charles Tobey, both liberal Republicans and early opponents of McCarthy, kept Pearson informed about what happened within the Senate Republican Conference, including Taft's conversations with other Republican senators at their luncheons. Taft had advised them that whether or not they believed McCarthy's wild charges, he was winning votes for their party. According to the column, Taft said: "I told Joe to keep talking. I don't think he's got anything. But the longer he talks, the more people will think he has something." Rather than deny these charges, Taft admitted to reporters from the *New York Times*, *Herald Tribune*, *Baltimore Sun*, and the Associated Press that he had privately advised McCarthy that "if one case didn't work out to bring up another." Taft had also drafted an explanation for not trying to rein in McCarthy that he chose not to release: "Confidentially, every Senator is a prima donna, and nobody who undertakes to tell them what to say and what not to say is going to have much influence very long." But Taft came to have second thoughts about being so candid and denied making the statements attributed to him. "I don't think I have ever read anything in Drew Pearson's column that is true," he told those who questioned him, "and I advise you to pay no attention to what he says."[53]

An irritated Taft mailed a form letter to every newspaper in Ohio refuting allegations that he had encouraged McCarthy. "Apparently this story originated in a column by Mr. Drew Pearson and it is not true," his letter asserted. Some of the editors who received this letter contacted Pearson for a response. He reminded everyone that when his column about Taft's encouraging McCarthy first appeared, Taft had substantiated the charge while answering other reporters. "Apparently he has since had a change of heart," Pearson added, attributing Taft's denials to a bad public reaction. The columnist quoted his wife, Luvie, as chiding him: "After all, when you list all those people like John Maragon, Parnell Thomas, Representative Andrew May who called you a liar, and then show that they went to jail—well, it makes people think you want to send Senator Taft to jail. And I know you don't mean anything like that." Of course not, Pearson replied, but when others similarly reported that Taft had buoyed McCarthy, the senator had not denounced them as liars.[54]

Pearson carried on a protracted campaign against Joe McCarthy, denouncing his tactics, dismissing his charges, and demanding his censure. The "Merry-Go-Round" also claimed credit for two other Senate censures. In 1946, after it revealed a scandal involving Mississippi Senator Theodore Bilbo and the awarding of war contracts, the Senate censured Bilbo. Twenty years later, the column's relentless exposé of Connecticut Senator Thomas Dodd's personal use of campaign funds also led to his censure.

Pearson took aim at "ghost voting" by absent members of the House of Representatives, who had friends cast ballots for them as if they were present. He exposed lobbying excesses and extravagant junkets, holding members of Congress accountable politically and legislatively. At the same time, he bolstered members whose actions he admired. In 1950, he took credit for enabling Tennessee Senator Estes Kefauver to chair an investigation into organized crime—a recurring subject in "Merry-Go-Round" columns. When Kefauver failed to win support for his resolution to authorize the investigation, Pearson went to Senate Majority Leader Scott Lucas and urged him to let it pass. He warned that people were saying Lucas took campaign contributions from gamblers, and it would look suspicious if he blocked the investigation. Pearson later repeated this story to an interviewer, who asked, "Couldn't that warning be interpreted as . . ." "Blackmail?" the columnist flushed. "Oh, no. Lucas was a good friend of mine."[55]

Conservatives complained that Pearson aimed only at them, but the column's exposés of greed, corruption, and abuse of power cut across ideological lines. Notably, the "Merry-Go-Round" conducted a sustained attack on the liberal Democratic Representative Adam Clayton Powell Jr. of New York for his flagrant abuses of power. Initially, Pearson had praised Powell as a "brainy Negro Congressman" who stood like David against the Goliath of Southern segregationists. Then a former political associate of Powell's, Frederick Weaver, advised the columnist that Powell had endorsed the Republican Dwight Eisenhower's reelection in 1956 in return for a promise to fix an income tax case against him. Concluding that Powell was corrupt, Pearson blasted Powell's chronic absenteeism and expensive, government-paid trips to Europe and the Bahamas, dubbing him the "Harlem globetrotter." In 1961, when Powell's seniority elevated him to chairman of the House Education and Labor Committee, Pearson returned to a more respectful treatment, publicizing his views on poverty in America. But before long Pearson complained that Powell's absences had delayed passage of anti-poverty legislation. When the column praised a committee counsel who helped shape a bill in the chairman's absence, Powell promptly fired the man.[56]

The "Merry-Go-Round" recorded how Powell fished off the island of Bimini in the Bahamas while his colleagues toiled in Washington. Such negative publicity eventually roused the House of Representatives to act. In January 1967 the Democratic caucus stripped Powell of his committee chairmanship. In March, the House voted not to seat him. In a special election six weeks later, his constituents reelected him. Rather than reclaim his seat, Powell sued. In 1969, the Supreme Court ruled that the House had unconstitutionally denied him membership, since he met the sole requirements of age, citizenship, and residence. Pearson agreed that the House had been foolish not to seat Powell first before voting to expel him. The next year, Charles Rangel, a reform candidate who would later face his own ethics charges, defeated Powell in the Democratic primary, ending his political career.[57]

Drew Pearson prodded Congress to establish stronger codes of ethics, to accept the same conflict-of-interest rules that applied to the rest of the government and cast more light on its members' outside activities. Internal review and punishment happened only rarely because the machinery of censure was too cumbersome and difficult to invoke. He proposed that each house create its own watchdogs, and eventually the House and Senate did establish ethics committees to weigh the type of improprieties that the

"Merry-Go-Round" reported. "This column has been writing about congressional misbehavior for about 20 years," Pearson reflected in 1963, "and has named names and printed facts." But the column had also paid tribute to productive members who made democracy work. "It is not fair to them—and I believe they are in the great majority—to have their reputations spoiled by the Congressmen who do cheat."[58]

7

Battling McCarthyism

A YOUNG, WEALTHY SOCIALITE, Louise Tinsley Steinman, known to her friends as Tinnie, threw a dinner dance at Washington's swank Sulgrave Club on December 12, 1950. Tinnie Steinman had made herself notorious by inviting guests who were at loggerheads and not telling them in advance who else would attend her parties. When Drew Pearson arrived at the ballroom, she laughed and said, "I hope you don't mind Joe is here." He was astonished to find himself seated at the same table with Senator Joseph R. McCarthy, whom the "Merry-Go-Round" had been denouncing for months. "I wouldn't have come to this damned thing if I had known Drew Pearson was going to be here, too," the senator growled, adding that he was getting ready to make a speech about him. "I'm really going to take you apart on the Senate floor tomorrow," McCarthy taunted, "I'm really going to tear you to pieces."[1] The badgering continued incessantly until Pearson walked around the table, leaned over, and inquired about reports of McCarthy's income tax problems back in Wisconsin. "When are they going to put you in jail?" the columnist asked before returning to his seat. "You take that back!" McCarthy shouted. The senator leapt up, followed him, and grabbed him by the back of the neck, inviting him outside to settle things. "Let's go," said Pearson, but other guests intervened. "Don't be a fool, sit down," said the wife of a congressman. "He has been drinking; don't embarrass your hostess." Pearson and his wife instead left the table to dance.[2]

Around midnight, the adversaries met again in the cloakroom. Pearson was reaching into his pocket for change to tip the attendant when McCarthy accused him of going for a gun. The senator pinned his arms, kneed him in the groin, and slapped him in the face. Just then, another guest at the dinner, California's newly elected Senator Richard Nixon, entered the cloak-room and stepped between them. McCarthy took one more swing and struck Pearson's head with the flat of his hand. In later years, Nixon often retold the story, insisting that if he had not separated them, the intoxicated senator might have killed the columnist. "And do you think it ever did me any good with that bastard Pearson?" Nixon would add. "Never!" When Pearson grabbed his coat and rushed from the room, McCarthy turned and said, "You shouldn't have stopped me, Dick."[3]

Afterwards, McCarthy bragged to the editor of the *Washington Times-Herald*, Frank Waldrop, about having kicked Pearson "in the nuts." Waldrop passed the story along to the conservative radio broadcaster Fulton Lewis Jr., who aired a version of the incident on his broadcast the next night. Publicly, McCarthy swore that he had only slapped his foe. "The senator kicked me twice in the groin," Pearson corrected the re-cord. "As usual, he hit below the belt." McCarthy's assault brought cheers from some of his colleagues. Utah Senator Arthur Watkins told him, "Joe, the newspapers differ as to where you hit him, but I hope both ac-counts were right." (This from the man who later chaired the committee that recommended McCarthy's censure for behavior contrary to Senate traditions.)[4]

The encounter at the Sulgrave Club marked the most violent incident in Pearson's protracted campaign against the rampaging, Red-hunting, Republican senator. For McCarthy, their four-year-long clash would end in his censure and ostracism. For Pearson, it would cause the loss of his radio and television sponsors, and a substantial cut in his income, along with the physical bruises.

Some 20 million listeners tuned in to Pearson's weekly radio broadcasts, carried on 250 stations nationwide. The radio show provided twice the in-come of the daily column. His fame appealed to a variety of sponsors, from Raleigh's cigarettes (although he did not smoke) to the antacid Bromo-Seltzer (because he led a "tense and busy life") and the laxative Serutan ("natures" spelled backward). After Lee Hats and later Adam Hats sponsored his programs, Pearson sported a fedora as his trademark headware. Adam Hats provided extra publicity by running a trailer beneath its newspaper and magazine ads urging people to listen to Drew Pearson on ABC radio. Despite the income and attention that radio brought him, however, the need for commercial sponsorship left Pearson politically vulnerable.[5]

In 1950, when the "Merry-Go-Round" assailed Senator McCarthy for making unproven and irresponsible accusations of internal subversion and espionage, the senator retaliated by branding Pearson "a sugar-coated voice of Russia" and "a Moscow-directed character assassin." McCarthy charged that Pearson was taking orders from his former leg man, David Karr, who had once written for the *Daily Worker*, which explained his demonization of such prominent anti-Communists as General MacArthur, James Forrestal, and himself. The senator called on newspapers and radio stations to "see this voice of international Communism is stilled," and he challenged the public to boycott the Adam Hat Company. "It should be remembered," McCarthy intoned ominously, ". . . anyone who buys from a store that stocks an Adam hat is unknowingly contributing at least something to the cause of international communism by keeping this Communist spokesman on the air." Leaving the Capitol after he made that speech, McCarthy nonchalantly donned a gray fedora—an Adam hat he had acquired compliments of Drew Pearson while they were still on good terms.[6]

Two weeks later, Adam Hats announced that it would not renew its contract to sponsor Pearson's radio program, although it claimed to have made the decision before McCarthy's call for a boycott. Pearson confirmed the sponsor's statement, speculating that McCarthy must have known about the cancellation in advance and had called for the boycott simply to take credit for killing the show. But Adam Hats's explanation had obscured the truth: they were still renegotiating the contract when the controversy erupted. Privately, Pearson blamed McCarthy's speech for scaring the sponsor away and diminishing his income. Pearson's television sponsor similarly cut him loose, professing that it was shifting all its advertising from news to entertainment programs. A sponsorship deal with Dunhill, the British cigarette firm, also collapsed. Although their advertising agency was all for it, Pearson noted, "the Dunhill boys finally replied, 'too controversial.'" No matter what their excuses, McCarthyism had intimidated Pearson's national sponsors.[7]

The clash also cost Pearson his longtime friendship with fellow radio commentator and columnist Walter Winchell. Both broadcast over the ABC network on Sunday nights and for years they had been political allies. They supported the same causes, made the same enemies, and came to each other's defense when either was attacked. After McCarthy's threatened boycott, Pearson phoned Winchell for help, but Winchell refused to intercede. By then, Winchell had found it more profitable to ally with the senator and his staff, collecting tips from them that allowed him to break the news about whom McCarthy planned to subpoena next. Winchell praised their anti-Communist crusade so slavishly that Pearson tagged him a "McCarthy cheerleader." The two commentators took swipes at each other on the air and never restored their relations.[8]

Determined not to let the loss of national sponsors silence him, Pearson taped a radio program on his own. With the blessing of Robert Kintner, the anti-McCarthy head of the ABC network, Pearson mailed the recordings to any ABC-affiliated station that would broadcast them using local sponsors. Very soon, 140 radio stations signed up for the program. Although his ratings held up proportionately with other radio commentators, all were losing listeners as Americans spent more time watching television. Pearson also aimed to make that transition. He began recording his own programs at a Washington television studio and—after an unprofitable year with Motion Pictures for Television handling the distribution—started selling the program himself. "It's not going to be any easy job," he predicted.[9]

Even local sponsorship put Pearson at the mercy of forces beyond his control. His television program suffered a significant financial reversal when its chief sponsor in Texas declared bankruptcy, losing twelve stations for the program. Worse still, he confided to his brother, the sponsor had been an insurance and loan company "in which a lot of small people invested" because they had confidence in him. So I have had to spend a lot of money with lawyers in Texas to try to help the situation and have been flooded with some very heartbreaking mail from people who lost their entire earnings."[10]

Beyond losing his sponsors, some newspapers, and a few friends, Pearson's battle with Joe McCarthy cost him one of the column's best sources on Capitol Hill: Senator McCarthy himself. In 1947, Pearson had yawned at McCarthy's arrival in the Senate, derisively noting that he came "with more publicity build-up than any colleague, but fizzled faster." The column showed the new senator snugly in the pocket of corporate interests and voting against veterans' housing rights. Pearson wrote that he "talked more and did less constructive work" than any other freshman. But after a year of negative coverage, the "Merry-Go-Round" highlighted McCarthy's "one-man crusade" to liberate millions of World War II prisoners still being held in Russia, France, and Britain, praising the humanitarian efforts of "the former Marine officer who flew as a tail gunner." It next reported that the senator "really got religion on public housing," having reversed his position and solicited Republican votes for slum clearance. From 1948 to 1950, the column provided McCarthy the kind of publicity that most freshmen senators could only dream about.[11]

In between those conflicting assessments, McCarthy had gone out of his way to befriend Pearson's Capitol Hill leg man, Jack Anderson. The senator yearned for publicity and Anderson needed a source within the conservative wing of the Senate GOP. McCarthy left his door open for the reporter and even allowed him to listen on an extension to his phone conversations with other senators. Since Anderson overheard everything for himself, McCarthy could deny having leaked anything to him. "This blot upon senatorial honor was for a reporter a professional coup of high rank," Anderson exulted, "and I rejoiced in it, prying out of McCarthy every last morsel of confidential information." The courtship grew so snug, Pearson recalled, that he received an angry phone call from William Evjue, publisher of the Madison, Wisconsin, *Capital Times*, ripping into him "for being too gentle with McCarthy."[12]

Once McCarthy started aiding the column, Pearson reassessed him as alert, smart, likeable, and "very charming." That favorable treatment ended abruptly in 1950, after McCarthy traveled to Wheeling, West Virginia, to deliver a Lincoln's Day speech to a Republican women's club. Instead of the standard fare, he made headlines by claiming to hold in his hand the names of 205 known Communists still at work in the State Department. At subsequent stops on his cross-country speaking tour, he muddled the numbers, claiming 57 or 81 subversives were undermining American diplomacy. Coming at a tense time in the Cold War, McCarthy's tactic of blaming setbacks in American foreign policy on internal subversion resonated with the general public. Pearson himself had long been critical of the State Department, but he regarded McCarthy's figures as "way off base." Congressional committees and loyalty boards for years had investigated suspected security risks and rooted out Communist sympathizers. In a column on February 18, 1950, Pearson refuted McCarthy's charges. Two of the people the senator named had resigned years earlier from the State Department; one never worked there; and another had been cleared and reinstated. Since not every newspaper initially reported or devoted much space to McCarthy's allegations, many readers got their first account of the controversy from Pearson's column. It marked the beginning of McCarthy's national news coverage and his emergence as the nation's leading anti-Communist.[13]

When a Senate subcommittee opened an investigation into the charges, McCarthy appealed to his friends in the press corps for help. "I don't have a thing. I shot my mouth off," he told Jack Anderson. "Do *you* have any facts?" Anderson rooted through Pearson's files in search of anything that McCarthy could use and passed along an unsubstantiated report about a White House speechwriter. McCarthy stunned him by using it raw, without any fact checking. Anderson was further perplexed to find himself working at cross purposes with his boss. After Pearson took after McCarthy, Anderson reminded him that the senator had fed them information. "He may be a good source, Jack," Pearson replied, "but he's a bad man."[14]

The "Merry-Go-Round" traced the inspiration for McCarthy's crusade to a dinner at the Colony Restaurant in Washington:

Originally, McCarthy got his Communist purge idea from a Catholic professor at Georgetown University, Father Edmund Walsh. The Senator had asked Father Walsh and Col. William A. Roberts, prominent Washington attorney, how he could keep his name before the public. McCarthy said that, in order to be reelected in Wisconsin, he would have to pick some important issue and become a national figure. Colonel Roberts suggested that, since Wisconsin is on the Great Lakes, McCarthy campaign for the St. Lawrence Seaway; also that he campaign for better social security benefits. Father Walsh advised that whoever campaigned on the issue of communism in Government would become the most popular figure in the country.[15]

McCarthy had already Red-baited his opponents in Wisconsin with some success and grasped its national potential. "The government is full of Communists," he agreed. "The thing to do is hammer at them." William Roberts happened to be Drew Pearson's lawyer and tipped him off about the dinner conversation. Georgetown University Professor Charles Kraus, another guest that evening, confirmed Roberts's account, but Father Walsh angrily denied the implication that he had inspired McCarthyism and later accused the columnist of having manufactured the incident. For decades, Walsh had been warning about the revolutionary tactics of American Communists, but he never anticipated McCarthy's Red Scare. In other columns, Pearson acknowledged that Father Walsh had not been happy with the outcome. "It was not Father Edmund Walsh who was really responsible for taking Joe up on the mountaintop," the columnist explained; he had only "planted the idea in Joe's mind."[16]

The columnist had tried to mend his fences with the Catholic Church after falling out over the Spanish Civil War, but he recorded in his diary that nearby Georgetown University was "backing McCarthy with poorly concealed enthusiasm," and that Father Walsh had given the senator "all sorts of support." Pearson concluded that many Catholic leaders disapproved of McCarthy but had just not been as vocal as his supporters.[17]

The "Merry-Go-Round"'s accusation that McCarthy had disrupted "our entire foreign service" at a dangerous time in the Cold War had encouraged the Senate investigation of McCarthy's charges—chaired, ironically, by the columnist's former nemesis, Senator Millard Tydings. "People at cocktail parties now almost faint when he comes by and slaps me on the back," Pearson chuckled. "Since the McCarthy fight, he and I have become quite friendly." He granted that his old adversary had shown courage in standing up to McCarthy, which led to Tydings's defeat in a brutal race for reelection in 1950.[18]

Anxious to divert press attention from his sparse evidence, Joe McCarthy announced that his whole case against the State Department would stand or fall on evidence against one man, whom he called the top Soviet spy in the United States. Before divulging the name publicly, McCarthy privately alerted Jack Anderson that he meant Johns Hopkins University Professor Owen Lattimore, an adviser to the State Department on Asian Affairs. Drew Pearson knew the professor slightly and doubted the charges. He decided to steal McCarthy's thunder by being the first to announce the name on his radio program. Other Washington reporters had also gotten Lattimore's name but had withheld it for fear of libel. They blasted Pearson's revelation as reprehensible. "When I take the risk of libel," he retorted sarcastically, "I am unethical." His friend Ernest Cuneo warned him that he was crazy to go after McCarthy, because public opinion had swung behind the Wisconsin senator's efforts to clean Communists out of the government. "I agree except I think that the Communists have been pretty well cleaned out," Pearson objected. "Now it has got to the point where anyone who was sympathetic to Russia during the war is in danger of being called a Communist."[19]

The national mood had changed dramatically. At the end of World War II, when Pearson wrote columns critical of Russian demands in Europe, readers had sent angry letters condemning him for upsetting Soviet-American relations. Five years later, the mail supported Senator McCarthy and vehemently denounced anything remotely favorable to the Soviet Union. "In other words," Pearson concluded, "the pendulum of public opinion, having swung violently one way, has now swung just as violently the other way." Americans now hated Russia beyond the point of objectivity.[20]

The columnist remained cordial enough with FBI Director J. Edgar Hoover in 1950 to consult with him about Owen Lattimore. Hoover advised him that Louis Budenz, the former editor of the *Daily Worker* who had turned informant against the party, planned to testify that the leaders of the party told him that they had used Lattimore. "Hoover doesn't think Lattimore was a member of the party but that he was easily used and is a poor security risk," Pearson noted in his diary. Budenz's testimony saved McCarthy from humiliation and emboldened him to escalate his crusade.[21]

Having revealed Lattimore's name, Pearson came to his defense and assailed McCarthy's financial ties to the Chinese Nationalists on Taiwan, known as the China Lobby. The attacks infuriated McCarthy. Assistant Attorney General Joseph Keenan warned Pearson that he overheard the senator threatening to bludgeon him. McCarthy, drinking heavily at a reception, bragged that he would be a hero to many senators if he could knock out his teeth, or break his ribs. The report steeled Pearson's determination to stand firm. "I will probably lose some newspapers and get some people mad," he noted in his diary, "but I wound up the radio program tonight with a comparison between Salem witch-burning and McCarthyism."[22]

Joe McCarthy renewed his threat in May 1950, while attending the Gridiron Club's annual white-tie dinner—where Washington reporters entertained politicians to relax tensions between them. McCarthy spotted Pearson, put his hand on his arm, and promised, "Someday I'm going to get hold of you and really break your arm." "I couldn't tell if he was joking or not," Pearson commented. That December, McCarthy made good on his threats by assaulting Pearson at the Sulgrave Club.[23]

Unrepentant after the beating, McCarthy rose in the Senate three days later to denounce Drew Pearson as the "voice of international Communism." Rather than accuse Pearson of being a card-carrying Communist, McCarthy portrayed him as having been manipulated by Communists on his staff, naming Andrew Older and David Karr. The stridently anti-Communist columnist Westbrook Pegler applauded McCarthy for challenging Pearson's "sly service to the Communist line," and discrediting Pearson's "strange, dangerous power to intimidate public men and to sway public opinion by means of deliberate, wanton lies, many of them plainly malicious." Pearson's attorneys later learned that McCarthy's speech had been written by James Walters, a reporter for the *Washington Times-Herald* who had worked as a temporary investigator for HUAC and gotten access to the committee's file on Karr. Walters bragged to colleagues at the *Times-Herald* that he had enough on Drew Pearson to ruin him.[24]

Although the two reporters were no longer on his staff, Pearson came to their defense. He issued a statement to the press explaining that Andrew Older had joined the Communist Party as a young man and been trying to extricate himself. But he insisted that David Karr was not a Communist.

Pearson pointed out that he had sent his leg man to Europe to organize the arrival of the Friendship Train that provided American aid to France and Italy and counteracted Communist endeavors in those countries. As for himself, he asserted that he was not and had never been a member of the Communist Party, and that he had been personally active in the fight against national and international communism. Pearson then challenged the senator to repeat his charges off the Senate floor where congressional immunity would no longer protect him. "I hope he will do so since I will then be able to sue him for libel." McCarthy replied that he would do so only if Pearson agreed to make all his and his wife's property available as collateral for a countersuit.[25]

Unable to circumvent congressional immunity, in 1951 Pearson sued Joe McCarthy for the assault and battery at the Sulgrave Club dinner, and for conspiring with conservative journalists and the *Washington Times-Herald*, in restraint of trade in violation of the antitrust laws, to discredit his column and drive him out of business. The unwieldy case drifted for years until being settled quietly in 1956, after the *Times-Herald* was purchased by the *Washington Post*, which carried the "Merry-Go-Round." As part of the settlement, Senator McCarthy sent Pearson a private letter of apology.[26]

On the Fourth of July 1951, a reporter in Madison, Wisconsin, solicited signatures on a petition that consisted of the Declaration of Independence and the Bill of Rights. All but one of the 112 people he approached refused to sign. Another reporter's repetition of the experiment in New Orleans produced similar results. Drew Pearson cited these dismal incidents in his column. "McCarthyism," he wrote, "had instilled such fear of any free doctrine or belief, that people were afraid to sign anything having to do with freedom."[27]

Having lost his radio sponsor to McCarthy's attacks, Pearson began hearing from some of his Republican editors who demanded that he stop writing about McCarthy in the column. Either because of public pressure or because of their own agreement with McCarthy, a few daily newspapers in Boston, Kansas City, Cleveland, and other cities canceled the "Merry-Go-Round." Pearson and his syndicate compensated by recruiting a larger number of local weeklies, crafting a condensed version of the week's columns to meet their needs. That Pearson kept up the fight despite the loss to his income impressed Jack Anderson, who concluded that "Drew's defenses were strong because he had lived his life as though in preparation for the contest now upon him," having coped for years with suspicious editors, angry politicians, and expensive libel suits.[28]

Persistence in the face of setbacks made Pearson a uniquely dangerous opponent for the Wisconsin senator. McCarthy had proved adept at manipulating his media coverage by making charges without substantiation, relying on hyperbole and half-truths, and rephrasing statements that witnesses before his investigating committee had made, giving them sinister twists. His victims lacked similar access to national publicity to make their rebuttals. But Drew Pearson's column appeared across the nation, as did his radio and TV broadcasts. He shunned the type of blind objectivity that led reporters to quote McCarthy without questioning the merits of his charges. Being a columnist gave Pearson a license for advocacy. Rather than repeating McCarthy's press releases, he called out their misstatements and lies.[29]

Revealing the truth required solid facts, and Pearson dispatched Jack Anderson to gather evidence. In that quest, Anderson teamed with Wisconsin reporter Ronald May to write the first biography of McCarthy. Anderson explored the senator's Capitol Hill reputation while May interviewed folks in McCarthy's hometown of Appleton. Most book publishers shied away from anything that might offend McCarthy, but the Unitarian-operated *Beacon Press* agreed to publish the biography in 1952. This connection gave the authors ready-made audiences for book talks at Unitarian churches, and it launched Jack Anderson's secondary career as a lecturer. Like Pearson, Anderson was as flamboyant on stage as he was quiet in person. He practiced the passionate oratory he had developed during his days as a Mormon missionary. *McCarthy: The Man, the Senator, the "Ism"* outlined McCarthy's exaggerations, fabrications, and contempt for the law. Hastily written, the book contained some errors and adopted what one reviewer called "jeepers-creepers-how-the-wind-blew prose," but it became an instant bestseller. True to form, McCarthy fired back by claiming that Jack Anderson had once joined a Communist organization to spy on it. Anderson called that bunk. "I have never joined any organization even remotely tainted with communism for any purposes whatsoever," he responded. "McCarthy obviously dragged my name into this affair in a left-handed attempt to discredit my book." (The FBI took the accusation seriously enough to track Anderson's every move, keeping him under surveillance even during his visits to the Capitol.)[30]

Drew Pearson similarly came under assault from the McCarthyites. He filed a lawsuit against a Pennsylvania paper, the weekly *Jefferson Republican*, for calling him a "Commie," and did not drop the suit until its publisher agreed to pay court costs and its editor declared that Pearson was "neither a Communist nor a Communist sympathizer." The *Atlanta Journal* also printed an apology after one of its typesetters changed "Columnist Drew Pearson" to "Communist Drew Pearson."[31]

On a broadcast that Pearson staged as a staff conference, Jack Anderson urged Pearson to answer the charges that he was a Communist. Pearson dismissed these allegations as ridiculous and countered with a list of reasons why he was anything but a Communist. Topping the list was his claim to have warned that Harry Dexter White was "un-American." White, a former Treasury Department official and "Merry-Go-Round" source, had been accused of providing information to Soviet espionage agents. Despite the evidence against him, he denied the accusation in his testimony before the House Un-American Activities Committee (HUAC) and died of a heart attack a few days later. In the "Merry-Go-Round", Pearson recalled that it was at the UN conference in San Francisco in April 1945 that he first became suspicious of White. He could not prove that White was spying, "but it certainly looked as if he was one of the men the Russians came to for secret information in Washington. The evidence was such that I took it to my old friend, Fred Vinson, who had just been made Secretary of the Treasury." He dated this event before the FBI had submitted its own report on White. Monitoring the broadcasts and columns, FBI agents suspected that Pearson had reshaped his memory to fit the times, recalling that even after the UN conference they had trailed White to Pearson's Georgetown address. In his diary, however, Pearson recalled that White had showed up at his home uninvited, to complain about a column he considered unfair to the Russians.[32]

The Red Scare made the FBI less cooperative with the muckraking columnist. A friend of Jack Anderson's, the lobbyist Irving Davidson, informed FBI agents that it was his impression—although he could not put his finger on anything definite—that Pearson's office was no longer as friendly to the bureau as it had once been. J. Edgar Hoover now categorized Pearson as mouthing the same sentiments as the Communists and the "bleeding hearts." When he learned that Anderson was trying to find evidence of FBI assistance to McCarthy, Hoover exploded that "This fellow Anderson and his ilk have minds that are lower than the regurgitated filth of vultures."[33]

During the 1952 elections, Pearson sided with candidates most likely to keep McCarthy in check. On the Republican side, he accused Senator Robert Taft of staunchly supporting Senator McCarthy and promoted Taft's rival, General Dwight D. Eisenhower, for the presidential nomination. But Pearson felt leery of Eisenhower's running mate, Senator Richard Nixon, who had acquired national fame as an anti-Communist member of HUAC and used the issue to win a Senate seat from California.[34]

Eisenhower's coattails restored Republican majorities in Congress, having the perverse effect of elevating Senator McCarthy to chair the Senate's Permanent Subcommittee on Investigations. Although that subcommittee had previously devoted its attentions to uncovering fraud and waste in government, McCarthy interpreted its mandate broadly enough to investigate anything he wanted. For his chief counsel, he recruited a twenty-six-year-old federal prosecutor, Roy Cohn. "They're trying to push me off the Communist issue," McCarthy told Cohn. "The sensible thing for me to do, they say, is start investigating the agriculture program or find out how many books they've got bound upside down at the Library of Congress. They want me to play it safe. I fought this Red issue. I won the primary on it. I won the election on it, and don't see anyone else around who intends to take it on. You can be sure that as chairman of this committee this is going to be my work."[35]

Chairman McCarthy could browbeat opponents in public and then embrace them in private. He seemed genuinely puzzled when someone he attacked gave him the cold shoulder. It was never clear whether McCarthy was a cynic, promoting his own career, or a true believer who became mesmerized by the spotlight. No matter what his motivations, his wantonly destructive tactics recklessly damaged lives and reputations. Skilled as a self-publicist, McCarthy proved inept as an investigator. He made poor staff choices, insufficiently prepared for hearings, and relied on his ability to bully witnesses in closed hearings and later twist their testimony when he stood before the press.[36]

McCarthy's name appeared regularly in the "Washington Merry-Go-Round" between 1950 and 1954, always in a negative light. Pearson paid similarly close attention to Roy Cohn and his friend G. David Schine, an unpaid consultant to the subcommittee, who traveled to Europe to investigate whether the US Information Agency's libraries stocked any books by Communist authors. On his broadcast, Pearson reported that the self-indulgent pair had run up a large bill at the Paris Hotel where they stayed for only sixteen hours. The American embassy had agreed to pay the bill, which meant, Pearson told his audience, that "you and I will probably foot the bill."[37]

Jack Anderson secured an interview with David Schine by identifying himself as a reporter for the Bell Syndicate rather than mentioning his connection to Drew Pearson. He encountered "a handsome, haughty kid" who bragged about writing an anti-Communist pamphlet that was distributed to all the guests at his family's hotel chain. Given Schine's age, Anderson questioned his draft status. Schine portrayed himself as a veteran, explaining that he had served in the Army Transport Service. "Were you in the army?" Anderson asked. "We carried army supplies," Schine replied, fudging his civilian status. "I had an army assimilated rank." When further pressed, Schine claimed instead to have been in the merchant marine (in fact, he sought a deferment from the army by enrolling in the Merchant Marine Academy, but never attended). The "Merry-Go-Round"'s inquiry into Schine's draft status would later play a critical part in the unraveling of McCarthyism.[38]

Like Pearson, Senator McCarthy depended on informants, some of whom proved unreliable—none more so than Harvey Matusow. In 1946, Matusow had joined the Communist Party, and in 1950 he offered himself to the FBI as an informer. Government investigators employed him to identify anyone he had known in the party, paying him monthly fees to cover his expenses. He exaggerated freely to satisfy their expectations and stay on the payroll. Brash and arrogant, Matusow made headlines with accusations about massive Communist infiltration of the news media, from the editorial staff of *Time* magazine to the New York bureau of the Associated Press. Pearson doubted his veracity. In a May 1953 radio broadcast, he noted that Matusow claimed that 126 Communists were working on the Sunday edition of the *New York Times*, which at the time had a staff of 93.[39]

After Matusow married one of Senator McCarthy's wealthiest supporters, his bride encouraged him to stop testifying at public hearings. But he had grown so addicted to publicity that he sacrificed his marriage and luxurious lifestyle to remain in the spotlight. Matusow later explained that he shaped his charges to attract the greatest media attention, coloring his testimony with half-truths, distortions, and innuendo. That pattern lasted until he underwent a religious conversion to Mormonism, thanks to Jack Anderson. Increasingly remorseful over his dishonest testimony, and having come to trust Pearson and Anderson implicitly, he began funneling them information. "When I was working with McCarthy," he later told his publisher, "I gave them a lot of stuff on Joe." As Pearson described it, the former McCarthy witness "decided he had been engaged in torturing innocent people, joined a church, confessed all, and swore under oath that he had lied" in his accusations.[40]

Harvey Matusow offered an affidavit to the *New York Times* about how he had lied, but its editors preferred to wait for *False Witness*, the tell-all book he was writing, to appear. Other reporters similarly sat on his story— all except Pearson and Anderson. "I went down to Washington, where I'd been very friendly with Drew Pearson," Matusow recalled. "I wrote the sample chapter of *False Witness* plus the outline on Jack Anderson's type-writer. Jack Anderson actually helped me with proofreading and stuff." Angus Cameron, a book editor who had been fired from his previous job as a victim of Redbaiting, read in the "Merry-Go-Round" that Matusow had confessed to lying. Now working for another publisher, he jumped at the opportunity. "So, we decided, hell, we'll get that book," he later recalled, "we can make these bastards eat crow." With its admission of perjury, however, the tell-all book led to Matusow's imprisonment. He spent much of the rest of his life as a circus clown. At his death, he was survived by his eleventh wife, indicating that he lied to more than just congressional committees.[41]

McCarthy and his staff concocted any number of ways to silence Drew Pearson's relentless criticism. Donald Surine, a former FBI agent working for McCarthy's subcommittee, knew that the bureau was tracking leaks from the Atomic Energy Commission. He called their attention to a chauffeur for AEC commissioners who had once driven for Pearson. The FBI had the man transferred to driving trucks. Another McCarthy staffer approached Peggy Palmer, widow of former Attorney General A. Mitchell Palmer, and offered to hire her "at most any price," if she could provide damaging information about the columnist, with whom she socialized. Palmer declined and notified the FBI, saying that she was "very fond of Drew Pearson and considers Mrs. Pearson like a member of the family." She told agents she had no unfavorable information about Pearson, and if she did, she would never furnish it to Joe McCarthy.[42]

Senator McCarthy even attempted to have Pearson indicted for violating the Espionage Act. When Roy Cohn had earlier worked as a Justice Department prosecutor, he had tried to get Pearson prosecuted for revealing military secrets, but his superiors ruled out the idea. After Cohn joined with Chairman McCarthy, they revived the charges. Although they were without merit, the allegations offered a glimpse into how Pearson's leg men operated, and how McCarthy manipulated the truth.[43]

As chair of the Permanent Investigating Subcommittee, McCarthy interrogated hundreds of witnesses in closed-door executive session, winnowing them down to those he would call before the cameras in public hearings. Witnesses who either groveled or stonewalled at these rehearsals were more likely to be summoned to appear in public as foils for the chairman; those who defended themselves with restraint usually got excused. An executive session "didn't really mean a closed session," army counsel John G. Adams recorded, "since McCarthy allowed in various friends, hangers-on, and favored newspaper reporters." Nor did it mean secret, because reporters would wait outside the door of each closed meeting for Senator McCarthy to come out and tell them what transpired. That strategy permitted him to rephrase the testimony, making it sound more dramatic and ominous, with little chance of rebuttal from the witnesses, who usually fled. "The 'secret' hearings were, after all, quite a show," Adams scoffed.[44]

Following a closed hearing on September 8, 1953, Senator McCarthy stepped outside the committee room to tell waiting reporters that a former employee of the War Munitions Board had been blackmailed into giving secret information on military arms production to Pearson's leg man Fred Blumenthal. As McCarthy sketched the story, Blumenthal had threatened to have the column attack the witness's superior officer unless he turned over classified information. The chairman indicated that he would not call the witness to appear at a public hearing unless "an espionage case is brought against Blumenthal and I think there should be, and against his boss Pearson who sent him there, the combination of espionage and blackmail, the Justice Department would have access to this and in any subsequent trial they might or might not use it." The senator predicted that once they started to expose a man with "a bad record as this Blumenthal apparently has," others among his victims would volunteer more information.[45]

McCarthy's assurances to the press had entirely misrepresented Donald Murray's testimony. The press officer for the Munitions Board had said that his boss appealed to him to try to mute the "Merry-Go-Round"'s criticism. Murray contacted Fred Blumenthal, who showed him information he had gotten elsewhere on how the production of military equipment had gotten bogged down. Blumenthal thought it likely that Pearson would run a story on it and asked if there was additional material available. According to Murray, Blumenthal never asked to see any classified documents. He was more interested in stories having to do with poor management than with national security. Murray swore that he had shown Blumenthal no secret information, and that nothing they discussed would have aided America's enemies.[46]

Donald Murray recalled another occasion when Fred Blumenthal came to his office asking about a report that tanks desperately needed in Korea were sitting at an arsenal in Detroit. Murray let him know that the tanks were awaiting modification and would be shipped when ready. As he often did, Senator McCarthy recast the testimony. "You find a fellow traveling around the building with confidential material," he confronted the witness. "You find him blackmailing you, if I may use the phrase, to get that information.

By blackmail, I am not referring to money blackmail but telling you, 'Unless you give me other information, I am going to print a bad story about your boss'" Instead, Murray denied being blackmailed, adding that Blumenthal had never threatened to write a story about him if he did not provide information. Nevertheless, the senator made his headlines by giving the press his fanciful version of the testimony, and then dropped the matter. Murray never testified in public; McCarthy never made a convincing case against Pearson and Blumenthal; and the Justice Department brought no charges against them.[47]

Privately, Pearson puzzled over what McCarthy was talking about. He checked his files and found a column on tank turrets, "which came from Don Murray . . . in the Munitions Board. Frankly, I don't think a jury would take action on that." Although Pearson had revealed secret documents in his column for decades, he began to worry that the climate of the Red Scare might put him in jeopardy. "Sure you printed classified material," Jack Anderson reassured him. "That was your job, digging up the inside news. But you always took great care not to print anything affecting the national security." Pearson indeed made a point of securing clearance from authorized spokesmen before revealing military stories drawn from classified records.[48]

On the radio, Pearson shared the news with his listeners that Senator McCarthy was trying to indict him for a story he had published two years earlier about the faulty manufacture of tanks. He noted that Walter Winchell, his old friend turned McCarthyite, had gleefully predicted his indictment. Pearson's former partner Robert Allen advised him that David Schine's family practically owned Winchell "because of his free boodling in their hotels, which is the real reason why he was been so all-out for those jackals."[49]

After McCarthy demanded that the Eisenhower administration prosecute Pearson, the columnist heard from sources inside the Justice Department that they had no incriminating evidence and might only submit a case in a pro forma manner. Pearson recognized that the case could jeopardize his status with some radio stations and newspapers, but he was not seriously worried. With Republicans now heading the Justice Department, Pearson assured Attorney General Herbert Brownell that he and his staff had acted responsibly. "I might say in passing that hardly a day passes that I do not discuss with certain public officials confidential matters which are not published," he added, ". . . and obviously no violation of the Espionage Act."[50]

Another ugly aspect of McCarthyism linked homosexuality to subversion, creating a "Lavender Scare" that paralleled the Red Scare. Some alarmists warned that Communists might blackmail homosexuals into betraying their country, and that their very nature might make them sympathetic to Marxism. "And here is why homosexual officials are a peril to us in the present struggle between West and East," a contributor to the anti-Communist tabloid *Human Events* argued in 1952: "members of one conspiracy are prone to join another conspiracy. This is one reason why so many homosexuals from being enemies of society in general, become enemies of capitalism in particular."[51]

Drew Pearson traded barbs with Joe McCarthy about each other's manhood. McCarthy often resorted to gay bashing, denouncing "those Communists and queers who have sold 400 million Asiatic people into atheistic slavery and have American people in a hypnotic trance, headed blindly toward the same precipice." He laced his speeches with references to "powder puff diplomacy" and accused his opponents of "softness" toward communism. In contrast, he portrayed himself in macho terms. Rooting out communism required him "to do a bare-knuckle job or suffer the same defeat that a vast number of well-meaning men have suffered over the past year. It has been a bare-knuckle job. As long as I remain in the Senate it will continue as a bare-knuckle job."[52]

In a May 1950 broadcast, Pearson warned that McCarthy's attacks on "sex perverts" in the State Department could soon backfire. He reported that one of McCarthy's staffers had been arrested for homosexual acts. McCarthy responded by accusing Pearson of being an unmanly degenerate enslaved by the Communists. Eager to discredit the columnist, a McCarthy researcher traveled to Reidsville, North Carolina, to unearth evidence concerning Pearson's arrest there in 1914. When Pearson and another teenager had bathed at a factory spigot after taking down the Chautauqua tents that night, they had been arrested for indecent exposure. A judge threw out the charge on the grounds a person had a right to get clean. Forty years later, McCarthy dangled threats about it. The senator told reporters that Pearson had sent one of his leg men to ask him not to use "certain photostats" that had found their way into his files. "I tell him here and now that if he sends another man to my office, either with threats or promises in regard to the use of those photostats," McCarthy intoned, "then on the next day those photostats will all be presented in the Senate." Without ever divulging what photostats he might have, McCarthy off the record spread false rumors that Pearson had been arrested for molesting an African American boy.[53]

Pearson compiled his own file on McCarthy's sexuality that included affidavits from men who claimed to have had relations with him, but never published those questionable allegations. The "Merry-Go-Round" generally avoided sexual gossip, and these accusations might also have offended some of the editors who published the column. Instead, Pearson passed the reports along to the editor and publisher of the *Las Vegas Sun*, Hank Greenspun, an ardent opponent of McCarthy, who used them in his own paper. McCarthy's staff provided the FBI with evidence that traced the *Sun*'s accusations back to Pearson and Anderson and encouraged the bureau to investigate. "Yes, and promptly," Director Hoover noted on the file, although nothing came of it. Nor did the accusations make any dent in McCarthy's popularity.[54]

Washingtonians also whispered about the personal relationship between the senator's aides Roy Cohn and David Schine. Senator McCarthy had grown increasingly dependent on Cohn, his chief counsel, while Cohn had grown increasingly obsessed with Schine. By the summer of 1953, Pearson had obtained Schine's draft records and launched a series of columns that pictured him as an otherwise healthy man who had gotten a medical deferment on suspicious grounds. Pearson even called Schine's draft board to demand that it reopen his case. Other reporters picked up the story until army doctors reexamined Schine and found him fit to serve. Senator McCarthy singled out Pearson for blame when the army drafted his aide.[55]

Immediately Roy Cohn began requesting weekend passes and other special privileges for Private Schine, who encouraged Cohn's indulgences but preferred dating voluptuous women—the reason for all those weekend passes. "For God's sake, don't put Dave in uniform and assign him back to my committee," McCarthy pleaded with the secretary of the army in a recorded telephone call. "If he could get off weekends—Roy—it is one of the few things I have seen him completely unreasonable about. He thinks Dave should be a general and work from the penthouse of the Waldorf."[56]

Pearson dated the beginning of the end for Senator McCarthy to December 1953, when the "Merry-Go-Round" broke the news that Private David Schine had been the object of favoritism since being drafted:

Gerald David Schine, the handsome, dreamy-eyed young man who gravitated around Europe at the taxpayers' expense on behalf of Joe McCarthy and who belatedly was drafted into the Army after various maneuvers and medical examinations, is now at Fort Dix, N.J. There, he has been the object of several phone conversations between his pal, Roy Cohn, and the commanding officer. . . . Two or three times a week for a while, Roy called the commanding officer to ask how Gerald David was getting along. "The Senator," said Cohn ominously, "wants to know." This had the desired effect among lower echelons at Fort Dix. Gerald David was kept off kitchen police, guard duty and other disagreeable chores.[57]

The column's revelation that Roy Cohn was intervening on behalf of Private Schine complicated Senator McCarthy's ongoing investigation of subversion within the Army Signal Corps. The army asserted that McCarthy was prolonging the investigation to blackmail it into giving Schine special treatment. McCarthy accused the army of holding Schine hostage to thwart him. The controversy triggered the nationally televised, three-month-long Army-McCarthy hearings, where McCarthy undermined his public image by exposing his bullying tactics and distorted evidence. Television viewers could see for themselves just what Pearson had been writing about for so long. The hearings culminated with army counsel Joseph Welch posing his searing question to the senator: "Have you no sense of decency?"[58]

On June 19, 1954, the staff of the Permanent Investigating Subcommittee planned to hold a party to celebrate the end of the Army-McCarthy hearings, sending out invitations in the form of subpoenas. They had to cancel that party because Wyoming Senator Lester Hunt committed suicide in the Senate Office Building that day. Months earlier, Earle Clements, who chaired the Senate Democratic Campaign Committee, had learned that two of McCarthy's supporters were blackmailing Hunt. Senators Styles Bridges of New Hampshire and Herman Welcker of Idaho told their colleague that they knew that his son had been arrested—but not prosecuted—on a morals charge and they would release this information to the press unless he resigned from the Senate. A vacancy would allow the Republican governor of Wyoming to appoint a replacement for Hunt, a Democrat, at a moment when the two parties were evenly divided in the Senate. Clements begged Hunt not to resign, arguing that his best chance to win reelection would be for the Republicans to use the story against him, calculating that it would surely backfire. But Hunt resisted this advice, worried about how the scandal would affect his wife.[59]

Senator Clements relayed the sordid story to Pearson, who admired Lester Hunt for having voted on the side of the underdog. Hunt seemed so emotionally spent, however, that Pearson withheld publication. Then McCarthy announced that he planned to investigate a senator who had fixed a case, an allusion to Hunt's son being let off with only a fine. After Hunt's suicide, Pearson wrote a column that laid out the facts of "one of the lowest types of political pressure this writer has seen in many years." The directors of the Bell Syndicate distributed the column but then had second thoughts about accusing two sitting senators of blackmail and considered asking editors not to print it. Sure that they could prove the truth, Pearson had a hard time convincing the syndicate, but finally got its directors to stand firm. Even so, most papers declined to publish the accusation, and some even berated him for dredging it up. One Wyoming newspaper decried that "the filth which at times is sent out by Drew Pearson is reprehensible."[60]

Other than Pearson's column, the news media largely shied away from delving into the cause of Lester Hunt's death. In 1959, *New York Times* correspondent Allen Drury wove a fictional account of a senator being blackmailed and committing suicide into his bestselling novel and later motion picture, *Advise and Consent*. Historians, biographers, novelists, and playwrights since then have relied on the details that only Pearson had the nerve to reveal.[61]

On radio and television, Pearson repeatedly assailed McCarthy and defended his victims. CBS reporter Edward R. Murrow usually gets the credit for highlighting the case of Annie Lee Moss by showing clips from her televised testimony in his national broadcast on March 16, 1954, but Drew Pearson invited Moss to appear in person on his TV program on April 4. The African American woman had once paid dues to a cafeteria workers' union that had Communists in its leadership, but she denied joining the party, paying dues, or subscribing to the *Daily Worker*. When she later took a job as a communications clerk at the Pentagon, a loyalty board investigated and cleared her, although the FBI had evidence from an informer that an Anna Lee Moss appeared in the Communist Party's membership rolls. McCarthy described Moss herself as "not of any great importance." What he wanted to know was: "Who in the military, knowing this lady was a Communist, promoted her from a waitress to a code clerk?" Although the army insisted that Moss was only a relay machine operator who could not decode the messages she transmitted, it transferred her to a supply room and then suspended her entirely. On Pearson's program, Moss related how difficult she had found it to get a hearing, and that when she did testify, Senator McCarthy had walked out before she finished. Since she hardly appeared a threat to national security, McCarthy could see that further interrogation would be a public relations disaster. When the uproar abated, the army found Moss another job.[62]

Having helped trigger the Army-McCarthy hearings, Pearson felt pessimistic about their results. On his television program he speculated that Senator McCarthy would reemerge with his feathers ruffled but relatively unscathed because the Senate acted as an exclusive club that protected its members. He expressed similar despair in July when Vermont Republican Senator Ralph Flanders filed a censure resolution against McCarthy, for behavior that ran contrary to Senate traditions. Pearson predicted that rather than confront McCarthy's misconduct, a majority of senators would try to duck voting on the resolution. His skepticism may have been his way of shaming the Senate into finally placing some restraints on their errant colleague. Still, Pearson's calls for censure infuriated some of his readers and listeners. A typical McCarthyite letter called him "a malicious contemptable LIAR [who] would smear anyone who opposed you. . . . Senator McCarthy is a honest God fearing MAN who is fighting the commies and their followers without gloves and no holds barred."[63]

During the summer and fall of 1954, Pearson devoted a score of columns to exposing the pressure being put upon senators to vote against McCarthy's censure, and reminding readers of the evidence against him. He kept up the drumbeat until December 1954, when the Senate voted 67 to 22 to censure Joseph R. McCarthy, demolishing his credibility. Reporters began ignoring his press releases or filing stories about him. President Eisenhower, who anticipated that the senator's influence would wane once he lost his headline allure, gloated that McCarthyism had become McCarthywasm. Denied the spotlight, McCarthy drank himself to an early death in 1957.[64] Pearson reported getting a surprise phone call from him not long before:

> Joe McCarthy telephoned me some days before he died. He and I had not conversed since I found myself looking in his face, arms pinned to my side, in the men's cloakroom of the Sulgrave Club. . . . Seven years had passed. Suddenly, I picked up the telephone to hear a cheery voice as if nothing had ever happened. "Drew," said the voice, "this is Joe McCarthy. Are you sitting down?" "Yes," I replied, also as if nothing ever happened. "I wanted to make sure you were sitting down, because if you were standing up you would faint," continued Joe. "I've just put your column in the Congressional Record. I haven't always agreed with your column," he said, "but in this case I'm sure it's completely accurate, and I wanted to tell you in advance what I'd done so you wouldn't faint."[65]

The column McCarthy liked so much had accused the United States of reneging on a commitment to Israel. "I suppose no one newspaperman suffered more economically than I did from Joe McCarthy," Pearson later reflected. "But I felt sorry for Joe in these latter years. He had been so famous once. He was so lonely later. He used to walk through the halls of Congress, a sheaf of handouts under his arm, offering them to newspapermen, offering to pose before TV cameras. But his press handouts hit the wastepaper basket and his face didn't appear on TV any more. . . . That was what killed Joe." His sympathetic column drove the McCarthyites wild. The editor of the New York *Mirror* advised him they had never received so many protests.[66]

Drew Pearson did as much as anyone to derail McCarthyism. Business executive William Benton, a Democrat who lost his Senate seat from Connecticut after clashing with McCarthy, asked Pearson how much he had suffered as a commentator. "My income dropped $100,000 a year, and I've been working harder than ever to keep my budget balanced," Pearson responded. "I no longer am on a network and have been unable to get any fat calf like yourself to sponsor me. But I do not regret the battle." In later years, Pearson continued to confront the John Birch Society and other lingering remnants of McCarthyism. "I recognize that I may be unpopular," he reflected. "During the old McCarthy days I was unpopular as hell with some people. I got a storm of letters in this office, and I am sure my editors got a storm of letters in protest. But I think history showed that I was right and McCarthy was wrong."[67]

Pearson's father, Paul M. Pearson, served as the first civilian governor of the American Virgin Islands. *Bain News Service, Library of Congress, LC-DIG-ggbain-18617*

Drew and Luvie Pearson after they returned to their home in Georgetown with her five-year-old son, Tyler, who had been abducted by his father, September 5, 1937. *Harris & Ewing, Library of Congress, LC-DIG-hec-23323*

Pearson's mother-in-law, newspaper publisher Eleanor "Cissy" Patterson, became his most vituperative critic. *New York World Telegram & Sun Collection, Library of Congress, LC-USZ62-12521*

Drew Pearson (*left*) and Robert S. Allen (*right*) interview FDR's campaign manager Jim Farley on their radio program in 1936. *Wisconsin Historical Society, WHS 74464*

President Roosevelt returns to Washington from a cruise with one of Pearson's chief targets, Secretary of State Cordell Hull, and two of his best sources, Under Secretary of State Sumner Welles and Assistant Secretary of War Louis Johnson. August 24, 1941. *Harris & Ewing, Library of Congress, LC-DIG-hec-47498*

Pearson broke the story that General George S. Patton had slapped two shell-shocked soldiers at army field hospitals in Europe. *Army Signal Corps, Library of Congress, LC-USZ62-25122*

Robert S. Allen left the "Merry-Go-Round" to rejoin the army during World War II and never resumed his partnership with Pearson. *Wisconsin Historical Society, WHS 126007*

Although Pearson made Harry Truman furious during his presidency, they reconciled in later years. *Harry S. Truman Presidential Library, 59-823*

Accusations in the "Merry-Go-Round" led to a congressional investigation of President Truman's military aide, General Harry H. Vaughn, here testifying before the Senate Subcommittee on Investigations. *Harry S. Truman Presidential Library, 99-1231*

Pearson targeted Secretary of Defense James Forrestal (*far right*), conferring here at a congressional hearing with Army Secretary Kenneth C. Royall, Navy Secretary John L. Sullivan, and Air Force Secretary Stuart Symington (*right to left*). *New York World Telegram & Sun, Library of Congress, LC-DIG-ds-07292*

Pearson works at his cluttered desk in his office at his Georgetown home, in December 1945. *Lyndon B. Johnson Presidential Library, B8514-4*

Two of Pearson's targets, Maryland Senator Millard Tydings (*left*) and Wisconsin Senator Joseph McCarthy, squared off against each other in 1950 over McCarthy's charges of subversion in the federal government. *Harris & Ewing, Senate Historical Office*

Press secretary Jim Hagerty, seated to the right of President Eisenhower during this press conference, oversaw his media relations. *Marion S. Trikosko, Library of Congress, LC-U9-1058-5 [P&P]*

President Kennedy met with Soviet Premier Nikita Khrushchev in Vienna, Austria, in June 1961. Soviet Foreign Minister Andrei Gromyko stands between them. *New York World Telegram & Sun, Library of Congress, LC-USZ62-135499*

Luvie Pearson snapped this photo of her husband (*left*) with Nikita Khrushchev during their meeting in August 1961. *Luvie Pearson, courtesy Drew Pearson Papers, Lyndon B. Johnson Presidential Library*

Pearson and his former leg man David Karr meet with President Johnson in the Oval Office in 1968. *Yoichi Okamoto, courtesy Lyndon B. Johnson Presidential Library, A6001-15a*

Luvie and Drew Pearson on the terrace at their Maryland farm, overlooking the Potomac River, in 1969. *Lyndon B. Johnson Presidential Library, B9481-8*

Pearson, who caused many headaches in Washington, endorsed Bromo-Seltzer for relief. *Jack Anderson Papers, MS2001, Series 10, Special Collections, George Washington University*

Jack Anderson (*standing*) became Drew Pearson's top leg man and eventual successor. *Walter Bennett/The LIFE Picture Collection via Getty Images*

Jack Anderson addressed the National Press Club in 1972 after winning a Pulitzer Prize. *William W. Fisk, National Press Club Archives*

8

Disliking Ike

WHAT WAS A DEMOCRATIC COLUMNIST to do when a Republican won the White House for the first time in twenty years? Unbound by the conventions of objective journalism, Drew Pearson had the liberty to express opinions and take political sides in his columns. As he assessed the election results in 1952, however, he knew that the largest share of his clients were Republican-leaning editors and publishers, as were many of his friends and sources, whom he wanted to keep. Rather than become a voice for the opposition, he intended to give the new administration the benefit of the doubt—while scrutinizing it thoroughly. So the "Washington Merry-Go-Round" expressed high hopes for General Dwight D. Eisenhower, assuring its readers that Ike would "lean over backwards against war," inject new blood into the government, and keep Senator McCarthy in check.[1]

"Eisenhower was the only President of the United States to spend eight years in office without referring to me in an uncomplimentary manner," Pearson liked to say. "I have not yet forgiven him." He repeated that joke often enough to indicate he really meant it. Ike's opaque leadership style and avoidance of public confrontations ran contrary to the columnist's quest for transparency and accountability. The columnist also found it hard to maintain his showmanship in that muted atmosphere. As he turned sixty, he reflected, "The fact that the Eisenhower Administration has been so mild-mannered has caused my wife to insinuate that perhaps the old man was slipping."[2]

Pearson's relations with Dwight Eisenhower started well but ended badly. They first met during the Hoover administration, when Ike was an inconspicuous major stationed at a desk outside the office of the army's chief of staff, General Douglas MacArthur. In 1932, unemployed military veterans, desperate to survive the Depression, marched on the capital to demand early payment of a promised bonus for their World War I service. They set up camp in Washington and lobbied Congress fruitlessly. President Hoover sent MacArthur to restore order, and the general dispatched mounted cavalrymen to route the Bonus Marchers and burn their shacks. On that dramatic day, Pearson spotted Major Eisenhower at police head-quarters, keeping track of the news while "reading westerns and studiously staying out of trouble." He got to know Eisenhower better after World War II, while Ike served as army chief of staff, although Pearson caused him grief by quoting from the army's classified records in the "Merry-Go-Round." Eisenhower ordered an investigation but failed to identify the leaker.[3]

In 1948, when Truman's reelection looked doubtful, the columnist promoted a movement to draft Eisenhower as a Democrat. He goaded his friend Harold Ickes into meeting with Eisenhower to urge him to run. Pearson then embarrassed Ickes by revealing the confidential conversation on his broadcast. Ickes denied knowing how Pearson could have gotten the information, after which Eisenhower wrote a letter to assure him that he had "lived too long in Washington to be amazed because some apparently impos-sible 'leak' occurs. I could not even take oath that I personally was not guilty of mentioning to some friend that you had been in my office. Conceivably I could have even given an indication of what we talked about."[4]

Eisenhower's diary shows that he listened to Pearson's broadcasts and read his column for political insights. Through Pearson he learned that Wisconsin Senator Joe McCarthy was "digging up alleged dirt with which to *smear* me *if* I run for Pres." (Denying this accusation, McCarthy called Pearson a "degenerate liar.")[5]

By 1951, Ike had become Supreme Commander Allied Forces Europe, leading NATO from its headquarters in Paris. Worried that the Republicans might nominate the isolationist Senator Robert Taft for president, Pearson encouraged his radio listeners to send Christmas cards urging Ike to be-come a candidate. Some 18,000 cards poured into his office, which he flew across the Atlantic to present to the general. Assessing the public's response, Pearson predicted that many people would cross party lines to vote for Ike. "It is probably brash of me to offer you advice," he told Eisenhower, "but I feel very deeply that, entirely aside from my personal regard for you, the foreign policies of the United States must not be reversed at this time." Aware of the good press Pearson was giving him, Eisenhower flattered him in return, assuring him that he found his estimate of national thinking and its effect on collective security convincing.[6]

As a New Dealer, Pearson really preferred Senator Estes Kefauver, a liberal Democrat from Tennessee, for president, and even drafted some campaign speeches for him. He felt confident that Kefauver had the know-how and idealism for the job, but worried that Republicans would likely tear him to pieces. The country needed unity, which pointed to Eisenhower.[7]

Pearson returned to Paris for another meeting in April 1952, this time to warn Eisenhower that Senator Taft's allies intended to "steal" the delegates from the Southern states, where Republican candidates rarely prevailed and whose delegates could be swayed by patronage promises. He advised Ike to have his supporters in the Senate call for an investigation (and admitted that he had already talked to several senators about doing just that), assuring him that there was nothing that Democratic senators enjoyed more than investigating Southern Republicans. Pearson recalled that he had earlier encouraged Eisenhower to run as a Democrat. The general replied that he thought a party change would be necessary to give Washington "a good clearing out, at least for four years." The meeting helped convince Ike that if he waited for the Republican convention to draft him, Senator Taft would likely prevail. In June, Ike retired from the military to return home and campaign for the nomination.[8]

During the national party conventions in 1952, Pearson and other veteran radio news broadcasters found themselves competing at a disadvantage with a new generation of television news reporters. The dean of the radio commentators, H. V. Kaltenborn, complained that television technology required too much nervous energy for him to do "anything important in this new form of radio." Radio newscasters scoffed that TV offered only the novelty of putting pictures to headlines, but the trend was unstoppable. Attempting to make the leap, Drew Pearson staged *Pearson's Parade*, his first TV show, while covering the conventions, but his hot radio style did not transfer well to the cool new medium. He pronounced his performance "a dubious success."[9]

After Eisenhower won the Republican nomination, Pearson remained favorably inclined toward him, but not toward his running mate, Richard Nixon. He had distrusted Nixon for what he saw as the ruthless tactics he used while running for the House and Senate. Nixon had been a member of Congress for only six months when he sent a mock letter of congratulations to other House colleagues whom Pearson had criticized in the column: "Now that you have been attacked by that arch character assassin and truth distorter, I am confident that your ratings . . . will be even higher than in the past."[10]

Richard Nixon believed that Pearson's animosity stemmed mostly from the Hiss-Chambers controversy. Whittaker Chambers testified before the House Un-American Activities Committee that he had been a Soviet agent in the 1930s and named former State Department official Alger Hiss as a clandestine contact. Liberals generally accepted Hiss's declaration of innocence, but Nixon sided with Chambers and procured some of the evidence that led to Hiss's conviction for perjury. Pearson took the charges against Hiss seriously but also regarded Nixon as a headline hunter with dubious ethics. After the Hiss-Chambers hearings, Pearson published a column portraying the congressman as a puppet of the "real estate lobby," claiming that he had allowed lobbyists to write statements for him. Outraged, Nixon sent a telegram to his staff to investigate the matter, signaling that he planned to demand a public retraction. His staff had to admit that Pearson got the story right. They had indeed allowed the lobbyist's statement to be published over Nixon's name. "I am afraid that we might let you in for further unfair treatment if we were to demand a retraction," a staffer advised. No matter the merits of the accusation, Nixon saw himself as the victim and Pearson the perpetrator.[11]

In 1952, Republicans ran on a platform of Korea, Communism, and Corruption, owing the corruption issue in large part to the "Merry-Go-Round"'s accounts of the Truman administration's mink coats and deep freezers. That September, Pearson boarded Eisenhower's campaign train just as three of his competitors, the columnists Stewart Alsop, Doris Fleeson, and Marquis Childs, were disembarking. "After they left and I arrived, the biggest event in the history of campaign trains and possibly the biggest event in 75 years of American history occurred when the Nixon storm broke and Eisenhower was called upon to dump his running mate," Pearson exulted. He had picked up revelations that the vice presidential candidate had benefited from a secret fund financed by wealthy contributors. When Nixon learned that Pearson was on his trail, he had William P. Rogers (a Nixon ally who was also one of Pearson's libel lawyers) pass the word that if Pearson published this story, Nixon would retaliate by branding him a Communist. Jack Anderson relayed the message to Pearson. "All right, I'll change the story," the columnist reacted. "I'll make it stronger." Before they could nail down the facts, however, a reporter for the *New York Post* broke the news first.[12]

Pearson closely monitored the Republican ticket's stand on McCarthyism. He learned that Ike's campaign staff had quarreled over how to handle the Wisconsin senator. One faction wanted to stage a showdown at a campaign stop in Milwaukee. Eisenhower instead accepted the advice of other aides who sought to avoid a confrontation entirely by deleting from his speeches any criticism of McCarthy or praise for General George C. Marshall, Ike's wartime mentor. McCarthy had wildly accused Marshall of having aided international communism in "a conspiracy so immense and an infamy so black as to dwarf any such venture in the history of man." Although seething, the candidate agreed to remain silent.[13]

Eisenhower's kowtowing to McCarthy cost him Pearson's support. "I had already come to the conclusion that Ike had no guts," he later wrote. "This confirmed it." The liberal instincts he had previously detected in Eisenhower seemed to have been "put on the shelf by those around him." Pearson's growing disillusionment with the Republican ticket prompted a dozen papers to cancel the "Merry-Go-Round." Other editors who liked Ike simply chose not to run Pearson's unfavorable columns.[14]

During his broadcast on the Sunday before the election in 1952, with the polls still close, Pearson predicted Eisenhower's victory. He assumed that the undecided vote that had gone to the Democrats four years earlier would swing to the Republicans this time. He also calculated if he was wrong, he could still live with his Democratic friends, but if he called the election incorrectly for Adlai Stevenson, "I can never live with my Eisenhower friends." Three days later, Ike won in a landslide.[15]

Eisenhower's presidency soon made the columnist nostalgic for Harry Truman. As a general, Ike had established warm relations with the newsmen who covered him under tight wartime censorship, but he would never be as open with reporters in peacetime. "His press relations are pleasant and cordial," Pearson judged, "but they are played according to his rules." The most remarkable aspect of the new administration was how well it kept secrets. Eisenhower pursued a significant share of his foreign policy through covert intelligence operations in Iran, Guatemala, Cuba, the Congo, and Southeast Asia. Those around the president adopted his penchant for secrecy. Ike's national security adviser, Robert Cutler, seemed to regard it as an insult if reporters dared approach him.[16]

Eisenhower's displeasure over unauthorized disclosures prompted New York Times columnist Arthur Krock to warn that a leak-free administration was an unattainable goal. Even if the White House sat on a story, members of Congress would inevitably keep reporters posted when it suited their purpose. In his column, Krock predicted that reporters would intensify their efforts to break through any curtain of secrecy. Leaks were "usually harmless," Krock advised, "and the intolerable alternative is total secrecy."[17]

At National Security Council meetings, Eisenhower vented his irritation whenever leaks appeared in Pearson's columns and griped that the FBI ought to get to the bottom of it. He assumed that the culprits were some clerks far down the line who talked loosely. A memorandum of one NSC meeting noted: "The President observed philosophically that he supposed that if one were engaged in intelligence activity there was reason to read Drew Pearson's column, but he could think of no other valid reason."[18]

Eisenhower's team succeeded in plugging leaks largely because of their determined gatekeeper, press secretary James Hagerty. Himself a former reporter, Hagerty knew what the press corps desired and spoon-fed it to them. For eight years he returned their phone calls and usually answered their questions. He assured reporters that he was there to serve them: "After all, you're my boys." Drew Pearson both admired and tangled with Hagerty, calling him the most efficient and ruthless press secretary who had ever operated in the White House, also one who willingly deceived the public. It did not help that Ike relegated his quarrels with the media to his press secretary. The absence of presidential involvement diminished the story. "In all frankness," Pearson later concluded, "I think he was wise."[19]

Jim Hagerty enjoyed total access to Eisenhower, spoke with authority, and allowed himself to be quoted on tough issues, which kept the president above the fray. A reporter who wanted to talk to anyone at the White House had to go through Hagerty, and usually got no further than him. If a cabinet member blundered, Hagerty would produce a press release to reshape the story and distance the president from any negative publicity. He manufactured favorable stories to distract attention from unfavorable ones. If all else failed, he was willing to fall on his sword for his chief. Once when Hagerty commented that if he told the press what Eisenhower wanted him to say, the reporters would give him hell, Ike patted him on the back and said, "My boy, better you than me."[20]

To protect the president, Hagerty lashed out at Pearson. Once, when the press secretary thought that the columnist had broken a White House release date by reporting a story prematurely, he delivered "a nasty lecture off-the-record about me," Pearson noted in his diary. Later in the afternoon, when the editor of the *Washington Post* set him straight, Hagerty phoned to apologize. On another occasion, the United Press veteran White House correspondent Merriman Smith berated Pearson for having mentioned him by name in a column. "For God's sake, don't mention me anymore. Every time you do, you get me in Dutch," said Smith. "Jim Hagerty accused me of leaking to you. If you are going to say anything, say something nasty."[21]

Recalling how he had alienated Harry Truman with only the slightest criticism of his wife, Pearson flattered Mamie Eisenhower. He recounted the war years when she lived alone in Washington while Ike commanded troops abroad, discreetly omitting the reports he had collected about Mamie's drinking during those lonely days. Nor did he write what he knew about Ike's contemplating a divorce in order to marry his wartime driver, Kay Summersby. He had also picked up rumors of Eisenhower's heart condition, but his radio network had balked at letting him mention this on the air. "Of course, it should have been mentioned before he was elected," he reflected. "I hinted at it as best I could, but tempers run so high that people won't believe you even if you do try to report a candidate's health."[22]

For twenty years, Pearson had relied on personal friendships with cabinet members to supply inside news to the column, but he found it harder to establish confidences with those around Ike. When the incoming secretary of agriculture, Ezra Taft Benson, met with the outgoing Charles Brannan, Benson asked whether his family could use the secretary's official car and chauffeur. He was chagrined when a version of this private conversation made it into Pearson's column, "intimating that I was in the job for all I could get." Benson stewed about the column until Pearson visited him one day with a proposal about food distribution. Rather than hear his ideas, the secretary lectured the columnist that he had misinformed his readers about the farm program, the Agriculture Department, and Benson personally. That closed another door for him.[23]

Once when a staff member quoted something in Pearson's column, the president "blew his top," according to notes of the meeting that Vice President Nixon took. Ike fumed that he wished everyone in his administration "would quit reading the columnists and quit reporting such incidents to him." The president was determined to "cool it" (in Jim Hagerty's words) and avoid controversy wherever possible. He accepted and expanded New Deal reforms rather than fighting to repeal them, committing congressional Republicans to legislation they had fought against for a generation. The status quo in domestic policy enabled Ike to win Democratic support for his foreign policies. Eisenhower's centrist, pragmatic approach worked well for him, but it did not generate much compelling news for a columnist who depended on controversy. The president's preference for operating from behind the scenes left the columnist and the public less than fully informed. From what he could see, Pearson believed that Eisenhower delegated too much and was unaware of much that was going on within his administration. He thought that the rest of the Washington press corps shielded

Ike because they liked him too much. "Few people realize how little time Eisenhower spends at work." Pearson grumbled. "He golfs at least three days a week."[24]

Adding to his sour mood, cancellations of the column were rising at an alarming rate. "I don't know whether it's the Littell suit or criticism of Eisenhower, or the difficulty of getting inside news," he puzzled. But his former leg man David Karr summed up the column's slippage as "No news and poorly written."[25]

The Littell case Pearson mentioned was the only libel suit he ever had to settle, paradoxically losing to a former friend. Pearson had earlier praised Norman Littell as FDR's "two-fisted young Assistant Attorney General" and invited him to relax at his farm. Littell later quit the Justice Department in a noisy feud with Attorney General Francis Biddle—one of Pearson's best sources in the cabinet—and drifted politically to the right. He got on the wrong side of Pearson's anti-colonial sentiments by defending Dutch rule in Indonesia. In the column, Pearson publicly accused Littell of serving as a propagandist for the Dutch government and not registering as a foreign lobbyist. In a radio broadcast, Pearson further called Littell a lobbyist for the Polish embassy and accused him having helped the Communist spy, Gerhardt Eisler, escape from the United States. Littell sued Pearson for libel and defamation, claiming that he had never worked for the Dutch government and for implying that he was pro-Communist. He asked for $600,000 in damages.[26]

With a little help from Truman's Justice Department, which slipped his attorney information on Pearson from its own files, Littell won his case. A jury awarded him $50,000 in the Dutch case and $1 in punitive damages. Pearson wanted to appeal, but his lawyers convinced him that it would be much cheaper to settle. They reminded him that Littell was demanding that newspapers that carried the "Merry-Go-Round" print retractions, and Pearson agreed not to appeal in order to protect his subscribers. Littell was "bombarding some of the newspapers in an effort to pressure me," he recorded, "and in order to save my newspapers further headaches, I have finally, at least to some extent, knuckled under." Although much of the payment was tax-deductible, the $40,000 settlement and $15,000 in legal fees required him to mortgage his Maryland farm.[27] Years later, Littell's lawyer Edward Bennett Williams confided to Luvie Pearson that Littell never should have won that case. "Drew didn't do anything wrong and by the time the case was over, I hated my client and I loved Drew," he said. Williams thereafter became one of Pearson's sources for Washington gossip.[28]

Simultaneously, Pearson had to defend himself against a defamation suit brought by Mary Gariepy, a Michigan woman he had named in his broadcasts. The Internal Revenue Service was prosecuting her former husband, and he testified that Father Charles Coughlin had paid him $68,000 for alienating Mrs. Gariepy's affections. Pearson repeated this story on the air to embarrass the pro-Franco, antisemitic Father Coughlin, but Mary Gariepy protested that the broadcast implied she had been an unchaste wife. Pearson based his defense on his First Amendment rights to publish what he believed was in the public's interest. A lower court ruled in his favor, but the District of Columbia Court of Appeals reversed the decision, arguing that question was "not whom they aimed at but whom they hit." After a second trial resulted in a hung jury, Mary Gariepy sued again. The case stirred support for Father Coughlin among the Catholic hierarchy and helped scare off Pearson's radio sponsor at the time, Lee Hats. After several more years of litigation, a jury found for Pearson and ordered Gariepy to pay the court costs. "I sometimes wonder how many days of my life I have spent in court," Pearson confided in his diary. "More cases have been named for me in the District of Columbia court than anyone else so far. I may have pioneered some new libel law, but I would just as soon forgo this distinction."[29]

On top of these libel suits, Senator Joe McCarthy pressed the Justice Department to prosecute Pearson for publishing military secrets. Just the threat of such legal actions caused several of his radio stations to cancel his program, and more papers threatened to drop the column. Pearson also found it hard to attract new sponsors at a time when so many business leaders were rallying for Eisenhower, which further diminished his income.[30]

In 1954, the Republican National Committee leaked a report of Pearson's tax problems to the conservative *Chicago Tribune*. The Internal Revenue Service claimed that he owed $15,290 (nearly four times the average American's annual salary at the time). The dispute involved $30,000 that he received from Lee Hats when it canceled its contract to sponsor his radio program. Pearson insisted that the money represented nontaxable payments for the damage to his reputation. After more than a year of negotiation he got the claim cut in half, but with lawyers' fees it still resulted in a financial setback.[31]

Further financial woes arose from Pearson's former partner, Bob Allen. They had remained friendly after Allen returned from the war, and he occasionally substituted for Pearson on his radio broadcasts and in the column. In 1954 the two talked of Allen once again becoming co-author of the column, but nothing came of the idea. For tax purposes, Pearson was paying Allen annual sums to buy out his co-ownership of the "Merry-Go-Round," but as Pearson's income declined, he found it difficult to meet the payments. "Bob Allen is chewing nails over my lag in paying him," Pearson moaned. Later he noted that Allen wanted $100,000 for his share of the column's trademark.[32]

Compounding his financial travails was the demise of so many afternoon newspapers that had subscribed to the column. During the 1950s, television's evening news programs steadily drained advertising away from once profitable papers. Revenue from Pearson's radio shows also diminished in the TV era, and his attempted transfer to television was less than stellar.[33]

Faced with declining income, Pearson considered an offer from the publisher of the sleazy and sensationalist *Confidential* magazine, Robert Harrison, to produce a Washington version called *Drew Pearson's News Beat*. Unlike its parent magazine, it would be devoted to cleaning up corruption, rather than sex. Pearson recalled that he had once played with the idea of creating a *Washington Merry-Go-Round* magazine to be circulated on the day of Franklin Roosevelt's inauguration in 1933 but had gotten too busy writing a column to start a magazine. "Now with more and more newspapers folding and with more and more papers refusing to print the truth," he ruminated, "I am sorely tempted by the magazine. But it would ruin me to be associated with Harrison." He wisely chose to stick with his corruption-fighting column.[34]

The hunt for big scoops to boost the column sometimes led to big embarrassments. Pearson began the election year of 1956 with a dramatic prediction that President Eisenhower would not run again. He made that mistake based on three clues: "First, a remark he once made to me that he wanted to be a one-term President; second, on his health; third, on the fact that he never seemed particularly happy in dealing with the political headaches that bedevil a President." He resisted making a judicious retreat until Eisenhower's announcement that he would run proved him wrong. "Having stuck my neck out, the old Pearson stubbornness my wife complains of got the better of me," he explained, "and I came crashing down with the limb I had gone out on."[35]

Then, a week before the election, in which Democrats had made an issue out of Eisenhower's dicey health, Pearson reported that the president had collapsed while on a campaign tour. Press secretary Jim Hagerty denounced the allegation, and the columnist's leg men could find no evidence to support it. They would refer to it ever after as "the boo-boo."[36]

It will be vigorously denied but President Eisenhower apparently suffered a mild relapse on his western campaign trip. . . . Whether it was campaign exhaustion or something more serious, it hit Ike while he was driving back to the airport from Minneapolis. He suddenly turned to others in the car and announced, "I can't take any more of this. Let's get out of here." The presidential limousine took off from the motorcade and sped to the airport, followed by a Secret Service car. Ike was hustled into his plane. . . . At the next stop, Seattle, Ike clenched his teeth and waved to the crowd along the route to the hotel. Then he collected himself in his suite for 24 hours, seeing no one but his family and physician.[37]

A reliable source in Minneapolis had alerted Pearson to Eisenhower's shaky condition. But Jim Hagerty pointed to news film that showed that the president's limousine had not pulled out of the motorcade and maintained that the president had kept to his schedule without interruption. "I am trying not to get mad," Hagerty told the press, "but I think this is about as worse a job of reporting as I ever saw." In fact, Hagerty deliberately misled reporters about Eisenhower's activities, making it seem as if he had kept busy. Years later, his doctor's notes showed that Ike had retreated to his hotel room for a day, exhausted and suffering from high blood pressure. The doctor called the president "emotionally upset because of exhaustion of these three days and at the prospect of the requirements for the days to come." Although Pearson had been wrong about some details, he had gotten the gist of the story correct.[38]

Pearson never conceded error on Eisenhower's health, but he had to back down from a column accusing Ike of intervening with the Interior Department to grant timberland rights to a friend. He initially wrote that he had wondered why Interior Secretary Douglas McKay had seemed anxious to unload such valuable property, until he learned that the Senate Interior Committee had in its possession a letter in which Ike had asked McKay to see what he could do to make the grant. Jim Hagerty promptly branded this claim a scurrilous lie, insisting that no such letter existed. Pearson felt confident that the facts would prove him correct. His source had been a Senate committee counsel, Robert Redwine, who claimed to have the letter. When further pressed, however, Redwine said that his files had been rifled and the letter was gone. This left the columnist defenseless. Without the letter—"if it ever existed, beyond one man's imagination"—he had to accept Hagerty's statement as truthful. But he drew a distinction: "I think he will agree with me that a 'scurrilous lie'—or in fact any kind of a lie is a deliberate telling of an untruth and does not apply to reporting something which one believes to be the truth but later turns out to be in doubt."[39]

Pearson found that year's Republican convention in San Francisco so tediously predictable that he wrote his column on Eisenhower's nomination three days before the event occurred. He assumed that if Ike had died on his way to the convention, Republicans would have "stuffed him and run him anyway." Feeling the same way about the election's outcome, the columnist went abroad to cover foreign affairs. He knew that his editors would not relish his leaving the country during an election campaign, but he had a hunch that bigger news was brewing in the Middle East. He judged those conditions correctly. Britain, France, and Israel invaded Egypt that fall, attempting to reopen the Suez Canal.[40]

Newspaper correspondents in Eisenhower's Washington described their job as a tedious waiting game. But in the effort to produce a daily column, Pearson lacked either time or patience. Beyond a general sparsity of news, he characterized Eisenhower's second term as dreary. Ike preferred to entertain at stag parties, to which Pearson was never invited, so there was little to write about. Other social events generated fewer items for the column, although he did get some critical feedback. At one dinner party, an army general and his wife each took Pearson aside individually "to tell me what an S. O. B. I was for having written about their daughter's marriage in Germany and the fact that they were sending some packages to her by air. For the life of me I can't recall the incident," he confessed to his diary. "It made me realize, however, how many people's toes I've stepped on and how many enemies I've made over the years."[41]

Another avenue closed to Pearson during the Eisenhower era was the Georgetown set of journalists who socialized with the top echelon of the Central Intelligence Agency and benefited from their highly classified leaks. Although Allen Dulles lived across the street from him in Georgetown, Pearson rarely did more than wave at the CIA director from a distance. Unlike the columnist Joseph Alsop, who fed copiously on his dinner guests' confidential information, Pearson remained an outlier. He regularly panned the secretive agency in his columns, portraying its "young socialite" agents as amateur detectives. Lack of access meant that the column missed most of the CIA's covert activity under Eisenhower. While he gave the agency credit for its ability to provide policymakers with timely alerts, he condemned its subterranean operations that American taxpayers had paid for but not known about. Polly Fritchey, wife of the journalist Clayton Fritchey and former wife of the CIA's chief of covert activity, Frank Wisner, confirmed the attitudes of her regular dining partners. "We didn't see Drew Pearson," she sniffed. "Nobody trusted him."[42]

Despite the drying up of many gossip streams, the "Merry-Go-Round" still managed to break news that the Eisenhower administration wanted to hold back. Pearson exposed some lower-level conflict-of-interest cases that cost officials their jobs, a list that included Peter Strobel from the General Services Administration, for approaching army engineers on behalf of his own firm; Carl Hansen, who conducted a wool-buying business while working for the Farmers Home Administration; and Federal Communications Commissioner Richard Mack, who took money from an applicant for a TV license in Miami. But they were small fish who produced few ripples in the news pages.[43]

The Dixon-Yates scandal gained more attention. Acting on a tip from Tennessee Senator Estes Kefauver, the "Merry-Go-Round" reported in 1954 that the Eisenhower administration intended to use government funds to finance construction of a private steam power plant near one of the Tennessee Valley Authority's dams. Edgar Dixon, president of Middle South Utilities, and Eugene Yates, board chairman of the Southern Company, had signed the contract. But Pearson revealed that the man who really swayed the Eisenhower administration on Dixon-Yates was Lewis Strauss, chairman of the Atomic Energy Commission. At that time, the AEC's operations in Oak Ridge and Paducah consumed nearly half of all the power that TVA generated.[44]

Democrats made Dixon-Yates a congressional election issue. When they won back majorities in both houses, they investigated the contract. What turned a policy dispute into a front-page scandal was the revelation that Adolphe Wenzell, vice president of the First Boston Corporation, had served as a consultant to the Bureau of the Budget to facilitate the contract, even though First Boston acted as financial agent for Dixon-Yates. The director of the Budget Bureau hung up on Pearson when he called to ask about this conflict of interest, but a House committee compelled Wenzell to testify.[45]

At a press conference, President Eisenhower denied that Wenzell had anything to do with the Dixon-Yates contract, calling him just a technical adviser on TVA bookkeeping. A week later the "Merry-Go-Round" revealed that Wenzell had attended secret sessions with Lewis Strauss when the contract with the AEC was being negotiated. "There were very hush-hush meetings held after hours in the AEC Building," Pearson recorded, "and it was only through the memory of an AEC guard that we were able to ascertain that Wenzell was present." Eisenhower's elaborate administrative machinery, to which he had delegated so much authority, had left him embarrassingly unaware. Despite having denied any wrongdoing, Ike had to cancel the contract.[46]

Although the Dixon-Yates brouhaha ended in 1955, it became part of an even bigger story four years later when the president nominated Lewis Strauss as secretary of commerce. "Eisenhower never knew of the role I played in this nor did the public," Pearson boasted. "But the strategy meeting of Senate leaders who decided to wage the battle to defeat Strauss was held at my home."[47]

Wall Street bankers like Strauss had never been Drew Pearson's heroes. Nor had he forgiven the AEC chairman for revoking the security clearance of physicist J. Robert Oppenheimer, calling it one of the most unfair purges of the McCarthy era. His persistent nettling of the AEC chairman prompted Strauss to telegraph the Bell Syndicate, threatening to sue. But with Oppenheimer in mind, Pearson continued his drumbeat, determined that Strauss get what he deserved when he came up for Senate confirmation. He counted on Senate Democrats to vote Strauss down, but initially they showed little interest. Senators generally assumed that presidents deserved the cabinet they wanted, making rejection of a nominee a rare occurrence.[48]

Both Drew Pearson and Jack Anderson testified at Strauss's Senate confirmation hearings, and behind the scenes Anderson admitted that they got "knee-deep in things journalists should never do." They visited key senators to urge rejection of the nominee, wrote anti-Strauss speeches for them, and devoted a stream of columns to attacking his record.[49]

Ultimately, Pearson's passion for defeating Strauss led to a slippery agreement with Democratic Majority Leader Lyndon Johnson. Since LBJ showed no desire to wage a fight over the cabinet nomination, Jack Anderson proposed that they offer him a deal. "If you expect him to do this for you," he told Pearson, "you're going to have to ease up on him." With a smile, Pearson agreed that "Lyndon Johnson is a fellow I like to make peace with, frequently." If Johnson would help defeat Strauss, Pearson would provide him with some immunity in the column. "Who do I have to kill?" Johnson asked when Anderson offered to get the column off his back. The majority leader agreed to the deal so long as the columnist shouldered the load and allowed him to remain publicly neutral. Johnson then coached Pearson on how to conduct his anti-Strauss lobbying, which helped defeat the nominee by a 46 to 49 vote. True to his promise, Pearson stopped assailing Johnson's leadership and began commending his legislative talents.[50]

The assault that hurt Eisenhower even more deeply, however, was the "Merry-Go-Round"'s demolition of his chief of staff, Sherman Adams. Widely regarded as the second most powerful man in the government, the abrasive Adams dominated Ike's vaunted staff organization and functioned essentially as acting president during the president's illnesses. Nearly everything filtered through the former governor of New Hampshire, who sheltered the president from problems he preferred to avoid. Eisenhower could remain beloved while his chief of staff said no to requests and fired anyone who embarrassed the administration. Sherman Adams projected the image of a flinty, incorruptible man, the embodiment of Eisenhower's pledge to clean up the "mess in Washington."[51]

Pearson had written favorably about Adams at first, but his thinking changed in 1954, when he heard Colorado Senator Edwin Johnson, ranking Democrat on the Commerce Committee, launch into a tirade about government corruption under Eisenhower. Senator Johnson claimed that commission after commission was "bent on robbing the public," and that all one had to do to get TV licenses, oil pipelines, and higher utility rates was to know Sherman Adams. This made Truman's deep freezers seem petty by comparison. Pearson began keeping tabs on Adams but felt he needed to move cautiously when going after such a powerful figure.[52]

In 1957, a special subcommittee of the House Committee on Interstate and Foreign Commerce opened an investigation into charges of influence peddling in the Federal Communications Commission (FCC) and other independent agencies. The subcommittee hired a New York University professor, Bernard Schwartz, as its chief counsel, expecting little more from him than an academic study of regulatory agencies. When Schwartz dug deeper than anticipated, the members who hired him turned against him. His investigation strayed too close to their friends, relatives, and contributors. Members heckled and interrupted their own counsel in order to protect witnesses, and they leaked information suggesting that the counsel had claimed improper expenses.[53]

Professor Schwartz prepared a memo detailing FCC members' acceptance of gifts, favoritism, and fraternizing with litigants, and it reached the "Merry-Go-Round" while still under seal. Subcommittee members planned to pin the blame on Schwartz but in a closed-door session he called their bluff by proposing that they all be put under oath and asked if they had given Pearson the memo. Schwartz then leaked the secret transcript of that meeting. "It spoils a good scoop for us," Pearson recorded in his diary, "but it's probably in the public interest to have it out."[54]

Sherman Adams's name flashed only briefly through the FCC story, but when Schwartz informed the subcommittee that he wanted to examine White House meddling in the independent agencies, Chairman Oren Harris moved to shut down the inquiry. Harris wanted to avoid anything that might dissuade Eisenhower from appointing him a federal judge. Through back channels, Jack Anderson picked up the story, which would eventually cost Adams his job. While Pearson was traveling in Europe, Anderson laid out in detail in the "Merry-Go-Round" how Adams had intervened with federal agencies on behalf of a Boston textile tycoon, Bernard Goldfine. Within a week, reporters for the *New York Herald Tribune* and *St. Louis Post-Dispatch* had confirmed Anderson's account. When Pearson returned, he expanded the story with an inventory of gifts, including a vicuna coat, that Adams had received in return for helping his wealthy friend evade government regulators.[55]

The betting odds in Washington are that Sherman Adams, for five years guardian of the presidential gate, correlator of White House decisions, the man who requires Cabinet members to check with him as to what they have discussed with the President, will have to retire as "assistant president." The secret evidence piling up in the House Legislative Oversight Committee is too embarrassing. It includes the fact that Bernard Goldfine paid other hotel bills for Sherman Adams. The $2,000 tab he picked up at the Sheraton-Plaza in Boston was just one case. Then there is also the case of a $1,300 hotel bill paid for the assistant president at Plymouth, Mass. . . . It develops that Goldfine paid for most of Adams clothes. He even presented Adams with a vicuna coat.[56]

In columns that followed, Pearson and Anderson upped the ante by charging that President Eisenhower had also received one of Goldfine's vicuna coats. This accusation spurred Jim Hagerty to an extraordinary display of spin control. "Drew Pearson has a story today which has in seven paragraphs at least ten complete falsehoods," Hagerty told a press conference, "and I sincerely hope that all the papers that carried this story will also carry what I am going to say now." It was not true, he declared, that Ike had received a vicuna coat. He had only received a bolt of vicuna cloth, which he gave to a friend—whose name he could not recall. Hagerty called it untrue that Adams had used an air credit card in the name of one of Goldfine's companies, or that he had received rugs and furniture. "That's still a lie. That's three in one sentence, which must set some sort of record." The list went on. Hagerty ended by denying Pearson's assertion that he had been friendly with Goldfine. "I have never met Mr. Goldfine in my life," he swore, unless it was to shake his hand in a crowd. "Eleven lies in one day is really something."[57]

Pearson retorted that this was not the first time the press secretary had denied a story that happened to be true. Hagerty had conceded that the president had received the vicuna cloth, he noted, only because Ike's thank-you note existed. The president could not remember to whom he had sent the vicuna: "Does the friend exist?" Pearson urged the House subcommittee to subpoena sales records from the Boston stores where Goldfine and Adams shopped together, to see who paid the bills. As for Hagerty's denial that he ever met Goldfine, Pearson advised the House subcommittee to subpoena the chef at Washington's Carlton Hotel and question him about the night in April 1956 when Hagerty dined in Goldfine's hotel suite. "Hagerty apparently forgot that the food made him sick and Goldfine complained to the chef."[58]

A day after Hagerty's defense of Adams, a haggard-looking Eisenhower held his own press conference and insisted that no one who knew his chief of staff doubted his personal integrity and honesty. Impatiently answering reporters' questions, he conceded that Adams might have been imprudent. "But I need him."[59]

Relentless pursuit of the Adams story drove Jack Anderson too far. On July 7, he advised Pearson that he been caught secretly trying to record Bernard Goldfine at a hotel near the White House. Anderson's friend Baron Shacklette, the chief investigator for the House subcommittee, suspected that Goldfine had hired private detectives to dig up dirt on the subcommittee's members. He proposed bugging Goldfine's hotel suite. More focused on the scoop than the ethics of achieving it, Anderson rented a hotel room next door to Goldfine's press relations staff under an assumed name. He and Shacklette set up a tape recorder and microphone by the adjoining door. Unfortunately for Anderson, when his wife, Olivia, delivered sandwiches to the hotel room, a private investigator recognized him as he answered the door. Alerted to their presence, Goldfine's staff called an impromptu news conference in their own room. Dramatically, they ran a coat hanger under the adjourning door and snagged the microphone wire. After some vigorous door pounding, Anderson and Shacklette emerged shamefaced. Shacklette lost his job with the subcommittee, and Anderson feared for his. When he told this tale to Pearson, however, Anderson could tell that his boss was enjoying it, "because his white mustache was twitching slightly." Pearson impishly announced to the press: "Jack Anderson, of course, has been imprudent, but I need him" (causing news broadcaster David Brinkley to break into laughter on the air as he reported the story).[60]

Although mortified, Anderson realized that the incident helped the column and himself: "Everyone thought it proved we were getting just the kind of keyhole evidence we were suspected of getting." The publicity also pulled him out from Pearson's shadow and established his own name recognition.[61]

Sherman Adams's resignation in September 1958 confirmed the columnists' allegations as facts. Pearson judged Adams less guilty than Eisenhower, who had also accepted lavish gifts. He cited the expensive farm machinery, cattle, landscaping, and miniature golf course that Ike had gotten from wealthy friends. But he found that a lot of his subscribers had trouble accepting news that conflicted with their preconceptions. Republican papers that had been grateful for his stories about Harry Truman's deep freezer now denied or deleted his reports on Eisenhower's expensive gift-taking.[62]

It later became evident that Adams's story had been even worse than what Pearson reported. Adams's landlady wondered why he always paid her in cashier's checks, and she had kept of a record of the different banks that issued them. Her files later helped the Internal Revenue Service build a case against him. Bernard Goldfine's secretary also contributed evidence that he gave Adams far more than previously suspected: some $300,000, on which Adams had paid no taxes. When Pearson reported that the Kennedy Justice Department was considering filing suit against Adams, former President Eisenhower intervened anxiously. Through the Senate's Republican leader, Everett Dirksen, Eisenhower implored President Kennedy not to prosecute his former chief of staff. Eager to ensure Eisenhower's indebtedness, Kennedy agreed to drop the case.[63]

By then, Bernard Goldfine had lost his friends in high places. He went to prison in 1959 for failing to provide income tax data to the IRS, and again two years later for underpaying his federal taxes by $790,000. His business enterprise collapsed, his textile mills and home were sold to satisfy creditors and tax claims, and he died broke.[64]

Ike's leak-free objective crumbled during his second term. In December 1956, Pearson obtained a "dynamite-laden" memo by Colonel John

C. Nickerson Jr., who managed the army's Jupiter intercontinental ballistic missile (ICBM) program at Redstone Arsenal at Huntsville, Alabama. Infuriated to learn that Defense Secretary Charles Wilson planned to turn future control of long-range missiles over to the navy, Colonel Nickerson wrote a twelve-page memo vehemently objecting to the decision and revealing the classified results of tests of the two systems: the army's Jupiter missile had soared 3,000 miles, whereas the navy's Thor had gone only three feet. The memo went to members of Congress, one of whom slipped a copy to Drew Pearson.[65]

Jack Anderson carried the classified memo to the Pentagon, to find out which portions the column could publish without risk, a custom that Pearson had followed since World War II. Alarmed officials instead confiscated the document, traced its origin to Colonel Nickerson, raided his home, and charged him with violating the Espionage Act, making him the first whistleblower to be prosecuted for leaking secret defense information to the press.[66]

When the Pentagon refused to return the Nickerson memo, Pearson made a rare appearance at one of Secretary Wilson's press conferences. Taking a front-row seat, he planned to have it out with the defense secretary, but Wilson surprised him with frank responses. Wilson explained that under normal circumstances the department would have returned the memo with its classified portions deleted, but that prosecutors had held it for evidence in Colonel Nickerson's court-martial. Pearson objected that such action would make it difficult for a newspaperman to check things that were classified. Wilson replied: "You'll sleep well with yourself as long as you do the right thing." The wind taken out of his sails, Pearson stopped asking questions and shook hands with Wilson. He described the encounter in the "Merry-Go-Round" on May 27, 1957—his first story about the Nickerson memo—which earned a letter of thanks from Wilson. After some delay and much effort, Pearson obtained a redacted copy of the memo, which he published in later columns.[67]

The rocket scientist Wernher von Braun testified for Colonel Nickerson, assuring the court that 90 percent of the memo could safely have been made public. The army dropped its Espionage Act charges and let the colonel plead guilty to mishandling classified information. Removed from the Jupiter program, Nickerson was reassigned to inspect construction projects in Panama. His ordeal demonstrated that the government's security classification system worked better at keeping information from the public than protecting national security. At the same time, Eisenhower's Commission on Government Security recommended that reporters who published secret data should be subject to fines and imprisonment. Pearson protested that under those strictures, journalists who consulted the Pentagon about leaked material risked jeopardizing themselves.[68]

Soon afterward came the missile-gap controversy. Intelligence agencies and defense officials, worried about Eisenhower's efforts to trim the military budget, secretly supplied Washington columnists with erroneous information that the United States had fallen behind the Soviet Union in producing long-range missiles. Pearson published the classified information, which he justified on the grounds that Cold War issues demanded a national response. A journalist had a moral obligation to keep the public informed, he insisted, especially when it came to weapons vital to the defense of the nation. That became the theme of Pearson and Anderson's 1958 book, *U.S.A.—A Second-Class Power?*, which asserted that Americans could not withstand the Communist challenge internationally "if they are fed sugar-coated half-truths and soothing syrup. They must know the facts."[69]

Eisenhower knew that no missile gap existed but would not reveal the evidence the government had gathered from secret U-2 surveillance flights over the Soviet Union. When the Soviets shot down a U-2 plane in 1960, Pearson dispatched Anderson to the Pentagon to get an inside account. He returned with the administration's cover story, swallowed whole. Pearson sent his papers an immediate release stating categorically that the plane had been on a weather reconnaissance mission and had crashed due to engine failure. That fable exploded when the Soviets displayed the plane's wreckage and revealed that the pilot had survived. Two days after the "Merry-Go-Round" published the air force's phony account, Pearson sent out a special column stating that the Central Intelligence Agency had charge of these spy plane operations and that very few knew about them, even within the government. He had to admit to being duped.[70]

    ▦ The dispatch of the American "observer" plane over the heart of the Soviet Union shortly before the summit conference highlights a situation that has plagued U.S. foreign policy since the war. It is the fact that we have two Secretaries of State. One is the official Secretary of State, Christian Herter. The other is Allen Dulles, head of the Central Intelligence Agency. . . . Last week, State Department and Pentagon officials were telling the truth—as far as they knew it— when they put out that phony alibi about Pilot [Francis Gary] Powers had oxygen trouble over Lake Van. This is what they were told by the CIA, and they seemed so confident the story was true that a good many newsmen, including this writer, believed them. This was how the United States, on the verge of the most important international conference in recent years, got caught, at first spying, and then lying.[71]

Eisenhower's admission that he had lied exposed the media's complicity in keeping government secrets. On the day that the story broke, the *New York Times'* military correspondent Hanson Baldwin could write an authoritative article about it since he had known about the flights for more than a year. Baldwin had spotted a U-2 plane at an air force base in Germany and informed his colleagues Arthur Krock and James Reston about the still-secret aircraft. All three sat on the story in the interest of national security. Secrecy prevailed not just because of Ike's no-leak policy, but because responsible journalists willingly suppressed stories they knew to be true. The rest of the press corps reacted furiously at having been tricked into printing lies, and the incident started press-government relations down the slope toward the credibility gap. Eisenhower's public admission also came as a shock to citizens who never expected their government to lie to them. With the U-2 debacle, Hagerty's desired, homogenized press coverage of the administration also crashed. The public kept on liking Ike, but the increasingly negative reporting undercut his party at the polls.[72]

Drew Pearson spent most of Eisenhower's presidency in the doghouse. He had hoped for better relations from a man he had encouraged to run for office but came to consider it foolish to think he could ever be on intimate terms with a president of the United States. "I do not believe this is entirely because of this certain streak of cantankerousness in my character," he concluded. "I think the problem of trying to report on the mistakes and foibles of human nature which crop up in any administration also has something to do with it."[73]

9

Between Kennedy and Khrushchev

APPEARING ON MIKE WALLACE'S POPULAR TV interview show in December 1957, Drew Pearson created a political shock wave that would complicate his future. Wallace confronted him with a recent "Merry-Go-Round" that described Senator John F. Kennedy's "millionaire McCarthyite father" as spending a fortune on a publicity machine to boost his son's visibility for a presidential race. "What significance do you see in this aside from the fact that Joe Kennedy would like to see Jack Kennedy President of the United States?" Wallace asked. "Jack Kennedy is a fine young fellow, a very personable fellow, but he isn't as good as that public relations campaign makes him out to be," Pearson replied. "He is the only man in history that I know who won a Pulitzer Prize on a book which was ghostwritten for him, which indicates the kind of public relations buildup he's had."

WALLACE: Who wrote the book for him?
PEARSON: I don't recall at the present moment, I—.
WALLACE: You know for a fact, Drew—
PEARSON: Yes . . .
WALLACE: *Profiles in Courage* was written for Senator Kennedy, by somebody else?
PEARSON: I do.
WALLACE: And he got a Pulitzer Prize for it, and—
PEARSON: He did.
WALLACE: And, and he has never acknowledged the fact?

PEARSON: No, he has not. There's a little wisecrack around the Senate about Jack who is a very handsome young man as you know, who some of his colleagues say, "Jack, I wish you had a little bit less profile and more courage."[1]

Off camera, Pearson regretted having blurted out the rumor that Kennedy's aide Theodore Sorensen (whose name he forgot) had ghostwritten the prizewinning book. His accusation put ABC-TV executives "in a dither," he realized. They insisted that he sign a statement to absolve the network if it was sued. Smart enough not to file a lawsuit, Senator Kennedy instead invited Pearson to his office to show him his original notes and rough chapters for the book. Kennedy convinced the columnist that although others helped him, he had lived with the book and made it so much a part of him that basically it was his book. The senator also explained that a substantial share of the royalties had gone to Sorensen for putting the manuscript together. "Sometimes I'm a sucker for a nice guy who presents an appealing story," Pearson concluded. "He didn't ask for a retraction, but I think I shall give him one." He concluded a column in February 1958 by quoting Norman Thomas as saying, "It is easy to write profiles in courage about men who are dead. What we need is profiles in courage among men who are living." To which Pearson added "Author of 'Profiles in Courage' is Sen. Jack Kennedy of Massachusetts."[2]

Pearson owed Kennedy the retraction, having mischaracterized an effort that had been more a collaboration than a matter of ghostwriting. The book project had kept Kennedy occupied while recovering from back surgery. Old friends researched and discussed with him a series of biographical profiles—one contributor described the senator as "managing editor" of the project, not unlike Pearson's management of the "Merry-Go-Round." Kennedy devoted most of his efforts to the opening and closing chapters, which set the tone and perspective for the rest. Ted Sorensen certified that Kennedy "immersed himself in the book's research, provided the philosophy, wrote or rewrote each of the chapters, chose its title, and provided constant directions and corrections to those of us supplying him with raw material." Yet even after Kennedy became president, he found it hard to shake off Drew Pearson's charge that he had not written *Profiles in Courage*. President Kennedy asked *New York Times* correspondent Arthur Krock if he remembered seeing him writing the book at Palm Beach. "I replied that I certainly had," Krock attested, "that I recalled seeing him lying flat on his back on a board with a yellow pad on which he was writing the book, and that I had read enough of those pages at the time to know that the product was his own."[3]

Kennedy never forgot or forgave Pearson for the flap over *Profiles in Courage*, which meant that the Democrat who succeeded Dwight Eisenhower in the White House would not embrace the columnist, despite his liberal leanings. "I was never an intimate at the White House and did not see the President too often," he admitted. Unlike Jack Anderson, he had not dealt directly with Kennedy in Congress. Nor had he gotten to know him all that well as a neighbor in Georgetown, although the Kennedys attended at least one of Drew and Luvie's garden parties. During Kennedy's presidency, Luvie complained to her husband that other journalists were being invited to the White House while they were excluded. "She begins to wonder whether I have typhoid fever," Pearson jotted in his diary. "As far as the Kennedys are concerned, I suspect I have."[4]

For the first time since he began the column, Pearson was covering a president of the United States a generation younger than himself. "The strange thing about President Kennedy is that I knew his father better than I really knew him," Pearson told his daughter. "It shows that I am growing old." He had befriended Joseph P. Kennedy in the 1930s during his chairmanship of the Securities and Exchange Commission, touting him in the column as brilliant and dynamic. Joe Kennedy rented an estate down the road from Pearson's farm in Maryland and invited him to swim in his pool. Pearson liked to tell about the afternoon when Joe hustled him out of the pool and off the estate because FDR was due to arrive. When Kennedy went to London as the American ambassador, he sent Pearson a running stream of correspondence and at Christmas "some of the loudest neckties I have ever worn." The ambassador's letters gave a breezy view of what was happening in Britain, but once the interventionist Pearson began criticizing Kennedy's tilt toward appeasement and isolationism his letters dwindled until they ceased altogether.[5]

John F. Kennedy came into Pearson's sights during World War II, when he carried on an affair with Inga Arvad, a columnist for the *Washington Times-Herald*. Pearson heard that Arvad had seen a lawyer about divorcing her husband and that Joe Kennedy was hot and bothered about it. Though he steered clear of sexual innuendo in the "Merry-Go-Round," Pearson considered this story provocative enough to pass along to Walter Winchell.[6]

The "Merry-Go-Round"'s first reference to JFK after his election to the House of Representatives identified him simply as a famous son. Illness kept Kennedy from establishing much of a record in the House, but in 1952 he audaciously challenged the incumbent senator from Massachusetts, Henry Cabot Lodge Jr. Pearson felt ambivalent about that race. He liked the liberal, internationalist Lodge and worried that Kennedy might revert to his father's way of thinking. When Kennedy won that election, Pearson judged privately that he had "the makings of a first-class Senator or a first-rate fascist." What alarmed him most was that the senator's younger brother, Robert, had joined the staff of Joe McCarthy's investigating committee, and that their father was providing heavy financial support to the Red hunter. Whatever John Kennedy thought of him, McCarthy posed a political problem back in Massachusetts, where Jacqueline Kennedy remarked that "anyone whose name was McAnything thought he was wonderful." It did not help that Kennedy, absent for back surgery, had been the only Senate Democrat not to vote for Joe McCarthy's censure. The "Merry-Go-Round" accused him of entering the hospital to dodge the vote—information that Kennedy assumed had come from his rival for power in the state, Governor Foster Furcolo. In a handwritten note to his staff, the recuperating Kennedy asserted that the facts were wrong, that the operation had been scheduled before the censure debate was announced. Kennedy authorized his staff to handle it as they saw fit but added, "I am inclined to say the hell with them."[7]

During John Kennedy's bid for the Democratic vice presidential nomination in 1956, Pearson was still steaming about Joe Kennedy's McCarthyite sympathies but concluded that the younger Kennedy had distanced himself from his father on policy and made a fine senator. Jack Anderson, however, further strained relations by publishing a *Parade* magazine article portraying the Kennedy brothers as "Papa's Boys," dependent upon the whims of their father.[8]

Four years later, when Senator Kennedy ran for president, he invited Pearson to breakfast at his Georgetown home and answered blunt questions about his record, his family, and his religion. "I have heard that you think I am against you because of your religion," said the columnist to open the conversation. "On the contrary I think it would be healthy to break down religious taboos and have a Catholic in the White House—if he's properly qualified." Kennedy replied that he expected his religion to cost him some votes. "But I think in the balance I may gain as much as I lose." Pearson raised the delicate subject of Joe Kennedy, expressing concern over his father's influence on him. "Well, father wants me to be President all right," John Kennedy replied wryly, but he insisted that the *Congressional Record* showed his independence.[9]

Joe Kennedy was not an issue that Pearson could let rest. During the Democratic convention in 1960 he infuriated the elder Kennedy with a column reminding readers of his behavior as American ambassador in London before the war, when he had been "soft on Hitler."[10] He reverted to that theme during the campaign:

> 🖼 Old Joe Kennedy, daddy of the Democratic candidate for president, has been dropping word around New York's café society that when his son gets into the White House, he, Joe, has a revenge list. No. 1 on the revenge list whom he plans to put out of business, says Joe, is a certain columnist named Drew Pearson. What irks Joe is a column reporting his operations as Ambassador to London before Pearl Harbor, which showed that he was chummy with the Nazi Ambassador in London and didn't seem to worry about Hitler's well-known operations against the Jews and his taking over of Austria. Several people have asked for more details on this—though not old Joe himself. And despite old Joe's well-known spirit of revenge, I am happy to supply further details.[11]

Should anyone wish to challenge this account, Pearson advised that the State Department had recently published its captured war documents, and he helpfully provided the title of the publication, its price, and the page where the incriminating evidence against Joe Kennedy began. Kennedy's press secretary, Pierre Salinger, protested that the column hurt their campaign, judging from the amount of mail they received about it. Admitting that Kennedy had not been his favorite candidate, Pearson offered to steer the column away from "Old Joe" if the campaign would give him inside information on the candidate's concessions to conservative Southern Democrats—a story that Kennedy was not about to divulge. The campaign staff grappled with how to respond to the columns on Joe Kennedy's insensitivity toward European Jews before the war until it finally concluded there was little to say that would not further fan the controversy. They decided to trust that Jewish voters' antipathy to Richard Nixon would counter negative publicity against the former ambassador.[12]

The "Merry-Go-Round" called candidate Kennedy inexperienced in foreign affairs. Kennedy rebutted with a list of all his international travels, which the columnist dismissed as superficial—some of them made while Kennedy was very young. "I couldn't see that he had any real foreign affairs background," he concluded. But he gave Kennedy credit for showing courage in leading the fight for aid to satellite countries "against the position taken by many of his own churchmen." Pearson claimed that an active Catholic Lobby existed in Washington, even though the church denied it. "As far as I know," he added, "the church of Vice President Nixon (and mine), the Quakers, is the only faith which registers under the Lobbying Act." But for years he had confronted Catholic clerics' lobbying for Franco's Spain and had watched some members of Congress turn "complete somersaults as a result of Catholic pressure." Jack Anderson wondered if Pearson did not want a Catholic in the White House because of the influence of the clergy, but Pearson assured his readers that as president, Kennedy would make sure not to favor the Catholic Church or its members. That column drew an outburst of protest mail from Protestants.[13]

Along with the rest of the Washington press corps, Pearson regarded Kennedy as an intelligent, candid, and charming man, but a backbench senator rather than a political leader. Only after he began to hear about Kennedy from *outside* of Washington, on the campaign trail, did he take him seriously. "What impressed me was the efficiency of his operations," Pearson wrote of Kennedy's primary campaigns. "He didn't miss a single trick. He covered all the bases in advance. He knew exactly what was going to happen before it happened—largely because he had been there first and cased the joint. He knew how each delegate was working and thinking and where the delegate was." This was the kind of leader America needed to cope with the Kremlin, Pearson judged. "Kennedy is not bombastic. He doesn't go out and attack Khrushchev. He knows that he may have to get along some day with Khrushchev."[14]

The columnist had never hidden his disdain for Richard Nixon, but after Nixon won the Republican nomination, Pearson surprised his readers by awarding him a few favorable columns. "It seemed to me he gave rather a good acceptance speech—not as good as Kennedy's but nevertheless it contained a lot of wholesome meat and if he lives up to it it will not be bad for the country." Pearson offered these concessions to appease his pro-Nixon subscribers, but his tolerance for Nixon did not last for long during the campaign. The editor of the *Deseret News* in Utah commented that he did not like what Pearson had been saying about Nixon but did not have to publish what he said. When Pearson stopped in St. Paul and Chicago, he discovered that papers there had failed to run his story tying Nixon's willingness to risk war with Communist China over the tiny islands of Quemoy and Matsu to the contributions he had received from the pro-Nationalist China Lobby. Such omissions illustrated "the difficulty in trying to tell the truth about the Republicans when 80 percent of the newspapers are pro-Republican."[15]

Despite their wariness of Pearson, Kennedy's campaign staff handed the columnist his biggest story of the election: that the billionaire Howard Hughes, whose empire thrived on federally assigned airline routes and government contracts, had provided Nixon's family with a generous loan. The candidate's hapless brother, Donald Nixon, had borrowed money from Hughes to finance his drive-in restaurants in the Los Angeles area, which had all the appearance of a political favor. Kennedy's campaign tried to slip this information to several reporters, but they could not get the story published during the last days of the campaign. An investigator for the Kennedy campaign, James McInerney, provided evidence to Jack Anderson, who knew he was being used but could not pass up such a hot tip.[16]

After Anderson drafted the column, Pearson hesitated in using it. If they were mistaken, his Republican editors would never forgive him. He suggested they hold it until after Election Day. "What good would it do to footnote it after the election?" Anderson demanded. Finally agreeing that they had a duty to inform the public, Pearson decided to run the story two weeks before the election, close enough to influence voters but with time enough for Nixon to rebut. To avoid looking like they were making a last-minute smear, Pearson devised a ploy. He hinted to the Nixon campaign that he was about to reveal the Hughes loan. That panicked Richard Nixon into preempting him by having his press secretary leak an advance alibi. The Nixon campaign provided columnist Peter Edson with a sanitized version of the loan story. Pearson and Anderson promptly jumped on Edson's misleading account. The "Merry-Go-Round" exposed both the nature of the loan and Nixon's lies about it. Calling a press conference, Pearson portrayed the timing of his own story as having been governed entirely by how long it took him to verify the details of the transaction.[17]

Some Republican papers sat on the Hughes loan columns, devoting more space to Nixon's denials. The *Washington Post* chose not to run them out of fear that if proven inaccurate it might create a sympathetic backlash for Nixon. But reporters picked up and corroborated Pearson's allegation on their own. A widely reprinted Associated Press account spread the sordid tale, inflicting maximum damage on Nixon's campaign just before the election. The *Los Angeles Herald-Express* tried to turn the story and make Drew Pearson the scapegoat, publishing four critical columns against him and reprinting a *National Review* article calling him a "smear artist." Robert Kennedy, who served as campaign manager for his brother, let Anderson know that they were not anxious to become identified with the loan story. Pearson suspected that they were afraid the Nixon camp might retaliate with something on

Kennedy's sex life. He himself had amassed evidence of Kennedy's extramarital affairs but kept them out of the "Merry-Go-Round."[18]

On November 8, 1960, John F. Kennedy defeated Richard Nixon by a minuscule 0.17 percent margin in the popular vote. Both Nixon and Robert Kennedy cited the Hughes story as a determining factor in the election, second only to the televised debates. Nixon blamed Pearson and Anderson rather than his own mishandling of the story, which deepened his antagonism toward the press. As for Pearson, when he surveyed the results, he concluded that the close vote might have been a good thing after all: "There is a lot of arrogance in the Kennedy family and this may dampen it."[19]

Meanwhile, the 1960 campaign had spawned new libel issues to plague Pearson. At the Democratic convention, Pearson, his old partner Bob Allen, and columnist George Dixon were set to appear on a news discussion program when ABC executives objected that Pearson had no libel insurance. He informed network officials that he had never carried libel insurance and did not intend to bow to any insurance company now. When he arrived at the studio, a network attorney stopped him. "I want you to know that if you go before the television cameras, the cameras will go black," he announced. "You are not insurable." Although Pearson encouraged the others to go on without him, all three walked off the set. He published a full-page advertisement in the *Los Angeles Mirror News* about being barred from the air and had the ad distributed to the convention delegates.[20]

More trouble developed later that fall when Pearson learned that Republican Senator Styles Bridges, running for reelection in New Hampshire, had schemed to place dubious candidates in the Democratic primary, attempting to derail a more competent Democratic contender, history professor Herbert Hill. Three days before the primary, the *Concord Monitor* and *New Hampshire Patriot* carried a "Merry-Go-Round" column that revealed that Frank Sullivan had been released from a prison work farm just in time to file for the Senate seat and identified candidate Alphonse Roy as a "former small-time bootlegger." Because of the ethnic divisions in New Hampshire, Irish Catholics might be inclined to vote for Sullivan while French Canadians could be attracted to a name like Alphonse Roy. The effect would be to cut down on Herbert Hill's chances. After Roy lost the race, he sued the paper and the syndicate that distributed the column for libel. The case would go all the way to the US Supreme Court and outlive both Alphonse Roy and Drew Pearson.[21]

"My family keeps telling me that I should avoid these political battles; and they point to many scars and many law suits to back them up," Pearson wrote attorney Joseph Millimet, a source for his story about the rigged primary, who was defending him in the lawsuit. "But it has seemed to me that I would be shirking my job as a newspaperman if I ran away from a scandal such as that which you outlined to me and which I reported in New Hampshire."[22]

Six years later, a New Hampshire jury awarded Roy $10,000 in damages from the *Concord Monitor* and another $10,000 from the syndicate. By previous agreement, Pearson would have to pay both fines. Pearson's attorney blamed the jury's decision on the poisonous atmosphere created by the *Manchester Union Leader*, the state's largest newspaper. "So many people have been publicly abused by that paper that nobody around here likes the idea that it's almost impossible for a public figure to recover." His attorney recommended he settle, but the columnist insisted on appealing the verdict. Pearson felt particularly upset that the judge had instructed the jury that even if Roy had once been a bootlegger, they had to decide whether it was a fair comment. "If you cannot dig into the record of a man who is running for US Senate," he fumed, "it will be a sorry day for clean politics."[23]

By then the US Supreme Court had made it much harder for public officials to win libel actions. In its 1964 ruling in *New York Times Co. v. Sullivan*, the court ruled that public figures could recover for libel only on proof that the accusation had been knowingly false and published with reckless disregard of the truth. The *Sullivan* case stemmed from a civil rights advertisement in the *New York Times* critical of the Montgomery, Alabama, police. City Commissioner L. B. Sullivan maintained that since he had charge of the police force, the ad had libeled him. Aiming to undermine press coverage of the civil rights movement, Sullivan sued the *Times* and the civil rights leaders who signed the ad. An all-white jury in Alabama awarded him $500,000. The Alabama Supreme Court upheld this verdict, asserting that the First Amendment did not protect libelous publications. Libel law varied among the states, but the *Times* appealed to the US Supreme Court on the grounds that public officials such as Sullivan were wielding libel suits to counter the constitutional freedom of the press. In March 1964, the Supreme Court unanimously reversed the Alabama decision, insisting that debate on public issues should be "uninhibited, robust, and wide open," even if that meant unpleasantly sharp attacks on public officials. The *Sullivan* decision replaced what had largely been a state-by-state approach to libel with a federal ruling that shifted the burden of proof from the journalists to the officials who were suing them.[24]

Despite this landmark ruling, New Hampshire's supreme court upheld the verdict in the Roy case, concluding that the jury had properly considered whether the libel was relevant to Roy's fitness for office. The state court pointed out that Alphonse Roy's only brush with the law had occurred in 1923, when he was caught in a raid on his brother's beer parlor; that the police had not charged him with any violation and had released him; and that the incident had occurred thirty-seven years before the "Merry-Go-Round" made its charge, long after Prohibition had ended. The defendants appealed to the US Supreme Court, which in *Monitor Patriot Co. v. Roy* (1971) held that publications concerning candidates for public office deserve the same protection under the First and Fourteenth Amendments as those concerning public officials, regardless of how much time had elapsed since the reported behavior.[25]

Jacqueline Kennedy shuddered that the *Sullivan* decision made it all right to print anything about anyone in the press. She called it "such an awful thing to do." But the decision liberated investigative reporters like Drew Pearson. He felt gratified that the US Supreme Court had cited some of his own pioneering libel cases to uphold journalists' rights under the First Amendment. Public officials could now be scrutinized and criticized without newspapers being subjected to expensive jury trials. Although the old libel laws had heightened his diligence for accuracy as his best defense, his career would have been less stressful, and far less expensive, if *New York Times Co. v. Sullivan* had been rendered earlier.[26]

On Inauguration Day in 1961, the "Merry-Go-Round" predicted that once the public festivities had ended Kennedy would doubtless retire to the Lincoln study in the White House to review the world problems he had inherited. Instead, Kennedy headed for a late-night party at columnist Joe Alsop's Georgetown house to which Drew Pearson had not been invited, even though it was just down the street. He took this as an omen that the new Democratic administration would not treat him as an insider.[27]

Kennedy's New Frontiersmen suspected that older columnists like Drew Pearson had difficulty accepting that young men were now running the government. Even so, they did their best to court his influence. In April 1961, Pierre Salinger telephoned to volunteer a story, which had never happened with Truman's or Eisenhower's press secretaries. Salinger let him know that Kennedy was promoting desegregation of the White House Press Photographers Association by refusing to attend their annual dinner unless they admitted black photographers. Pearson obliged by running it in the "Merry-Go-Round" but warned Salinger that while he was for Kennedy on most things, he could not possibly refrain from criticism. "I suggested that when the going got tough and I got too much hell from Republican editors I would ask Kennedy a favor—namely, that he do to me what Harry Truman did, blast me off the face of the map. This would really set me up with the press." Being blasted by Democrats had always raised his standing with his Republican editors. A bemused Salinger agreed that when the time was desperate the columnist could call on him.[28]

Early on, Pearson visited the White House to invite Kennedy to participate in one of the charitable dinners he sponsored for Big Brothers, a volunteer organization that mentored young boys who had their first brush with the law. It was his first visit to the Oval Office since 1945, when Harry Truman had berated him for writing about his family. This time, Kennedy greeted him warmly, even though their relations remained uneasy. The new president appreciated whatever positive treatment the column gave him but bristled at any criticism. After reading one column he considered hostile to his family, he exclaimed, "Here I am, President of the United States, and I can't do anything to stop someone like Drew Pearson!"[29]

Pearson promptly staged a public fight against Kennedy's nominee to the Export Import Bank, Charles Meriwether, who had been close to the Imperial Wizard of the Alabama Ku Klux Klan and had backed the campaign of an antisemitic candidate for governor of Alabama. Kennedy had been seeking to curry favor with powerful Southern Democrats in Congress, but Pearson made it clear this was not the sort of appointment a liberal president should make. When Kennedy read these charges against Meriwether, he considered withdrawing his name, but decided that might be taken as a sign of weakness. At Kennedy's urging, and despite Pearson's lobbying, the Senate confirmed Meriwether, regardless of his record.[30]

In July 1961, speechwriter Ted Sorensen called the columnist to ask a favor, reminding him, "We've done some favors for you." The White House wanted to plant a story about Florida Senator George Smathers, who had accepted Kennedy's hospitality and then opposed him in the Senate. "I wish he could read your column just before he comes to breakfast tomorrow morning," said Sorenson. Senator Smathers sent protest letters to Pearson's Florida editors whenever the column criticized him, and Pearson had no qualms about retaliating. Three days later he wrote about Smathers's conflict-of-interest problems. On another occasion, Smathers complained (in a recorded phone call) that he heard that "Drew Pearson is getting ready to write a mean one on me again." JFK reassured him, "Oh, well, we don't even think about that crap. We got so many that I don't read all those."[31]

The "Merry-Go-Round" treated Attorney General Robert Kennedy even more roughly. The attorney general's press secretary, Edwin Guthman, called Pearson whenever he felt a column had been unfair. "Why didn't you at least give us an opportunity to tell you what we think's happened, or give our side of it?" he complained. Pearson would invariably answer, "Well, I got that from such a good source, I didn't think I needed to check it." Although it irritated Guthman that Pearson rarely bothered to call him in advance of a story, it disconcerted him even more whenever he did. "And if he did call you, you were so goddamned scared [about] what you said, because you had to be so careful! You didn't know what he'd do with it!"[32]

Unlike Dwight Eisenhower, whose doctors advised him to avoid reading newspapers to keep his blood pressure down, John Kennedy consumed copious quantities of news. He had almost made a career in journalism, reporting for Hearst's International News Service (alongside Pearson's brother Leon) when he left the navy in 1945. His father once considered buying the *Washington Times-Herald* and installing him as editor or publisher. But unsatisfied with being an observer to events, Kennedy had wanted to be a more active participant. His brief experience as a reporter left him more at ease around journalists than was usual for a politician. His friend Ben Bradlee, later editor of the *Washington Post*, thought that Kennedy liked reporters "because they shared a craving to know what was going on, and to know what people were like. Like reporters, he was always hungry for gossip, giving and getting the hints of what others were thinking and doing."[33]

Beyond charm and grace, it was Kennedy's incisive mind that impressed the Washington correspondents. Whenever Jack Anderson met with Kennedy, he would go straight to the heart of each issue, with an impressive lack of fluff. He never wasted reporters' time, giving the impression of competence, good intentions, and a keen sense of what was practical and possible. Journalists who sought intimacy with a president, however, ran the risk of manipulation. Kennedy favored columnists Joseph Alsop, Joseph Kraft, and Rowland Evans, to whom he handed inside information directly from the Oval Office. He invited them and others from the media to intimate dinners at the White House, trips on the presidential yachts, and visits to his weekend retreats, which produced more scoops. Another willing collaborator, Philip Graham, publisher of the *Washington Post*, periodically declined to print "Merry-Go-Round" columns critical of the president he supported.[34]

Drew Pearson rated the Kennedy administration the most public relations minded he had ever encountered. The veteran Washington correspondent

Arthur Krock shared that opinion and published an article in *Fortune* magazine that accused Kennedy of managing the news to an unprecedented degree. Krock's charges generated a heated debate; he took satisfaction that "it has made a number of members of the Washington press corps very anxious to prove that they are immune to what I described in the *Fortune* article, and it has made the Administration narrow the definition of the 'national interest' as a justification for man-handling the legitimate news." Like Pearson, Krock stood among the older journalists on the other side of a generation gap from the young circle of "natty, well-combed" Ivy Leaguers who covered Kennedy. Where the veterans regarded the Kennedy administration as manipulative, the younger reporters saw it simply having less pretense than its predecessors about shaping the news it wanted.[35]

Press secretary Pierre Salinger attempted to coordinate all important news from the executive branch through the White House, which heightened accusations of news management. The Kennedy administration tried hard not to repeat the mistakes of the Eisenhower administration during the U-2 affair, when press officers in four different agencies put out conflicting stories about what the plane was supposedly doing before it crashed. Yet by channeling news through the White House, Salinger alienated reporters like Jack Anderson at the Pentagon, who had their own regular sources of news. Unnerving also was Pentagon press officer Arthur Sylvester's order after the Cuban missile crisis in 1962 that all Defense Department officials submit memos on any contacts they had with the press. Reporters protested that this order reeked of censorship and would inhibit officials from talking to them. Sylvester did not help matters by defining news as a weapon for the government to use in times of crisis and suggesting that it was sometimes a necessity of national security for the government to lie.[36]

Although they were generally kept at a distance, Drew and Luvie Pearson received an invitation to a state dinner for the visiting president of Venezuela in February 1963. This marked the first time since the beginning of the Roosevelt administration that Pearson attended a social event at the White House. When he proceeded through the receiving line, he told Jacqueline Kennedy that he was trying to look benign that night—making a reference to their earlier meeting in Caracas, when she had said. "Oh, Mr. Pearson, you look so much more benign in Venezuela than you do in Washington." "That's because you don't see me much in Washington," he had replied.[37]

Pearson felt more at ease with a political leader five years his senior, Soviet Premier Nikita Khrushchev. In 1961, Pearson and Walter Lippmann became the first two American journalists to interview the mercurial Soviet leader. During that crucial year in US-Soviet relations, the building of the Berlin Wall and the resumption of nuclear testing heightened tensions between the superpowers. "We both came away with the same impressions and reported virtually the same conclusions," Pearson noted, "namely, that Nikita Khrushchev wanted peace; that Berlin could be negotiated; that atomic war was so catastrophic that it must be avoided." Unlike Lippmann's columns, however, his own generated a storm of criticism.[38]

During the Cold War, Pearson assumed a hardline stance toward the Soviet Union. His old leg man Dave Karr, always more sympathetic to the Soviets, encouraged him to promote friendship efforts and not just to listen to the "hard boiled guys." Having a lifelong fascination with foreign policy, Pearson had traveled extensively and interviewed world leaders whenever he could, aspiring to be more esteemed for his commentary on foreign affairs. In April 1961, when he learned that Khrushchev had granted Lippmann an eight-hour interview, Pearson began lobbying the Soviet ambassador to Washington to wrangle an interview for himself.[39]

That summer, Drew and Luvie Pearson vacationed in Scandinavia. In Stockholm, Pearson wrote a "Merry-Go-Round" column phrased as a letter to one of his grandsons, explaining that Khrushchev had once boasted that American grandchildren would one day live under communism. "I am on my way to Russia to report on whether it is likely to come true." In Moscow, the Pearsons waited for several days and placed numerous phone calls, until word came that "Mr. K" would see them at Gagri, in the Soviet Republic of Georgia. At Khrushchev's dacha overlooking the Black Sea, the Soviet leader played the affable host, taking them swimming and feasting with them on caviar and vodka. A Soviet official inquired of Luvie Pearson, "What we want to know is: Are you like Mrs. Lippmann?" Noticing her puzzled look, he explained, "The important thing we wish to know is: Do you insist on sitting in on the interview? Or will you go swimming with the daughters and the grandchildren?" Luvie asked her husband, "Am I like Helen Lippmann?" "For heaven's sake, at a time like this don't ask me any of your silly questions," Pearson snapped. She joined him at the interview and turned the experience into a piece for the Saturday Evening Post, "My Thirty-Six Hours with Khrushchev"—beating her husband to the article he had expected to write himself.[40]

Believing that a nuclear war would be catastrophic for both sides, Pearson was relieved to find Khrushchev in a temperate mood. The Soviet leader reiterated that he wanted peace with the West and reminisced amicably about his meetings with Eisenhower and Kennedy. Intent on reaching an American audience, Khrushchev provided the columnist with an English-language transcript of their talks, which Pearson turned into four columns. Jack Anderson pleaded with him for caution, predicting a brutal reaction from the anti-communist John Birch Society. "We'll lose papers," Anderson warned. "I don't care," Pearson replied. "It's what I think, and I've got to print it."[41]

The "Merry-Go-Round" reported the interview under a Gagri dateline. The columns included some of Khrushchev's ribbing about the benefits of communism over capitalism, and his insistence that he meant their grandchildren would live under communism as a result of healthy compe-tition. Pearson painted a portrait of a leader who was cold and calculating politically yet warmhearted personally, a fierce competitor who sought peace rather than war. After their two days of conversation, he credited Khrushchev with being "completely frank in telling me what he would or would not do regarding future relations with the United States."[42]

▣ GAGRI, Georgia, U.S.S.R. The dacha or villa in which Premier Khrushchev spends a few weeks each summer was built for Soviet cab-inet members to vacation in. It is comfortable but not ornate, with a wide upstairs veranda on which the Khrushchev family breakfast, lunch and dine and from which they can look out on several hundred miles of the Black Sea. . . . His talks with Kennedy's disarmament adviser, John J. McCloy . . . were held beside the swimming pool. . . . "When our discussions got hot," Khrushchev jokes, "McCloy and I would quit talking and go for a swim. Despite that we didn't get anyplace."[43]

At Khrushchev's request, Pearson briefed President Kennedy on their talks, relaying the Soviet premier's assurance that there was not going to be a war. Kennedy listened more than he asked questions during the hour-long meeting. He suggested that when Pearson wrote to thank the Soviet leader for his hospitality, he should mention that if the two nations could get the situation in Laos straightened out, they could move on to other is-sues. When Pearson wrote to Khrushchev, he also advised that any decision to resume nuclear testing would likely "arouse American public opinion to a state of resentment which will not be easy to overcome."[44]

To Pearson's surprise, the Central Intelligence Agency invited him to ad-dress its top Russian experts, despite his frequent criticism of the agency.

"You have had an experience which all these gentlemen would like to have had: that of spending some time with Khrushchev," General Charles Caball, the acting director, introduced him. "You are a trained and expert observer. They've all read your column. Just give us your impressions, and you can save time by not duplicating what you've already written." When asked whether he thought Khrushchev wanted war, he said he had the impression that Khrushchev would instead follow Secretary of State John Foster Dulles's lead and go right up to the brink of war but no further. Khrushchev admired Dulles, he explained, because he knew where Dulles stood and that he would not go to war. "He doesn't know where Kennedy stands, and it worries him."[45]

Another unexpected outcome of Pearson's interview was that it inspired a twenty-six-page letter from Premier Khrushchev to President Kennedy. This began the Kennedy-Khrushchev private correspondence, Pierre Salinger attested, that would play a role in mitigating the Cuban missile crisis the following year.[46]

Drew Pearson delivered lectures on "My Two Days with Khrushchev," but found the reaction to his columns less favorable than he had hoped. Newspapers carried angry letters from those objecting to being spoon-fed Soviet propaganda. One writer called Pearson's "Black Sea romance with Nikita Khrushchev" nauseating. Another protested that his columns had made Khrushchev seem "more bearable to the great number of unthinking persons among us." The *New York Times* columnist C. L. Sulzberger also dismissed such interviews as simply one of Khrushchev's propaganda devices, facilitated by a reservoir of Western journalists eager to accept his invitations. Syndicated columnist Joseph Alsop jeered that Khrushchev just wanted to be friends so long as he got everything—including Berlin—his own way.[47]

Pearson sent a "Dear Boss" letter to all the editors who published the column, assuring them of his certainty that Khrushchev wanted peace. He soon realized that his letter made some of his editors doubt his judgment, and infuriated others. Sensitive to criticism|that he had interviewed more communist dictators than any other American columnist, he urged his editors to remind their readers how often he had talked to such anti-communist leaders as Nationalist Chinese President Chiang Kai-shek.[48]

In some parts of the United States, Pearson's reporting on Kennedy and Khrushchev was equally unpopular. The editor of the *Tempe Daily News*, a conservative Democrat, complained that the column was turning his stomach. "You've slid so far to the left you might be right against the leftfield fence—ready to jump over! . . . What the hell is going on? We've carried you on the front page for 17½ years." Reviewing such protests from his editors, Pearson concluded that what irked them most was his critical reporting on right-wing extremists.[49]

Only the Southern California *Wilmington Daily Press-Journal* canceled the column because of the Khrushchev interviews. In a front-page editorial, "Goodbye Drew Pearson," its editors explained that they had published the column because he had done such a good job as a watchdog in Washington. "We admired the fact that regardless of party he went after the crooks at the public trough. He has been, in his day responsible for sending more dishonest Congressmen to jail, for exposing more shady practices in our nation's capital than perhaps any other single individual. He has also been merciless with the self-anointed and self-appointed bureaucratic fat-heads who infest Washington." So long as Pearson stuck to exposing scoundrels, he was worth reading, despite his "ultra-left-wing" political views. But they could no longer tolerate his efforts to brainwash the American people into appeasement of the Kremlin. Calling him a virtual mouthpiece for Khrushchev, the paper replaced the "Merry-Go-Round" with a column by the more dependably anti-communist Ralph de Toledano.[50]

Pearson filed a million-dollar defamation suit against the paper, charging that the editorial had been defamatory, that it exposed him to hatred, and that it would injure him as a newspaperman. He agreed to drop the suit after the *Wilmington Press-Journal* apologized for claiming that his ideas bordered on treason.[51]

When he visited Miami, picketers outside the columnist's hotel demanded that Pearson "go back to Russia." The retrograde evangelist Billy James Hargis heaped denunciations upon him, and letters from John Birch Society members streamed into his editors. Pearson noted that his hate mail far exceeded the outcry over Lippmann's earlier interview. "I have occasionally told Walter how much trouble he causes me," he ruminated. "I'm quite aware, of course, that I cause the trouble for myself. And there are moments, probably well concealed from the public, when I yearn to be loved, when I would give my eye-teeth to get away from controversy." But even when he tried to step away from muckraking and adopt a Lippmann-like role as a statesman and international pundit, he attracted howls of protest.[52]

Extremists in the United States reminded Pearson of the widening split between Moscow and Beijing. Just as Kennedy had the right wing waiting to blast him if he made concessions over Berlin, he wrote in October 1961, "so Khrushchev has Mao Tse-tung, the John Birchite of the Communist world, breathing down the back of his neck." Both extremes, he warned, were doing their best to undermine chances of peaceful coexistence.[53]

Despite Pearson's hopes for détente, tensions between the United States and the Soviet Union spiraled dangerously. In August 1962, he received a telegram from an American reporter who had covered Cuba but shifted to the Dominican Republic after Fidel Castro came to power. Thayer Waldo alerted him that the Soviets were shipping nuclear weapons to Cuba. Pearson rushed this message to Richard Goodwin, Kennedy's deputy assistant secretary of state for inter-American affairs, but Goodwin dismissed the idea that Khrushchev would send atomic weapons outside his borders. The consensus within the Kennedy administration, Goodwin assured him, was that the Soviet Union intended to turn Cuba into an economic showplace, not a military stronghold. Disagreeing, Pearson interpreted Khrushchev's actions as an effort to contain the United States in Cuba, the way the United States had done in Berlin and Turkey, but when he wrote a column about it, John Wheeler, the head of his syndicate, called to urge caution. They were already in hot water with their editors over the Khrushchev interviews, Wheeler warned, and could face more cancellations. Pearson obliged by toning it down.[54]

In October 1962 came the Cuban missile crisis. As the world braced for nuclear confrontation, the "Merry-Go-Round" outlined the geopolitical reasons Kennedy took a tough stand against missiles in Cuba but concluded that national politics had really tipped the scales. Vice President Johnson had warned the president that Cuba was hurting Democratic candidates in the congressional elections and that the public was getting the impression that Kennedy was indecisive. "Military fear of Cuba actually had very little at all to do with it," Pearson asserted. However, he was impressed with Kennedy's firmness and astonished that Khrushchev would knuckle under. The dramatic events in October sobered both Kennedy and Khrushchev and confirmed Pearson's opinion that the Soviet leader did not want war, assuring readers that Khrushchev had been quite serious in telling him that a year earlier.[55]

"Pearson sounds like a real stooge for Khrushchev!" J. Edgar Hoover scrawled on a "Merry-Go-Round" column. Although the McCarthy era had ended, the columnist and the FBI director never restored their once-cordial relations. Hoover put Pearson in the FBI's "Junk Mail" file, its code name for items drawn from illegal wiretaps and burglaries. He labeled Pearson a "muckraking yellow dog," and ranked him "over [Martin Luther] King as a liar."[56]

Hoover's testy linkage of Pearson and Dr. King occurred just as the civil rights movement roiled the columnist's relations with his Southern editors.

As a Quaker, Pearson promoted human equality and opposed racial, religious, and ethnic prejudice, but he also lived in largely segregated Washington, DC, and like other white Northerners at the capital took its Southern mores for granted. He also knew that most of his Southern subscribers stood committed to segregation. When the column exposed Southern efforts to sabotage FDR's Committee on Fair Employment Practice in 1942, the editor of the *Dothan Eagle* in Alabama had chastised him for taking up the NAACP's cause to abolish racial segregation laws. Pearson assured the Alabama editor that his own views on race were not far out of line with the paper's. He had once worked side by side with African Americans on the Chautauqua circuit, "pounding stakes and putting up tents and doing farm work," but he accepted a distinction between social and political equality. Lingering resentment over Paul Pearson's difficulties contributed to this prejudice. "My father was Governor of the Virgin Islands where they practically crucified him," he explained. "You simply cannot please a Negro politically. I think it would be the most dangerous thing in the world to let them have any political power, and I view with alarm the growing power of the Negroes in Harlem, Philadelphia, Pittsburgh and Chicago. Here in Washington we have a very real problem ourselves, and it isn't getting any better."[57]

A compassionate but paternalistic governor, Pearson's father had come under fire not only from the island's white population for economic and social policies that aided blacks, but also from leaders of the black majority who demanded a role in the government. Accusing him of running a regime "dominated by a little clique of rich and predatory half-castes," they held a referendum on whether he should remain in office. The vote was 3,614 to 72 against the governor, which later contributed to his removal.[58]

Drew Pearson did not expect to pursue racial equality to any great extent in the column, although he warned his editors that the pressure for civil rights made it almost impossible to keep out of the news. What jolted him from indifference was the revival of the Ku Klux Klan in the United States, soon after the defeat of Nazi Germany. Pearson had witnessed the heyday of the Klan in the Midwest in the 1920s and recalled how his Grandmother Pearson had once asked whether she should join its women's auxiliary. People at her church had become members and the preacher seemed to approve. He suggested that her family might not agree, and she never joined. In 1924, as a young freelancer, Pearson had gone to Kansas to report on William Allen White's gubernatorial campaign against the Klan. By the 1930s the hooded band stood discredited, with many of its leaders in jail, but reports indicated that it had sprung to life again after the war.[59]

In 1946, Pearson learned of the Klan's revival from Stetson Kennedy. A Florida folklorist, Kennedy had a bad back that kept him out of the military during World War II. He dedicated the war years instead to unmasking racial intolerance at home. Kennedy conducted an undercover investigation of the Klan Klavern at Stone Mountain, Georgia, developing an informant within the Klan and passing his findings along to Drew Pearson. On his Sunday night radio program, Pearson read from the minutes of the Klan's meetings, naming the police, judges, prosecutors, and businessmen who had attended the meetings. In the column, he provided a secret survey of KKK activities in the South, which documented Klan meetings, cross burnings, and the intimidation of Jewish merchants.[60]

Klansmen sent anonymous letters threatening dire harm if Pearson kept reporting on their activities. "They seem to be laboring under the impression that not only can they strike terror into the hearts of defenseless minority groups, but also enjoy torturing others without even being written up in the newspapers," he scoffed. "So long as this typewriter has a ribbon, it will continue to expose the nightshirt boys despite their threats to bump off the operator." He filled the column with more inside news on the Klan's operations.[61]

The Klan dared Pearson to broadcast from its Konclave at Stone Mountain in Georgia. His worried wife and friends urged against bearding the lion in its den. They insisted that he was giving the Klan too much publicity and should write it off as not amounting to anything. But leg man David Karr egged him into accepting the offer. "Dave had a habit of catapulting me into these things," Pearson recalled, "and in retrospect he was right." His own sense of showmanship finally convinced him to go. Once in Georgia, however, he discovered there were no radio facilities at Stone Mountain. Governor Ellis Arnall, then leading a fight to revoke the Klan's state charter, instead set up a broadcast on the steps of the state capitol in Atlanta. On July 21, 1946, Arnall introduced Pearson as "a valiant crusader for good-will among men." Facing a national radio audience and a hooting, jeering crowd in front of him, Pearson denounced the Klan and its political supporters, but tempered his criticism with words of praise for the more tolerant elements of the South.[62]

During his absence from Washington, the "Merry-Go-Round" ran a letter to the columnist from his secretary, Marian Canty: "The Atlanta radio station which had so much pressure brought on them not to carry your Ku Klux Klan broadcast is now feeling happier." Despite threats from sponsors, the general reaction in Atlanta had been positive. "Incidentally, mail on your KKK broadcast would do your heart good. I am saving all the letters until you get back; know you will want to read them. They came from all sorts of people, big and little, with—this surprised me—a lot of fine letters from the South." For the next two decades, the "Merry-Go-Round" kept a close watch on the KKK.[63]

Challenging the Klan put Pearson on the honor roll of the African American *Chicago Defender* that year. At Dave Karr's suggestion, the syndicate sent out announcements of the award, but not to their Southern clients. Having gotten more caught up in the movement, Pearson applauded when President Truman blasted the KKK, integrated the armed forces, and supported the civil rights plank in the Democratic platform of 1948.[64]

Within his own profession, Pearson took a stand for racial integration. The White House Correspondents' Association had admitted African American journalists since 1944 and the congressional press galleries were integrated in 1947, but National Press Club membership remained limited to white men. Northern reporters had been unwilling to challenge this racial exclusion for fear of being regarded as troublemakers, but in 1955 Pearson and Lee Nichols, a United Press reporter and fellow Quaker, nominated Louis Lautier for membership in the club. As Washington correspondent for the National Negro Publishers Association, Lautier furiously assailed Jim Crow laws and racial segregation in print, while maintaining a quiet and dignified demeanor in person. All that prevented his membership in the Press Club was his race. Sponsoring Lautier set off more of a battle than he had expected, Pearson recorded, "and a lot of hot words have been exchanged all the way around." Angry members accused him of disrupting a club that he rarely used, and it was true the columnist kept his distance. "A lot of members don't like me," he acknowledged. "I could name quite a few colleagues and fellow members who might well be persuaded to poison my soup at lunch." When the membership committee approved Lautier's nomination, dissident members filed a petition of disapproval. At a club meeting, Pearson pointed out that their rules contained no racial restrictions, and he seconded a motion to put the issue to a vote of the membership. In this unique balloting—the only one held to admit an individual member—Lautier was accepted into the club by a vote of 377 to 281. Pearson said he was quite aware of his colleagues' disapproval. "I find that when you stick out your neck on issues, even unobtrusively, a hundred brickbats come your way."[65]

The columnist went on to defend the two African American women then serving as Washington correspondents, Ethel Payne for the *Chicago Defender* and Alice Dunnigan for the Associated Negro Press. Unlike the Republican Lautier, both women were liberal Democrats who got under President Eisenhower's skin by asking questions about civil rights at his press conferences. Ike simply stopped calling on them. Press secretary Jim Hagerty went a step further by threatening to remove Ethel Payne's press credentials because she had done some part-time work for CIO unions. The underpaid correspondent conceded that she had edited some campaign material for the CIO-PAC but insisted that she remained a full-time Washington correspondent. The "Merry-Go-Round" speculated that Hagerty had accessed her income tax returns to discover the sources of her income.[66]

Speaking at Howard University, Pearson accused the Eisenhower administration of intimidating journalists who dared to ask embarrassing questions about racial discrimination. In contrast to Ike, he said, Harry Truman never tried to suppress reporters—he simply called them names. Pearson concluded his address by urging a united effort to fight fear and preserve the freedoms that belonged to every American. Howard University President Mordecai Johnson added that while many might disagree with Pearson, he represented "the eternal pricking of consciences of decent people to make them aware of threats to their liberties."[67]

Jim Hagerty denied that he had accessed Ethel Payne's income tax returns or that his treatment of her had anything to do with the questions she tried to ask Ike, but he never explained how he had discovered such information about her finances. Although Payne had violated the press corps rules by working for an organization that engaged in lobbying, the White House Correspondents' Association took no action against her and she held on to her press pass. Ethel Payne and Alice Dunnigan continued attending presidential press conferences but had to wait until the Kennedy administration to have a president take their questions again.[68]

In 1958, a high school in Clinton, Tennessee, was dynamited after obeying a court order to admit nine African American students. Pearson traveled to Clinton and devoted several columns to the community's struggle to rebuild its schoolhouse and live up to the court rulings. Reporting on how the federal government had turned down the town's request for funds for the reconstruction, he launched a "Buy a Brick for Clinton" movement to raise money in the United States and abroad to fund the reconstruction. "Have read Pearson's column," read one letter containing a contribution. "We in this old U.S.A. will take care of ours when they deserve it."[69]

Violence shook Drew Pearson personally in 1961, in the form of a letter from a postal worker in Baltimore. William Moore, a white man, let Pearson know that he planned to hike from Chattanooga, Tennessee, to Jackson, Mississippi, wearing a sandwich board sign reading "Equal Rights for All Men" in front and "End Segregation in America" on the back. "I have no idea what, if anything, the press plans to do about my walk," Moore wrote. "I would feel better if I knew that if I was shot or arrested, somebody would be informed of what it was all about." He asked permission to visit with the columnist before he left, and enclosed a stamped, addressed envelope for his reply. Pearson ignored the letter—until Moore was found shot to death alongside an Alabama highway. Stunned by the killing, Pearson devoted two columns to the letter Moore sent him. He kept the envelope from the doomed mailman on his desk with the image of George Washington on its stamp staring at him reproachfully.[70]

As he focused increasingly on civil rights, Pearson criticized President Kennedy for not speaking out on the issue. In 1963 he pointed out that Kennedy had delivered three speeches in the South without once mentioning race relations. Instead, Pearson praised Vice President Lyndon Johnson for being more forthright on civil rights. The "Merry-Go-Round" credited Johnson, as head of the President's Committee on Equal Employment Opportunity, with pressuring defense contractors to provide better-paying jobs to African Americans. (That committee paved the way for creation of the Equal Employment Opportunity Commission in 1965.)[71]

When President Kennedy finally proposed a sweeping civil rights bill in 1963, Pearson responded approvingly and sought to explain JFK's activist tactics and moderate policies:

Seldom has any President of the United States fought so hard to shape any piece of legislation as John F. Kennedy did the Civil Rights bill all last week—even before it passed the House Judiciary Committee. Through friendly Democratic mayors back in the home districts, and by both nocturnal and daylight secret White House conferences, Kennedy did his best to get Civil Rights back on a more moderate track. He did this despite the risk of antagonizing Negro leaders, for the following reasons:

1. A tough Civil Rights bill will either get voted down or be debated into 1964—an election year.—

2. Already the Civil Rights issue has turned against the President in many parts of the North. Kennedy put it this way to one group of Democrats: civil rights has lost us four times as many votes as it has

won, but we have to pass it for moral reasons. It's much better to do it now than let it get snarled in the 1964 elections.

3. JFK, who once served in the House of Representatives, knows the difficulty of effectively amending a bill once it leaves a House committee. This was why he held night conferences and even stalled a committee vote until this week so he could break the weird alliance of Northern liberals and Southern Democrats who want a thorough bill (Southerners want it, of course, because a tough bill would be easier to defeat or sidetrack).[72]

The Civil Rights Act did not pass until 1964. In its aftermath, the "Merry-Go-Round" encouraged African Americans living in the North to boycott companies whose Southern branches continued to ignore civil rights practices. Defending civil rights made Pearson more willing to sacrifice some of his Southern papers. In Mississippi—the state Pearson labeled the most resistant to the new federal law—the *Meridian Star*, which had carried his column since 1933, declared that he had outlived his usefulness for them. "We simply cannot, in good conscience, continue to pay for and support this man's attempts to destroy our state. Drew Pearson's column has been cancelled. It will appear no more in this newspaper."[73]

By then, Kennedy was gone. Pearson had changed planes in Dallas on November 22, 1963, but did not learn of John F. Kennedy's assassination until he reached Austin. The Johnsons had invited him to spend a few days at the LBJ Ranch after Kennedy's visit to Texas ended. With all those plans canceled, he flew immediately back to Washington. Writing to his family about his relations with the slain president, Pearson observed that the Kennedys never really forgot the opposition he gave them before the Democratic convention "even though I went to bat for Kennedy hard afterwards." The late president had his weak points but also some great strengths, Pearson assessed. "His greatest was his genuine desire to push for peace. His greatest weakness was his timidity. He was inclined to pull back when he encountered too many obstacles." Some years later, after the nation had plunged into war in Vietnam, Pearson expressed second thoughts about Kennedy's militarism and felt wistful for Eisenhower, whom he deemed a more mature president who had kept the peace.[74]

After Kennedy's assassination, the "Merry-Go-Round" reported that the FBI had been keeping tabs on Lee Harvey Oswald and had interviewed him just a week before the shooting without informing the Secret Service.

J. Edgar Hoover's deputy, Cartha "Deke" DeLoach, saw an advance copy of the column and protested indignantly that Pearson had fallen for erroneous information. Seeking to kill the column, DeLoach insisted that the FBI had not bungled its part of the job in Dallas. Pearson took the occasion to remind DeLoach that he had been unable to see Hoover in recent years to check his facts and had to rely on reputable sources in the Pentagon instead. DeLoach advised Hoover that friends in the news media had offered to "take Pearson apart," but Hoover reminded him that the FBI was "not in a position to completely contradict Pearson," privately acknowledging the negligence they denied publicly.[75]

Secretly, Pearson also gave the CIA a memo on his last interview with Nikita Khrushchev before the Soviet leader was deposed in 1964. He reported that Khrushchev felt sure that JFK had been the victim of a conspiracy. When Pearson replied that he believed that Oswald had acted alone, Khrushchev gave him a tolerant smile. At the request of officials in both the United States and the Soviet Union, Pearson agreed not to publish that interview.[76]

A decade after Kennedy's death, revelations about his compulsive womanizing raised questions about whether the Washington press corps had been too protective of the young president. Pearson knew well enough what was going on. After one dinner party he recorded in his diary that "We spent most of the evening discussing the favorite topic of conversation: the sex life of the President of the United States." Such stories never appeared in his column. Those sorts of revelations did not surface until after the women's movement, together with Watergate and other scandals, revised media attitudes about protecting the privacy of public figures. Considering the abuse Drew Pearson sustained for being too intrusive, the muckraker and public guardian's greater offense might have been what he refrained from revealing.[77]

IO

Lyndon's Lackey?

WHEN DREW PEARSON RETURNED FROM Texas after John F. Kennedy's assassination, a White House car met him at Dulles Airport. With him was his daughter-in-law, Bess Abell, who was working as Lady Bird Johnson's secretary. She had brought the Johnsons' luggage from their ranch, where they had been expecting to host the Kennedys for the weekend. The ride in the official limousine reminded Pearson that the new president of the United States was "an old and very dear friend," who might open doors for him at the White House. "I have been thirty-seven years in Washington and still have never been really in the good graces of a president," he mulled in his diary. "Probably I won't be in Lyndon's graces very long." He got that prediction wrong. Lyndon Johnson had worked far too hard to win approval in the "Washington Merry-Go-Round" to let the columnist slip away. Johnson ran for election in 1964 under the slogan "All the Way with LBJ," and Pearson managed to go almost all the way with him, staying sufficiently close to be jeered by Johnson's critics as "Lyndon's lackey."[1]

Before the Johnsons moved into the White House, they invited Drew and Luvie to a family dinner at their Washington home, The Elms. Sitting before a blazing fire made with wood from Pearson's farm, the new president played on the columnist's predilections by expressing his desire to get along with the Russians. He said that Premier Khrushchev had sent him a dossier on Kennedy's assassin, and while the State Department had discouraged him from thanking Khrushchev, he intended to do it anyway. Then he signed the letter in the columnist's presence.[2]

Their families had grown socially and politically intertwined. The Johnsons gave a wedding reception for Pearson's stepson, Tyler Abell, and his wife, Bess, following their elopement. Her father, Kentucky Senator Earle Clements, had been Johnson's whip in the Senate. After working for the Johnsons during his vice presidency, Bess would serve as their social secretary in the White House, and Tyler would become assistant postmaster general and chief of protocol. The Abells named one of their sons Lyndon. But such intimacy created problems for the columnist. Whenever he published anything critical about the First Family, his daughter-in-law scolded him. He assured her that he would much rather praise the president. "But when he or his family deserve criticism, I cannot withhold it—even though, as you said, it hurts."[3]

"We had a kind of love/hate relationship with Drew," Lady Bird Johnson explained. "Every now and then he would cut Lyndon up in his column and every now and then he would praise him." Because she considered Pearson sincere in trying to make democracy live up to its potential, she could tolerate his occasional criticism. It was his sniping at her family that irritated her. Lyndon Johnson would laugh and say, "You are just like George Smathers's brother." It was an old family joke. For years, whenever Senator Smathers objected to Pearson's criticism, his banker brother would tell him, "Now George, you just ought not to pay that any mind, nobody reads it much, it doesn't matter." Then one day Pearson turned his fire on the banker brother, making him forget his advice and turn livid.[4]

Pearson was well aware of the drawbacks to their relationship. "Lyndon will always try to write your stories if you'll let him," he rued. His easy access to the president, and a fountain of leaks from the White House, complicated his efforts to report candidly. If he wrote something complimentary, critics charged that LBJ had dog-collared him. If he wrote something unfavorable, Johnson—who read the column every day—protested bitterly. As Johnson faced a widening credibility gap with the press corps, he became determined to hang on to Drew Pearson's allegiance, even when he felt irked. "I can always tell when I'm up or when I'm down, according to what Drew writes," Johnson said. "When I am down, Drew goes to my defense. When I am up, Drew takes a nick at me."[5]

Lyndon Johnson worked obsessively to achieve good press. Charles Roberts, the *Newsweek* correspondent who coined the phrase "credibility gap," observed that LBJ wanted to overcome what he saw as the prejudices of the press, particularly those journalists who had so admired Kennedy. Many reporters recoiled from Johnson's embrace, however, because they knew that there would be a quid pro quo required to remain intimate with the president. The bargain meant sacrificing objectivity. Reporters wanted to see a president up close but still observe him with detachment. It did not help that Johnson had the thinnest skin of any politician. "Sometimes I think he couldn't understand why people who were friends of his and who liked him," Roberts reflected, "how they could possibly write anything the least bit critical of him."[6]

Washington correspondents expected presidents to try to manage the news. The question was how well they did it. FDR and Eisenhower manipulated the media effectively because of their personalities and their masterful press secretaries. Truman stumbled because of his bluntness and inclination to argue with reporters. Kennedy got away with a lot because of his charm. Johnson thought he was being effective, but his excessive efforts to flatter, cajole, and court them often made the effect counterproductive.[7]

Drew Pearson had liked Lyndon Johnson from their first meeting in 1937, at the Washington mansion of Texas newspaper publisher Charles Marsh. Pearson reported, tongue in cheek, on the newly elected representative from a land-locked district in Texas who had managed to get assigned to the Naval Affairs Committee. In 1940 the "Merry-Go-Round" awarded a brass ring to Representative Johnson for his successful heading of the Democratic Campaign Committee, praising the young Texas congressman who had "political magic at his fingertips." Johnson had funneled campaign contributions from the wealthiest oil and gas men in Texas to endangered Democrats (of his choice) and turned an expected rout into a national triumph. Republicans, having gained eighty-one seats two years earlier, had expected to win the House of Representatives this time; instead they lost seven seats. The column proclaimed Johnson a born politician, identifying him as a New Dealer and favorite of President Roosevelt, who somehow managed to remain on cordial personal terms with the anti–New Dealers too.[8]

Congressman Johnson made himself a source for Pearson to keep in the column's good graces and inflate his image. The "Merry-Go-Round" touted his brief naval service in the Pacific in 1942 and intimated—incorrectly— that the president was considering him for secretary of the navy. When Johnson ran for the Senate in 1948, he faced a formidable primary opponent in former Governor Coke Stevenson. Johnson appealed to Pearson to raise questions about his rival's support for the Taft-Hartley Act. Stevenson opposed that labor-restricting law, despite its popularity among Texans. Pearson sent David Karr to an airport press conference, and Karr fired off so many questions that the candidate protested he was trying to cross-examine him. The "Merry-Go-Round" then accused Stevenson of dodging its questions to duck the labor-management issue. Johnson reprinted that column and mailed it to hundreds of thousands of voters across the state. He assured Pearson that the column had tipped the scales in his favor, helping him eke out an 87-vote victory.[9]

Once Lyndon Johnson arrived in the Senate, however, his politics shifted to the right as he tried to please both his wealthy donors and the down-to-earth Texans who elected him. LBJ rose to Senate Democratic whip in 1951 and aimed for the top post following Democratic Majority Leader Ernest McFarland's defeat in the 1952 elections. Hoping to stave him off, Drew Pearson convened nineteen liberal Democratic senators at his Georgetown home to identify an alternative candidate. They reasoned that Southerners in the caucus would oppose a Northern liberal and tried to convince the moderate Alabama Senator Lister Hill to run. When Hill turned them down, their second choice, the aging Montana Senator James Murray, stood no chance. With the support of Georgia Senator Richard Russell and other Southern committee chairmen, Johnson easily won his party's floor leadership. After the fight, Pearson ran into LBJ. "He had just been made Democratic leader by the Southern reactionaries," Pearson recorded in his diary, "and he felt supremely in the saddle," having forgotten his earlier pleas for help.[10]

The "Merry-Go-Round" began ripping into Lyndon Johnson as "Lyin' down," a slur that Pearson picked up from liberals in the Democratic caucus. "They figure that 'Lyin' down,' as he is nicknamed, will follow a pro-Republican line and there won't be much Democratic opposition to GOP policies," Pearson wrote. While he gave the leader credit for showing remarkable talents in keeping his discordant party together, Pearson's repeated use of the abusive title stung the hypersensitive Johnson. "He was pretty sore at me for a long while there," Pearson recalled. The columnist described Johnson's dual nature as alternately "harsh, brusque, and demanding" and "warm, generous and kind," with a massive ego that was easily bruised.[11]

When Joe McCarthy challenged Pearson's patriotism the columnist sought help from the Democratic leader. Reminding him of his help in opposing Coke Stevenson, he said, "I assume that I might have a little help from you on the Senate floor tomorrow showing that I'm not a Communist." Johnson gave him an icy stare and replied, "Drew, you've not been kind to me lately." And when Pearson wrote about Johnson being afraid to tackle McCarthy, the Texas senator called publishers in his state to ask them to cancel the column, which several did.[12]

As minority leader, Lyndon Johnson adopted a strategy of biding his time on McCarthy. Pearson complained that Johnson "ran like a scared rabbit" when liberal senators tried to block McCarthy from taking his seat at the start of the new Congress, pending an investigation of his financial improprieties. Pearson claimed that LBJ stood silent while McCarthy "crucified people inside and outside Government" and that he made no move until after the Army-McCarthy hearings had undermined McCarthy's credibility. "By that time, it was easy," Pearson belittled.[13]

Democratic victories in the congressional elections of 1954 made Johnson Senate majority leader, after which Pearson tried to patch their frayed relationship. He went to the Capitol on a peace mission but walked out when Johnson kept him waiting for forty-five minutes. The new majority leader soon had second thoughts about alienating the columnist. "He called me up and asked me to come back, which I did, and we had a nice talk." Pearson recorded. The column began lauding "the astute Lyndon, who in one term became one of the most powerful leaders in recent Senate history." Privately, however, Pearson worried about Johnson's slippery nature.[14] After hearing reports that the majority leader bowed to the Texas oil and gas lobby, Pearson revealed that Johnson had pressured the Internal Revenue Service to refrain from investigating the Brown and Root contracting firm, a major source of his campaign funds. In March 1956, the column explained how things worked:

Here are more details on how employees of the giant Brown and Root contracting firm, which has received many lush contracts from the Government, contributed in 1941 to the first senatorial primary of Lyndon Johnson, now Democratic leader of the Senate, and then deducted the contributions from income taxes. The case history is important for several reasons. First, this unfortunately is a practice used by other companies. They hand out bonuses to vice presidents, then require that a percentage of that bonus be contributed to a certain pet candidate. Afterward, that candidate, if elected, is in hock to the company. It controls his vote, which is why the Congress today, more and more, is losing its independence. Second, the Brown and Root history is important because they were active during the gas bill debate. George Brown has entertained Sen. Lyndon Johnson and other bigwigs at his Middleburg, Va., estate on weekends. . . . Finally, Sen. Johnson has exerted his influence to sidetrack the original forthright probe of the gas lobby proposed by Sen. Thomas C. Hennings (D-Mo.), and is now exerting his influence against the recording of political contributions in primary campaigns. Yet, it is primaries, including his own in Texas, that really elect Senators in about one-third of the states.[15]

"When I wrote the details of this story during Lyndon's Senate career, he almost died," Pearson later recalled. "He did his best to kill the story in the *Washington Post*, but they finally stood their ground." Pearson also used the column to defeat Johnson's efforts to pass a natural gas deregulation act. At the 1956 Democratic convention, Pearson occupied the hotel suite next to LBJ's, but found they were not on speaking terms. The senator's staff then approached him with a deal: if Pearson would quit harping on Johnson's tax deal for Brown and Root, he would throw his support behind Pearson's favored candidate for the party's presidential nomination, Tennessee Senator Estes Kefauver. "With some reservations and considerable doubt, I agreed," Pearson confided to his diary. He felt he had exhausted the Brown and Root tax story anyway and wanted to help Kefauver. "This is the first time I've ever made a deal like this, and I feel a little unhappy about it," he wrote. "With the Presidency of the United States at sake, maybe it's justified— maybe not—I don't know." In the end, Johnson gave Kefauver no help at all, reneging on the deal Pearson thought he had made, and Adlai Stevenson won the nomination.[16]

Despite his boss's fractious relationship with the majority leader, Jack Anderson maintained good sources in Johnson's office. In his struggles to keep that door open, he persuaded Pearson to once again award LBJ a brass ring in 1958 and stop referring to "Lying-Down' Lyndon." The "Merry-Go-Round" credited his impressive record of bipartisan legislation: "Johnson passed all the legislation President Eisenhower requested, and then some, and he wrangled it out of a Senate in which, part of the time, he had a paper majority of only one vote." He scored his victories by "out-talking, out-persuading, and out-maneuvering" his opponents. Pearson took heart that while Johnson had wrapped himself in some of the conservatism of the Texas oil men who supported him, he fundamentally had not lost all of the fervor of his days as a "rootin' tootin' New Dealer."[17]

Agreeing to mute his criticism of Johnson in return for the majority leader's helping to block Senate confirmation of Lewis Strauss for secretary of commerce in 1959, Pearson signed on as a Johnson loyalist for the presidential campaign in 1960. He had come to genuinely admire LBJ's ability to take command of legislation and enact constructive programs. The "Merry-Go-Round" praised the majority leader for doing great things for the Democratic Party, the Senate, and the country. Yet Johnson focused more on the negative than the positive, using one meeting to gripe about the column's criticism. "I went back to my office and made a compilation of my stories on Johnson," Pearson recorded after one such encounter. "It showed two critical stories and about one hundred favorable. I sent this to Lyndon, but never got a response."[18]

Johnson reminded the columnist of Franklin Roosevelt. Whenever he called on either of them, they did most of the talking. During the presidential primaries in 1960, when Pearson coached Johnson on running for president, he always carried strategy memoranda to their meetings. He could prevent the senator from monopolizing the conversation by telling him what was in the memo before Johnson had a chance to read it. Pearson helped draft Johnson's speech announcing his availability for the Democratic nomination but excusing himself from active campaigning so that he could tend to his duties as Senate majority leader. Seeing Johnson as the man most fit to hold the presidency, the "Merry-Go-Round" boosted his candidacy, promoting him as able and astute, and arguing that he "would give the Negroes a better break than any previous president, partly because he came from the South."[19]

Reluctant to enter any fight unless he felt sure he could win, Johnson preferred to let surrogates challenge the front-runners and take his own chances at the convention. But when the Democrats convened in Los Angeles, Pearson watched Johnson get hopelessly outmaneuvered by John F. Kennedy's "young upstart campaign manager," brother Robert Kennedy. Despite Pearson's record for farsighted predictions, Johnson caught him off guard by accepting Kennedy's offer to run for vice president. "I never thought Lyndon would do it," he recorded with astonishment. "The majority leadership is too important."[20]

During the presidential campaign, Pearson continued offering private advice and public praise to the vice presidential nominee. He applauded Johnson's homey campaign style and took note that liberals who had opposed his nomination now cheered at his campaign stops. After the Kennedy/ Johnson ticket eked out a narrow victory in November, Pearson discussed potential cabinet appointments with Johnson, who was promoting Arkansas Senator J. William Fulbright for secretary of state. Pearson expressed doubts about Fulbright's record on race and his relations with Israel, but Johnson reminded him: "You had a party at your house when Fulbright was there, and you plotted to try to keep me from being Senate majority leader back in 1952." "Your intelligence is awfully good," Pearson conceded. By then, Johnson had forgiven him. LBJ told Pearson he did not owe Fulbright anything, "not as much as I do you."[21]

Pearson published glowing reports on the vice president's international trips, excusing his exuberant Texas war whoop at the Taj Mahal and insisting that he won a friendly reaction from his crowds of onlookers. More importantly, LBJ followed through on international issues when he returned to Washington. After returning from touring Asia in 1961, Johnson called Pearson's former leg man, David Karr, then president of the Fairbanks-Whitney Company, which manufactured engines, pumps, and industrial equipment. "We've got to do something about the poverty and misery out there," the vice president implored. Recalling the old water-powered generator that his family had used when he was a boy, Johnson asked whether the company was still manufacturing them. He wanted to fly one out to India immediately. The pump had been discontinued, and when the company began manufacturing it again, Johnson cut through the red tape to pressure American officials in charge of foreign aid to distribute it.[22]

Still, Johnson remained an inviting target for muckraking. In 1962, Jack Anderson picked up rumors about a Texas con man, Billie Sol Estes, who had gotten rich off the federal farm program. Anderson heard rumors that Estes's plane had landed frequently at LBJ's personal airfield in Johnson City, and that Johnson had intervened with the Agriculture Department on Estes's behalf. Johnson angrily denied the allegations, insisting that he had met Estes only as part of a Texas delegation at the inauguration. "You let people get at me through you," Johnson complained to Pearson. Since Secretary of Agriculture Orville Freeman had assured him that Johnson had called only to complain about Estes, he accepted Johnson's denial as true and steered the column away from implicating him in the scandal, while other reporters remained skeptical. Estes went to jail, but an FBI investigation found no evidence of Johnson's involvement in his schemes.[23]

A more threatening cloud developed during the fall of 1963 regarding the wheeling-dealing Bobby Baker, who had risen from Senate page boy to become Senator Johnson's right-hand man as secretary to the majority party. Known as "Little Lyndon," Baker was a skilled vote counter, able to predict the outcome of tense legislative battles, often winning them by procuring campaign funds and other inducements to change enough votes. Johnson had kept him too busy to get into trouble, he later reminisced, but the relaxed style of the next majority leader, Senator Mike Mansfield, gave Baker more latitude. Before long, his deal making had expanded into lucrative outside business ventures, from vending machines to real estate and a beachside motel. Jack Anderson counted Baker as a regular source but rarely mentioned him in the "Merry-Go-Round" until Delaware Senator John J. Williams began asking how he had managed to get rich on the modest income of a Senate staffer. Among the shady transactions that Williams uncovered was a kickback scheme involving LBJ. An insurance agent, Don Reynolds, said that Bobby Baker had persuaded him to give Lyndon Johnson an expensive hi-fi set and buy ads on the Johnsons' Texas radio and TV stations in return for Johnson's purchase of two large life in-surance policies. As news of other questionable deals broke, Baker resigned his Senate post in October 1963.[24]

Pearson had barely known Bobby Baker. A year before the scandal broke, he was embarrassed when the young man had to introduce himself to him at a reception. But when Baker got into trouble he trusted Jack Anderson enough to show him his income tax returns to dispute charges that he had amassed a fortune (what later sent him to prison, however, was not the in-come he had filed but what he had failed to claim). In mid-November 1963, the "Merry-Go-Round" reported that the Baker investigation would soon blow the lid off a Pandora's box of Senate secrets about sex and money in Washington. At the same time, Jack Anderson was working on what Pearson called "quite a devastating story" about Lyndon Johnson's role in awarding the controversial TFX fighter plane contract to General Dynamics, con-necting Baker with that deal. Pearson distributed a column for release the following week on Bobby Baker's ability to raise campaign money from the oil companies for Kennedy and Johnson. "When Jack's column on Lyndon comes out on Saturday, our name will be mud with the Vice President," Pearson wrote in his diary. "When my column comes out on Monday about oil money behind Kennedy, I am sure that nobody in the White House will ever speak to me again." John Kennedy's assassination that Friday aborted both of those potentially ruinous columns.[25]

Drew Pearson listed the Bobby Baker investigation as the new president's top political problem. When Baker broke his silence, he gave his first in-terview to Pearson, offering a rebuttal to Don Reynolds's claims. Accepting

Baker's word, the "Merry-Go-Round" dismissed the charges of entangle-
ment that Republicans were raising against Johnson. Pearson reported that
his own investigation showed that Johnson had not been involved with
Baker's financial deals, which had developed after he had left the Senate to
become vice president.[26]

With Reynolds set to testify at the Senate hearings, the "Merry-Go-
Round" cited confidential FBI and Pentagon files that challenged his
reliability.

> Don B. Reynolds, the star witness against President Johnson in
> the Bobby Baker case, has brought reckless charges in the past against
> people who crossed him, accusing them of being Communists and
> sex deviates. He went to the FBI on Oct. 9, 1952, with a list of alleged
> spies. After a costly investigation, the FBI cleared all and concluded
> Reynolds merely had been taking out his "personal grievances" against
> the accused. Indeed, he made so many false accusations that the FBI
> in May, 1953, turned the tables on him and began an investigation
> on his own activities [as an air force officer and American consular
> officer].[27]

Pearson insisted that these revelations resulted from sleuthing rather than
any White House leaks. Few in the media believed him, largely because
Johnson's staff had told other reporters that Reynolds was an unreliable witness, implying that background facts about him "could be had." *New York
Times* columnist Arthur Krock shook Washington with a scathing column
dismissing claims that the information came from reportorial enterprise
rather than a handout from the White House. Even Bobby Baker believed
that President Johnson had done "a dumb thing" by leaking information.
The leak created sympathy for Reynolds and provided fodder to Republican
senators eager to allege White House whitewashing of the Baker case. It also
made the "Merry-Go-Round" look like a mouthpiece for the president.[28]

In his defense, Pearson pointed to the column he had written ten years
earlier blasting Reynolds's reckless congressional testimony. There were
investigations of Reynolds's past behavior underway at the State Department
and FBI, but it had been an air force major who had handed Jack Anderson
a confidential report on Reynolds's military service. "Our investigation
took about two weeks," Pearson assured his editors, providing them with a

summary of the air force report. "At no time during this period did I consult with the White House."[29]

Pearson tried to balance the column's attack on Reynolds by raising a few doubts about the new president. He pointed out that while Johnson served on the Senate Armed Services Committee, he had grown close to the generals and the admirals who were wary of the chance of peace with Communist nations. Johnson also had the Texas right wing "setting off firecrackers behind him" whenever he appeared less belligerent. "Will they succeed again?" the columnist wondered. "This is the biggest question mark facing President Johnson and the American people." As always, Lyndon Johnson proved sensitive to criticism and muttered that the columnist was just a troublemaker. When Pearson attended a White House luncheon and shook hands with the president in the receiving line, Johnson said without explanation, "There's about as much truth in that story as some of those other Drew Pearson columns." Pearson had no idea what he meant, since his most recent columns had defended him against Reynolds's charges.[30]

Having been at odds with every president since Herbert Hoover, the columnist tried not to lose the highest-possible source in Washington. "I am a little prejudiced, I admit, in favor of Lyndon," he told his assistants. There were times when Johnson would gnash his teeth over the column and when hosts at dinner parties had to keep them carefully separated. Now either he had grown more benign or Johnson had evolved. "At any rate I want to try to give Lyndon the breaks which I think he deserves. In other words, if he stubs his toe on some minor matter which is likely to make him see red if we report it, let's be charitable. Of course, if he rapes his grandmother in Lafayette Square we will have to report it." Johnson was bound to make some mistakes, and if they were major ones, the column could not overlook them, but he wanted to be as constructive as possible "without slobbering too much."[31]

Yet it became increasingly clear that his friendship with the president posed risks to his standing as a journalist. On December 22, 1963, LBJ invited Pearson to ride in his motorcade back from a candlelight memorial service for President Kennedy. Based on their conversation during that drive, he revised some of the predictions he would make about the president's plans on his upcoming radio program. The next day, while talking with Congressman Hale Boggs, Pearson boasted that the president had become his number-one leg man. But when a United Press story revealed that the columnist had ridden in the presidential limousine, his editors began complaining that they missed some of the needling he had given to past presidents. Pearson had found himself in the doghouse in every administration but Johnson's, which now caused more problems for maintaining his credibility than all those presidential accusations of lying.[32]

Although he recognized the inherent danger in preferential access, Pearson could not resist it. He scoffed at other reporters who could be influenced simply by a phone call from the White House or an invitation to lunch. Yet after one of his own calls from the president he scratched some critical paragraphs from a column he had written about Johnson's stand on federal aid to parochial schools. At least the replacement material was timely, he rationalized, "even if I did chicken."[33]

The columnist held high hopes for LBJ's presidency. He greatly admired the Great Society's anti-poverty programs, which promised to continue the New Deal and push on even further. What troubled him was the situation in South Vietnam. Pessimistic, Pearson concluded that the United States should withdraw its troops, yet he could see that Johnson wanted to avoid that painful decision in an election year. "If he pulls out, the Republicans could accuse him of giving up South Vietnam to the Communists," he reminded his readers. "If he chooses to fight, the Republicans could harp on the old theme that the Democratic Party is the 'war party.' "[34]

Pearson regarded 1964 Republican presidential candidate Barry Goldwater as too bellicose, and his running mate William E. Miller as too sleazy. He heard that former Mississippi Representative Frank Smith was claiming that Miller had once tried to bribe him. Years earlier, Miller promoted a private power plant at Niagara Falls and offered the Mississippi congressman a lucrative job handling public relations for the Lockport Felt Company, on whose board he served. He made the offer just before the House Public Works Committee was due to vote on the bill Miller favored. When Smith voted against that bill, the public relations offer vanished. Pearson learned this tale circuitously. Congressman Smith told it to Eric Goldman, a historian serving as special assistant to LBJ. Goldman got word to President Johnson, who instructed his aide Walter Jenkins to pass it along to Jack Anderson. Once the "Merry-Go-Round" carried a detailed account of the incident, other reporters picked it up in their own articles. Miller predictably called it a smear but could not shake off the charges.[35]

In October, Pearson got word that Walter Jenkins had been arrested on a morals charge for a homosexual liaison at the YMCA near the White House. He had known Jenkins for years as LBJ's most faithful and overworked assistant, as well as a reliable inside source whenever Johnson wanted something leaked. Ironically, Jenkins had been keeping the columnist informed about Barry Goldwater's sex life. Jack Anderson interviewed Goldwater's girlfriend, but Pearson chose not to print it. He wavered on a financial angle to the story, but added, "Certainly I will not use the sex part of it."[36]

Reflecting the prevailing sentiments about sexual orientation, Pearson wrote a column citing past incidents involving homosexuals in the government and called it a "disease which is completely bipartisan." Such an illiberal attitude passed for compassionate at the time. Since the column seemed to excuse Jenkins, the *Washington Post*, along with many other papers, declined to print it. "The *Post* has killed about three columns lately in its efforts to lean over backwards to be fair to Goldwater," he regretted. In his diary, but not in print, Pearson recorded that J. Edgar Hoover had astonished Republicans by concluding that Jenkins had not violated national security. "The Republicans, of course, don't seem to realize that Hoover has been in the same category with Jenkins for years," he noted, "only he has been careful not to use the YMCA."[37]

Thanks to the 23rd Amendment, Drew Pearson voted for president in 1964 for the first time since moving to the District of Columbia four decades earlier. He cast his ballot for Lyndon Johnson, contributing to the national landslide he predicted. Pearson called most of the states correctly, except that Goldwater carried five Southern states rather than the three he projected. Pearson expected the Democrats' loss of the Deep South to have positive results: It would make Johnson less beholden to the Southern senators and restore a two-party system to that region. On election night he also took satisfaction that New York Representative John Pillion, who "continually saw Communists under the bed," and who had sued him for libel, had gone down to defeat: "No wonder he was nervous."[38]

A month after the election, Pearson urged Johnson to pull American advisers out of Vietnam:

When you read over the complete file on Vietnam and French Indochina, you get no tingle of American pride. For after 18 years of western civilian and military aid—eight under the French and 10 under the United States—and after seven billions of American dollars plus the services of thousands of western advisers, South Vietnam is worse off than at the end of World War II. Furthermore, if a vote were held in South Vietnam today, the majority of its people would probably vote to have the United States, with all its aid, all its advisers, and all its troops, go home. These are the facts, unpleasant as they may be.[39]

Both Democrats and Republicans had waved the flag and pledged to protect South Vietnam from a Communist takeover, yet the situation had only grown worse. Pearson's anti-intervention columns prompted a barrage of letters from high-level officials, which he assumed were "all obviously inspired by the President." Jack Anderson told Pearson of a conversation he had with President Johnson in a corridor at the White House. "Why does Drew keep writing these columns about Vietnam?" Johnson had challenged him. "Doesn't he understand that we have to draw the line someplace? . . . We cannot keep on retreating." By contrast, Vice President Hubert Humphrey praised the columns, calling him the only journalist who was getting the Vietnam story right and assuring him that it was good for the president to have this interpretation given to the public. "Lyndon, however, is very sensitive," Pearson sighed.[40]

On March 23, 1965, as he prepared to leave for Moscow to meet the Soviet leaders who had ousted Nikita Khrushchev, Drew Pearson placed a courtesy phone call to President Johnson. The call came as LBJ was meeting with the House leadership and he tried to deflect it, but then changed his mind. "This is the worst day of the year for me," the president told his secretary as he took the call. With Pearson on the line, Johnson launched into a rapid-fire fifteen-minute monologue on why the United States had to defend South Vietnam militarily, talking so fast that the columnist had trouble taking notes. "I feel awfully sorry for Lyndon," Pearson recorded in his diary. "He has done such a terrific job on the domestic front. He was on the way to becoming one of the greatest Presidents. And then he gets bogged down in Vietnam—a morass in which no President can win. He inherited it. He could have pulled out immediately after the election. But now he's listened to the Pentagon . . . and he's in deeper than ever."[41]

When Pearson returned from Moscow, he convened a group of senators, both supporters and opponents of LBJ's Vietnam policies, at his home. He usually charged $1,000 for a lecture, he told them, but that evening they were getting one for free, along with a meal. The discussion soon shifted from the Russians to the bombing of North Vietnam, which Pearson considered futile. Pearson met with LBJ a few days later and begged him to remain a peacetime president. "Where do you want to stand?" Johnson responded fiercely. "Do you want to stand with [Air Force General Curtis] LeMay and bomb with nuclear weapons? Then the war would be over in a few weeks. Or do you want to stand with Wayne Morse and pull out?" Or did he want to take the middle stance that Secretary of State Dean Rusk and Secretary of Defense Robert McNamara advocated? Meekly, Pearson replied that he would stand with Rusk and McNamara.[42]

The hawkish columnist Joseph Alsop pressed Johnson either to seek a military solution in Vietnam or face the greatest defeat in American history. On alternating days on the same op-ed pages that Alsop clamored for war, Walter Lippmann urged a negotiated peace. While trying to appease both columnists, Johnson steered a middle course. He planned to escalate the American role gradually to extract a settlement from North Vietnam. Despite Pearson's reservations, he followed Johnson's middle path into the quagmire.[43]

Johnson flattered Pearson enough for him to believe he had been elevated to the president's inner circle of policymakers, perhaps even as a potential secretary of state. Jack Anderson scoffed at his boss's visits to the Oval Office: "Johnson was the only man I know who ever conned Drew Pearson by puffing him up." Aware of Johnson's sensitivity, Pearson engaged in his own share of puffery. He assured the president that he sympathized with him and blamed Jack Anderson for the occasional criticism in the column. Johnson caught on. "Whenever you write a column that's critical of me, you claim Jack writes it," he said. "You've been writing columns and blaming it on Jack for thirty years."[44]

At a Women's Press Club dinner, Pearson sat beside columnist Ymelda Dixon, who berated him for capitulating to Johnson. "Everybody has sold out," she thundered. "We thought you had real courage. But now you're gone." She accused him of trying to protect his stepson, Tyler, who held a job in the administration. "They either suck you in at the White House or they go out to get you," she insisted. "They are now passing out the report that Walter Lippmann is senile because he doesn't agree with them on Vietnam." Feeling torn, Pearson met with Lippmann, who explained that he had stopped trying to see the president because he demanded complete support and the conversations were too one-sided. Pearson recognized the truth in Lippmann's observation but could not resist the president's wooing. "I need the support fellows like you," Johnson begged. Whenever the columnist felt like criticizing him, he should just pick up the phone and call. "Just remember, your poor old President is working for all the country, and he's got to have your help."[45]

In April 1965, Johnson ordered US marines into the Dominican Republic to prevent a Communist takeover. Pearson criticized this unilateral action and insisted that the United States had itself to blame for much of the turmoil on that island for recognizing the military junta that had overthrown a democratically elected president. On his television program, he declared that the Dominicans saw the marines as fighting "for the military cabal, not just protecting Americans." In response, Bill

Moyers called to read him the latest public opinion poll showing that 69 percent of the American people supported Johnson's landing marines in the Dominican Republic. That was the trouble with Johnson's foreign policy, Pearson reflected. "He plays it according to what he thinks the American people will like, not according to what is good for them, and good for the country."[46]

United Nations Ambassador Adlai Stevenson died unexpectedly in July 1965, and Arthur Goldberg resigned from the Supreme Court to take his place. Goldberg offered his good friend Drew Pearson the post of deputy ambassador. "After fifty years I would get back to what I once dreamed of doing when I got out of college, being a diplomat," he mused. As a young man he had lacked the money to pursue that dream. Now he had wealth but still could not relinquish the income as a columnist and broadcaster and maintain his lifestyle. Not only could they not afford it, Luvie interjected, but they did not agree with Johnson's policy in Vietnam. Goldberg pressed the case, arguing that Pearson was "a Johnson man." Pearson speculated that the Senate would never confirm him, and Goldberg said he had not thought of that. "Actually of course, I would be confirmed overwhelmingly," Pearson privately recorded, "but we let it drop."[47]

By then, Luvie Pearson had turned passionately against the war in Vietnam. "She is considerably stronger than I and is almost developing an anti-Johnson complex as a result," her husband observed. The fact that his wife picketed the White House while his daughter-in-law worked inside created family tension. Bess Abell's position as social secretary helped him arrange for his best sources to get invited to White House events. But he also felt proud that his wife marched with the antiwar demonstrators.[48]

Readers sent so much mail protesting his support for the war that the columnist had his secretary, Katherine Raley, prepare a four-page response, justifying his position. "He wasn't happy with the war," she recalled, "but he didn't want to lose his contacts with Lyndon Johnson, so he was treading a fine line all the time on that. So, this letter had to tread that same fine line and that was really tough."[49]

Attending a party at Walter Lippmann's home, the antiwar journalist I. F. Stone asked Luvie why her husband did not go after LBJ on Vietnam. The growing criticism nettled Pearson, especially since Johnson was complaining that he had "taken out on him rather vigorously and for some time." Arthur Goldberg urged Johnson to listen to Pearson, assuring him, "He's your friend." "Drew's not my friend," Johnson replied—as Goldberg relayed the message to Pearson. "He's a peacenik. He's always criticizing my policy in

Vietnam." Pearson recognized that Johnson would never be satisfied if the column did not give him 99 percent support, which would make him look like a presidential press agent.[50]

By the summer of 1966, Pearson's contacts around the country confirmed that LBJ's political stock had slumped. The tragedy, in Pearson's opinion, was that the war, and the inflation it caused, had undercut his domestic achievements. Most Democratic candidates for Congress did not want the president to campaign for them. "They don't like to tell him this, but they haven't invited him to come, and he knows the handwriting on the wall," he observed privately, but not in the column. "The press, which he courted rather assiduously during the early days of his administration, has now turned against him about 90 percent."[51]

As Pearson approached his seventieth birthday, David Karr assured him that the only significant change that he had seen in his old boss as he aged was that for the first time he was on excellent terms with a president of the United States. Looks could be deceiving. After Pearson published a mildly critical column, White House staff called Jack Anderson to offer him an interview with the president for *Parade* magazine, where he was Washington correspondent. "Jack interpreted this as punishing me by favoring him," Pearson noted, "which is more or less standard procedure around the White House."[52]

Although he was shocked by the strident behavior of the young antiwar activists in the streets, Pearson admired their idealism. He feared that his own generation had become callused after enduring two world wars and a depression. The still zealous Dave Karr, then living in Paris, returned to Washington to march in an antiwar demonstration, and expressed pessimism about the war's impact on the Great Society. Karr reported that European sentiments had turned against the United States "for picking on little nations far away from our shores." The "Merry-Go-Round" pictured Johnson as having grown philosophical about his unpopularity and confident that history would treat him well. Luvie Pearson chided her husband for such saccharine sentiments. "Luvie thinks that I'm being too pro-Johnson in the columns," he noted morosely. "All her friends have remarked that I have sold out to Lyndon."[53]

Despite their courtship, the president did not always keep Pearson well informed. When the White House announced that Robert McNamara would resign as secretary of defense to become head of the World Bank, Pearson fumed that "The story made a fool out of me." Johnson had been assuring him that he had no problems with his defense secretary, even though Jack

Anderson had picked up rumors of a growing rift between McNamara and the commanding general in Vietnam, William Westmoreland. Anderson was convinced that Johnson had turned against McNamara and would remove him from office, but Pearson had resisted believing that could be true, based on all he had heard from Johnson.[54]

An interviewer asked Pearson whether he was offering advice to the president. "Look, I know he reads the column, and I think it influences him, but I don't want him to think I'm bragging about my influence," he responded. Herman Klurfeld, the friendly biographer whom Pearson recruited to counteract some savagely critical books that had been written about him, had Pearson review a draft chapter on his relations with LBJ. Blanching at how much space it devoted to Vietnam, Pearson whittled the text down to: "He has differed with the President on some things, such as sending troops to the Dominican Republic and some of the moves in the Vietnam war, such as bombing the north."[55]

The columnist helped write some of the president's speeches on the war and implored LBJ to stop referring to "my planes" and "my troops," which made Vietnam sound like "his war." But Pearson never saw the need to visit the war zone himself. He felt he was getting better information from the secret communiqués and cables Jack Anderson had obtained from deep within the Pentagon. "In all modesty," said Anderson, "I would say that we know more about what's going on than we could if we were there."[56]

The surprise North Vietnamese Tet offensive in January 1968, followed by news that General Westmoreland wanted 200,000 more American troops in Vietnam, finally compelled Pearson's break with Johnson on the war. Rising before dawn on March 10, he wrote to the president: "Regretfully I have arrived at the conclusion that your policies in the Far East are taking us down a perilous road which can end only in disaster for you personally and for the nation; and that I must leave you." Pearson promised to remain an enthusiastic supporter for his domestic policies, but let Johnson know that he was preparing a series of columns in disagreement with his policies in Vietnam. Johnson responded with yet another defense of his policies: "I know that you have always fought and worked for the underdog—for the innocent victim of injustice and aggression, no matter what his race or ethnic background. That is what America is attempting to do now in Southeast Asia."[57]

History would be kind to Lyndon Johnson, Pearson later assured an oral historian from Johnson's presidential library. He would certainly stack up as one of the greatest presidents on the domestic front. "Unfortunately, his success was partly hurt by the war in Vietnam," he accepted. "If it wasn't for that he would be head and shoulders over many other presidents."[58]

For two years during the war in Vietnam, the "Merry-Go-Round" diverted much of its attention to a protracted assault on one of the war's staunchest defenders. On January 24, 1966, there appeared the first of what would become a hundred columns bashing Connecticut Senator Thomas Dodd. This extraordinary campaign involved surreptitious entry into the senator's offices, an FBI investigation, libel suits, and a reluctant Senate ethics inquiry, culminating in a rare censure of a United States senator.

Pearson disapproved of Tom Dodd, dismissing him as an alcoholic. Rather than call the senator drunk during an intemperate, extemporaneous harangue on the Senate floor, Pearson had twitted him as "the Connecticut rambler." Yet Dodd's friendship with Lyndon Johnson gave him prominence. Dodd had been the only Democrat from New England to endorse Johnson rather than John Kennedy for the Democratic nomination in 1960. Four years later, Dodd became a finalist for vice president on the Johnson ticket. Johnson then got him a seat on the Senate Foreign Relations Committee, where he defended military intervention in Vietnam. But Pearson smelled something fishy about the senator's practice of starting and then abruptly ending promising investigations. He advised Jack Anderson to watch Dodd carefully since it seemed obvious to him that somebody was paying to halt those investigations.[59]

In March 1965, Senator Dodd got wind that someone from Pearson's office was asking questions about him. Although Dodd's staff assured him that the columnist would surely not embarrass a friend of the president's, the senator told them to contact Jack Anderson to find out what was going on, not realizing that Anderson had been asking the questions. A former Connecticut congressman alerted Anderson that Dodd maintained an unusually close relationship with a registered German agent, Julius Klein, and that the lobbyist never entered the senator's office without carrying a wad of cash. Another source in the Connecticut delegation let Anderson know that Dodd was having staff troubles, which led him to the senator's former chief of staff, James Boyd. Anderson pleaded that it would be in the public interest to help him understand what was going on, and Boyd admitted that he and other staff members suspected the senator of pocketing campaign funds for personal use. Anderson pledged that he would publish any incriminating evidence they could find and would turn the documents over to the FBI. The disgruntled staff entered Dodd's offices over several weekends, spiriting away files, photocopying, and then returning them. They provided

Anderson with six thousand letters and other documents, enabling him to quote from "secret correspondence" to make specific allegations.[60]

Despite this abundance of evidence, the effort nearly failed at its start. The *Washington Post* initially declined to publish the columns. After several unanswered calls, *Post* editor Russell Wiggins told Pearson that repeated criticism of one man looked like malicious intent, which would open them to a libel suit. Pearson rebutted that he had "amazing documentation" on Dodd and the fact that he was being used—and paid—by a German agent. He assured the editor that the senator's former staff had cooperated because of Dodd's shocking behavior. The *Post* agreed to publish the articles only after cutting out paragraphs that might be libelous. Other editors shared the *Post*'s apprehensions, claiming the column had overstated its case.[61]

Senator Dodd called on the FBI and the Senate Ethics Committee to investigate those who had robbed his files and published "distortions" and "half-truths." Deke DeLoach from the FBI contacted Jack Anderson to let him know that Attorney General Nicholas Katzenbach had ordered an investigation into the theft of Dodd's files. DeLoach implied that former Attorney General Robert Kennedy was behind the move because of his hatred of Pearson. "I can't really figure out how Bobby would have that much influence over Katzenbach," Pearson wondered, "and I suspect the FBI was just trying to cross a few wires." DeLoach left the impression that the FBI was conducting the inquiry under orders and that "theirs was not to reason why."[62]

Jack Anderson gave the FBI complete access to his six months' worth of research, the leads he ran down, the interviews he conducted, and the documents he amassed. FBI agents came to his home to photograph the papers, and then interviewed Dodd's renegade staff. Instead of asking questions about the senator's suspicious behavior, however, the agents were only concerned with how they had gotten the documents. "Suddenly the story developed an O. Henry twist," Anderson realized. "*We the investigators found ourselves being investigated.*" The relentless grilling indicated that the government intended to protect Senator Dodd—himself a former FBI agent—and prosecute his adversaries.[63]

At the Justice Department, Pearson and Anderson met with Katzenbach, who also invited the head of the criminal division to attend, stoking suspicion that they would be indicted. Pearson laughed the threat off, reminding Katzenbach that Roy Cohn had once tried to indict him for obtaining secret intelligence reports on the strength of the Chinese army during the Korean War. Jack Anderson took a more bellicose approach. "He talked rather vigorously and indiscreetly about the manner in which Dodd's employees had come to him with these documents," Pearson recorded disapprovingly. That same evening Pearson encountered the attorney general again at a reception at the White House, pleased to remind him that he too was a friend of the president. The Justice Department then disavowed any investigation of the columnists, insisting that it was only looking into allegation that documents had been stolen.[64]

The *Washington Post*, whose management stayed close to President Johnson, stung Pearson with a front-section story by reporter Richard Harwood that belittled the Dodd exposé. The article twitted that the columns had neither affirmed their allegations nor had any impact on the senator's reputation. *Newsweek*, also owned by the *Post* company, quoted a friend of the senator saying that Pearson and Dodd were on a collision course where "one or the other must be gravely injured or even destroyed by the outcome." Newspapers in Connecticut largely ignored the confrontation. The two dailies and three weeklies that carried the "Merry-Go-Round" had a combined readership of 50,000 in a state of 3 million, and three of those papers chose not to print the Dodd columns. The only reason Connecticut reporters covered the story at all was to explain the senator's denials.[65]

After publishing twenty-three columns on Dodd, Pearson brought the series to a halt for three weeks. "I don't know why Drew is holding this up," Jack Anderson told James Boyd. "I know some editors are kicking, but I've never known him to back away from a fight. He'll take on battles that even I would duck." In April, Anderson drove the conspirators to Pearson's Maryland farm to make an emotional appeal for continuing the exposé. "So you think I've got cold feet, eh," he replied. "Well, I can't say I blame you. I agree with everything you've been saying." He had just returned from a speaking tour, where audiences had asked questions about the case. He agreed to resume the columns if they could find more damaging material. "I'm looking for fresh stories, new subjects that have a moral to them, things that affect *people*." Over the next year another eighty columns on Dodd appeared, all but two written by Jack Anderson. "We should have done this before," Anderson told the group as they left the meeting. "When Drew Pearson gets personally involved in something, there's no holding him." (Pearson also found a job for the unemployed Boyd at the Big Brothers of the District of Columbia, a charity whose board he chaired.)[66]

By then, President Johnson had decided he needed the "Merry-Go-Round" more than he needed Senator Dodd. Vice President Humphrey assured Pearson and Anderson that the president had completely reversed himself on the Connecticut senator. Having first tried to save Dodd, Johnson came to believe that Dodd had exploited their friendship by prompting the FBI investigation and intimidating their sources. Johnson made Nick Katzenbach the scapegoat, sending word to Pearson that he planned to replace his attorney general.[67]

Speaking at the University of Bridgeport in Connecticut, Pearson called for Dodd's censure. A bipartisan Senate Ethics Committee was investigating, but Dodd doubted that the committee would pursue the matter vigorously. Dodd knew he was not the only senator to have dealt with Julius Klein. When the committee opened its public hearings in June 1966, it dismayed Pearson by shifting the focus of its inquiry away from the senator's errand running for the lobbyist to his diversion of contributions raised at testimonial dinners. Dodd contended that proceeds from his dinners had been intended as tax-free gifts to him, but both President Johnson and Vice President Humphrey, who spoke at the dinners, said they understood they were raising funds for campaign expenses. The Senate Ethics Committee therefore recommended Dodd's censure for conduct that was "contrary to accepted morals, derogates from the public trust expected of a Senator, and tends to bring the Senate into dishonor and disrepute." On June 23, 1967, the US Senate censured Thomas Dodd, 92 to 5.[68]

Senator Dodd filed a $5 million libel and conspiracy suit against Pearson and Anderson. "I've been sued before," Pearson told the press, "and I hope to be in the business long enough to be sued again." Dodd's attorneys persuaded the senator to withdraw the libel suit while continuing a $1 million claim against the columnists for violating his privacy and for receiving stolen goods. Judge Alexander Holtzoff, who heard the case, lamented that the Supreme Court's decision in *New York Times Co. v. Sullivan* required proof of actual malice to sustain a judgment of libel. "It may be said that it is a hardship to a high-ranking public official to be subject to having his reputation ruined, but apparently in the eyes of the Supreme Court this is one of the burdens of public office," he added archly. The judge ruled that Dodd had the right to sue for damages caused by the theft of property. "We did in fact use stolen documents," Pearson admitted, "but did so to improve the ethics of the Senate." The US Court of Appeals later overturned Judge Holtzoff's ruling, concluding that even if the documents were wrongfully obtained, the columnists were not civilly liable for publishing accurate information. The Supreme Court finally quashed the case by declining to hear it.[69]

When the "Merry-Go-Round" reported that Dodd's subcommittee on juvenile delinquency had suppressed studies on the ill effects of television violence, an angry Tom Dodd rose in the Senate to denounce Drew Pearson as a liar and a monster. "Someday the American people will recognize it," Dodd ranted. "Those associated with him are thieves, liars and monsters . . . his business is lying. He is a devil." Dodd had sent yet another investigator to Reidsville, North Carolina, to dig into the old charges involving Pearson's arrest for public indecency as a teenager, after using a warehouse spigot to wash late one night. Dodd added a malicious twist that Pearson was a child molester who had gotten his arrest records destroyed. It was a distortion of the old story, Pearson responded, about his "taking a bath after taking down a Chautauqua tent at four o'clock in the morning." His detractors had invented the charge of child molestation. At his Maryland farm, Pearson professed not to be bothered by Dodd's attack, writing in his diary: "Out here at the farm the focus is on entirely different things, particularly getting our hay in at White's Ferry and whether the hail damaged the pea crop to such an extent that the cannery won't accept it."[70]

"It Doesn't Take Much to Be Drew Pearson: Just Guts," the Bell-McClure Syndicate headlined an ad touting his crusade against Tom Dodd. Pearson described his role more modestly. "That was Jack Anderson's story," he said. "All the best stories are Jack Anderson's." By then he was sharing the column's bylines with Anderson. The two-year battle had won them few friends. The conservative columnist and Connecticut resident William F. Buckley Jr. organized an Ad Hoc National Committee for Justice for Dodd, calling the columns a smear and attributing them to the senator's anti-communism rather than dishonesty. Buckley also organized a spurious Committee to Horsewhip Drew Pearson, for which he sold memberships and distributed buttons. The *Washington Post*, Pearson's flagship paper, ran articles so sympathetic to Dodd that the columnist dared the paper to cancel him. His old friend Tommy Corcoran, who lobbied Congress, warned Pearson that "everyone on Capitol Hill" was sore at him.[71]

In the months before the Senate Ethics Committee held hearings, only a few other reporters had bothered to interview members of Dodd's disgruntled staff, most seeing it as a Connecticut story. Yet the Connecticut press generally took a charitable attitude toward their senator. Home state reporters were not anxious to anger publishers who had endorsed Dodd in his campaigns, nor alienate an important news source at the Capitol. One Connecticut paper dropped the "Merry-Go-Round" entirely.[72]

Seeking vindication, Tom Dodd ran for reelection in 1970. The uneven news coverage had left him in surprisingly good standing in the polls. Many voters had not paid attention to the column's accusations. Some saw Dodd as an underdog prize fighter getting up from a knockdown to the cheers of fans. "The mystery of Dodd's political future grows alternately darker and brighter," the Washington correspondent for the *Hartford Courant* commented. But Dodd's prowar stance caused Connecticut Democrats to pass over him and nominate an antiwar activist as their Senate candidate. Dodd then ran as an independent, coming in third in a three-way race. A jury of journalists unanimously recommended awarding the Pulitzer Prize to Pearson and Anderson for their sustained exposé of Senator Dodd, but the trustees of Columbia University overruled them. Jack Anderson attributed their loss to his boss's unjust reputation as a "hip-shooting outlaw reporter." Drew Pearson agreed that "The brass hats in the industry have no love for me."[73]

The Dodd columns had largely distracted the "Merry-Go-Round" from other issues, and Pearson was as surprised as anyone on March 31, 1968, when Lyndon Johnson informed the nation that he would not seek reelection. Pearson realized he had missed the opportunity to make that prediction, having ignored multiple hints from Johnson over the past two years. "I wish that I had stuck to those hints and my own hunch, rather than listening to others," he lamented. His skeptical wife had convinced him there was no chance of Johnson's stepping down voluntarily.[74]

In the political scramble that followed, Pearson preferred Hubert Humphrey for the Democratic nomination, even hosting a fundraiser for Humphrey at his home. He counted on Humphrey as a fighter for liberal causes and a reliable inside source. Luvie Pearson campaigned for the antiwar icon Senator Eugene McCarthy, but Pearson felt less confidence in him. The "Merry-Go-Round" had criticized Gene McCarthy's tendency to vote with the oil and gas lobby. Pearson similarly disliked the other antiwar candidate, Senator Robert Kennedy. The column's frequent attacks on Bobby Kennedy pained *Washington Post* editor Ben Bradlee. "Why don't you dig up some stuff on Hubert Humphrey or McCarthy?" he badgered.[75]

Drew Pearson and Robert Kennedy shared a mutual disdain. The columnist still distrusted Kennedy for having worked for Joe McCarthy, and Kennedy never forgave the columnist for the "Merry-Go-Round"'s attacks on his father during the 1960 campaign. At their first meeting after Kennedy became attorney general, Pearson described him as a "gimlet-eyed, cold young man who sits in his shirtsleeves with his tie undone, looking at you in a much more fierce manner than Khrushchev does." He saw Kennedy as too young for the presidency and shuddered at his shaggy hairstyle.[76]

In March 1967, Jack Anderson produced two columns that exposed the CIA's efforts to recruit Mafia hit men to assassinate Fidel Castro.

The column cited an unconfirmed report that Robert Kennedy approved the plot, which might have backfired against his brother. Kennedy's staff considered these allegations absurd. "Well, it's not that absurd in this sense," he cautioned them, and then related a CIA plan to get Castro that he had called off. Kennedy acknowledged, "there is a germ of something in there." The column prompted President Johnson to order an investigation, and a month later the CIA inspector general's report confirmed that the story had been correct, and that the agency could not plausibly deny the "Merry-Go-Round"'s version.[77]

Pearson followed with another damaging accusation that then–Attorney General Kennedy had ordered wiretapping to probe the activities of then–Vice President Johnson. This time, Kennedy called the columnist to deny responsibility and blame J. Edgar Hoover. "Robert F. Kennedy is a man with a terrific Senate record, a lot of courage—sometimes bordering on gall—and a strong belief in the divine right of the Kennedys," wrote the "Merry-Go-Round," feigning praise. The question it raised was whether he had learned anything from his past mistakes. The column compared his wiretapping as attorney general to the "witch-hunting tactics of his Joe McCarthy days." Some liberal papers objected. The *Chicago Daily News* ran the column but published a disclaimer that its "juxtapositions and distortions of fact" conveyed a misleading impression. The column had not mentioned that after Bobby Kennedy resigned from McCarthy's committee staff he came back to work for the Democratic minority, who opposed McCarthy. ("He didn't come back to fight McCarthy," Roy Cohn scoffed, "he came back to fight me.")[78]

J. Edgar Hoover habitually covered his tracks by blaming others. On May 9, 1968, Deke DeLoach lunched at Pearson's home and showed him documents involving Bobby Kennedy's approval of wiretaps. They confirmed that Kennedy had signed an authorization to wiretap Martin Luther King Jr. "I suspect Deke was prompted by the president to talk to me," Pearson reasoned. Given Dr. King's recent assassination, revelations that Kennedy had tapped his phones would be politically explosive. Just prior to the Oregon primary fight between Kennedy and Eugene McCarthy, the column broke the story:[79]

The question of whether Bobby Kennedy, when Attorney General, ordered widespread wiretapping and eavesdropping by the FBI has become the subject of some controversy. It is also very important in gauging Kennedy's qualifications to be President, and whether he is telling the truth. After all, the credibility gap has become something of an issue these days. In this connection, this column has learned that Mr. Kennedy ordered a wiretap put on the phone of the Rev. Martin Luther King, Jr. Kennedy denies this, and other statements that he ordered or condoned the wide-scale wiretapping or eavesdropping by the FBI while he commanded the Justice Department. He states that nowhere in the Justice Department is there to be found a single eavesdrop order signed by him. However, the facts in the eavesdropping of Dr. King are irrefutable, and we can report them in detail.[80]

The "Merry-Go-Round" disclosed that the wiretaps had been intended to investigate reports of Communist influence on Dr. King but had also uncovered King's extramarital sex life—although many papers deleted this part of the story from the column. It further asserted that the attorney general had ordered the taps over the FBI's objections, rather than the other way around. Kennedy's campaign responded that he had authorized wiretapping only in response to written requests from the FBI. Jack Anderson later came to believe that the FBI had deliberately given him misleading information to smear both King and Kennedy.[81]

As soon as the syndicate distributed advance copies of the column, editors began raising concerns. Ben Bradlee at the *Post* telephoned Deke DeLoach to ask about the allegations. This made DeLoach nervous about being identified as the leaker. Pearson had counted on getting more confidential FBI memos before publication, but now realized they would not be forthcoming. The FBI was running scared, he noted in his diary: "In fact, they demand that we modify the column I have written for today for release on Monday. They want some of the good quotes taken out."[82]

Covering Kennedy's race for the nomination, reporter Jules Witcover judged the charges "a tempest in a teacup, but in a campaign in which the ruthlessness tag on Kennedy again had become a factor, it was still another headache." Robert Kennedy concluded that the issue was too complicated to explain and chose not to talk about it. Once he lost the Oregon primary, however, he accused the Johnson administration of having leaked the wiretapping story to influence the outcome. His campaign moved on to California, where, during a televised debate, Kennedy was asked about the King wiretaps but responded evasively. "It would have been great if he called me a liar," Pearson reflected, "but he didn't."[83]

On the morning of June 5, Pearson arose as usual at 4 A.M. and heard the UPI news teletype clattering loudly in his office, very much out of the ordinary for such an early hour. He read on the wires that Robert Kennedy had been shot. It was too late to pull that day's column, but Pearson scrapped the next several columns that continued his attacks on Kennedy and instead addressed the issue of violence in American life and the need for stronger gun control.[84]

Bobby Kennedy's death replaced Pearson's animosity with ambiguity. He regarded Kennedy as able, dynamic, dedicated, but ruthless. The columnist resented how Kennedy had made his own candidate, Vice President Humphrey, seem old and out-of-date, perhaps taking that depiction personally. Still, he published a memorial tribute and devoted a television broadcast to the slain senator. A few readers blamed him for Kennedy's death, and Pearson himself questioned whether the column had been too hard on him. "He was a man who kept his goals for the common man," he agreed. "He was thoughtful of other people though ruthless toward his enemies."[85]

Promoting Hubert Humphrey, the "Merry-Go-Round" analyzed his predicament in being yoked to President Johnson's war policies: "There is no possible way he can differ with the president yet remain as a loyal member of the team." When the Democrats held their nominating convention in Chicago, battles erupted between pro- and antiwar forces among the delegates, and between demonstrators and police in the streets. Intent on waging an upbeat campaign based on the politics of joy and happiness, Humphrey desperately tried to forge a compromise peace plank for the party platform, but the disruptive debate that followed left wounds that Pearson doubted could heal before the election. Pearson blamed the president for sabotaging Humphrey's efforts. "If LBJ, sitting at his ranch in Texas, had taken his hands off the reins of the convention it wouldn't have happened at all," he argued in the column. "But he didn't. Instead he seemed more interested in vindication for his own Vietnam policy than in the election of Hubert Humphrey next November."[86]

Republicans in 1968 presented their candidate as a New Nixon, rested and ready to take command. Drew Pearson held him to be the same opportunist he had written about for decades. He accused Nixon of running a slick campaign that avoiding engaging with the news media and hid his nasty side from the public. Once again, Pearson dredged up the Howard Hughes loan that he had used against Nixon in 1960, but by then that accusation had grown shopworn.[87]

The columnist obtained a more damaging story at the end of October via a letter marked "urgent & confidential." Peter Blake, editor of the *Architectural Forum*, informed Pearson that for years Nixon had been under the psychiatric care of Dr. Arnold Hutschnecker. Pearson telephoned Blake, who quoted the psychiatrist as saying that Nixon "ought not to have his finger on the nuclear trigger" but that he was reluctant to speak out against a former patient. At nine that morning, Pearson called Dr. Hutschnecker, appealing that it was in the national interest for people to know about Nixon's stability. The therapist excused himself because of a busy schedule and asked Pearson to call back at four that afternoon. Meanwhile, Jack Anderson had called Nixon's campaign for confirmation. Nixon's staff quickly contacted the doctor, persuading him to state that Nixon had been his patient for internal medicine not psychiatry. Pearson had already dictated a column but decided to kill it, concerned about making the allegation without more proof so close to election day. A disappointed Jack Anderson felt that Pearson seemed torn by concerns that would never have inhibited him in the past.[88]

To Pearson's regret, Hubert Humphrey lost to Richard Nixon. The columnist found it inconceivable that anyone so "ruthless, unfair, and cowardly" could become president, and wondered if publishing the Hutschnecker story might have made a difference. A week after the election, he addressed a luncheon at the National Press Club. When the club's president asked how he dealt with spectacular but unsubstantiated or inane stories, he joked that his instinct was naturally to take the inane. Pearson then offered as a serious illustration the unused story of Nixon's psychiatric treatment. That revelation opened floodgates of complaints. Newspapers like the *Washington Post* assailed Pearson for raising the issue at all. Others complained that he should have published it before the election and not waited until the votes had been counted. Nixon's press secretary, Ron Ziegler, called the account false, but Pearson provided verification from the doctor's other patients who had seen Nixon at his offices. He warned that the new president was in danger of creating his own credibility gap. Later evidence indicated that Pearson's reporting rather than Ziegler's denial had been accurate.[89]

The 1968 election closed Drew Pearson's brief interlude as a White House insider. That December, he and Luvie attended what they assumed would be their last White House dinner. "Nixon will not be inviting me, and he may be there for eight years," Pearson calculated, when he would be nearly eighty. At least the departing president remained friendly. He invited Pearson to visit him at his ranch, where the two men reminisced about their long on-again, off-again relationship. "Now you may cut up on me. And you can be mean," said Lyndon Johnson. "But you usually do have the facts."[90]

II

Prisoner of the "Merry-Go-Round"

EVEN BEFORE HE COMPILED AN enemies list, Richard Nixon banned his entire administration from ever speaking to Drew Pearson. Five days prior to his inauguration in January 1969, the new president instructed his chief of staff, H. R. Haldeman, to have someone read Pearson's columns to make sure that no one around him violated his order. He made an exception only for Secretary of State William Rogers, formerly Pearson's attorney, whom Nixon assumed was "smart enough to handle the situation." He had no doubt that Pearson would try to cause him trouble. "The time to deal with this kind of problem is right at the outset of an Administration," Nixon contended, "rather than waiting until we get burned."[1]

The White House staff created a Drew Pearson file to collect not only his latest columns but all previous references to Nixon. Considering that Pearson had covered him for three decades, and that his column appeared daily, this posed a formidable task in the days before digital searches. To their dismay, the staff could find no central repository of Pearson's columns outside of his own office. Their only other option was to crank through the rolls of microfilm of newspapers that carried the column. They began the laborious process, tagging each column as "favorable, unfavorable, or nondescript."[2]

Despite Nixon's suspicions, Pearson gave him a presidential honeymoon by muting criticism in the column. After six months of this, his staff were ready to take off the gloves, but the columnist wanted to give Nixon more time to reveal his true intentions. "Nixon was working for ambition until he became president," he reasoned. "Now he is working for the history books." Pearson was also curious about the effect of the only thing he had in common with Nixon—a Quaker background.[3] In January 1969 he observed:

> Most members of the Society of Friends believe in letting bygones be bygones, and hope that the new President has permanently abandoned political witchhunting. More important, they are concerned over their fellow member's current outlook on peace. . . . Will he continue Mr. Johnson's talks with the Soviet Union seeking long-range peace? Will he push the Paris start toward an early peace in Vietnam? These are "concerns" which Quaker leaders had hoped to discuss with their fellow member before he entered the White House. They will be watching—as will be most Americans—to see how he acts, when he is President, regarding his most important tenet of the Quaker faith.[4]

Age had mellowed Drew Pearson's attitudes toward Nixon, while at the same time it stirred resentment towards his attention-seeking partner, Jack Anderson. Pearson objected when a TV interviewer gave the younger man all the credit for focusing the spotlight on congressmen who cheated. "I suppose it has been twenty years since I started this crusade," he griped. On another occasion he stayed up late to listen to Anderson being interviewed by television talk show host Joe Pyne, who asked why Pearson was still working at sixty-nine. "That's up to him," Anderson replied, suggesting that his senior colleague was "moving over" to make room for him. "I thought Jack handled the whole thing with inexcusable bad taste," Pearson wrote indignantly in his diary.[5]

Anderson retained a mixture of fear and respect for Pearson, even as they shared the column's byline. Having grown used to his boss's habit of sniffing before he began a sentence, he said that "The only jump start I needed in my workday was to pick up the phone and hear that telltale sniff on the other end of the line." Anderson attributed the survival of their partnership to his willingness to disagree. He could speak his mind with confidence that Pearson trusted his opinions, because he "knew that 'yes' from a yes man didn't mean anything." While Pearson wrote the largest share of the column, his contribution increasingly tended toward personal commentary, leaving Anderson to handle the investigative reporting. "The reason for that was he was tied up with the front office; he had to make the contracts. He had to deal with the editors. He had to give the speeches," Anderson explained.

"So, he wasn't free to go digging out the stories . . . and I wound up doing far more than he did."[6]

For years Pearson had goaded the old-timers in Congress to retire, and he wondered now whether he should follow his own advice. His younger brother Leon had died of a heart attack in 1963, which he took as a warning about the strain of constant work. "I feel rather a prisoner of my own Merry-Go-Round," he had confided to his brother a year earlier, "and am making lectures all over the USA in order to balance my budget—which is still unbalanced because of decreasing radio revenue and the attempted boycott against me by the John Birch Society and Rev. Billy Hargis and other right-wing groups." Extremists picketed his speeches and passed out leaflets demonizing him. The Liberty Lobby, which claimed to represent the right-wing spectrum in Washington, sued him. "All of this scares away timid sponsors and timid publishers," Pearson regretted, "of which there are many."[7]

The routine of writing a daily column, weekly newsletter, and radio and television scripts had become a grind. One diary entry noted that he had gotten to bed at 2:30 in the morning, arose at 6:00 to write a column, and was still working at midnight. He continued writing columns at airports while waiting for flights. "Got up at 4:00 and finished most of the radio script, then caught a 6 A.M. plane to Los Angeles," he recorded on another occasion. In a prospectus for his proposed memoirs, he boasted of rarely taking a full day off, seven days a week.[8]

Pearson spent much of his life on the road, toting the old Corona typewriter his father had given him and pounding out columns on the way to his next speaking engagement. In the days when he traveled by train and reserved a sleeping compartment, other passengers complained about his late-night typing. Friendly porters would try to find him a more isolated compartment. At the next station he would telegraph the column to his syndicate. As train schedules cut back, he flew more frequently but found plane seats too cramped for typing.[9]

"I'm not sure whether I can continue indefinitely to travel all night and work all day," he admitted in May 1965. "This time I was bushed; however, I had a column and a broadcast to finish." Later that month he described "trying to write four columns, plus a radio program, in order to leave town for a few days. I succeeded in writing two columns but will have to lug a typewriter along to finish the others." A year later he was complaining of a hectic week. Thursdays and Fridays were always difficult because he prepared columns in advance for the weekends and the newsletters, from which he was trying to exit. In 1969 he tried to persuade his favorable biographer, Herman Klurfeld, to take over the business-oriented newsletter. It had been limping along and was about to go in the red. "I sure would like to get rid of it," he moaned. David Karr had started the newsletter when he needed a job in 1950, and then dumped it on Pearson when he went on to bigger things. Adversaries on the far right predicted that when Pearson retired, "David Katz, alias Karr" would inherit the newsletter. The Liberty Lobby hyped it as "a lucrative racket concocted by Katz-Karr about 15 years ago and nets Pearson and Katz-Karr $150,000 per year. How victims are induced to subscribe to this newsletter is a story in itself." Pearson would have been happy if any of that had been true.[10]

Rather than retiring, Pearson expanded his reach. He invested in local newspapers, the weekly *Maryland News*, and daily Annapolis *Capital Gazette*. When the Bell Syndicate came up for sale in 1965, Pearson took out an additional mortgage on his farm to buy a share, along with Leonard Marks, President Johnson's radio and TV adviser, and publisher Fortune R. Pope (for whose Italian American newspaper, *Il Progresso*, Pearson provided a weekly column). They bought the syndicate for $250,000. After years of squabbling with syndicate executives, Pearson relished taking charge of his own distribution. He congratulated himself for having come a long way from the 1920s, when he peddled features for a news syndicate for a 50 percent commission rather than a salary. He had made a good living at it, "but that was the day when there was competition among newspapers, not monopolies."[11]

Owning his own syndicate freed him from being second-guessed, but the deal did not reap the expected financial rewards. Television ads had drained revenue from radio and newspapers at an alarming rate. In 1967 he lamented the demise of the New York *World Journal Tribune*—itself an amalgam of three defunct newspapers. That left only four major papers in the nation's biggest city (the *Times, Daily News, Post,* and *Wall Street Journal*), where there had once been a dozen. He lost more papers in the South, including the *Atlanta Journal*, that had carried the column for thirty-three years, because of his defense of federal civil rights policies, and papers in the West because of lobbying by the John Birch Society. His syndicate drifted financially downhill. Pearson had to take out additional mortgages and borrow money from his wife to meet his payroll. By 1969 he was hunting for a buyer for the syndicate.[12]

At the same time, Pearson renewed efforts to buy a radio station. In 1966, he and his friend John Duncan, the District of Columbia's first African

American city commissioner, organized an interracial group of investors into the Washington Community Service Broadcasting Company to buy radio station WOOK. Founded after World War II by a white news commentator, Richard Eaton, WOOK had been the first station to aim its programming toward the District's black community. Believing that the station pandered to its audience, Pearson, Duncan, and their associates appealed to the FCC for WOOK's license, pledging to improve the station's offerings. "The Negro population of Washington has been treated to a mixture of rock and roll far beneath its dignity and educational standards," said Pearson, whose taste in music was his least progressive attribute. (In 1956 he predicted that Elvis Presley's star would fall unless he cleaned up his act.) Their well-meaning effort failed to anticipate Richard Eaton's resourcefulness. He tied up their application with technicalities for years, outlasting Drew Pearson.[13]

The biggest financial losses came from Pearson's greatest passion, his farms in Maryland. Pearson had never had any hobbies other than farming, his stepson Tyler Abell noted. He did not golf, and he wrote more than he read, but the farm brought back memories of his childhood summers with his grandparents in Kansas. His farming began with a victory garden during World War II and expanded into a dairy. He also raised hay and packaged and sold his "All Cow, No Bull" manure. He bought two other nearby farms, which required hiring more farmhands and extending his payroll. His earnings from the column and the radio broadcasts were usually enough to sustain the farms' losses, part of which he could deduct from his taxes. In 1967, Pearson calculated that he earned $225,534 from his newspaper columns, television broadcasts, and lectures, and spent $151,209 on staff salaries and other professional expenses. That would have left him a comfortable income, except that the farms lost $64,153.[14]

Pearson's lawyers advised him that his only real asset was himself, so when his income from broadcasting shrank, he made up the difference by lecturing. People assumed that Pearson earned a fortune, without calculating his burden of paying his office staff, farm workers, and libel lawyers. He supported his daughter after she divorced, urging her not to buy him any expensive presents "when there are so many unpaid bills, some of which have been sent to me. I am trying to keep my own expenses down to the very minimum and I have a lot of unpaid bills myself." But he also spent extravagantly to maintain his desired lifestyle. "He'd love to have first-class things," Tyler Abell recalled. The expensive cars he drove and the two servants at his house ate into his income. He paid his staff perpetually low salaries, and they regarded him as a skinflint, but he had to stretch his dollars to meet his payroll. His secretary Kay Raley recalled how heavily his financial responsibilities bore down upon him. Despite their being underpaid, she reflected, "he was such a wonderful man it was really hard to leave him."[15]

Legal fees from all those libel suits had cost him an estimated half million dollars over the years (a figure that multiplies more than tenfold when calculating for later inflation). Legal battles left scars, he confessed, but he would have had to shirk his obligations as a columnist to avoid confrontations. He puzzled over why at the apex of a career as a successful newspaperman he found himself in serious financial straits. His bookkeeper sent him occasional reminders that he was overdrawn. The financial decline seemed to be accelerating, he realized, "and unfortunately, as my 70th birthday approaches, I find myself in a position where the harder I work to increase my income, the more I incapacitate my ability to work."[16]

Further complicating Pearson's life was the discovery in 1967 of some indiscreet letters he had written to a former secretary. The Justice Department alerted him that the woman he knew as Margaret Herring Laughrun, then remarried as Margaret McSurely, had been arrested in Kentucky and charged with sedition. He remembered her as "a beautiful girl and an efficient secretary," who opened his mail, answered his fan letters, and typed the daily entries in his diary in 1963 and 1964. She regarded her boss as having a gruff manner, but a twinkle in his eye. "He saw the trouble in the world," she said, "but also the humor." With her marriage breaking up, they began an affair.[17]

During the summer of 1964, the mail she opened dealt mostly with civil rights and included press releases from the Student Non-Violent Coordinating Committee (SNCC). She urged Pearson to write something about SNCC, but he hesitated because powerful friends in Washington had labeled SNCC organizers troublemakers or even revolutionaries. In August, when she accompanied Pearson to the Democratic National Convention in Atlantic City, he said, "If you think so much of these people, when you finish your work go out and interview them, write something up, and I'll see about putting it in the column." At the convention Laughrun met Fannie Lou Hamer of the Mississippi Freedom Democratic Party, who so inspired her that she quit her job to go work for SNCC in Mississippi. Perplexed and concerned, Pearson wrote affectionate letters encouraging her to come back.[18]

In the spring of 1967, Margaret Laughrun and her new husband, Alan McSurely, relocated in Pikesville, Kentucky, to fight strip mining and campaign for economic reform. On August 11, a politically ambitious county attorney, sure that a Communist conspiracy was about to seize Pike County, raided their home, confiscated their books and papers, and had them arrested. They spent a week in a Kentucky jail. "Probably it was not a good idea to hang a portrait of Che Guevara over the fireplace," she conceded.[19]

A federal court struck down Kentucky's sedition law as unconstitutional, but by then John Brick, an agent of the Senate's Permanent Subcommittee on Investigations, had secured copies of their correspondence. (Brick knew of the couple because his wife had worked for Margaret McSurely's psychiatrist.) The subcommittee's chairman, Arkansas's dour Senator John McClellan, was seeking to connect the urban riots of the 1960s to LBJ's anti-poverty programs and made a tenuous connection to the McSurelys to justify taking their private papers. The correspondence included the letters Pearson had written to Margaret. A grinning John Brick first made Alan McSurely read portions of his wife's personal diary. "It was the most intimate details of her relationship with Mr. Pearson," he said later in court, "and I wasn't stunned by what I was reading, but I was stunned by the fact that, you know, it just dropped on me like a pipe, a lead pipe right on my shoulders, that these guys, this guy standing right here in front of me . . . had taken this stuff, taken it up to the Senate and kept it up there for a year." Brick them showed him a letter that Pearson had addressed to "Dearest Cucumber." "Did this help you investigate the riots?" Alan McSurely asked after reading it.[20]

Drew Pearson had long feuded with Senator McClellan, and Margaret McSurely feared that the senator's possession of the letters might mute the column. Seeing the inquiry as a vendetta against Pearson, she and her husband refused to cooperate. In 1969 they were convicted of contempt of Congress and given one-year prison terms for refusing to hand over the originals of documents that McClellan already had. An appeals court overturned their convictions and ordered the subcommittee to return their papers. The couple went on to sue state and federal officials for the illegal seizure. At the trial, which took place years after Pearson's death, Jack Anderson confirmed that his boss had been fearful that Senator McClellan would use the intimate letters to blackmail him. The McSurelys' eighteen-year legal battle ended with all criminal charges overturned and the US Senate paying damages for having breached their privacy, but their marriage did not survive the ordeal.[21]

Although Pearson avoided mentioning his own embarrassment in the "Merry-Go-Round," he paid attention to allegations of sexual misconduct within the staff of California Governor Ronald Reagan. Unintentionally, Pearson had helped Reagan win his first election in 1966. The columnist got a tip from the incumbent Democratic Governor Pat Brown about a blot on the record of San Francisco's Republican Mayor George Christopher, then seeking the Republican nomination to run against him. Brown regarded the moderate Christopher as a more formidable opponent than the conservative Reagan, whom he dismissed as a mere movie actor. Based on Brown's information, Pearson's columns revealed that Christopher had been arrested in 1940 for buying and selling underpriced milk and watering the cream at his dairy. Although half the newspapers in California declined to publish these columns, Pearson called a press conference to announce that he would sue Christopher for calling him a liar—a ploy to get the story in those papers. He felt foolish bringing a libel suit, having been sued so often himself, but justified it on the grounds of overcoming political news management in California.[22]

The attack on George Christopher backfired spectacularly. It not only cleared the way for Ronald Reagan to win the Republican primary but then go on to defeat Pat Brown for governor. The next year, still smarting from his loss, Brown alerted Pearson that two close aides whom Governor Reagan had inexplicably fired were gay. Overcoming his usual reluctance to inject sex into the column, Pearson wrote about a "homosexual ring" within Reagan's staff that had been eased out of office for engaging in a "sex orgy" in a cabin near Lake Tahoe, omitting any names. Once again, California papers refused to carry these columns (as did most other newspapers). Governor Reagan responded by calling him a liar. "If Pearson's going to hang around California anymore," he told reporters, "he better not spit in the street." But to Reagan's chagrin, his press secretary had already confirmed the story to show that the governor had cleaned house. Confronted with the contradiction, Reagan backed down, admitting that his threat to Pearson had been an injudicious remark he should not have made. That took the wind out of Pearson's sails and he withdrew a column announcing that he was going to California to test Reagan's warning. But Pearson believed that the incident had "pretty well knocked Reagan out of the box as a Republican candidate for President."[23]

Pearson's descent into homophobia inspired Richard Nixon's hatchet man, Murray Chotner, to attempt a little chicanery. Angry over not getting a White House job, Chotner retaliated by slipping Jack Anderson a fabrication that the president's top aides, H. R. Haldeman and John Ehrlichman, were lovers. Seeking substantiation, Anderson contacted Deke DeLoach at the FBI. DeLoach became suspicious that Anderson wanted only to be able to say that the bureau had gotten the information. If the FBI did not investigate,

Anderson could say the story had been hushed up. J. Edgar Hoover agreed, although he raised the possibility that Pearson and Anderson might be relying on a White House source, since they had seemed to have contacts everywhere. Hoover added that Anderson was no friend of the bureau, although he was a "rather nice-looking fellow," whereas Pearson "looks like a skunk and is one."[24]

Relations between Pearson and the FBI director had hit rock-bottom. Hoover sent off protest letters about the column to the Bell Syndicate and Pearson retorted that Congress should have forced the director to comply with a mandatory retirement age. Even when Pearson occasionally commended the FBI for good work, Hoover remained unmoved: "Beware! Praise from this source is like a brickbat!" he jotted on one such favorable column.[25]

Hoover defused the Haldeman-Ehrlichman rumor by interviewing Nixon's aides under oath. He accepted their denials of a "gay cell" in the White House and pronounced Jack Anderson misinformed. The "Merry-Go-Round" never circulated the story. But the White House aides feared that Hoover had used the situation to ingratiate himself with the new president, as Haldeman noted, and "keep us in line, remind us of his potential."[26]

On Christmas Day in 1967, Drew Pearson signed $10,000 worth of checks, unsure whether he had enough funds in the bank to cover them. Being overdrawn was not uncommon for him and anxiety about it was taking a toll. Two days later, a bleeding ulcer sent him to the hospital. "This marks the fourth trip to the hospital for me in approximately three years," he recorded, "which is not a good record."[27]

What saved him from financial disaster was the successful end to several libel suits now that the Supreme Court's *Sullivan* ruling had made it so much harder for public officials to win damages. "This fall we have knocked off the [Thomas] Dodd libel suit, the [Charles Patrick] Clark suit, thanks to his death, the [Philip] Corso suit, thanks to his failure to prosecute, and the [Representative John R.] Pillion suit in Buffalo," Pearson wrote with relief. But the losses from his three farms continued to drain his resources. As much time as he devoted to his cattle and crops and attending farm auctions, he remained an amateur. He made all of the day-to-day operating decisions, often by long-distance telephone, but his mismanagement showed in the farms' declining production. Faced with mounting debts, he concluded that "writers are just never too efficient. Perhaps it's a good thing to keep us spurred on, otherwise I would take things easy."[28]

Book royalties and lecture fees propped up Pearson's accounts. *The Case against Congress,* co-authored with Jack Anderson, became a bestseller—although he contributed only the last chapter. Under his own name Pearson published a Washington novel, *The Senator*, ghostwritten by Gerald Green (author of *The Last Angry Man*). One reviewer decried "a pacing that makes the *Congressional Record* seem brisk," but the book sold swiftly based on Pearson's reputation. Its success inspired Doubleday to send him a check for $100,000 for a second novel, *The President*—about a chief executive who strongly resembled LBJ—which Green would also write under Pearson's name. The second novel appeared posthumously, and the lack of Pearson's input was readily apparent. In May 1969, Pearson signed a contract with Harper's for his memoirs, with a $250,000 advance, receiving a first installment payment of 10 percent.[29]

As he contemplated writing the memoir, Pearson reflected that despite all his successes he had missed the brass ring on two of his goals. He never got the Pulitzer Prize he had hoped for, recalled Kay Raley, who did research for the biography, "and he never got to be secretary of state, which he really wanted." He told her about his early aspirations for a career in diplomacy and how Lyndon Johnson had led him to believe he might be appointed secretary of state. But given the animosities he had stirred for so long, that dream had been farfetched and unattainable.[30]

The deaths of old friends and enemies reminded him of his own mortality. Another chapter in his life ended with the termination of his long-frayed relations with his first co-author, Bob Allen. In 1966, Pearson delivered a lecture in Cleveland and was asked about a decades-old allegation that Roy Howard, head of the Scripps-Howard chain, had cheated on his taxes. When he blamed that column on his former partner, Allen called to complain that the comment embarrassed his wife, Ruth Finney, who wrote a "Washington Calling" column for Scripps-Howard. The hot-tempered Allen cursed so fiercely that Pearson hung up on him. They never spoke again. In later years, Allen vented his anger in interviews with anyone writing about Pearson. He had also begun his own column, paired with the conservative writer Paul Scott. The "Allen-Scott Report" beat the drum for a strong national defense but never matched the "Merry-Go-Round" in circulation. Aged, ill, and lonely after his wife died, Bob Allen could be seen pacing the halls of the National Press Club, rarely speaking to anyone. In 1981, he shot himself at his Georgetown home, and was buried at Arlington National Cemetery.[31]

When President Eisenhower died in 1969, Pearson could not bring himself to praise the man he had criticized so often, even though he knew that his sour opinion would be sure to incite protest mail. Readers strongly objected to his reference to Ike's affair with Kay Summersby during the war, and one newspaper in Minnesota canceled in protest. In retrospect, he decided his memorial had been too frank.[32]

Rival columnist Westbook Pegler also died in 1969, and reporters called on Pearson to comment. It was not easy for him to say much, since they had been on opposite sides of almost every issue, and Pegler had hated him with relish. Publicly, he asserted that the world would miss his "brilliant and acid pen," adding privately in his diary: "Actually he won't be missed a bit." The two had once been friendly before tangling over a trivial item. On the radio, Pearson had recounted some election-night horseplay in 1944. While celebrating FDR's victory the singer Frank Sinatra persuaded a hotel maid to let him into Pegler's suite at the Waldorf-Astoria. Once inside he punched a pillow "as if it were Peg." Pearson's source had been the actor Orson Welles, who relayed it from Sinatra. Vehemently denying that it had ever happened, Pegler called Pearson a "faker as a news reporter." Despite regarding the story as inconsequential, Pearson sued for $50,000. Pegler's apology settled that case amicably, but the acerbic columnist could not hold his temper for long and broke their truce by accusing Pearson of having driven Defense Secretary James Forrestal to suicide. Pearson again sued for libel, this time for $250,000. Pegler's Hearst-owned syndicate had contracted to pay any libel judgments against him, and the Hearst newspaper chain settled the case by agreeing that all its papers, from then on, would carry the "Washington Merry-Go-Round."[33]

Constant work and worry over finances eroded Pearson's own health. In 1965 he contracted malaria on a trip to Africa. Two years later he suffered a stroke but concealed it from the public. "We have diagnosed my illness as a return of malaria," he confided in his diary. The stroke affected his arm and speech, and hospitalized him for a time, but he recovered. "He was killing himself just working so hard," his secretary shuddered. When she urged him to slow down, he replied, "I can't. I've got to go give this speech in Seattle tomorrow." He would sometimes fly home, dictate a column, and turn around and fly out again.[34]

In July 1969, after Senator Edward Kennedy drove off a bridge at Chappaquiddick, killing his passenger, the senator backed out of his commitment to speak at the International Platform Association for professional lecturers. Pearson, who chaired these meetings, "chased him from hell to breakfast for days trying to make him honor the engagement anyway," the IPA director recalled, although his frantic efforts failed.[35]

The columnist looked exhausted while hosting that IPA convention. At the end of July, he awoke with a fever he could not shake. A virus kept him in bed for a week. On the night of August 2, he found it hard to breathe and could not sleep. In the morning, he called his doctor for an oxygen tank, and the doctor ordered him hospitalized. "Things were something of a blur here for several days, except for a very painful test to photograph the heart," he recorded. "They have concluded that I can recover if I take things slowly, but never regain full strength of one heart valve." He had suffered a heart attack and spent much of August at Georgetown University Hospital. Jack Anderson took over the column in his absence. Luvie told the staff not to send her husband anything that might remind him of the news business. When Pearson returned to his farm to recuperate, he drafted a column on the state of modern medicine and instructed his staff to bring him an extra carbon of each new column.[36]

Pearson spent his last days resting at his farm. "He didn't want to know why he was sick," said Tyler Abell; "he wanted to know how to get well." On a warm and sunny September 1, 1969, he read through the newspapers on his terrace and then asked Tyler to drive him around the farm. They toured the dairy barn and bean fields, stopping to talk to fieldhands, until Pearson said they had better turn back. Suddenly he collapsed and had such trouble breathing that his family called for an ambulance. Pearson died on the way to the hospital, with Luvie and Tyler riding beside him. Tyler telephoned Jack Anderson, who put out a press release. Since the office was closed for Labor Day, some of his staff learned the news over the radio.[37]

A thousand people gathered for a memorial service at the Washington National Cathedral. Jack Anderson eulogized Drew Pearson as "a man of courage and conviction, yet never without compassion." Oregon Senator Wayne Morse hailed him as a citizen-statesman who had fought against dishonest and corrupt officials. Fellow journalists offered more mixed assessments. An editorial in the *New York Times* asserted that "beneath the pugnacity, sometimes marred by signs of vindictiveness and irresponsibility, there was always the fearless dedication to the belief that the independent and resourceful reporter is the indispensable guardian of good government." The *Washington Post*, which had found many reasons to cut his columns, acknowledged that "when Mr. Pearson printed the stories that others were too fastidious to be the first to print, the others suddenly had no compunction about printing them." A tribute in *The Times* of London judged that Pearson "brought a good deal of trouble upon himself. Perhaps because of his Quaker background, and his own private vision of what the United States should be, he expected too much of his fellow Americans."[38]

Drew Pearson's family interred his ashes at his farm, on a quiet hillside overlooking the Potomac River. His estate was far less placid. At his death, his bank account was overdrawn. The Bell Syndicate terminated his contract the day after he died. Two publishers demanded return of the advances for books not yet written. His estate also faced some unfinished libel suits and—although Pearson had intended to fight them—chose to settle two cases to avoid the trial costs. His stepson Tyler ended the money-losing "Personal from Pearson" newsletter, dismantled his office staff, and trimmed the labor force on his farms. The legendary Washington lawyer Edward Bennett Williams, once an opponent in court, volunteered to help Luvie settle the estate.[39]

Disconcertingly, they discovered that Pearson had left seven different wills, only one of which had been witnessed, and that in 1938. Pearson typed that will on a train going to give a speech in Council Bluffs, Iowa, and asked the two teachers who met him at the station to witness it. While on the road over the years, he wrote other wills on hotel stationery and blank telegraph forms. None of the others was witnessed, including the last, which he handwrote while in Louisville in 1967, and they were therefore invalid in the District of Columbia, his primary residence. Since the last would have divided his estate between his wife and his daughter from his first marriage, Luvie Pearson chose to honor his wishes and gave Ellen a 160-acre farm near their main farm in Maryland. Her husband's negligence in not leaving a valid current will deprived his grandchildren of inheritances and left his longtime staff without severance pay or pensions. "I was certainly struck by the irony of the situation," observed Tyler Abell in a letter to the register of wills. "Here was a man who had devoted his life to revealing the personal secrets of others but had taken elaborate measures to keep part of his personality shielded even from his closest confidants, friends and family."[40] He had kept hidden his inability to sort out and resolve his own personal affairs and responsibilities.

Drew Pearson intended to turn over his most invaluable tool, a massive name, date, and subject card index for the thousands of "Merry-Go-Round" columns, to Jack Anderson. But his 1938 will had specified that the index go to Robert S. Allen. Even though Pearson had bought out Allen's share in the column, his unforgiving former partner sued the estate to recover the cards. The estate wound up paying Allen $4,000 to drop his claim so that Anderson could have the index. The remaining staff boxed up Pearson's enormous collection of letters and other documents for Lyndon Johnson's presidential library in Austin. Luvie Pearson had never liked sharing her Georgetown home with his office and had the files hauled off by the truckload to a warehouse before shipment to Texas. She said she was sick of the whole business and wanted the building empty. His staff could not blame her, Pearson's secretary confirmed, because "he'd saved every piece of paper that he had ever written on in his life." He never knew when he might need something for the column.[41]

Epilogue

A Muckraker's Legacy

A YEAR BEFORE HIS DEATH, Drew Pearson autographed copies of *The Case against Congress* at Washington's Woodward & Lothrop department store. He recalled that the same store had refused to carry his first book, *Washington Merry-Go-Round*, for being too salacious, while another store had hidden it under the counter and sold it only on request. By the 1960s, muckraking had grown more reputable. Pearson died just before the scandals of the 1970s elevated and bestowed honors on those who followed in his path. His long career linked the old-time muckrakers and the Watergate-spawned investigative reporters.[1]

Jack Anderson became his immediate heir. Although in later years the two had shared the byline, Pearson and Anderson never signed a formal agreement spelling out the column's future. Anderson grieved the death of his mentor but also felt freed from his long apprenticeship. Resentful at being underpaid and treated more as an employee than a partner, he was determined to assume full control of the column. Anderson negotiated a settlement with Pearson's family and the syndicate, paying Luvie Pearson a monthly stipend for use of the "Washington Merry-Go-Round" name. He also agreed to a reduced payment from the syndicate, recognizing that some editors had kept the column only because Drew Pearson had been a household name and might use his death as an excuse to cancel—as thirty-six quickly did.[2]

Everyone advised Anderson not to change the format of what he called "the world's most successful column," but he intended to cut down the commentary and gossip to make it a mostly investigative outlet. After some initial losses, the subscriptions stabilized when editors realized the risk of letting rival papers pick it up and draw away readers. Gradually, more papers signed on, but Anderson declined the credit. "Drew made the column," he said, "and I started at the peak of its power and success."[3]

Pearson had hoped that the "Washington Merry-Go-Round" would survive his death, and Anderson insisted its voice would never be stilled. In his own clumsy way, Richard Nixon helped fulfill that wish. On the assumption that Anderson did not share Pearson's hostility toward him, Nixon sent his courier Murray Chotiner with a peace offering. When Anderson needed to know something, he could call Chotiner, who would call Nixon. Anderson accepted, saying he never turned down an offer. For a while, that arrangement turned the column more sympathetic to the Nixon administration. Before long, however, the president's obsession with secrecy and plugging leaks raised Anderson's hackles and prompted a revival of investigative journalism. "Drew died a pariah before Watergate suddenly transformed his heirs into folk heroes," Anderson affirmed.[4]

In 1972, Anderson achieved a goal that had always eluded Drew Pearson. He won a Pulitzer Prize for the revelation that the Nixon administration had secretly tilted toward Pakistan during its war with India, despite a public pledge to maintain neutrality. Anderson's source, navy yeoman Charles Radford, was a stenographer on Henry Kissinger's National Security Council staff. The yeoman had funneled classified documents from the White House to the Joint Chiefs of Staff, and Anderson, who knew Radford as a fellow Mormon, persuaded him to share them with him. In a column that appropriately opened with a tribute to Drew Pearson on what would have been his seventy-fourth birthday, Anderson wrote that his mentor, were he still alive, "would not spare our own leaders who have been less than candid in dealing with the Indian-Pakistani crisis." Henry Kissinger denounced the column for taking his words out of context, which opened the door for Anderson to release the classified material verbatim as a rebuttal. This reinforced his credibility, elevated his stature, and helped convince another three hundred newspapers to subscribe to the "Merry Go-Round," bringing the total to nearly a thousand.[5]

"This son of a bitch Anderson really knows how to work us," President Nixon complained in remarks captured on one of his secret Oval Office tape recordings. "He has more people around the government than, I guess, anybody ever had," Attorney General John Mitchell agreed. "Far more than Drew Pearson ever had." "Got more out of 'em, too," Nixon griped. Within the Nixon White House fanciful plots churned to eliminate Anderson, with schemes that ranged from killing him to drugging him to make him sound incoherent on the air.[6]

At Washington's National Airport, on June 16, 1972, Anderson bumped into Frank Sturgis, a soldier of fortune he had known since the Bay of Pigs fiasco in 1961, when Fidel Castro's forces defeated a CIA-funded Cuban refugee invasion. Four edgy companions accompanied Sturgis. "What are you doing in town?" Anderson asked. "Oh, we're here on some private business," Sturgis smiled noncommittally. In Cleveland, Anderson read news accounts that the same five men had been arrested the next day for breaking into the Democratic National Committee's headquarters at the Watergate. Over the next two years, Anderson devoted his attention overwhelmingly to the Watergate story, focusing 418 columns on the scandal, but the glory went to two Metro reporters for the *Washington Post*, Bob Woodward and Carl Bernstein, thanks to Deep Throat, their secret source high inside the FBI. The *Post* cut many of Anderson's Watergate columns to lessen his competition with its own reporters. He resented the national accolades showered on Woodward and Bernstein, regarding his own contributions as much bigger than theirs. "I have to do almost daily what Woodward and Bernstein did once," he insisted. At the end of 1972, Anderson presented the Drew Pearson Foundation's Drew Pearson Prize for investigative reporting to Woodward and Bernstein.[7]

Watergate converted Anderson to Pearson's more judgmental style. He had intended to avoid the personal animosities for which his mentor had been famous, and even tried getting along with Richard Nixon. "But I sense the ghost of Drew Pearson hovering restlessly over my typewriter," Anderson wrote in the "Merry-Go-Round." "He must be in a magnificent rage over the Watergate revelations, which confirmed the worst he ever wrote about Richard Nixon." Anderson himself had reached a breaking point. "No longer can I suppress my outrage over the abuse of power at the pinnacle," he declared. A quarter century earlier, Pearson had sensed the fatal flaw in Nixon's character, he noted. "Drew was all too right about Nixon."[8]

Lacking Pearson as an anchor, however, Anderson drifted. The pressure to produce revelations led him to stumble into some appalling mistakes. During the 1972 election, he reported that the Democratic candidate for vice president, Thomas Eagleton, had a record of drunk driving. Without hard proof, Anderson rushed to make the charge on national television to avoid being scooped. He insisted that his source possessed the photostatic evidence, but the informer—an unsuccessful candidate who had run against Eagleton for the Senate—never produced the promised documents. By the time Anderson finally retracted the spurious charge, he had damaged his own reputation as much as Eagleton's. His staff puzzled that he could produce worldwide headlines with scoops about corruption but also fail so spectacularly by putting his faith in bad sources and having to issue embarrassing retractions.[9]

Parkinson's disease, diagnosed in 1986, eventually ebbed Anderson's strength and diverted his attention from the column. "The digging, the slogging, I leave that to others now," he admitted. With the column losing money, he sustained the enterprise by delivering high-paying lectures and television commentary. Anderson also made some risky business deals. In 1992 came a distressing revelation that the Exxon Corporation had paid him to deliver a positive TV analysis of the company's efforts to clean up the *Exxon-Valdez* oil spill in Alaska.[10]

"Nobody portrays me as noble as I think I am," Anderson complained. As his ethics came under fire, he tended to compare himself favorably to his predecessor. He pictured Drew Pearson as a knee-jerk liberal whose penchant for making a better world had led him to lobby politicians to support his causes. He blamed Pearson's personal politics for restricting the column by treating some politicians kindly in return for their support on favored issues. Anderson called these tactics unscrupulous—without specifying which had been his own inspiration or Pearson's. Drawing on these confessions, the veteran journalist Richard Harwood held the two columnists as cautionary examples for future journalists. "Pearson and Anderson were brilliant muckrakers, successful and influential," he wrote, "able to remedy specific problems in the political process and to punish many villains in public life. But at the end of the day, as Anderson is aware, a big question remains: at what price to the soul?" Pearson would have recognized this as a case of guilt by association.[11]

In January 1997, the *Washington Post* reorganized its comics page and dropped the "Merry-Go-Round," after a forty-four-year run. The paper did not bother to mention this omission to its readers, and no one seemed to notice. Cutting off its Washington outlet diminished the column's clout at the White House and on Capitol Hill. Anderson stopped contributing to the column in 2001, though he did not announce his retirement until 2004, a year before he died.[12]

Under Drew Pearson, Robert Allen, and Jack Anderson, the "Merry-Go-Round" countered official secrecy and made a forceful case for openness. They contended convincingly that the US government classified far too much information for reasons of national security—or national insecurity—suppressing information that was more embarrassing than damaging. State secrecy withheld what citizens ought to know. Closed proceedings and selectively released information too often constituted misinformation. Unlike autocracies, whose rulers make decisions unfettered, democracies require informed citizens, who judge their leaders by casting their ballots. Pearson did his best to assure that government did not operate in the dark.[13]

The federal government's confrontation with secret-breakers expanded during the decades following Drew Pearson's death, and accelerated after the terrorist attacks on September 11, 2001. Prying open closed doors, demanding accountability, and exposing corruption remained hallmarks of investigative journalism, but national security violations led to renewed threats of prosecution under the Espionage Act. Despite governmental efforts at restraint, many in the Washington press corps challenged official versions of events more assertively, checking facts and overtly identifying lies. Politicians in turn accused the media of sensationalism and fake news. Leaks continued to dog official Washington, and reporters persevered in refusing to reveal their sources, risking imprisonment rather than betray a confidence. Successful suits for libel, by contrast, diminished in the wake of the *Sullivan* case, which shifted the burden of proof to frustrated officials who felt maligned. During the 2016 campaign, Donald Trump expressed his personal outrage by pledging to "open up our libel laws so when they write purposely negative and horrible and false articles, we can sue them and win lots of money."[14]

Since Pearson's days, the proliferation of talk radio, cable television networks, and twenty-four-hour news broadcasts intensified heated rhetoric in news commentary. In 1987 the Federal Communications Commission dropped the Fairness Doctrine, which had required stations to present contrasting viewpoints to retain their licenses, further contributing to the stridency. During the 1990s, the Internet began luring advertising revenue away from the print media. Newspapers and magazines slashed their newsroom staffs as online news services developed. Beyond organized news sites, an array of social media provided the public with greater ability to respond on their own, making universal the field of discourse once available almost exclusively to columnists and commentators.[15]

The decades after Drew Pearson's death saw storehouses of government documents, intelligence reports, personal manuscripts, and once-secret recordings opened for research. They offered means to assess the numerous accusations that appeared in the "Washington Merry-Go-Round." Presidential press secretaries, cabinet members, senators, representatives, and other targets, high and low, repeatedly denounced the columnist as a liar, but the subsequent archival evidence more often verified his accusations than the protests of his accusers, and validated Drew Pearson's sense of smell. Despite Pearson's intermittent mistakes, the evidence affirms his claim that he performed a public service by revealing how politicians and government really worked.

Like all media legends in their own times, Pearson's name faded in the public's mind after he ceased reporting and commenting. For decades, he had appeared daily in most everyone's newspapers, and weekly on radio and television, so that his name worked its way into cartoon captions and board games. In later years, the Dallas Cowboys' wide receiver Drew Pearson preempted his prominence. That Drew Pearson's parents had named their future football-playing son for their favorite newspaper columnist. Memory of the journalist Drew Pearson lingered through the publication of much of his revealing diary, which historians and biographers have found ever useful to quote. In a broader sense, his influence persisted through the investigative reporters who followed him, in print, on the air, and online. Willing to challenge prevailing opinion and unwilling to take officials at their word, these new muckrakers continued to reveal hidden truths and unmask deception. As Pearson instructed his staff, whenever those in power betrayed their trust, "then it is your job to be ruthless in exposing that betrayal. You must be their watchdog. You must let them know what the publicity penalty is—if they fail." His admonition remains valid today.[16]

A NOTE ON SOURCES

———✦———

DREW PEARSON SPENT HIS LIFE writing, preserving what was on his mind, in abundance. His papers are primarily located at the Lyndon B. Johnson Presidential Library in Austin. His father, Paul Martin Pearson, left an extensive collection of records at the Friends Historical Library at Swarthmore College. Drew Pearson's sister, Barbara Lange Godfrey, gave a small collection of the family's correspondence to American University's Special Collections. Files relating to the Friendship Train are in the Manuscript Division of the Library of Congress.

From 1949 until his death in 1969, Pearson kept an almost daily diary. Substantial portions of his diaries were published in Tyler Abell, ed., *Drew Pearson Diaries, 1949–1959* (1974), and Peter Hannaford, ed., *Washington Merry-Go-Round: The Drew Pearson Diaries, 1960–1969* (2015). Tyler Abell generously provided me with access to the previously unpublished portions of the diaries, including the last months that had earlier gone missing, as well as other Pearson papers in his possession. Katherine (Kay) Raley Watkins, Pearson's last secretary, also contributed two boxes of documents that Pearson had personally selected to help him write his never-completed autobiography, which will also go to the Johnson Library.

A thousand pages of FBI reports and correspondence about Drew Pearson are open for research at the National Archives. These files trace the arc of Pearson's association with J. Edgar Hoover, from friendship to animosity, recorded by Hoover's increasingly heated comments handwritten in the margins of memoranda. Hoover directed that an FBI agent monitor Pearson's Sunday night radio and television shows and prepare a memorandum for Monday morning, summarizing and rebutting anything he said about the bureau. These reports now provide a handy survey of Pearson's broadcasts. Extensive FBI files for Jack Anderson during his collaboration with Pearson are also available through the National Security Archives' Internet Archive, documenting the bureau's failed attempts to "fix responsibility" for the leaks.

Michael Binstein, a partner of Jack Anderson's, donated a complete collection of "Washington Merry-Go-Round" columns, from 1932 to 1969, to American University. That collection consists of 50,000 pages of yellowing and brittle copies of the column as distributed by their syndicate. American University has digitized all the columns and posted them online. In addition, those columns that appeared in the *Washington Post* from 1942 to 1969 are online and searchable through ProQuest. For someone who began researching with brittle volumes of newsprint and hand-cranked microfilm readers, these websites made Pearson's thousands of columns remarkably accessible and convenient for review.

Both Drew Pearson and Robert Allen gave oral history interviews to the Johnson Library. Tyler Abell sponsored an oral history project with members of Pearson's family and former staff, ably conducted by Brien Williams. Other helpful oral histories are located at the Truman, Eisenhower, Kennedy, and Johnson presidential libraries, as well as the interviews that I conducted for the Senate Historical Office. Additional interviews are Drew Pearson's appearance on the television show, *The Mike Wallace Interview*, December 7, 1957, in the C-SPAN archive; Jack Anderson's interview, May 23, 1979, in the Studs Terkel Radio Archive; Anderson's interview with Tim Chambless, March 15, 1986, in the Jack Anderson Papers; Stetson Kennedy's interview on National Public Radio's *Talk of the Nation*, May 23, 2005; and Tyler Abell's interview on C-SPAN's *Q&A*, December 28, 2015.

Beyond the columns, Drew Pearson authored or co-authored seven books and lent his name to two ghostwritten novels. In November 1956, he published a four-part autobiographical series, "Confessions of an S.O.B.," in the *Saturday Evening Post*—a magazine with a record of having published unflattering articles about him in the past. The popularity of the series prompted publishers to propose the memoir that he never found the time to write.

During Pearson's lifetime, several books about him were published. Morris A. Beale's *All America Louse: A Candid Biography of Drew A. Pearson* [*sic*] (1965) is a nasty smear, lacking all credibility. Not much more reliable, Frank Kluckhohn and Jay Franklin's *The Drew Pearson Story* (1967) offers the opinions of Pearson's harshest detractors in the press corps, which prompted J. Edgar Hoover to encourage his associates to "Get a copy if you do not have it." Kluckhohn, a former reporter, had worked for Defense Secretary James Forrestal, the Republican National Committee, and the Liberty Lobby, all Pearson opponents. To balance these negative assessments, Pearson recruited Herman Klurfeld to write *Behind the Lines: The World of Drew Pearson* (1968), and revised portions himself, producing a more respectable but unchallenging assessment.

Four years after Pearson's death, Oliver Pilat published *Drew Pearson: An Unauthorized Biography* (1973), a title he explained in a letter to Luvie Pearson, on November 5, 1972:

> A decade ago I did a bio of Westbrook Pegler, which led to Drew's original recommendation that I do one about him. I have included as subtitle for my book "An Unauthorized Biography" because you told somebody in Washington that I was pretending to write it as an authorized biography, which is how it started out not how it ended. Oh, oh, what I started to say about Peg is that no new biography of him appeared since then and I don't think any will, since the memory of a newspaperman however great his impact, swiftly fades. From a historic point of view, this may be the only Pearson biography.

Pilat's book contained no citations and indicated only that he relied heavily on interviews, "too numerous to list." Some sources had been "promised immunity from mention," but he specifically cited Pearson's sisters, office manager Marian Canty, partner Robert Allen, leg man Jack Anderson, biographer Herman Klurfeld, and Margaret and Alan McSurely. Suspicious of his motives, Luvie and her son Tyler kept him at a distance and denied him access to Pearson's papers and diaries.

Lacking manuscripts, Pilat made dubious assumptions about Drew Pearson's life, motives, and sources. Among these was his misidentification of Pearson's mother, Edna Rachel Wolfe Pearson, as a Jewish convert to Quakerism, news that surprised her surviving children. Pilat concluded that Edna's father, Dr. Morris Ezra Wolfe, a dentist, had been "unobtrusively Jewish," and that she became a Quaker at Swarthmore because she felt unsure "how she would be received as a Jew in that closed campus atmosphere." Family records instead show that Drew Pearson's grandfather had been baptized Ezra (after his father) Morris (after a Methodist bishop) Wolf. As a young man he reordered his first and middle names and added an "e" to his surname. There is no indication that he or his thirteen siblings were Jewish. This matters only because Pilat made Pearson's supposed Jewish roots an explanation for the frequent accusations of antisemitism that appeared in the "Washington Merry-Go-Round." Pilat called antisemitism "a highly offensive and difficult-to-prove adjective, in excoriating the isolationists." It was true that fascism and antisemitism offended Pearson, but his passion reflected an abhorrence of bigotry, not his family's heritage.

The first volume of Pearson's diaries, which Pilat did not have while writing the biography, appeared the next year. Writing a critical review in the *Philadelphia Inquirer* (February 24, 1974), he exposed his own attitudes. "Drew generally used scandal to advance his rad-lib causes," he wrote. "Pearson made large contributions to a better world but his lobbying for his causes was often incredibly crass." Pilat's unreliable biography stood for years as the primary book on Pearson and contributed to some of the negative assessments the columnist received in other accounts. For all his faults, Drew Pearson's contributions to American journalism were far more significant than his detractors acknowledged.

NOTES

Introduction

1. James Boyd, *Above the Law* (New York: New American Library, 1968), 170–72; Peter Hannaford, ed., *Washington Merry-Go-Round: The Drew Pearson Diaries, 1960–1969* (Lincoln, NE: Potomac Books, 2015), 389.
2. "Washington Merry-Go-Round" (WMGR), *Washington Post*, April 1, 1966.
3. Nigel West, ed., *The Secret History of British Intelligence in the Americas, 1940–1945* (New York: Fromm International, 1999), 127–28; Michael L. Gillette, *Lady Bird Johnson: An Oral History* (New York: Oxford University Press, 2012), 247; Richard L. Strout, "Pearson 'Kept on Exposing Them,'" *Christian Science Monitor*, September 5, 1969.
4. "Querulous Quaker," *Time* 52 (December 13, 1948): 70–71.
5. Curt Heseltine, "Drew Pearson at the Brink of 70: Meet the Man Behind the Column" [c. December 1968], advertisement for Bell-McClure Syndicate, Jack Anderson Papers, George Washington University.
6. Timothy Mark Chambless, "Columnist Jack Anderson, the Secular Evangelist: Five Speeches in Utah between 1972 and 1975" (master's thesis in Speech Communication, University of Utah, 1977), 44; Matt Mitchell oral history, 7–8, Tyler Abell Papers, Potomac, Maryland; Katherine Raley letter to the editor, *Washington Post*, September 6, 1969; Pearson on *The Mike Wallace Interview*, December 7, 1957, C-SPAN.
7. Jack Anderson, "Looking Back at Pearson," *Atlanta Constitution*, January 2, 1977; Pearson to John N. Wheeler and Henry M. Snevily, December 21, 1945, Drew Pearson Papers, Lyndon B. Johnson Presidential Library.
8. Pearson memo to Jack Anderson, December 3, 1949, Anderson Papers; William L. Rivers, *The Opinionmakers* (Westport, CT: Greenwood Press, 1965), 111; Jack Anderson with James Boyd, *Confessions of a Muckraker: The*

Inside Story of Life in Washington during the Truman, Eisenhower, Kennedy and Johnson Years (New York: Random House, 1979), 13; WMGR, *Washington Post*, February 28, 1951; October 21, 1954.

9. Patrick Anderson, "The Truth about Drew Pearson," *Washingtonian* 3 (June 1968): 41; Robert Sherrill, "The Revealing Diaries of Drew Pearson," *Chicago Sun-Times*, February 24, 1974; Arthur Schlesinger, "I Shall Tell You All," *Washington Post*, February 24, 1974; Anderson, *Confessions of a Muckraker*, 145.

10. Mark Clague, ed., *The Memoirs of Alton Augustus Adams, Sr.: First Black Bandmaster of the United States Navy* (Berkeley: University of California Press, 2008), 199; Tyler Abell oral history #5, 5–6, Abell Papers; Drew Pearson, "Confessions of an S.O.B.," *Saturday Evening Post* 229 (November 3, 1956): 23.

11. Anderson, "The Truth about Drew Pearson," 38.

12. Carlisle Bargeron, "Washington's Mighty Penmen," *Nation's Business* 34 (May 1, 1946): 58–64, 106, 110–11; see Donald A. Ritchie, *Reporting from Washington: The History of the Washington Press Corps* (New York: Oxford University Press, 2005), 133–58.

13. Michael Hopkins alerted me to this report from R. H. Brand to the Chancellor of the Exchequer, Sir John Anderson, August 23, 1944, Robert Brand Papers, 197/1, C folder, Bodleian Library, Oxford; Ronald Steel, *Walter Lippmann and the American Century* (Boston: Little, Brown, 1980); Stewart Alsop, *The Center: People and Power in Political Washington* (New York: Harper & Row, 1968), 180–81.

14. Joseph Alsop with Adam Platt, *"I've Seen the Best of It": Memoirs* (New York: W. W. Norton, 1992), 119; see also Robert W. Merry, *Taking on the World: Joseph and Stewart Alsop—Guardians of the American Century* (New York: Penguin, 1996).

15. Charles Fisher, *The Columnists* (New York: Howell, Soskin, 1944), reviewed the leading columnists of the 1930s and 1940s; [Robert S. Allen and Drew Pearson], *Washington Merry-Go-Round* (New York: Horace Liveright, 1931), 351.

16. Bargeron, "Washington's Mighty Penmen," 111.

17. Pearson described himself in his "Confessions of an S.O.B." series in the *Saturday Evening Post* 229 (November 3–24, 1956); Fisher, *The Columnists*, 238–39.

18. Peter Edson, "Interpretation and Analysis of Washington News," in *The Press in Washington: Sixteen Top Newsmen Tell How the News Is Collected, Written, and Communicated from the World's Most Important Capital*, ed. Ray Eldon Hiebert (New York: Dodd, Mead, 1966), 320.

19. Pearson, unpublished diary, December 10, 1964, Pearson Papers; Seymour K. Freidin, *A Sense of the Senate* (New York: Dodd, Mead, 1972), 83; Hannaford, ed., *Washington Merry-Go-Round*, 205; see also Frank Rich, "Confessions of a Recovering Op-Ed Columnist," *New York Times*, March 13, 2011.

20. WMGR, *Washington Post*, September 2, 1969; Donald A. Ritchie, *Press Gallery: Congress and the Washington Correspondents* (Cambridge, MA: Harvard University Press, 1991), 179–94.

21. Ritchie, *Reporting from Washington*, 221–23; [Allen and Pearson], *Washington Merry-Go-Round*, 349.

22. Al Aronowitz, "A Talk with America's Number One Muckraker, Jack Anderson," *Gallery* [undated], 31–38, Jack Anderson Papers, George Washington University; Rivers, *The Opinionmakers*, 123–24; David Cooper, "The Drew Pearson Story: Hated, Feared, Scorned and Read by Everybody," *Detroit Free Press*, August 5, 1973; C. E. Hennrich to A. H. Belmont, December 20, 1951, Jack Anderson FBI files, National Security Archives; Drew Pearson, "Confessions of an S.O.B.: How to Make Enemies," *Saturday Evening Post* 229 (November 24, 1956): 37.

23. Anderson, "The Truth about Drew Pearson," 40; Dan Tyler Moore to Tyler Abell, August 20, 1974, Abell Papers.

24. Carl Elliott, "Kept 'Em Honest at Top," Jasper, Alabama, *Daily Mountain Eagle*, December 21, 1973. Elliott was more critical of Pearson in his memoirs: "He shot from the hip, spraying the landscape with his off-the-cuff conclusions. A fellow who fires his rifle as often as Pearson did is bound to hit the target once in a while, but he missed much too often for my comfort." Carl Elliott Sr. and Michael D'Orso, *The Cost of Courage: The Journey of an American Congressman* (Tuscaloosa: University of Alabama Press, 2001), 150–51.

25. Henry F. Pringle, "SRL Washington Poll: Surveying the Capital Correspondents," *Saturday Review of Literature* 27 (October 14, 1944): 17–19; George Carlin to Si Cassady, February 6, 1942, Pearson Papers; Frank Kluckhohn and Jay Franklin, *The Drew Pearson Story* (Chicago: Chas. Hallberg & Company, 1967), 1.

26. WMGR, *Washington Post*, October 5, 1953; Brit Hume, *The Inside Story* (Garden City, NY: Doubleday, 1974), 31; Rivers, *The Opinionmakers*, 126; George A. Carlin to Hugh Kane, April 4, 1942, Pearson Papers.

27. Scott I. Peek Oral History, Senate Historical Office, 1992, 65; Tom Dowling, "Who Knows What Evil Lurks in the Hearts of Men?: Jack Anderson Knows," *Washingtonian* 6 (May 1971): 91; Alden Whitman, "Watchdog of Virtue," *New York Times*, September 2, 1969.

28. Rivers, *The Opinionmakers*, 117–18; Leonard Downie Jr., *The New Muckrakers* (Washington, DC: New Republic Book Company, 1976), 139–40; Cabell Philips, "The Pearson Treatment," *New York Times*, November 9, 1958.

29. United Features Syndicate to editors, April 30, 1937, Pearson Papers; WMGR, *Washington Post*, May 4, 1967.

30. Seymour M. Hersh, *Reporter: A Memoir* (New York: Random House, 2018), 327; "Satanic," *Washington Post*, May 25, 1944; Anderson, "The Truth about Drew Pearson," 41; L. B. Nichols to Clyde Tolson, November 20, 1946, FBI files, 94-HQ-8-350, Serials 283–374, RG65, National Archives and Records Administration (NARA).

31. *Meridian* (Mississippi) *Star*, November 12, 1964.

32. Drew Pearson, "Confessions of an S.O.B.: How to Make Enemies," 36; Pearson to T. C. O'Donovan, February 7, 1935, Benjamin Bradlee to Luvie Pearson, September 10, 1969, Pearson Papers.

33. WMGR, *Washington Post*, November 24, 1960; Julie Hall oral history, 6, Tyler Abell oral history #4, 4, Abell Papers.

34. William V. Shannon, "Drew Pearson Diaries," *New York Times*, March 17, 1974; Fisher, *The Columnists*, 225; Anderson, *Confessions of a Muckraker*, 14; Pearson, "Confessions of an S.O.B.: How to Make Enemies," 37; David Cooper, "The Drew Pearson Story."

35. Pearson, "Confessions of an S.O.B.: How to Make Enemies," 148; Jack Anderson interview, May 23, 1979, Studs Terkel Radio Archive; "Drew Pearson," *Washington Post*, September 3, 1969.

36. Pearson, unpublished diary, August 26, 1965, Pearson Papers; WMGR, *Washington Post*, May 20, 1953, October 27, 1959; *Congressional Record*, 91st Cong., 1st sess. (1969), 28047.

37. "Chronic Liar," *Time* 42 (September 13, 1943): 18–20; Winston Churchill telegram to Field Marshal Sir Harold Alexander, December 14, 1944, Churchill Archives Online; Jack Anderson with Daryl Gibson, *Peace, War, and Politics: An Eyewitness Account* (New York: Forge, 1999), 63; S. W. Reynolds memo to D. M. Ladd, December 14, 1944, FBI files, 94-HQ-8-350, Serials 283–374, RG65, NARA.

38. Hannaford, ed., *Washington Merry-Go-Round*, 428.

39. WMGR, January 1, 1950.

Chapter 1

1. Richard L. Strout, "Washington in 1931: Politics, People and the Press," *Washington Post Book World*, July 22, 1984; Charles Fisher, *The Columnists* (New York: Howell, Soskin, 1944), 234–35; Tyler Abell, ed., *Drew Pearson Diaries, 1949–1959* (New York: Holt, Rinehart & Winston, 1974), 440.

2. [Robert S. Allen and Drew Pearson], *Washington Merry-Go-Round* (New York: Horace Liveright, 1931), 350, 358.

3. "Robert S. Allen, Political Columnist," *New York Times*, February 24, 1981; Jack Eisen, "Robert S. Allen, Colorful Newsman in Washington," *Washington Post*, February 25, 1981; WMGR, July 1, 1942; American University Digital Research Archive (AU); John Nelson Rickard, ed., *Forward with Patton: The World War II Diary of Colonel Robert S. Allen* (Lexington: University Press of Kentucky, 2017), 1–4; Ishbel Ross, *Ladies of the Press: The Story of Women in Journalism by an Insider* (New York: Harper & Brothers, 1936), 339–42.

4. Bennett Cerf, *At Random: The Reminiscences of Bennett Cerf* (New York: Random House, 2002), 31; Lawrence Rainey, *Institutions of Modernism: Literary Elites and Public Culture* (New Haven: Yale University Press, 1998), 48.

5. Strout, "Washington in 1931"; WMGR, July 1, 1942, AU; WMGR, *Washington Post*, January 25, 1946; Robert S. Allen oral history, 2, Lyndon B. Johnson Presidential Library.

6. Donald A. Ritchie, *Reporting from Washington: The History of the Washington Press Corps* (New York: Oxford University Press, 2005), 95; [Allen and Pearson], *Washington Merry-Go-Round*, 11.

7. Allen oral history, 2–3; Allen to Pearson [c. June 1939], Drew Pearson Papers; [Allen and Pearson], *Washington Merry-Go-Round*, 39.

8. John Earl Haynes, Harvey Klehr, and Alexander Vassiliev, *Spies: The Rise and Fall of the KGB in America* (New Haven: Yale University Press, 2009), 159–60; Steven T. Usdin, *Bureau of Spies: The Secret Connections Between Espionage and Journalism in Washington* (Amherst, NY: Prometheus Books, 2018), 19–28. Alexander Vassiliev's Yellow Notebook #4 at the Library of Congress includes entries for Allen only in January and February 1933.

9. Genevieve Forbes Herrick, "Capital Gets Another Ride in New Satire," *Chicago Tribune*, August 25, 1932.

10. Drew Pearson, "Confessions of an S.O.B.," *Saturday Evening Post* 229 (November 3, 1956): 87; Pearson to Monte [unnamed], December 9, [1932], Pearson Papers; "Co-Authorship of Capital Book Costs His Job," *Chicago Tribune*, September 3, 1932; Abell, ed., *Drew Pearson Diaries*, 228.

11. Pearson to Felicia Gizycka, September 15, 1932, Pearson Papers.

12. His middle name, Russell, was for his grandmother, Abigail Russell Wolfe, Edna Pearson's stepmother. Pearson, chapter 1 of a proposed memoir, Pearson Papers.

13. "Unorthodoxy Quakers" referred to the liberal Quakers who founded Swarthmore College; Barbara Pearson Lange, "Keep Your Suspenders Up!," *Swarthmore College Bulletin* (March 1966): 6–10; Paul M. Pearson and Barbara Pearson-Lange, "'Unorthodoxy Quakers' at Swarthmore," *Friends Journal* 12 (June 1, 1966): 284–85; Barbara Pearson Lange Godfrey, *Man of Chautauqua and His Caravans of Culture: The Life of Paul M. Pearson* [Swarthmore, PA: privately printed, 2001].

14. Drew Pearson, "Paul Martin Pearson: 1871–1938," *Today's Speech* 7 (September 1959): 9; Pearson, unpublished diary, August 11, 1964, Pearson Papers; Julie Hall oral history, 10–15, Abell Papers; Daisy Yuhas, "A Glance at Swarthmore's Quaker Roots," *The Phoenix*, November 14, 2006.

15. Drew Pearson, "Growing Up in Swarthmore," in *Swarthmore Remembered*, ed. Maralyn Orbison Gillespie (Swarthmore, PA: Swarthmore College, 1964), 51–55; Pearson, unpublished diary, January 21, 1960; Pearson, notes for a memoir, chapter 1, Pearson Papers; Pearson, "Confessions of an S.O.B." (November 3, 1956): 23; Tom Pearson, "Portrait of an Uncle," *South Dakota Union*, May 12, 1974; Tyler Abell oral history, 4–5, Abell Papers.

16. Paul Pearson to Drew Pearson, 1902, 1903, Paul Pearson Papers, Friends Library, Swarthmore College; Julie Hall oral history, 5–6, Abell Papers; Pearson, unpublished diary, February 22, 1964, Pearson Papers.

17. Paul M. Pearson, "The Chautauqua Movement," *Annals of the American Academy of Political and Social Sciences* 40 (March 1, 1912): 211–16; "Chautauqua System to Bring Drama into Provinces," *Theatre Magazine* 36 (September 1922): 194.

18. Pearson, unpublished diary, April 2, 1962, Pearson, chapter 1 of a proposed memoir, Pearson, unpublished diary, August 9, 1965, Pearson Papers; see Morris A. Beale, *All America Louse: A Candid Biography of Drew A. Pearson* [*sic*] (Washington, DC: Columbia Publishing Company, 1965), 22–25; WMGR, *Washington Post*, April 5, 1943.

19. Drew Pearson to Paul Pearson, August 7, 1914, Paul Pearson to Edna Pearson [1914], Paul Pearson Papers; Pearson, unpublished diaries, May 28, 1965, Pearson to his grandsons, June 7, 1965, Pearson Papers.

20. Pearson to grandsons, January 25, 1965, Pearson, chapter 1 of a proposed memoir, Pearson Papers; "Washington Merry-Go-Round," May 2, 1963, AU; "The Smileage Book Campaign," *Lyceum Magazine* 27 (February 1918): 19–20.

21. Pearson, "Our Debt to Humanity," 1919, Paul Pearson Papers; Pearson, unpublished diary, August 28, 1957, Pearson Papers.

22. Pearson, chapter 1 of a proposed memoir, Pearson Papers; Pearson to Leon Pearson, July 27, September 13, 1919, March 19, 1920, Paul Pearson Papers; WMGR, May 2, 1963, AU.

23. Pearson to Grandpa and Grandma, November 23, 1921, Pearson Family Papers, American University; Pearson oral history, 1–2, Johnson Library; Pearson, chapter 1 of a proposed memoir, Pearson Papers; on the status of the diplomatic corps, see Martin Weil, *A Pretty Good Club: The Founding Fathers of the U.S. Foreign Service* (New York: W. W. Norton, 1978).

24. WMGR, *Washington Post*, December 20, 1943; Pearson, notes for a memoir, chapter 1, Pearson Papers.

25. Pearson, notes for a memoir, chapter 1, Pearson Papers.

26. Pearson, notes for a memoir, chapter 3; Paul M. Pearson to Drew Pearson, August 13, 1922, Drew Pearson to Father and Mother, September 23, 1925, Paul Pearson Papers; Pearson to Edna Pearson, March 17, 1923, Pearson newspaper releases, 1924, "India Should Stay in British Empire, but Must Have Home Rule, Says Gandhi," "Mussolini Predicts Communism in U.S.," Pearson Family Papers, American University.

27. Pearson, unpublished diary, March 8, 1965, Pearson Papers.

28. Ralph G. Martin, *Cissy* (New York: Simon & Schuster, 1979), 198; [Allen and Pearson], *Washington Merry-Go-Round*, 11.

29. Drew Pearson, "Confessions of an S.O.B.," *Saturday Evening Post* 229 (November 17, 1956): 88.

30. Mary E. Plummer, "Eleanor Patterson's Daughter Decries Modern Home," *Hartford Courant*, April 23, 1939; Martin, *Cissy*, 207–9.

31. Amanda Smith, *Newspaper Titan: The Infamous Life and Monumental Times of Cissy Patterson* (New York: Alfred A. Knopf, 2011), 265; Martin, *Cissy*, 227–29.

32. Drew Pearson, unpublished diary, February 14, 1925, March 28, 1962, Pearson Papers; Pearson, "Growing Up in Swarthmore," 54; Pearson, "Confessions of an S.O.B." (November 17, 1956): 88; Pearson to Father and Mother, September 23, 1925, Paul Pearson Papers.

33. Lewis E. Pierson to Drew Pearson, December 8, 1924, Paul Pearson Papers; Felicia Gizycka Pearson to Eleanor Patterson, [c. 1926], Pearson Papers.

34. Martin, *Cissy*, 239; Paul Pearson to Grace [no last name], April 17, 1929, Paul Pearson Papers.

35. Felicia Gizycka Pearson to Drew Pearson, August 24, 31, 1927; Pearson to Felicia Gizycka Pearson, August 28, September 3, 1927, Pearson Papers.

36. Pearson, notes [undated], Eleanor Patterson telegram to Drew Pearson [c. 1931], Pearson Papers; Peter Hannaford, ed., *Washington Merry-Go-Round: The Drew Pearson Diaries, 1960–1969* (Lincoln, NE: Potomac Books, 2015), 185.

37. Pearson, "Paul Martin Pearson," 12; Julie Hall oral history, 6, Abell Papers; Paul Pearson to Friends, April 1, 1930, Paul Pearson Papers; Godfrey, *Man of Chautauqua*, 333; Drew Pearson to Joe Arnold, March 23, 1964, Pearson Papers.

38. Drew Pearson, "Two Rows Develop in Virgin Islands," *Baltimore Sun*, December 16, 1930; "Brown Assails Absurd Jobs in Virgin Islands," *Washington Post*, August 4, 1931.

39. Dorothy Pearson to Pearson, October 22, 1931, Pearson to Monte, December 9, [c. 1933], Paul Pearson to Pearson, November 10, 1931, Pearson Papers.

40. [Allen and Pearson], *Washington Merry-Go-Round*, 321–26; Donald A. Ritchie, *Electing FDR: The New Deal Campaign of 1932* (Lawrence: University Press of Kansas, 2007), 321–26.

41. Paul Pearson to Drew Pearson, May 22, 1931, November 10, 1931, Pearson Papers; "Dr. Pearson, 66, Ex-Governor of Islands, Expires," *Washington Post*, March 27, 1938.

42. Fisher, *The Columnists*, 237; United Features Syndicate, "Advance Story— The Daily Washington Merry-Go-Round," AU; Pilat, *Drew Pearson*, 133.

43. United Features Syndicate advertisement, 1933, Paul Pearson Papers; George A. Carlin to Pearson and Allen, October 31, 1932, Pearson Papers.

44. WMGR, December 12, 1932, AU.

45. Ritchie, *Electing FDR*, 185–88; Eric Rauchway, *Winter War: Hoover, Roosevelt, and the First Clash over the New Deal* (New York: Basic Books, 2018), 202–3; Allen, "My Pal, Drew Pearson," 14; Jack Alexander, "Pugnacious Pearson," in *More Post Biographies: Articles of Enduring Interest about Famous Journalists and Journals and Other Subjects Journalistic*, ed. John E. Drewry (Athens: University of Georgia Press, 1947), 223–25; Fisher, *The Columnists*, 214–15, 243; Paul Pearson to Drew Pearson, August 12, 1936, Paul Pearson Papers.

46. For the New Deal's impact on Washington news bureaus, see Ritchie, *Reporting from Washington*, 7–27.

47. Luvie, pronounced "Loo-vy," was an inherited name. Her mother had been Luvie Butler Moore, and her grandmother Luvean Boone Butler. Martin Weil, "Luvie Pearson Dies," *Washington Post*, March 22, 1992; Sarah

Booth Conroy, "The Legend That Was Luvie," *Washington Post*, May 10, 1999; Gore Vidal, *The Golden Age: A Novel* (New York: Random House, 2000), 72–73.

48. Walter Winchell to Pearson, September 15, 1941, Pearson Papers; Frank Kluckhohn and Jay Franklin, *The Drew Pearson Story* (Chicago: Chas. Hallberg & Company, 1967), 26; Drew Pearson to Mrs. Fessner, August 24, 1933, Pearson Papers.

49. Smith, *Newspaper Titan*, 277–79, 430; Martin, *Cissy*, 248, 263–64, 294; Conroy, "The Legend That Was Luvie."

50. *Congressional Record*, 76th Cong., 1st sess. (1939), 745; Allen oral history, 11–12.

51. Alexander, "Pugnacious Pearson," 223–26; Paul Pearson to Drew Pearson, August 12, 1936, Paul Pearson Papers.

Chapter 2

1. Herman Klurfeld, *Behind the Lines: The World of Drew Pearson* (Englewood Cliffs, NJ: Prentice-Hall, 1968), 51; WMGR, April 13, 1933, AU.

2. Drew Pearson, "Confessions of an S.O.B.: My Life in the White House Dog House," *Saturday Evening Post* 229 (November 10, 1956): 38.

3. Pearson to Harry E. Northam, July 20, 1939, Pearson to James R. Rhodes, August 24, 1939, Pearson Papers.

4. Donald A. Ritchie, *Reporting from Washington: The History of the Washington Press Corps* (New York: Oxford University Press, 2005), 7–27; Arthur Krock, *Memoirs: Sixty Years on the Firing Line* (New York: Funk & Wagnalls, 1968), 175–77.

5. WMGR, March 11, 1933, AU.

6. Pearson, Memo, "Roosevelt Five Years Later," 1938, Pearson Papers; Klurfeld, *Behind the Lines*, 52–53.

7. Washington Merry-Go-Round to Subscribers, April 2, 1938, AU; Tracy Campbell, *Short of the Glory: The Fall and Redemption of Edward F. Prichard, Jr.* (Lexington: University Press of Kentucky, 1998), 86–87.

8. Harold L. Ickes, *The Secret Diary of Harold L. Ickes: The Lowering Clouds, 1939–1941* (New York: Simon & Schuster, 1954), vol. 3: 644; Pearson to Paul B. Cousley, April 3, 1943, Pearson Papers.

9. [Allen and Pearson], *Washington Merry-Go-Round*, 350; WMGR, March 29, 1933, AU; Pearson Notes, 1933, Pearson to Paul B. Cousley, October 6, 1944, Pearson Papers; George Martin, *Madam Secretary, Frances Perkins* (Boston: Houghton Mifflin, 1976), 286–91.

10. WMGR, *Washington Post*, August 25, September 24, 1942, July 5, 1957; Natalie Robins, *Alien Ink: The FBI's War on Freedom of Expression* (New York: William Morrow and Company, 1992), 144–45; Mathew Cecil, *Branding Hoover's FBI: How the Boss's PR Men Sold the Bureau to America* (Lawrence: University Press of Kansas, 2016), 14–26.

11. Cecil, *Branding Hoover's FBI*, 74; J. Edgar Hoover memo to Clyde Tolson, June 23, 1934, A. L. Dixon to Hoover, August 20, 1937, Hoover to Dixon,

September 2, 1937, FBI Files, 94-HQ-8-350, Serial 1-40, RG 65, NARA; Robins, *Alien Ink*, 145.

12. Pearson to J. Edgar Hoover, August 6, 1936, Gordon Dean memo to Hoover, March 8, 1938, Hoover memo to Clyde Tolson, February 1, 1939, FBI Files, 94-HQ-8-350, Serial 1-40, RG 65, NARA.

13. Gary Dean Best, *The Critical Press and the New Deal: The Press Versus Presidential Power, 1933–1938* (Westport, CT: Praeger, 1993); Charles Fisher, *The Columnists* (New York: Howell, Soskin, 1944), 211; Klurfeld, *Behind the Lines*, 52–55.

14. Fisher, *The Columnists*, 211; Pearson to Robert H. Winn, August 14, 1934, Pearson Papers; To Washington Merry-Go-Round Subscribers, November 9, 1940, AU.

15. WMGR, May 11, 1933, AU; Robert C. Albright, "Ten Billions Public Works Fund Sought," *Washington Post*, April 12, 1934; "Election Effect on Peace Debated," *New York Times*, October 2, 1944.

16. Arthur M. Schlesinger Jr., *The Age of Roosevelt: The Coming of the New Deal* (Boston: Houghton Mifflin Company, 1959), 564; Pearson, "Confessions of an S.O.B." (November 10, 1956): 38; George A. Carlin to F. H. Bartholomew, July 3, 1934, Pearson Papers; Douglas A. Anderson, *A Washington Merry-Go-Round of Libel Actions* (Chicago: Nelson-Hall, 1980), 99; Tyler Abell memorandum re: Douglas MacArthur, Abell Papers; Tyler Abell to author, October 30, 2018.

17. WMGR, March 9, April 5, April 25, 1934, AU; Tyler Abell, ed., *Drew Pearson Diaries, 1949–1959* (New York: Holt, Rinehart and Winston, 1974), 412; George A. Carlin to F. H. Bartholomew, July 3, 1934, Pearson Papers.

18. Pearson to Paul Pearson, December 22, 1934, Paul Pearson Papers; Pearson to George Carlin, November 21, 1934, Pearson Papers; Janie Frank, "Enquirer Avoids Legal Action," clipping, December 3, 1976, Dan Schwartz to Tyler Abell, September 16, 1976, Tyler Abell Papers. After a failed attempt at a movie career, Isabel Rosario Cooper committed suicide in Los Angeles in 1960.

19. Pearson to S. S. Hahn, January 21, 1935, Pearson Papers; William Manchester, *American Caesar: Douglas MacArthur, 1880–1964* (Boston: Little, Brown, 2008), 156.

20. Drew Pearson to Paul Pearson, December 22, 1934, September 22, 1937, Paul Pearson Papers.

21. Pearson, "Confessions of an S.O.B." (November 10, 1956): 38–39; Suggested Promotion Box to Accompany Today's Washington Merry-Go-Round Column, May 14, 1938, AU; Pearson to Bess Abell, September 6, 1966. Pearson Papers; Doris Farber, *The Life of Lorena Hickok: E. R.'s Friend* (New York: William Morrow, 1980), 138.

22. Pearson, "Confessions of an S.O.B." (November 10, 1956): 38–39.

23. WMGR, March 31, 1938, AU.

24. WMGR, March 31, 1938, AU; Klurfeld, *Behind the Lines*, 56–58; Fisher, *The Columnists*, 212.

25. Arthur Krock, *Memoirs: Sixty Years on the Firing Line* (New York: Funk & Wagnalls, 1968), 185.

26. Drew Pearson to Paul Pearson, December 11, 1935, Paul Pearson Papers; WMGR, October 19, 1936, AU; Robert S. Allen, "Landon's Sure of Carrying Only 3 States," *Philadelphia Record*, November 1, 1936; Pearson to Judge Ben B. Lindsey, August 30, 1935, Pearson to Max Elser Jr., August 31, 1935, Pearson to Charles Michelson, October 9, 1936, Pearson Papers.

27. Drew Pearson and Robert S. Allen, *The Nine Old Men* (Garden City, NY: Doubleday, Doran & Company, 1936), 29–30; WMGR, January 28, 1937, AU; Kenneth G. Crawford, "Sells 'The Nine Old Men' on Their Doorstep; Hughes Has Him Arrested," *Philadelphia Record*, March 2, 1937.

28. Drew Pearson to Dorothy Pearson, November 27, 1936, Paul Pearson Papers; Pearson to Edith D. Moses, October 22, 1935, Pearson Papers.

29. Klurfeld, *Behind the Lines*, 58; Pearson, unpublished diary, February 10, 1969, Pearson Papers.

30. WMGR, October 13, 1936, April 12, May 11, 1938, AU; Klurfeld, *Behind the Lines*, 59; Abell, ed., *Drew Pearson Diaries*, 121–23, 314–15; WMGR, *Washington Post*, December 23, 1958.

31. WMGR, May 18, 1938, AU; Robert S. Allen to Pearson, October 10, 1942, Pearson, unpublished diary, January 25, 1966, Pearson Papers.

32. Paul Pearson, "My Family Letter," February 1934, March 7, 1934, Drew Pearson to John T. Flynn, September 23, 1934, Paul Pearson Papers; Pearson to Joseph Arnold, March 23, 1964, Paul Pearson to Drew Pearson, May 15, 1935, Pearson Papers; WMGR *Washington Post*, March 4, 1965; Blanche Wiesen Cook, *Eleanor Roosevelt, 1933–1938* (New York: Viking, 1999), vol. II: 169–70.

33. Paul Pearson to E. K. Burlew, August 20, 1934, Drew Pearson to Paul Pearson, September 25, 1934, Paul Pearson Papers; Franklyn Waltman Jr., "Gov. Pearson Target of Strong Opposition," *Washington Post*, April 21, 1935; Julian M. Pleasants, *Buncombe Bob: The Life and Times of Robert Rice Reynolds* (Chapel Hill: University of North Carolina Press, 2000), 83–85; Harold Ickes, *The Secret Diary of Harold L. Ickes: The First Thousand Days, 1933–1936* (New York: Simon & Schuster, 1953), vol. 1: 391.

34. "Ickes Called an Intruder by Tydings," *Washington Post*, September 11, 1935; "Tydings Recesses Quiz after Call at White House," *Washington Star*, September 11, 1935; "Territories: Fight & Fantasy," *Time* (July 22, 1935): 16–17; Franklin D. Roosevelt to Paul Pearson, July 23, 1935, Paul Pearson Papers.

35. J. Edgar Hoover memo to Attorney General, May 6, 1940, FBI Files, 94-HQ-8-350, Serial 1-40, RG 65, NARA; Caroline H. Keith, *"For Hell and a Brown Mule": The Biography of Senator Millard E. Tydings* (Lanham, MD: Madison Books, 1991), 209; Abell, ed., *Drew Pearson Diaries*, 171–72; Drew Pearson to Paul Pearson [c. 1938], Pearson to Robert S. Allen, June 28 [c. 1939], Pearson Papers; Drew Pearson to Paul Pearson, March 7, 1938, Paul Pearson Papers.

36. E. A. Tamm memo for J. Edgar Hoover, April 22, 1940, FBI Files, 94-HQ-8-350, Serial 1-40, RG 65, NARA; Jack Alexander, "Pugnacious Pearson," in *More Post Biographies: Articles of Enduring Interest about Famous Journalists and Journals and Other Subjects Journalistic*, ed. John E. Drewry (Athens: University of Georgia Press, 1947), 235.

37. O. John Rogge to Edward M. Curran, May 15, 1940, FBI Files, 94-HQ-8-359, Serials 41–100, RG 65, NARA; *Congressional Record*, 77th Cong, 1st sess. (1941), 5830; Drew Pearson to Edna Pearson, April 7 [1938], Pearson Papers; "Senate Puts O.K. on Jackson for Supreme Court," *Chicago Tribune*, July 8, 1941.

38. J. Edgar Hoover memo to Clyde Tolson, August 27, 1938, FBI Files, 94-HQ-8-350, Serials 1–40, RG 65, NARA; Robert S. Allen to Pearson, [c. June 1939], Allen to Pearson, October 10, 1942, Pearson Papers.

39. Pearson to George Carlin, July 24, 28, 1939 James A. Noe to Pearson, October 27, 1939, George Carlin to the Advisory Board of the Graduate School of Journalism, Columbia University [c. 1939], Pearson, unpublished diary, April 28, 1969, Pearson Papers.

40. Oliver Pilat, *Drew Pearson: An Unauthorized Biography* (New York: Harper's Magazine Press, 1973), 163–66.

41. Robert S. Allen to Pearson, c. 1941, Pearson Papers; Harold Ickes, *The Secret Diary of Harold L. Ickes: The Lowering Clouds, 1939–1941* (New York: Simon & Schuster), vol. 3: 539–41.

42. "Capital Columnist Predicts Roosevelt Candidacy in 1940," *Los Angeles Times*, November 22, 1938; Ickes, *The Secret Diary of Harold L. Ickes*, vol. 3: 616.

43. Pearson to James R. Rhodes, September 30, 1940, Pearson Papers.

44. To Washington Merry-Go-Round Subscribers, November 14, 1940, AU; Pearson to James R. Rhodes, November 11, 1940, Pearson Papers.

45. WMGR, November 16. 1940, AU.

46. WMGR, *Washington Post*, June 20, 1965.

47. WMGR, October 12, 1936, AU.

48. Fifteen-minute news shows were standard at the time. Deducting time for advertisements, each program had thirteen minutes and twenty seconds of air time for substance. Drew Pearson to Paul Pearson, December 11, 1935, Paul Pearson Papers; Pearson to Allen, January 13, 1936, Pearson Papers.

49. Fisher, *The Columnists*, 241.

50. Allen to Pearson, [c. June 1939], Pearson Papers; Anthony Weitzel, "Notes on Bob Allen," December 18, 1940, AU.

51. Pearson to Allen, June 28 [1939], Pearson Papers.

52. Allen to Pearson, August 8, 1942; Allen to Pearson, undated [c. June 1939], Pearson Papers.

53. Fisher, *The Columnists*, 239, 242; Allen to Pearson [c. June 1939], Pearson Papers.

54. Allen to Pearson, undated [c. June 1939], Pearson Papers.

55. Allen to Pearson, undated [c. 1942], Pearson Papers.
56. "To Merry-Go-Round Editors," January 26, 1943; Fisher, *The Columnists*, 216–17; Pilat, *Drew Pearson*, 168. Pearson took offense over an assertion in Kluckhohn and Franklin, *The Drew Pearson Story*, 7, that he had "euchred" Allen out of his share of the column, but his lawyer dissuaded him from suing for libel. JD [John Donovan] memorandum, April 4, 1967, Pearson Papers.
57. Pearson to George Carlin, July 25, 1942, Allen to Pearson and George Carlin, July 28, 1942, Pearson Papers.
58. Allen to Pearson, October 10, 1942, Pearson Papers.
59. WMGR, July 1, 1942, AU; Allen to Drew Pearson, August 8, 1942, Pearson Papers.
60. Michael S. Sweeney, *Secrets of Victory: The Office of Censorship and the American Press and Radio in World War II* (Chapel Hill: University of North Carolina Press, 2001), 155–62; John N. Wheeler to Pearson, October 8, 1946, Pearson Papers; WMGR, *Washington Post*, September 4, 1966.
61. WMGR, *Washington Post*, December 3, 1943; Sweeney, *Secrets of Victory*, 162; Pearson to Ellen Pearson, November 23, 1943, Pearson Papers; George S. Patton diaries, November 21, November 24, December 1, 1943, Patton Papers, Library of Congress; William M. Hammond, *Public Affairs: The Military and the Media, 1962–1968* (Washington, DC: Center of Military History, United States Army, 1988), 6. See also John Nelson Rickard, ed., *Forward with Patton: The World War II Diary of Colonel Robert S. Allen* (Lexington: University Press of Kentucky, 2017).
62. L. B. Nichols memo to Clyde Tolson, December 15, 1944, FBI files, 94-HQ-8-350 Serials 21-282, RG65, NARA.
63. Lee Kirsch Brenneisen to Pearson, April 8, 1946, Pearson to John Perry, November 10, 1944, Pearson to Ellen Pearson, December 15, 1944, Pearson to Ruth Finney, [c. 1944], Pearson Papers.
64. John N. Wheeler to Pearson, October 8, 1946, Pearson Papers; Jack Anderson with James Boyd, *Confessions of a Muckraker: The Inside Story of Life in Washington during the Truman, Eisenhower, Kennedy and Johnson Years* (New York: Random House, 1979), 102–7; Jack Anderson with Daryl Gibson, *Peace, War, and Politics: An Eyewitness Account* (New York: Forge, 1999), 187; Robert S. Allen, *Lucky Forward, The History of Patton's Third US Army* (New York: Vanguard Press, 1947); "Settlement Ends $20,750 Job Suit by Colonel Allen," *Washington Post*, October 19, 1948.
65. WMGR, *Washington Post*, January 25, 1946; Robert S. Allen, "My Pal, Drew Pearson," *Collier's* 124 (July 30, 1949): 14–16, 55; "Straight Reporting, No Hoopla Is Bob Allen's Goal on Radio," *Washington Post*, October 19, 1947.

Chapter 3

1. WMGR, June 10, 1943, Note to Editors, December 10, 1941, AU.

2. Pearson to George Carlin, January 27, 1939, Pearson Papers; Charles Fisher, *The Columnists* (New York: Howell, Soskin, 1944), 225; William P. Carney, "Washington Gadfly," in *Molders of Opinion*, ed. David Bulman (Milwaukee: Bruce Publishing, 1945), 120; Adam Hochschild, *Spain in Our Hearts: Americans in the Spanish Civil War, 1936–1939* (Boston: Houghton Mifflin Harcourt, 2015), 154–55; WMGR, *Washington Post*, November 6, 1955.

3. "Times Rated First for Capital News," *New York Times*, October 12, 1944.

4. Nigel West, ed., *The Secret History of British Intelligence in the Americas, 1940–1945* (New York: Fromm International, 1999), 129.

5. Frank Kluckhohn and Jay Franklin, *The Drew Pearson Story* (Chicago: Chas. Hallberg & Company, 1967), 7, 33; Jack Alexander, "Pugnacious Pearson," in *More Post Biographies: Articles of Enduring Interest about Famous Journalists and Journals and Other Subjects Journalistic*, ed. John E. Drewry (Athens: University of Georgia Press, 1947), 221–22 (Alexander's article appeared in the January 6, 1945, issue of the *Saturday Evening Post*).

6. Peter Edson, "Interpretation and Analysis of Washington News," in *The Press in Washington: Sixteen Top Newsmen Tell How the News Is Collected, Written, and Communicated from the World's Most Important Capital*, ed. Ray Eldon Hiebert (New York: Dodd, Mead, 1966), 40.

7. Pearson to George Carlin, January 2, 1941, Pearson Papers.

8. See, for instance, WMGR, December 8, 1933, AU; Michael S. Sweeney, *Secrets of Victory: The Office of Censorship and the American Press and Radio in World War II* (Chapel Hill: University of North Carolina Press, 2001), 138; Fisher, *The Columnists*, 32.

9. Pearson to Eleanor Patterson, April 8, 1939, Pearson to George Carlin, January 2, 1941, Pearson Papers.

10. WMGR, August 15, 1940, AU.

11. WMGR, September 7, September 20, 1940, AU; Herman Klurfeld, *Behind the Lines: The World of Drew Pearson* (Englewood Cliffs, NJ: Prentice-Hall, 1968), 17–18.

12. Klurfeld, *Behind the Lines*, 18–19; William L. Rivers, *The Opinionmakers* (Westport, CT: Greenwood, 1965), 127.

13. Chalmers M. Roberts, *The Washington Post: The First 100 Years* (Boston: Houghton Mifflin, 1977), 243–44; Pearson, unpublished diary, November 22, 1968, Pearson Papers; Drew Pearson, "Confessions of an S.O.B.," *Saturday Evening Post* 229 (November 17, 1956): 89, 91.

14. Pearson, "Confessions of an S.O.B." (November 17, 1956): 91.

15. Kluckhohn and Franklin, *The Drew Pearson Story*, 29; Oliver Pilat, *Drew Pearson: An Unauthorized Biography* (New York: Harper's Magazine Press, 1973), 168–69, 171; Klurfeld, *Behind the Lines*, 16.

16. Ruth Wagner, "For a Writer, a Woodsy Hideaway," *Washington Post*, September 29, 1968; Sarah Booth Conroy, "Condos for Horses—and That Ain't Hay," *Washington Post*, November 16, 1989; Amanda Smith,

Newspaper Titan: The Infamous Life and Monumental Times of Cissy Patterson (New York: Alfred A. Knopf, 2011), 478–80.

17. Walter Trohan, *Political Animals: Memoirs of a Sentimental Cynic* (Garden City, NY: Doubleday, 1975), 238; WMGR, *Washington Post*, July 31, 1948.

18. Roberts, *The Washington Post*, 243–44, 265; Carol Felsenthal, *Power, Privilege and The Post: The Katherine Graham Story* (New York: G. P. Putnam's Sons, 1993), 129, 192–93, 217–18.

19. Drew Pearson and Constantine Brown, *The American Diplomatic Game* (Garden City, NY: Doubleday, Doran, 1935), 395; Drew Pearson to Paul Pearson, March 29, 1935, Paul Pearson Papers; Fisher, *The Columnists*, 225; Sweeney, *Secrets of Victory*, 138; Drew Pearson, "Confessions of an S.O.B.: My Mother-in-Law Troubles," *Saturday Evening Post* 229 (November 17, 1956): 91.

20. Tyler Abell, ed., *Drew Pearson Diaries, 1949–1959* (New York: Holt, Rinehart and Winston, 1974), 132.

21. WMGR, December 13, 1941, AU.

22. WMGR, December 13, 1941, AU; Pearson and Allen, "Confidential to Washington Merry-Go-Round Editors," December 1941, Pearson Papers.

23. George Carlin to Si Cassady, February 6, 1942, Pearson Papers; WMGR for release on December 13, 1941, FBI Files, 94-HQ-8-359, Serials 41–100, RG 65, NARA.

24. George Carlin to Si Cassady, February 6, 1942, Pearson, unpublished diary, October 9, 1961, December 27, 1966, Pearson Papers; Peter Hannaford, ed., *Washington Merry-Go-Round: The Drew Pearson Diaries, 1960–1969* (Lincoln, NE: Potomac Books, 2015), 452; Hoover memo to C. Tolson, E. A. Tamm, and D. M. Ladd, December 12, 1941, FBI Files, 94-HQ-8-359, Serials 41–100, RG 65, NARA.

25. J. Edgar Hoover series of memos to Clyde Tolson, E. A. Tamm, and D. M. Ladd, December 12, 1941, FBI Files, 94-HQ-8-359, Serials 41–100, RG 65, NARA.

26. WMGR, *Washington Post*, March 17, 1944.

27. Pearson to L. J. Wilhoite, December 13, 1941, Allen's handwritten note on William Allen White to Pearson, December 19, 1941, Pearson and Allen to Washington Merry-Go-Round editors, December 13, 1941, Pearson Papers; note to editors, January 9, 1942, AU.

28. WMGR, *Washington Post*, December 13, 1945; George Carlin to Pearson, December 19, 1941, Pearson to Carlin, October 13, 1941, Pearson Papers; "George Carlin, 54, of News Syndicate," *New York Times*, November 29, 1945.

29. Pearson to Jack Harris, December 19, 1941, Pearson Papers.

30. Pearson to George Carlin, January 2, 1942, Pearson Papers; D. M. Ladd memo to J. W. Cannon and W. S. Crawford, August 31, 1942, R. R. Roach to D. M. Ladd, January 11, 1945, FBI Files, 94-HQ-8-350, Serials 101–130, RG 65, NARA.

31. Pearson to George Carlin, April 9, 1942, Pearson Papers; Sweeney, *Secrets of Victory*, 139–41; Abell, ed., *Drew Pearson Diaries*, 92–93.

32. George A. Carlin to Hugh Kane, April 4, 1942, Pearson Papers.

33. Pearson to George Carlin, July 2, 1942, Pearson Papers.

34. Klurfeld, *Behind the Lines*, 66; Pearson to George A. Carlin, July 2, 1942, Pearson Papers.

35. D. M. Ladd memo to J. Edgar Hoover, May 12, 1942, FBI Files, 94-HQ-8-350, Serials 101–130, RG 65, NARA.

36. D. M. Ladd memo for J. W. Cannon and W. S. Crawford, August 31, 1942, FBI Files, 94-HQ-8-350, Serials 101–130, RG 65, NARA; Sweeney, *Secrets of Victory*, 135–36, 142–45.

37. Sweeney, *Secrets of Victory*, 135–36.

38. Pearson to Byron Price, June 5, 1942, Pearson to John H. Sorrells, March 7, 1942, Pearson, "Notes on the Censor (WWII)," Pearson Papers.

39. N. R. [Nat] Howard to George Carlin, January 23, 1943, Pearson Papers; Sweeney, *Secrets of Victory*, 148–50.

40. Pearson to George Carlin, April 19, 1943, Pearson Papers.

41. Larry I. Bland, ed., *The Papers of George Catlett Marshall*, vol. 2 (Baltimore: Johns Hopkins University Press, 1986), 651–52; Robert F. Burk, *Dwight D. Eisenhower: Hero and Politician* (Boston: Twayne, 1986), 49.

42. Forrest C. Pogue, *George C. Marshall: Organizer of Victory* (New York: Viking, 1973), 266–67, 278; Sweeney, *Secrets of Victory*, 138; Daniel Kurtz-Phelan, *The China Mission: George Marshall's Unfinished War, 1945–1947* (New York: W. W. Norton, 2018), 15; WMGR, *Washington Post*, January 25, 1965; Rivers, *The Opinionmakers*, 115.

43. Alexander, "Pugnacious Pearson," 222–23.

44. Pearson to Oswaldo Aranha, August 26, 1941, Pearson Papers; "Halifax Statement on Relief Arouses Rome, Stars and Stripes Reports Pearson Story," *New York Times*, January 7, 1945; Mary E. Glantz, *FDR and the Soviet Union: The President's Battles over Foreign Policy* (Lawrence: University Press of Kansas, 2005), 72–75, 107–11.

45. Herbert Romerstein and Eric Briendel, *The Venona Secrets: Exposing Soviet Espionage and America's Traitors* (Washington, DC: Regnery Publishing, 2000), 137–38. See also New York to Moscow, July 15, 1944, Venona Online; and John R. Deane, *The Strange Alliance: The Story of Our Efforts at Wartime Co-Operation with Russia* (New York: Viking, 1947).

46. Irwin F. Gellman, *Secret Affairs: Franklin Roosevelt, Cordell Hull, and Sumner Welles* (Baltimore: Johns Hopkins University Press, 1995), 128–30; Benjamin Welles, *Sumner Welles: FDR's Global Strategist, A Biography* (New York: St. Martin's Press, 1997), 185–86.

47. Pearson memo on Hull [1933], Pearson Papers; Hannaford, ed., *Washington Merry-Go-Round*, 351.

48. Gellman, *Secret Affairs*, 145; Frank Warren Graff, *Strategy of Involvement: A Diplomatic Biography of Sumner Welles* (New York: Garland, 1988), 220–22; Hannaford, ed., *Washington Merry-Go-Round*, 351.

49. Welles, *Sumner Welles*, 197; West, ed., *The Secret History of British Intelligence in the Americas, 1940–1945*, 128; Molly M. Wood, "Diplomacy and Gossip: Information Gathering in the US Foreign Service, 1900–1940," in *When Private Talk Goes Public: Gossip in American History*, ed. Kathleen A. Feeley and Jennifer Frost (New York: Palgrave Macmillan, 2014), 139–59; Kati Marton, *True Believer: Stalin's Last American Spy* (New York: Simon & Schuster, 2016), 56.

50. Welles, *Sumner Welles*, 199; Gellman, *Secret Affairs*, 155–56; WMGR, May 6, May 13, 1938, AU; "Hull Clashes with a Columnist on Arms Exports to Germany," *New York Times*, May 7, 1938; The Ambassador in Germany (Wilson) to the Secretary of State, April 13, 1938, Document 365, the Acting Secretary of State to the Ambassador in Germany, April 20, 1938, Document 366, the Secretary of State to the Ambassador in Germany, May 12, 1938, Document 369, *Foreign Relations of the United States Diplomatic Papers, 1938, The British Commonwealth, Europe, New East, and Africa* (Washington, DC: Government Printing Office, 1954), vol. 2: 458–61.

51. WMGR, December 19, December 28, 1940, AU; Welles, *Sumner Welles*, 212; Gelman, *Secret Affairs*, 163, 201, 311–12, 322, 326; William D. Leahy, *I Was There: The Personal Story of the Chief of Staff to Presidents Roosevelt and Truman, Based on His Notes and Diaries Made at the Time* (New York: McGraw-Hill, 1950), 128; "Hull Says Story of Franco Loan Was Made 'Out of Whole Cloth,'" *New York Times*, December 22, 1940; "Welles Answers Report of Discord," *New York Times*, December 29, 1940; Kluckhohn and Franklin, *The Drew Pearson Story*, 84.

52. Pearson to Earle Godbey, January 3, 1941, Pearson to Oswaldo Aranha, February 17, 1941, Pearson Papers.

53. WMGR, *Washington Post*, April 9, 1943; Gellman, *Secret Affairs*, 319–21, 325; "The World of Felix Frankfurter," *Washington Post*, August 10, 1975.

54. WMGR, *Washington Post*, August 21, 26, 27, 1943.

55. Edward M. Bennett, *Franklin D. Roosevelt and the Search for Victory: American-Soviet Relations, 1939–1945* (Wilmington, DE: Scholarly Resources, 1990), 95; The Secretary of State to the Ambassador in the Soviet Union (Standley), August 30, 1943, *Foreign Relations of the United States: Diplomatic Papers, 1943, The British Commonwealth, Eastern Europe, the Far East* (Washington, DC: Government Printing Office, 1963), vol. 3: 417; Edward T. Folliard, "3-Power Talks Taking Shape, President Says: Roosevelt Attacks Columnist's Stories on Soviet Situation," *Washington Post*, September 1, 1943; Walter Trohan, "Hull Denounces Columnist for 'Diabolical Lies,'" *Chicago Tribune*, August 31, 1943; Arthur Krock, "Amity with Russia," *New York Times*, September 1, 1943; "Roosevelt Blast at Pearson as 'Liar' Climaxes Longtime Feud with Press," *Newsweek* 22 (September 13, 1943): 79–80; Welles, *Sumner Welles*, 350; Gellman, *Secret Affairs*, 323.

56. Pearson on *The Mike Wallace Interview*, December 7, 1957, C-SPAN; Vera Glaser, "Things Drew Pearson Didn't Tell," *Philadelphia Inquirer*,

February 17, 1974; Pearson, "To Washington Merry-Go-Round Editors," September 20, 1943, Pearson Papers; West, ed., *The Secret History of British Intelligence in the Americas, 1940–1945*, 130.

57. "Pearson's Replies to FDR and Hull Suppressed," *PM*, September 12, 1943; Pearson, "draft column," Pearson to Karl A. Bickel, September 9, 1943, Pearson Papers.

58. Gellman, *Secret Affairs*, 323–25; Abell, ed., *Drew Pearson Diaries*, 85; Carlisle Bargeron, "Washington's Mighty Penmen," *Nation's Business* 5 (May 1, 1946): 106.

59. "Chronic Liar," *Time* 42 (September 13, 1942); "Rooseveltian Rampage," *Washington Post*, September 2, 1943.

60. Abell, ed., *Drew Pearson Diaries*, 221.

61. "Navy Ends 'Shadowing' of Pearson," *PM*, March 5, 1943.

62. West, ed., *The Secret History of British Intelligence in the Americas*, 123–24.

63. West, ed., *The Secret History of British Intelligence in the Americas*, 130–31.

64. West, ed., *The Secret History of British Intelligence in the Americas*, ix, 130; Jennet Conant, *The Irregulars: Roald Dahl and the British Spy Ring in Wartime Washington* (New York: Simon & Schuster, 2008), 146.

65. WMGR, July 25, 1944, AU.

66. William Phillips to Franklin D. Roosevelt, May 14, 1943, Pearson Papers; WMGR, *Washington Post*, July 6, 25, August 28, 1944; Kenton J. Clymer, *Quest for Freedom: The United States and India's Independence* (New York: Columbia University Press, 1995), 193–96; US Department of State, *Foreign Relations of the United States: Diplomatic Papers, 1944, The Near East, South Asia, and Africa, The Far East* (Washington, DC: Government Printing Office, 1965), vol. 5: 236–47.

67. Pearson, "Memorandum Regarding Developments Following Phillips Letter Publication," [undated], Pearson to Wendell Willkie, August 23, 1944, Pearson to William Randolph Hearst, August 25, 1944, Pearson Papers; WMGR, *Washington Post*, January 30, 1958.

68. Pearson to Luvie Pearson, August 2, 1944, Pearson Papers; Sweeney, *Secrets of Victory*, 139.

69. Kluckhohn and Franklin, *The Drew Pearson Story*, 36; Harold A. Gould, *Sikhs, Swamis, Students, and Spies: The India Lobby in the United States, 1900–1946* (New Delhi: Sage Publications, 2006), 373–77; David A. Hollinger, *Protestants Abroad: How Missionaries Tried to Change the World but Changed America* (Princeton: Princeton University Press, 2017), 217–18; Harvey Klehr and Ronald Radosh, *The Amerasia Spy Case: Prelude to McCarthyism* (Chapel Hill: University of North Carolina Press, 1996), 101–2.

70. Conant, *The Irregulars*, 221–22; West, ed., *The Secret History of British Intelligence in the Americas*, 130–32, 267.

71. WMGR, *Washington Post*, August 16, 1944; Pearson to John Wheeler, January 17, 1945, Pearson Papers; Michael Hopkins alerted me to R. H. Brand's warning to the Chancellor of the Exchequer, Sir John Anderson,

about American perceptions of the British military, August 23, 1944, Robert Brand Papers, 197/1, C folder, Bodleian Library, Oxford.

72. Winston Churchill telegram to Field Marshall Sir Harold Alexander, December 14, 1944, Churchill Archives Online; Pearson to Wendell Willkie, January 6, 1943, Pearson to Alexander Esway, September 6, 1944, Pearson Papers.

73. Winston Churchill telegram to General Sir John Scobie, December 5, 1944, Churchill Archives Online; WMGR, *Washington Post*, August 19, 1944; J. Edgar Hoover memo to Tamm, Ladd, and Tolson, January 5, 1945, FBI files, 94-HQ-8-350, Serials 21–282, RG65, NARA.

74. Winston Churchill telegram to Field Marshall Sir Harold Alexander, December 14, 1944, and to Field Marshall Sir Henry Wilson, June 18, 1945, Churchill Archives Online; Conant, *The Irregulars*, 219–20; WMGR, *Washington Post*, December 12, 1944, January 4, 1945.

75. WMGR, *Washington Post*, January 25, 1965; William Manchester and Paul Reid, *The Last Lion: Winston Spencer Churchill, Defender of the Realm, 1940–1965* (New York: Little, Brown and Company, 2012), 884–86.

76. The FBI made a transcript of Pearson's broadcast on Gouzenko. See A. H. Belmont memo to D. M. Ladd, February 15, 1954, 94-HQ-8-350, Serials 541–599, FBI files, RG 65, NARA; Klurfeld, *Behind the Lines*, 126–27.

77. Amy Knight, *How the Cold War Began: The Igor Gouzenko Affair and the Hunt for Soviet Spies* (New York: Carroll & Graf, 2005), 104–8.

78. L. B. Nichols memo to Clyde Tolson, February 16, 1946, FBI files, 94-HQ-8-350, Serials 283–374, RG65, NARA.

79. Carlisle Bargeron, "Washington's Mighty Penmen," *Nation's Business* 34 (May 1, 1946): 61; Knight, *How the Cold War Began*, 106; Klurfeld, 140–42; see "The New Republic Mail Bag," *New Republic* 114 (April 8, 1946): 480.

80. Dennis Molinaro, "How the Cold War Began . . . with British Help: The Gouzenko Affair Revisited," *Labour* 79 (Spring 2017): 143–55.

81. Kluckhohn and Franklin, *The Drew Pearson Story*, 40–41.

82. Fisher, *The Columnists*, 211–13, 223–24; Alexander, "Pugnacious Pearson," 237–38; Kluckhohn and Franklin, *The Drew Pearson Story*, 83–84.

83. Sweeney, *Secrets of Victory*, 150.

84. WMGR, *Washington Post*, May 29, 1944; Oliver Burtin, "'A One-Woman Tea Party': Tax Resistance, Feminism, and Conservatism in the Life of Vivien Kellems," *Journal of Policy History* 28 (January 2016): 162–90.

85. Sweeney, *Secrets of Victory*, 153–55.

86. "Miss Kellems Hits Nazi Love Story as Plot," *Chicago Tribune*, April 2, 1944; Willard Edwards, "Senate Group Votes Probe of Drew Pearson," *Chicago Tribune*, May 5, 1955; "Senator M'Kellar Calls Drew Pearson 'Liar,'" *Los Angeles Times*, April 26, 1944.

87. Subcommittee of the Senate Committee on Post Offices and Post Roads, *Investigation Concerning the Disclosure of Information Obtained Leaked Through Censorship* (June 10, 1944), 128, Kellems's testimony, December

4, 1944; Senate Committee on Post Offices and Post Roads, *Censorship of Communications under Section 303 of the First War Powers Act*, 78th Cong., 2nd sess., Report 857; Willard Edwards, "Kellems Smear Blamed on Leak in Hull's Office," *Chicago Tribune*, May 24, 1944; "A Determined Lady Who Won't Pay Income Taxes," *People* magazine, April 15, 1974.

88. Walter Trohan to Major General Clayton L. Bissell, March 20, 1944, J. Edgar Hoover memo to Tolson, Tamm and Ladd, April 11, 1944, FBI Files, 94-HQ-8-350, Serials 130X–210; Charles L. Greene report, July 1, 1944, FBI files, 94-HQ-8-350, Serials 21–282, RG65; S. W. Reynolds memo to D. M. Ladd, December 14, 1944, L. B. Nichols memo to J. Edgar Hoover, January 16, 1945, FBI files, 94-HQ-8-350, Serials 283–374, RG65, NARA; J. Edgar Hoover to Pearson, November 20, 1945, Pearson Papers.

89. Drew Pearson, "Morgenthau Was Right," *Washington Post*, February 12, 1967.

90. Pearson, notes for a chapter "The Distrust Deepens," c. 1969, Pearson Papers.

91. WMGR, *Washington Post*, September 21, 1944; R. Bruce Craig, *Treasonable Doubt: The Harry Dexter White Spy Case* (Lawrence: University Press of Kansas, 2004), 161, 174; Stephen Casey, "The Campaign to Sell a Harsh Peace for Germany to the American Public, 1944–1948," *History* 90 (2005): 62–92; Minutes of a Meeting of January 17, 1945, *Foreign Relations of the United States, Diplomatic Papers, 1945, European Advisory Commission, Austria, Germany* (Washington, DC: Government Printing Office, 1968), vol. 3: 390.

92. David Rees, *Harry Dexter White: A Study in Paradox* (New York: Coward, McCann & Geoghegan, 1973), 244–65, 280–81; WMGR, *Washington Post*, September 21, October 5, 1944; Henry Morgenthau Jr., "Occupying Germany No Job for GI," *Washington Post*, August 26, 1945.

93. Jack Lockhart to Pearson, June 6, 1944, Pearson to Lockhart, June 7, 1944, Pearson Papers; Sweeney, *The Secret War*, 3, 153.

Chapter 4

1. Charles Fisher, *The Columnists* (New York: Howell, Soskin, 1944), 238–39; Louis Heren, "Son of a Bitch," *Times of London*, January 16, 1975.

2. Tyler Abell oral history #1, 15, #5, 6, Tyler Abell Papers; *Congressional Record*, 91st Cong., 1st sess. (1969), 28047.

3. WMGR, August 20, 1941, AU.

4. Jack Anderson with James Boyd, *Confessions of a Muckraker: The Inside Story of Life in Washington during the Truman, Eisenhower, Kennedy and Johnson Years* (New York: Random House, 1979), 6–7; Tyler Abell interview, July 21, 2011, Citizens Association of Georgetown, www.cagtown.com; Edward A. Tamm memo to J. Edgar Hoover, May 29, 1942, FBI Files, 94-HQ-8-350, Serials 101–130, RG 65, NARA.

5. "The Pearsons' 3-in-1 Home," *Washington Post*, April 2, 1954; Pearson to Leon Pearson, December 12, 1945, Pearson Papers.

6. Anderson with Boyd, *Confessions of a Muckraker*, 15–16; Vera Glaser, "Things Drew Pearson Didn't Tell," *Philadelphia Inquirer*, February 17, 1974.

7. Drew Pearson to Paul Pearson, August 7, 1937, Paul Pearson Papers; Tyler Abell oral history #2, 3; #4, 12–13; #5, 5.

8. Tyler Abell interview #2, 3–4; Pearson to Leon Pearson, December 12, 1945, Pearson to David Karr, June 8, 1967, Pearson Papers; Lawrence A. Armour, "Corporate Cinderella," *Barron's National Business and Financial Weekly* 43 (May 6, 1963): 18.

9. Harvey Klehr, *The Millionaire Was a Soviet Mole: The Twisted Life of David Karr* (New York: Encounter Books, 2019), 7–19; Spencer Klaw, "Dave Karr in the President's Chair," *Fortune* 63 (June 1961): 154–57, 261–66; Roy Rowan, "The Death of Dave Karr and Other Mysteries," *Fortune* 100 (December 1979): 94, 96.

10. "Dies Gives Names of 'Radicals' in Attack on Bureaucrats," *Washington Post*, February 2, 1943; *Congressional Record*, 81st Cong., 2nd sess. (1950), 16912; *Counterattack [Facts to Combat Communism and Those Who Aid Its Cause]*, April 28, 1961, David Karr to Pearson, November 9, 1967, Pearson Papers; Klehr, *The Millionaire Was a Soviet Mole*, 20–39.

11. Edward A. Tamm memo to J. Edgar Hoover, April 11, 1947, FBI files, 94-HQ-8-350, Serials 283–374, Record Group 65, NARA; "Writer Threatens Action in Court," *Washington Post*, December 16, 1950.

12. WMGR, *Washington Post*, October 26, 1948; Pearson to editor, *San Diego Union*, October 30, 1948, Pearson Papers; Abell, ed., *Drew Pearson Diaries*, 75.

13. John Earl Haynes and Harvey Klehr, *Venona: Decoding Soviet Espionage in America* (New Haven: Yale University Press, 1999), 138–43, 245–47; Klehr, *The Millionaire Was a Soviet Mole*, 45–46; LJL, SAC, Washington Field, memo to J. Edgar Hoover, July 16, 1944, FBI files, 94-HQ-8-350, Serials 21–282; A. H. Belmont memo to D. M. Ladd, November 13, 1953, FBI files, 94-HQ-8-350, Serials 541–599, RG 65, NARA; R. Bruce Craig, *Treasonable Doubt: The Harry Dexter White Spy Case* (Lawrence: University Press of Kansas, 2004), 309.

14. David Karr to Philip Murray, October 14, 1949, Pearson Papers.

15. Klaw, "Dave Karr in the President's Chair," 157; William L. Rivers, *The Opinionmakers* (Westport, CT: Greenwood Press, 1965), 122; Pearson to Morris Katz, November 29, 1949, Katz to Pearson, December 4, 1949, Drew Pearson, to whom it may concern, May 20, 1958, Pearson Papers.

16. Tyler Abell, ed., *Drew Pearson Diaries, 1949–1959* (New York: Holt, Rinehart and Winston, 1974), 3; Westbrook Pegler Deposition, July 2, 1953, in *Drew Pearson v. Joseph McCarthy, et al.*, Civil Action No 897-51, in the US District Court for the District of Columbia, Maurice Rosenblatt Papers, Library of Congress; Pegler, "Sen. McCarthy and the A.P.," Madison, Wisconsin, *State Journal*, February 16, 1951; Pearson to David

Karr, June 4, 1950, Pearson unpublished diary, February 26, 1969, Karr to Pearson, April 20, 1968, Pearson Papers; Lingthingham Hall letter, March 24, 1953, FBI files, 94-HQ-8-350, Serials 471–540, RG 65, NARA; Klehr, *The Millionaire Was a Soviet Mole*, 121–83.

17. W. H. Shippen, "McCarthy Faces Quiz Today on Report He Threatened to Maim Pearson," *Washington Evening Star*, October 5, 1951; Pearson notes for a statement, Pearson to J. Edgar Hoover, April 10, 1947, Pearson Papers; Pearson, unpublished diary, July 5, 1951, Abell Papers.

18. "Asks Public to Aid Purges," *Washington Post*, January 3, 1947; "Pearson Repeats Rap vs. Cong Wood as Key to 1946 Nix of Pix Red Probe," *Variety* (July 18, 1951): 2; Ethel J. Older to Pearson, July 15, 1951, Pearson Papers.

19. Susan Sheehan, "The Anderson Strategy: 'We Hit You—Pow! Then You Issue a Denial, and—Bam!—We Really Let You Have It," *New York Times Magazine* (August 13, 1972): 79; Neil A. Grauer, *Wits & Sages* (Baltimore: Johns Hopkins University Press, 1984), 15–34; Jack Anderson interview, May 23, 1979, Studs Terkel Radio Archive; Anderson with Boyd, *Confessions of a Muckraker*, 6.

20. Timothy Mark Chambless, "Muckraker at Work: Columnist Jack Anderson and the Watergate Scandal, 1972–1974" (PhD diss., University of Utah, 1987), 18–30; Mark Feldstein, *Poisoning the Press: Richard Nixon, Jack Anderson, and the Rise of Washington's Scandal Culture* (New York: Farrar, Straus & Giroux, 2010), 37.

21. Jack Anderson with Daryl Gibson, *Peace, War, and Politics: An Eyewitness Account* (New York: Forge, 1999), 61–62.

22. Al Aronowitz, "A Talk with America's Number One Muckraker, Jack Anderson," *Gallery* [undated], 36, and Andy Rosenblatt, "The Muck Stops Here," [Florida] *Tropic*, August 2, 1978, Jack Anderson Papers, American University; Chambless, "Muckraker at Work," 33.

23. Jack Anderson interview, May 23, 1979, Studs Terkel Radio Archive; Sheehan, "The Anderson Strategy," 10; Britt Hume, *Inside Story* (Garden City, NY: Doubleday, 1974), 85; Anderson with Gibson, *Peace, War, and Politics*, 62–63; interview with Jack Anderson by Tim Chambless, March 15, 1986, 4, Anderson Papers.

24. Anderson with Gibson, *Peace, War, and Politics*, 61–62; Hume, *Inside Story*, 85–86.

25. Hume, *Inside Story*, 85–87.

26. Chambless, "Muckraker at Work," 49; Anderson with Gibson, *Peace, War, and Politics*, 78, 80.

27. Oliver Pilat, *Drew Pearson: An Unauthorized Biography* (New York: Harper's Magazine Press, 1973), 188; Leon Pearson to Drew Pearson, December 10 [1933], Drew Pearson to Paul Pearson, August 7, 1934, Paul Pearson Papers; Pearson to Ellen [Pearson] Arnold, April 19, 1963, Pearson to George Carlin, July 25, 1942, Pearson Papers; WMGR, May 2, 1963, AU; "The Other Pearson," *Newsweek* 39 (June 23, 1952): 78.

28. Tristram Coffin to Pearson, July 20, 1942, Coffin to Pearson, December 20, 1949, Pearson Papers; Robert McG. Thomas Jr., "Tristram Coffin Is Dead at 84; Created Washington Spectator," *New York Times*, June 16, 1997.

29. Sheehan, "The Anderson Strategy," 11; Anderson with Gibson, *Peace, War, and Politics*, 80–81; Grauer, *Wits & Sages*, 19; Drew Pearson, "Confessions of an S.O.B.: How to Make Enemies," *Saturday Evening Post* (November 24, 1956): 148. Fred Blumenthal reported for Pearson from 1949 to 1953, after working in the Office of Price Stabilization and the Democratic National Committee.

30. Anderson with Gibson, *Peace, War, and Politics*, 78; Leonard Downie Jr., *The New Muckrakers* (Washington, DC: New Republic Book Company, 1976), 139; Douglas A. Anderson, *A "Washington Merry-Go-Round" of Libel Actions* (Chicago: Nelson-Hall, 1980), 7–8; Natalie Robins, *Alien Ink: The FBI's War on Freedom of Expression* (New York: William Morrow and Company, 1992), 146.

31. Jack Anderson interview, May 23, 1979, Studs Terkel Radio Archive; Downie, *The New Muckrakers*, 141; Anderson with Gibson, *Peace, War, and Politics*, 9, 81; Katherine [Raley] Watkins oral history, Abell Papers.

32. Ralph J. Lamphere with Tim Shachterman, *The FBI-KGB War: A Special Agent's Story* (Macon, GA: Mercer University Press, 1995), 114; Donald A. Ritchie, *Reporting from Washington: The History of the Washington Press Corps* (New York: Oxford University Press, 2005), 77.

33. L. B. Nichols memo to Clyde Tolson, May 1, 1951, May 17, 1947, FBI files, 94-HQ-8-350, Serials 375–424, RG 65, NARA.

34. Carol McCabe Booker, ed., *Alone Atop the Hill: The Autobiography of Alice Dunnigan, Pioneer of the National Black Press* (Athens: University of Georgia Press, 2015), 118–19; Jack Anderson with George Clifford, *The Anderson Papers* (New York: Random House, 1973), 5–8.

35. Edwin R. Bayley oral history #2, 78, John F. Kennedy Presidential Library.

36. David Karr to George Mintzer, January 21, 1947, Pearson Papers; Anderson with Clifford, *The Anderson Papers*, 8–9.

37. John M. Henshaw Memorandum: Interview with Mr. J. B. Hasselman, AAA, February 27, 1937, Pearson Papers.

38. J. E. Milnes memo to H. B. Fletcher, April 16, 1949, FBI files, 94-HQ-8-350, Serials 283–374, RG65, NARA.

39. Anderson with Boyd, *Confessions of a Muckraker*, 11–12; Matt Mitchell oral history, 6; Tyler Abell oral history #2, 5–6, #4, 12–13, Pearson to David Karr, April 10, 1951, Leon Pearson to Pearson, December 11, 1955, Pearson Papers.

40. Sonia Stein, "Drew Pearson Plotting a 'Bull Session' Show," *Washington Post*, March 7, 1953; A. H. Belmont memo to D. M. Ladd, April 20, 1953, FBI files, 94-HQ-8-350, Serials 471–540, RG 65, NARA; see Ritchie, *Reporting from Washington*, 67–68, 190–91.

41. WMGR, November 5, 1955, AU.

42. Matt Mitchell oral history, 4–5, Abell Papers; WMGR, *Washington Post*, October 26, November 5, 11, 1955.

43. Matt Mitchell oral history, 2–4, Abell Papers.

44. Anderson with Boyd, *Confessions of a Muckraker*, 15.

45. Ibid., 12; Matt Mitchell oral history, 6–8, Abell Papers.

46. Lee Kentosh to the "Old Gang" Vintage 1957: Marian Canty, Maggie Leguia, Bill Neel, Larry Berlin, September 1969, Pearson Papers.

Chapter 5

1. WMGR, *Washington Post*, April 15, 1945; Herman Klurfeld, *Behind the Lines: The World of Drew Pearson* (Englewood Cliffs, NJ: Prentice-Hall, 1968), 89–92.

2. WMGR, November 15, 1941, AU; WMGR, *Washington Post*, July 20, 1944; April 16, 1945; Tyler Abell, ed., *Drew Pearson Diaries, 1949–1959* (New York: Holt, Rinehart and Winston, 1974), 27.

3. WMGR, November 15, 1941, AU; WMGR, *Washington Post*, July 20, 1944; April 16, 1945; Abell, ed., *Drew Pearson Diaries, 1949–1959*, 27.

4. Robert H. Ferrell, ed., *Off the Record: The Private Papers of Harry S. Truman* (New York: Harper & Row, 1980), 40–41, 156; Ferrell, ed., *Dear Bess: The Letters from Harry to Bess Truman, 1910–1959* (New York: W. W. Norton & Company, 1983), 407; *Congressional Record*, 78th Cong., 1st sess. (1943), 895.

5. Klurfeld, *Behind the Lines*, 93, 96.

6. Pearson, Personal Notes, April 14, 1945, Pearson Papers; Ferrell, ed., *Dear Bess*, 521.

7. WMGR, June 11, 1945, AU.

8. WMGR, *Washington Post*, June 11, 1945; A. J. Baime, *The Accidental President: Harry S. Truman and the Four Months That Changed the World* (New York: Houghton Mifflin Harcourt, 2017), 238.

9. Klurfeld, *Behind the Lines*, 98–99; Charles J. Greene oral history, 33–34, Harry S. Truman Library, Independence, Missouri; Drew Pearson, "Confessions of an S.O.B.: My Life in the White House Dog House," *Saturday Evening Post* 229 (November 10, 1956): 74.

10. Michael Janeway, *The Fall of the House of Roosevelt: Brokers of Ideas and Power from FDR to LBJ* (New York: Columbia University Press, 2004), 83, 86; Tracy Campbell, *Short of the Glory: The Fall and Redemption of Edward F. Prichard, Jr.* (Lexington: University Press of Kentucky, 1998), 99, 102–3; Alexander Charns, *Cloak and Gavel: FBI Wiretaps, Bugs, Information, and the Supreme Court* (Urbana: University of Illinois Press, 1992), 25–26.

11. WMGR, *Washington Post*, April 18, 1945.

12. Margaret Truman, *Harry S. Truman* (New York: William Morrow & Company, 1973), 291.

13. Ferrell, ed., *Off the Record*, 95.

14. WMGR, *Washington Post*, June 8, 1945; D. M. Ladd memo to J. Edgar Hoover, April 2, 1947, FBI files, 94-HQ-8-350, Serials 283–374, RG65, NARA.

15. Cornelius J. Mara oral history, 46, Truman Library; J. Edgar Hoover to George E. Allen, June 20, 1946, E. G. Fitch memo to D. M. Ladd, July 16, 1946, FBI files, 94-HQ-8-350, Serials 283–374, RG65, NARA.

16. "Truman Hits 'Vicious Lie,'" *Washington Post*, March 12, 1948; Guy Hottell memo to J. Edgar Hoover, March 15, 1948, FBI files, 94-HQ-8-350, Serials 283–374, RG65, NARA.

17. "George A. Smathers, United States Senator, 1951–1969," oral history, 26, Senate Historical Office, Washington, DC; John Fisher, "Smathers Rips 'Carpetbagger' Aid to Pepper," *Chicago Tribune*, April 28, 1950; Pearson unpublished diary, May 3, 1950, September 15, 1968, Pearson Papers; Brian Lewis Crispell, *Testing the Limits: George Armistead Smathers and Cold War America* (Athens: University of Georgia Press, 1999), 76.

18. Peter Hannaford, ed., *Washington Merry-Go-Round: The Drew Pearson Diaries, 1960–1969* (Lincoln, NE: Potomac Books, 2015), 250; WMGR, *Washington Post*, September 15, October 27, 1948; Pearson, unpublished diary, August 24, 1968, Pearson to Karl Bickel, November 23, 1948, David Karr to Harold Keller, October 22, 1948, Karr to Charles Breitel, October 25, 1948, Pearson Papers.

19. Hannaford, ed., *Washington Merry-Go-Round*, 270; *Evening Statesman* telegram to Drew Pearson, November 9, 1948, Pearson to Leon Pearson, November 9, 1948, Pearson Papers; Richard L. Strout oral history, 39, Truman Library; WMGR, *Washington Post*, November 8, 1948.

20. Tyler Abell to author, October 20, 2018; "Querulous Quaker," *Time* 52 (December 13, 1948).

21. WMGR, April 7, 1945, AU; Abell, ed., *Drew Pearson Diaries*, 26–27, 139; Drew Pearson, "Morgenthau Was Right," *Washington Post*, February 12, 1967; R. B. Hood memo to J. Edgar Hoover, May 1, 1945, FBI files, 94-HQ-8-350, Serials 283–374, RG65, NARA.

22. Pearson to John N. Wheeler, March 27, 1946, Pearson Papers.

23. A.H. Belmont memo to D. M. Ladd, June 1, 1953, FBI files, 94-HQ-8-350, Serials 471–540, RG 65, NARA; Abell, ed., *Drew Pearson Diaries, 1949–1959*, Pearson, unpublished diary entry, January 13, 1949, Pearson Papers; Pearson, "Morgenthau Was Right;" Jack Anderson with James Boyd, *Confessions of a Muckraker: The Inside Story of a Life in Washington during the Truman, Eisenhower, Kennedy and Johnson Years* (New York: Random House, 1979), 123–26, 133–34.

24. WMGR, *Washington Post*, October 11, October 27, November 10, November 25, December 30, 1947, February 2, February 14, 1949; Earl Warren address on receiving the annual Drew Pearson Prize, December 13, 1973, Pearson Family Papers, American University.

25. WMGR, *Washington Post*, February 12, 1948, October 5, 1967; "Drew Pearson Proposed for Nobel Peace Prize," New York *Herald Tribune*, February 24, 1949; "Taft Sees Export Surplus Raising Prices," *Washington Post*, December 31, 1947.

26. WMGR, *Washington Post*, November 25, 1947; Pearson to Tyler Abell, Aug. 6, 1952, Jefferson Caffery to Pearson, January 12, 1948, Drew Pearson Papers, Library of Congress; Donald J. Gonzales, "Ike Enlists Americans to Sell Ideas Abroad," *Washington Post*, June 1, 1956.

27. Abell, ed., *Drew Pearson Diaries*, 52; Pearson, unpublished diary entry, January 13, 1949, Pearson Papers; Pearson, "Morgenthau Was Right"; Anderson with Boyd, *Confessions of a Muckraker*, 123–27.

28. Jack Anderson memo to Pearson, June 5, 1948, Pearson Papers; Alexander Wooley, "The Fall of James Forrestal," *Washington Post*, May 23, 1999; James C. Olson, *Stuart Symington: A Life* (Columbia: University of Missouri Press, 2003), 166–77.

29. WMGR, June 10, 1948, AU.

30. Abell, ed., *Drew Pearson Diaries*, 17; Jack Anderson Memo, "Source: Louis B. Nichols," November 1948, Pearson Papers; WMGR, *Washington Post*, July 2, 1957.

31. Arthur Krock telegram to Pearson, January 16, 1949, Krock to Pearson, January 21, 1949, Krock Papers, Princeton University; John N. Wheeler to Pearson, January 25, 1949, Pearson to Wheeler, January 27, 1949, Pearson Papers.

32. J. M. Henshaw to Pearson, April 27, 1949, Pearson Papers.

33. Abell, ed., *Drew Pearson Diaries*, 12; David McCullough, *Truman* (New York: Simon & Schuster, 1992), 737; Arthur Krock, *Memoirs: Sixty Years on the Firing Line* (New York: Funk and Wagnalls, 1968), 186, 237–39, 250–51, 256.

34. Anderson with Boyd, *Confessions of a Muckraker*, 123, 126–27, 139; *Congressional Record*, 81st Cong., 1st sess., A3220; Krock, *Memoirs*, 237; Abell, ed., *Drew Pearson, Diaries*, 35, 38–39, 42.

35. "Critics of Forrestal Flayed in Congress," *Washington Post*, May 24, 1949; Margaret Truman, *Bess W. Truman* (New York: William Morrow & Company, 1986), 146–47; Frank Kluckhohn and Jay Franklin, *The Drew Pearson Story* (Chicago: Charles Hallberg, 1967), 63. Kluckhohn had been a press aide to James Forrestal.

36. Abell, ed., *Drew Pearson Diaries*, 52; Pearson to Philip Graham, May 25, 1949, Pearson Papers.

37. Drew Pearson, "Pearson Replies," *Washington Post*, May 30, 1949.

38. Anderson with Boyd, *Confessions of a Muckraker*, 144; Pearson, unpublished diary, August 9, 1965, Pearson Papers.

39. WMGR, *Washington Post*, March 18, 1947. Evidence of the Truman administration's close attention to Pearson's criticism can be found in the papers of Cornelius J. Mara, assistant military aide to the president; Harry S. Truman Library, Independence, Missouri.

40. WMGR, February 12, 1945, AU; Ken Hechler, *Working with Truman: A Personal Memoir of the White House Years* (Columbia: University of Missouri Press, 1982), 54–58; Ken Hechler oral history, 176–77, Jonathan Daniels oral history, 113–14, Truman Library. In defense of Vaughn, see Cornelius J. Mara oral history, 39–45, Truman Library.

41. WMGR, April 7, 1947, AU.

42. Stephen J. Spingarn oral history, 152–53, Truman Library; Madeline Karr to Mr. Buckley [c. December 1953], *New York Journal American*, Pearson Papers; WMGR, *Washington Post*, March 18, April 1, 1947; Harvey Klehr, *The Millionaire Was a Soviet Mole: The Twisted Life of David Karr* (New York: Encounter Books, 2019), 53–57.

43. Nathan Miller, "The Mess in Washington," *Washington Post*, June 1, 1981; Bert Cochran, *Harry Truman and the Crisis Presidency* (New York: Funk and Wagnalls, 1973), 244–46; Cornelius J. Mara oral history, 75–81, Harry S. Truman Presidential Library.

44. Klurfeld, *Behind the Lines*, 101–7; WMGR, *Washington Post*, April 28, 1956.

45. Douglas A. Anderson and Dan Pingelton, "Examination of the Content of the 'Washington Merry-Go-Round,'" *Newspaper Research Journal* 3 (April 1982): 45–51; Alonzo L. Hamby, *Man of the People: A Life of Harry S. Truman* (New York: Oxford University Press, 1995), 485–86; Heckler, *Working with Truman*, 56.

46. Robert S. Allen, "My Pal, Drew Pearson," *Collier's* 124 (July 30, 1949): 14; Abell, ed., *Drew Pearson Diaries*, 24; Public Papers of the Presidents of the United States, *Harry S. Truman, January 1 to December 31, 1949* (Washington, DC: Government Printing Office, 1964), 143.

47. "Pearson Puts New Meaning on That 'S.O.B.' from Truman," *Washington Post*, February 28, 1949; WMGR, *Washington Post*, March 3, 1949.

48. Truman, *Harry S. Truman*, 423; Klurfeld, *Behind the Lines*, 109.

49. Harry H. Vaughn oral history, 107, Truman Library; WMGR, *Washington Post*, September 6, 1949; Klurfeld, *Behind the Lines*, 108–10; Westbrook Pegler Deposition, July 2, 1953, *Drew Pearson v. Joseph McCarthy, et al.*, Civil Action No 897-51, US District Court for the District of Columbia, Maurice Rosenblatt Papers, Library of Congress.

50. Abell, ed., *Drew Pearson Diaries*, 399.

51. "Pearson Gets Punch in Eye from Lawyer," *New York Times*, June 19, 1952.

52. Jack Anderson with Daryl Gibson, *Peace, War, and Politics: An Eyewitness Account* (New York: Forge, 1999), 63–64; Edward Bliss Jr., *Now the News: The Story of Broadcast Journalism* (New York: Columbia University Press, 1991), 257.

53. WMGR, *Washington Post*, July 19, 1950, January 25, 1969.

54. Anderson with Gibson, *Peace, War, and Politics*, 156, 169–71; draft manuscript for *Peace, War, and Politics*, Jack Anderson Papers; see also David Halberstam, *The Coldest Winter: America and the Korean War* (New York: Hyperion, 2007).

55. Anderson with Boyd, *Confessions of a Muckraker*, 161–71; WMGR, *Washington Post*, January 23, 1951, February 12, 1964.

56. The US army is organized into five units: G-1, personnel; G-2, intelligence; G-3, operations; G-4, logistics; and G-5, civil-military operations.

57. V. P. Keay memo to A. H. Belmont, January 6, 1951, V. P. Keay to A. H. Belmont, January 6, 1951, 94-HQ-8-350, Serials 375–424, RG 65, NARA.

58. FB [Fred Blumenthal] to Pearson, January 19, 1952, Pearson Papers; "Harry Costello, Hoya Great, Dies at 76," *Washington Post*, August 27, 1968.

59. Daily Staff Meeting, 22 August 1951, General CIA Records, www.cia.gov/library.

60. Fulton Lewis Jr., "Washington Report" [c. 1953], Jack Anderson Papers; WMGR, *Washington Post*, January 29, 1952.

61. Natalie Robins, *Alien Ink: The FBI's War on Freedom of Expression* (New York: William Morrow and Company, 1992), 148; C. E. Hennrich memo to A. H. Belmont, December 15, 1951, J. Edgar Hoover to Tolson, Ladd, and Nichols, March 6, 1952, Jack Anderson FBI files, National Security Archive; Pearson unpublished diary, January 16, 1952, Pearson Papers.

62. D. M. Ladd memo to J. Edgar Hoover, January 19, 1951, FBI files, 94-HQ-8-350, Serials 375–424, RG 65, NARA.

63. Pearson to Army Secretary Frank Pace, February 1, 1951, Pearson Papers.

64. WMGR, *Washington Post*, June 24, 1949; J. Edgar Hoover to Joseph H. Biben, January 25, 1949, Hoover to Tolson, Ladd, Nichols, June 29, 1949, FBI files, 94-HQ-8-350, Serials 283–374, RG65, NARA; Hoover to Pearson, July 12, 1941, May 9, 1949, Pearson Papers; Daniel Patrick Moynihan, *Secrecy: The American Experience* (New Haven: Yale University Press, 1998), 63–68.

65. Robins, *Alien Ink*, 108, 145; A. H. Belmont memo to L. V. Boardman, March 8, 1954, FBI files, 94-HQ-8-350, Serials 541–599, L. B. Nichols memo to Clyde Tolson, January 12, 1955, 94-HQ-8-350, Serials 600–677, RG 65, NARA; Matthew Cecil, Jessica Freeman, and Jennifer Tiernan, "Jackals, Vultures, Scavengers, and Scoundrels," *Journalism History* 43 (Spring 2017): 2–11.

66. David M. Noyes to Pearson, August 7, 1963, Pearson Papers; WMGR, *Washington Post*, November 6, 1967; Anderson and Boyd, *Confessions of a Muckraker*, 277–78.

Chapter 6

1. *Congressional Record*, 85th Cong., 1st sess. (1957), 9835; see Drew Pearson and Jack Anderson, *The Case against Congress: A Compelling Indictment of Corruption on Capitol Hill* (New York: Simon & Schuster, 1968); WMGR, *Washington Post*, January 5, 1969.

2. Donald R. Matthews, *US Senators and Their World* (Chapel Hill: University of North Carolina Press, 1960), 264.

3. Carlisle Bargeron, "Washington's Mighty Penmen," *Nation's Business* 34 (May 1, 1946): 59; "Hoffman Charges Reds Set Policies," *New York Times*, March 14, 1944; "Senate Ban Asked on Some Writers," *New York Times*, October 18, 1940; WMGR, *Washington Post*, January 13, 1943.

4. *Congressional Record*, 76th Cong., 1st sess. (1939), 745–46, 5412–26; "Senator Attacks Columnists for 'Trying to Destroy Me,'" *Los Angeles Times*, May 12, 1939; "Reynolds Denies 'Pro-Nazi' Charges," *New York Times*, May 12, 1939.

5. WMGR, October 21, 1940, AU; J. W. Cannon memo to D. M. Ladd, October 18, 1942, FBI Files, 94-HQ-8-350, Serials 101–130, RG 65, NARA; "Fish Raises Ante in Pearson Clash," *New York Times*, November 2, 1940; *Congressional Record*, 76th Cong., 3rd sess. (1940), 13685–86; Nivel West, ed., *The Secret History of British Intelligence in the Americas, 1940–1945* (New York: Fromm International, 1999), 73–80; Thomas E. Mahl, *Desperate Deception: British Covert Operations in the United States, 1939–44* (Washington, DC: Brassey's, 1998), 107–35.

6. *Congressional Record*, 78th Cong., 1st sess. (1943), 4722–24; Jack Anderson with James Boyd, *Confessions of a Muckraker: The Inside Story of Life in Washington during the Truman, Eisenhower, Kennedy and Johnson Years* (New York: Random House, 1979), 233.

7. Anderson with Boyd, *Confessions of a Muckraker*, 20–21; Oliver Pilat, *Pegler: Angry Man of the Press* (Boston: Beacon Press, 1963), 236–39; Finis Farr, *Fair Enough: The Life of Westbrook Pegler* (New Rochelle, NY: Arlington House, 1975), 193, 199–200; Drew Pearson to Edna Pearson, December 15, 1939, Pearson Papers.

8. WMGR, December 23, 1938, AU.

9. WMGR, December 23, 1938, AU; *Congressional Record*, 76th Cong., 1st sess. (1939), 6163–64; 76th Cong., 3rd sess. (1940), 4446; 78th Cong., 1st sess. (1943), 4722–24; Douglas A. Anderson, *A "Washington Merry-Go-Round" of Libel Actions* (Chicago: Nelson-Hall, 1980), 102–5.

10. Anderson, *A "Washington Merry-Go-Round" of Libel Actions*, 103, 127.

11. Anderson, *A "Washington Merry-Go-Round" of Libel Actions*, 104–6, "Rep. Sweeney Loses Libel Suit," *Washington Post*, May 26, 1942; "Sweeney Loses a Round," *New York Times*, May 26, 1942.

12. "Rules Bias Charge Libelous If False," *New York Times*, April 14, 1942; William R. Spear, "High Court Upholds Sweeney Libel Suit," *Washington Post*, April 14, 1942; *Congressional Record*, 77th Cong., 2nd sess., A37941; WMGR, January 27, 1951.

13. Anderson, *A "Washington Merry-Go-Round" of Libel Actions*, 107, 110.

14. Anderson, *A "Washington Merry-Go-Round" of Libel Actions*, 122–23; Drew Pearson to Washington Merry-Go-Round Editors, January 27, 1943, AU.

15. Anderson, *A "Washington Merry-Go-Round" of Libel Actions*, 125–26.

16. Anderson, *A "Washington Merry-Go-Round" of Libel Actions*, 127; *New York Times Co. v. Sullivan*, 376 U.S. 254 (1964).

17. Pearson to G. H. Leggett, May 17, 1944, Pearson Papers; WMGR, *Washington Post*, April 25, 1944.

18. Dean Pope, "The Senator from Tennessee," *The West Tennessee Historical Society Papers* 22 (1968): 103; *Congressional Record*, 78th Cong., 1st sess. (1944), 3683–84.

19. "Senator M'Kellar Calls Drew Pearson 'Liar,'" *Los Angeles Times*, April 26, 1944; Pearson to Galt Braxton, May 12, 1944, Pearson Papers.

20. Galt Braxton to Kenneth McKellar, May 8, 1944, Pearson to W. F. McAuliffe, May 23, 1944, Pearson Papers; W. H. Shippen, "McCarthy Faces Quiz Today on Report He Threatened to Maim Pearson," *Washington Evening Star*, October 5, 1951; Murray Marder, "Pearson Says McCarthy Threatened to Maim Him," *Washington Post*, October 5, 1951.

21. *Congressional Record*, 78th Cong., 1st sess. (1943), 4722–24, 6185.

22. Drew Pearson, "Confessions of an S.O.B.: How to Make Enemies," *Saturday Evening Post* 229 (November 24, 1956): 148; WMGR, *Washington Post*, October 21, 1954.

23. WMGR, *Washington Post*, October 21, 1954.

24. WMGR, *Washington Post*, May 13, 1952.

25. H. Belmont memo to D. M. Ladd, June 1, 1953, FBI files, 94-HQ-8-350, Serials 471–540, RG 65, NARA.

26. WMGR, *Washington Post*, October 21, 1954.

27. WMGR, *Washington Post*, May 21, 1946, January 3, 1947; Drew Pearson, "Confessions of an S.O.B.: My Mother-in-Law Troubles," *Saturday Evening Post* 229 (November 17, 1956): 148.

28. Pearson, "Confessions of an S.O.B.," *Saturday Evening Post* 229 (November 17, 1956): 148; John W. Ball, "Thomas Cotton Speculation Being Probed by Senate Unit," *Washington Post*, January 16, 1948.

29. WMGR, *Washington Post*, October 21, 1954.

30. WMGR, *Washington Post*, April 4, 1948; Jack Anderson interview, May 23, 1979, Studs Terkel Radio Archive.

31. Tyler Abell, ed., *Drew Pearson Diaries, 1949–1959* (New York: Holt, Rinehart and Winston, 1974), 94; Howard Durkin, "Jury Quizzes Thomas Aides on 'Kickbacks,'" *Washington Post*, October 23, 1948; Howard Durkin, "'New Low in Politics,' Thomas Calls Clark's Payroll Probe," *Washington Post*, October 24, 1948; Robert D. McFadden, "J. Parnell Thomas, Anti-Red Crusader, Is Dead," *New York Times*, November 20, 1970.

32. "Thomas Begs President to Free Him," *Washington Post*, May 31, 1950; Tyler Abell oral history #2, 3, Abell Papers.

33. WMGR, *Washington Post*, October 21, 1954.

34. Drew Pearson, "Confessions of an S.O.B.," *Saturday Evening Post* 229 (November 3, 1956): 24; Pilat, *Drew Pearson*, 172–73.

35. WMGR, *Washington Post*, July 12, 1946; "May the Martyr," *Washington Post*, June 30, 1946; "Full Pardons Granted May and Thomas," *Washington Post*, December 26, 1952.

36. WMGR, *Washington Post*, October 21, 1954.

37. WMGR, *Washington Post*, September 26, October 2, 1950.

38. WMGR, *Washington Post*, October 9, 1950; "Rep. Walter Brehm Indicted on Salary Kickback Charges," *Washington Post*, December 21, 1950; WFO [Washington Field Office] memo, August 16, 1950, Jack Anderson FBI files, National Security Archive.

39. Drew Pearson, "Confessions of an S.O.B.: How to Make Enemies," *Saturday Evening Post* 229 (November 24, 1956): 148; House of Representatives, Committee on Government Operations, *Government Contracts for Small Business*, 83rd Cong., 1st sess. (1953), 1–35; "Pearson Admits Error before Hoffman Group," *Washington Post*, March 25, 1953.

40. Subcommittee of the Senate Committee on Interstate and Foreign Commerce, *Hearings on the Nomination of Robert F. Jones to the Federal Communications Commission*, 80th Cong., 1st sess. (Washington, DC: GPO, 1947), 9; Jack Anderson interview, May 23, 1979, Studs Terkel Radio Archive.

41. "Robert F. Jones Dies; Former Congressman," *Washington Post*, June 23, 1968.

42. *Hearings on the Nomination of Robert F. Jones*, 11.

43. *Hearings on the Nomination of Robert F. Jones*, 5–7; Jack Anderson interview, May 23, 1979, Studs Terkel Radio Archive; Anderson with Boyd, *Confessions of a Muckraker*, 32–46.

44. *Hearings on the Nomination of Robert F. Jones*, 84–85.

45. *Hearings on the Nomination of Robert F. Jones*, 14–16, 21–27; Kenneth G. Crawford, "He Refused to Be Smeared by Pearson," *Saturday Evening Post* 222 (November 26, 1949): 93.

46. *Hearings on the Nomination of Robert F. Jones*, 10, 14; William A. Roberts to Pearson, December 28, 1950, Jack Anderson Papers.

47. Jack Anderson interview, May 23, 1979, Studs Terkel Radio Archive; Anderson with Boyd, *Confessions of a Muckraker*, 44–47; Mary Spargo, "Jones Okayed by Committee for FCC Post," *Washington Post*, July 11, 1947; "FCC Grants WBAL License Renewal," *Baltimore Sun*, June 19, 1951; Walter Trohan, "Capital Radio Scene Shifted under FCC Boss," *Chicago Tribune*, March 19, 1950.

48. Abell interview 2, 13–14, Abell Papers.

49. Clarence W. Wunderlin Jr. et al., eds., *The Papers of Robert A. Taft, 1945–1948* (Kent, OH: Kent State University Press, 2003), vol. 3: 300–1.

50. James Patterson, *Mr. Republican: A Biography of Robert A. Taft* (Boston: Houghton Mifflin, 1972), 402–3; Wunderlin Jr. et al., eds., *The Papers of Robert A. Taft*, vol. 3: 118–19, 261.

51. WMGR, *Washington Post*, July 18, 1947.

52. Ibid.; Wunderlin Jr. et al., eds., *The Papers of Robert A. Taft*, vol. 3: 304; Scott I. Peek Oral History, Senate Historical Office, 66.

53. "Drew Pearson Says Taft Told McCarthy to 'Keep on Talking,'" *Washington Post*, March 21, 1950; WMGR, *Washington Post*, March 22, 1950, January 28, 1953; Abell, ed., *Drew Pearson Diaries*, 112; Wunderlin Jr. et al., eds., *The*

Papers of Robert A. Taft, 1949–1953 (Kent, OH: Kent State University Press, 2006), vol. 4: 162–63.

54. "Taft Denies Urging Steps by McCarthy," *Washington Post*, May 19, 1950; WMGR, *Washington Post*, June 9, 1950.

55. Patrick Anderson, "The Truth about Drew Pearson," *Washingtonian* 3 (June 1968): 39.

56. WMGR, *Washington Post*, May 29, 1955, July 25, 1958, September 26, 1962, September 3, 1964, July 26, 1966; William Chapman, "Powell Aide Dismissed after Pearson's Praise," *Washington Post*, August 3, 1966; Abell, ed., *Drew Pearson Diaries*, 424; Charles V. Hamilton, *Adam Clayton Powell, Jr.: The Political Biography of an American Dilemma* (New York: Atheneum, 1991), 267–69, 411.

57. WMGR, *Washington Post*, September 15, 1966, January 4, 1967; Peter Hannaford, ed., *Washington Merry-Go-Round: The Drew Pearson Diaries, 1960–1969* (Lincoln, NE: Potomac Books, 2015), 469; *Powell v. McCormack*, 395 U.S. 486 (1969).

58. WMGR, *Washington Post*, April 13, 1963, December 8, 1966. His last piece on the subject, published posthumously, was Drew Pearson, "The Senate," *Playboy* 16 (November 1969): 119–20, 267–69.

Chapter 7

1. Judy Bachrach, "Louise Ansberry: A Tale of Changes," *Washington Post*, February 17, 1975; Murrey Marder, "Pearson-McCarthy Pre-Trial Hearing Closed to Public," *Washington Post*, September 26, 1951; Russell Long statement, Warren Woods interview, August 11, 1951, Maurice Rosenblatt Papers, Library of Congress.

2. W. H. Shippen, "McCarthy's Income Taxes, War Record Figure in Bristling Hearing on Pearson Suit," *Washington Evening Star*, September 27, 1951; Haynes Johnson, *The Age of Anxiety: McCarthyism to Terrorism* (Orlando, FL: Harcourt, 2005), 196–207.

3. "That Sulgrave Club Battle Marked by Two Encounters," *Washington Post*, December 15, 1950; Walter Trohan, "How Pearson Got Slapped: The Full Story," *Chicago Tribune*, December 17, 1950; Richard M. Nixon, *RN: The Memoirs of Richard Nixon* (New York: Grosset & Dunlap, 1978), 138–39; Robert Sam Anson, *Exile: The Unquiet Oblivion of Richard M. Nixon* (New York: Simon & Schuster, 1984), 219.

4. Warren Woods, memo for the files, November 2, 1951, Anderson Papers; "Sen. McCarthy Either Kicked, Slapped or Mauled Pearson," *Washington Post*, December 14, 1950; WMGR, *Washington Post*, December 15, 1954.

5. Pearson's ratings had also boosted his previous sponsor, Lee Hats: "Crusading Pays Lee . . . It Took Them from Sixth to *First!*" *Sponsor* 1 (February 1947): 9–14.

6. McCarthy sent franked copies of his speech to 1,800 editors, demanding that they cancel Pearson's column: "To Washington Merry-Go-Round Editors," December 7, 1954, AU; "Senator Calls Him 'Unprincipled Liar,'"

Washington Post, December 16, 1950; Jack Anderson and Ronald W. May, *McCarthy: The Man, the Senator, the "Ism"* (Boston: Beacon Press, 1952), 276.

7. "Pearson Job Over Anyway, Sponsor Says," *Washington Post*, December 31, 1950; Murray Marder, "Pearson Says McCarthy Threatened to Maim Him," *Washington Post*, October 5, 1951; Sonia Stein, "Drew Pearson Plotting a 'Bull Session' Show," *Washington Post*, March 7, 1953; Edwin R. Bayley, *Joe McCarthy and the Press* (New York: Pantheon Books, 1981), 166–67; Tyler Abell, ed., *Drew Pearson Diaries, 1949–1959* (New York: Holt, Rinehart and Winston, 1974), 254.

8. Walter Winchell, *Winchell Exclusive* (Englewood Cliffs, NJ: Prentice-Hall, 1975), 256–57; Neil Gabler, *Winchell: Gossip, Power, and the Cult of Celebrity* (New York: Vintage, 1995), 477–80; Donald A. Ritchie, *Reporting from Washington; The History of the Washington Press Corps* (New York: Oxford University Press, 2005), 89.

9. Peter Hannaford, ed., *Washington Merry-Go-Round: The Drew Pearson Diaries, 1960–1969* (Lincoln, NE: Potomac Books, 2015), 479; Tyler Abell Interview with Charles Warner, January 28, 2016, 3–5, Abell Papers; Pearson to Tyler Abell, June 20, 1955, Pearson Papers; Abell, ed., *Drew Pearson Diaries*, 258.

10. Pearson to Leon Pearson, January 8, 1956, Pearson Papers.

11. WMGR, *Washington Post*, August 1, 1947, August 10, 1947, July 18, 1948, November 22, 1948.

12. Jack Anderson interview, May 23, 1979, Studs Terkel Radio Archive; Ritchie, *Reporting from Washington*, 77; Jack Anderson with James Boyd, *Confessions of a Muckraker: The Inside Story of Life in Washington during the Truman, Eisenhower, Kennedy and Johnson Years* (New York: Random House, 1979), 205; Pearson, unpublished diary, June 19, 1969, Pearson Papers.

13. Jack Anderson notes McCarthy for *Parade* article [c. 1957], Jack Anderson Papers; Drew Pearson oral history, 9–10, Johnson Library; Memo, Sen. Joseph McCarthy—Drew Pearson Column References [1951], Pearson Papers; WMGR, *Washington Post*, March 14, 1950; Bayley, *Joe McCarthy and the Press*, 56–57.

14. McCarthy made the same confession in the same words to William Randolph Hearst Jr.: Lindsey Chaney and Michael Cieply, *The Hearsts: Family and Empire—The Later Years* (New York: Simon & Schuster, 1981), 79–82. Mark Feldstein, *Poisoning the Press: Richard Nixon, Jack Anderson, and the Rise of Washington's Scandal Culture* (New York: Farrar, Straus & Giroux, 2010), 42; Thomas C. Reeves, *The Life and Times of Joe McCarthy* (New York: Stein and Day, 1982), 247; Ritchie, *Reporting from Washington*, 71–72, 77, 79.

15. WMGR, *Washington Post*, November 29, 1951.

16. WMGR, *Washington Post*, March 14, 1950, November 29, 1951, May 6, 1957; Anderson and May, *McCarthy*, 172–73; Richard M. Fried, "The Idea of Conspiracy in McCarthy-Era Politics," *Prologue* 34 (Spring 2002): 45–47;

Reeves, *The Life and Times of Joe McCarthy*, 196, 202–3; Donald F. Crosby, *God, Church, and Flag: Senator Joseph R. McCarthy and the Catholic Church, 1950–1957* (Chapel Hill: University of North Carolina Press, 1978), 47–52; "Edmund A. Walsh," *Washington Post*, November 3, 1956; Larry Tye, *Demagogue: The Life and Long Shadow of Senator Joe McCarthy* (Boston: Houghton Mifflin Harcourt, 2020), 174–76, 501.

17. Abell, ed., *Drew Pearson Diaries*, 118; WMGR, *Washington Post*, July 11, 1953.

18. WMGR, *Washington Post*, March 14, April 19, 1950, February 14, 1961; "Lustron Pay to McCarthy Put in Record," *Washington Post*, June 16, 1950; Drew Pearson to Leon Pearson, January 8, 1956, Pearson Papers.

19. Abell, ed., *Drew Pearson Diaries*, 116, 118; Robert P. Newman, *Owen Lattimore and the "Loss" of China* (Berkeley: University of California Press, 1992), 207–22.

20. WMGR, *Washington Post*, April 21, 1950.

21. Abell, ed., *Drew Pearson Diaries*, 116.

22. WMGR, *Washington Post*, April 13, 1950; Abell, ed., *Drew Pearson Diaries*, 123–24.

23. Murrey Marder, "Pearson Says McCarthy Threatened to Maim Him," *Washington Post*, October 5, 1951.

24. "Senator Calls Him 'Unprincipled Liar,'" *Washington Post*, December 16, 1950; Westbrook Pegler, "Sen. McCarthy and the A.P.," Madison, Wisconsin, *State Journal*, February 16, 1951; Warren Woods, memo for the files, November 2, 1951, Anderson Papers.

25. FB [Fred Blumenthal] to Pearson, June 28, 1950, Pearson notes for a statement [1950], Pearson Papers; "Writer Threatens Action in Court," *Washington Post*, December 16, 1950.

26. Warren Woods to Jack Anderson, June 18, 1968, Jack Anderson Papers, George Washington University; Morris A. Bealle, *All America Louse: A Candid Biography of Drew A. Pearson [sic]* (Washington: Columbia Publishing Company, 1965), 19–25; Reeves, *The Life and Times of Joe McCarthy*, 350; Douglas A. Anderson, *A "Washington-Merry-Go-Round" of Libel Actions* (Chicago: Nelson-Hall, 1980), 227.

27. WMGR, *Washington Post*, July 4, 1952; Norman K. Risjord, *Wisconsin: The Story of the Badger State* (Madison, WI: Trails Books, 2007), 208.

28. Pearson to Jonathan Daniels, February 15, 1951, Pearson Papers; Oliver Pilat, *Drew Pearson: An Unauthorized Biography* (New York: Harper's Magazine Press, 1973), 221; Anderson and Boyd, *Confessions of a Muckraker*, 232.

29. See Ritchie, *Reporting from Washington*, 70–91, and Ritchie, "McCarthyism in Congress: Investigating Communism," in *The American Congress: The Building of Democracy*, ed. Julian Zelizer (New York: Houghton Mifflin, 2004).

30. Jack Anderson interview, May 23, 1979, Studs Terkel Archive; Timothy Mark Chambless, "Columnist Jack Anderson, the Secular Evangelist: Five

Speeches in Utah between 1972 and 1975" (master's thesis in Speech Communication, University of Utah, June 1977), 51; Alfred Friendly, "A Devastating Job on McCarthy," *Washington Post*, October 19, 1952; [Jack] Anderson statement to the press [c. 1952], Pearson Papers; Ronald W. May to Maurice Rosenblatt, December 30, 1952, Rosenblatt Papers; Bureau Memo, 3/22/51, Re: Physical Surveillance in the Capitol, FBI Files, the Internet Archive.

31.   Associated Press clipping, Charles Town, West Virginia, February 6, [1952], Pearson Papers; William Bryan to Pearson, June 23, 1952, Pearson Papers.

32.   WMGR, *Washington Post*, September 13, 1953; A. H. Belmont to D. M. Ladd, June 1, 1953, November 13, 1953, A. H. Belmont memo to D. M. Ladd, November 13, 1953, FBI files, 94-HQ-8-350, Serials 541–599, RG 65, NARA; Abell, ed., *Drew Pearson Diaries*, 282, 287.

33.   A. Rosen memo for J. Edgar Hoover, November 19, 1953, FBI files, 94-HQ-8-350, Serials 541–599, RG 65, NARA; Natalie Robins, *Alien Ink: The FBI's War on Freedom of Expression* (New York: William Morrow and Company, 1992), 148; Douglas M. Charles, *Hoover's War on Gays: Exposing the FBI's "Sex Deviates" Program* (Lawrence: University Press of Kansas, 2015), 296.

34.   Pearson to Brigadier General C. T. Lanham, March 20, 1952, Pearson Papers.

35.   Roy Cohn, *McCarthy* (New York: American Library, 1968), 46.

36.   See David M. Oshinsky, *A Conspiracy So Immense: The World of Joe McCarthy* (New York: Free Press, 1983); and Reeves, *The Life and Times of Joe McCarthy*.

37.   Abell, ed., *Drew Pearson Diaries*, 194; A. H. Belmont memo to D. M. Ladd, May 18, 1953, FBI files, 94-HQ-8-350, Serials 471–540, RG 65, NARA.

38.   Jack Anderson to Pearson, March 30, 1953, Pearson Papers; Christopher C. Lovett, "On the Side of the Angels and the Fall of Joe McCarthy," *Emporia State Research Studies* 51 (2016): 12.

39.   Harvey Matusow told his story in *False Witness* (New York: Cameron & Kahn, 1955); A. H. Belmont memo to D. M. Ladd, May 11, 1953, FBI files, 94-HQ-8-350, Serials 471–540, RG 65, NARA.

40.   Robert M. Lichtman and Ronald D. Cohen, *Deadly Farce: Harvey Matusow and the Informer System in the McCarthy Era* (Champaign: University of Illinois Press, 2004), 85, 121; Murrey Marder, "M'Carthy Ties in 1952 Cited by Matusow," *Washington Post*, February 23, 1955; WMGR, *Washington Post*, July 2, 1957.

41.   Murrey Marder, "McCarthy in Press Probe Demands All the Names of Communists Who 'Infiltrated' News Media," *Washington Post*, May 7, 1953; Griffin Fariello, *Red Scare: Memories of the American Inquisition* (New York: Avon Books, 1995), 107, 352; Martin Weil, "Anti-Communist Witness, Harvey Matusow, 75, Dies," *Washington Post*, January 28, 2002.

42.   A. H. Belmont memo to D. M. Laff, February 5, 1953, FBI files, 94-HQ-8-350, Serials 471–540, RG 65, NARA; Anthony Champagne and Reed

Penny, "Margaret Fallon (Peggy) Palmer: A Portrait of Sam Rayburn's 'Lady Friend,'" *Southwestern Historical Quarterly* 120 (October 2016): 203–4.

43. Pearson to Herbert Brownell, March 24, 1954, Pearson Papers.

44. Senate, Committee on Governmental Affairs, *Executive Sessions of the Senate Permanent Subcommittee on Investigations of the Committee on Government Operations, Eighty-Third Congress, First Session, 1953,* vol 1, xiii–xxviii; John G. Adams, *Without Precedent: The Story of the Death of McCarthyism* (New York: W. W. Norton, 1983), 53–66.

45. Senate, Committee on Governmental Affairs, *Executive Sessions of the Senate Permanent Subcommittee on Investigations of the Committee on Government Operations, Eighty-Third Congress, First Session, 1953,* vol. 2, 1774; "M'Carthy Accuses Pearson and Aide," *New York Times,* March 25, 1954.

46. *Executive Sessions of the Senate Permanent Subcommittee on Investigations of the Committee on Government Operations,* vol. 2: 1747–49.

47. *Executive Sessions of the Senate Permanent Subcommittee on Investigations of the Committee on Government Operations,* 1751, 1759, 1769, 1772–73.

48. Philip Dodd, "Pearson Prints Army Secrets; Probe Started," *Chicago Tribune,* January 13, 1951; Abell, ed., *Drew Pearson's Diaries,* 279; Jack Anderson memo to Pearson, October 23, 1953, Heber H. Smith to William Burke, January 4, 1954, Pearson to Hugh B. Mitchell, January 22, 1954, Pearson Papers.

49. A. H. Belmont to D. M. Ladd, October 26, 1953, FBI files, 94-HQ-8-350, Serials 471–540, RG 65, NARA; Robert Allen to Pearson, July 26, 1954, Pearson Papers.

50. Pearson to Hugh B. Mitchell, January 22, 1954; Pearson to Herbert Brownell, March 24, 1954, Pearson Papers.

51. R. G. Waldeck, "Homosexual International," *Human Events* 9 (April 16, 1952): 1, 3.

52. "Senator Declares His Attack Made Him 'a Revolving S.O.B.' Automatically," *Washington Post,* April 21, 1950; *Congressional Record,* 81st Cong., 2nd sess. (1950), A7249, A3426–28; Gail Collins, *Scorpion Tongues: Gossip, Celebrity, and American Politics* (New York: William Morrow and Company, 1998), 169–71.

53. Andrea Friedman, "The Smearing of Joe McCarthy: The Lavender Scare, Gossip, and Cold War Politics," in *When Private Talk Goes Public: Gossip in American History,* eds. Kathleen A. Feeley and Jennifer Frost (New York: Palgrave Macmillan, 2014), 203–23; Bealle, *An America Louse,* 22–25.

54. WMGR, *Washington Post,* July 17, May 1, 1954; Athan G. Theoharis and John Stuart Cox, *The Boss: J. Edgar Hoover and the Great American Inquisition* (Philadelphia: Temple University Press, 1988), 290; Bayley, *Joe McCarthy and the Press,* 134–35; FBI Memo, May 13, 1954, Serial 639–681, FBI Files, The Internet Archive.

55. M. Stanton Evans, *Blacklisted by History: The Untold Story of Senator Joe McCarthy and His Fight against America's Enemies* (New York: Crown Forum, 2007), 544; Oshinsky, *A Conspiracy So Immense*, 363–64; Johnson, *The Age of Anxiety*, 332–33; WMGR, *Washington Post*, July 17, 1953, November 22, 1953, February 14, May 1, 1954, June 5, 1954.

56. Schine's frequent date at the time, Iris Flores, testified at a closed hearing during the Army-McCarthy hearings. Schine eventually moved to California, became a movie producer, and married an actress with whom he had six children. See *Executive Sessions of the Senate Permanent Subcommittee on Investigations*, vol. 5, xvi–xix, 223–39.

57. WMGR, *Washington Post*, December 22, 1953.

58. WMGR, *Washington Post*, December 22, 1953, July 3, 1967; Cohn, *McCarthy*, 181, 208, 223, 275, 277; see Donald A. Ritchie, "The Army-McCarthy Hearings, 1954," in *Congress Investigates: A Critical and Documented History*, eds. Raymond Smock, Roger Bruns, and David Hostetter (New York: Facts on File, 2011).

59. "Ruth Young Watt, Chief Clerk, Permanent Subcommittee on Investigations, 1948–1979," oral history, 136, Senate Historical Office; Jack Anderson memo to Pearson, June 25, 1954, Pearson Papers.

60. Abell, ed., *Drew Pearson Diaries*, 321, 323, 325; WMGR, June 21, 1945, AU; Lester C. Hunt to Pearson, January 6, 1954, Pearson Memorandum to Ernest Cuneo, and John Wilson, June 22, 1954, editorial, *Kemmerer Gazette*, June 25, 1954, Pearson Papers.

61. See David K. Johnson, *The Lavender Scare: The Cold War Persecution of Gays and Lesbians in the Federal Government* (Chicago: University of Chicago Press, 2004), and Rodger McDaniel, *Dying for Joe McCarthy's Sins: The Suicide of Wyoming Senator Lester Hunt* (Cody, WY: WordsWorth, 2013).

62. Abell, ed., *Drew Pearson Diaries*, 304; US Senate Committee on Governmental Affairs, *Executive Sessions of the Senate Permanent Subcommittee on Investigations of the Committee on Government Operations, Eighty-Third Congress, Second Session, 1954* (Washington, DC: Government Printing Office, 2003), vol. 5: xiv–xvi; A. H. Belmont to L. V. Boardman, April 5, 1954, FBI files, 94-HQ-8-350, Serials 541–599, RG 65, NARA.

63. *Washington Post*, May 4, 1967; A. H. Belmont memos to L. V. Boardman, March 22, 1954, May 3, 1954, and July 26, 1954, FBI files, 94-HQ-8-350, Serials 600–677, RG 65, NARA; Arthur L. Lloyd to Pearson, November 19, 1954, Pearson Papers.

64. WMGR, *Washington Post*, September 20, October 2, November 8, 14, 17, 24, 1954; Dwight D. Eisenhower, *Mandate for Change, 1953–1956* (New York: Doubleday and Company, 1963), 388–89; Ritchie, *Reporting from Washington*, 88–91; Tye, *Demagogue*, 462–72.

65. WMGR, *Washington Post*, May 6, 1957.

66. WMGR, *Washington Post*, March 15, 1957, May 6, 1957; Abell, ed., *Drew Pearson Diaries*, 375, 379, 384.

67. Pearson to William Benton, June 5, 1957, Pearson to Francis N. Connolly, February 20, 1962, Pearson Papers.

Chapter 8

1. WMGR, *Washington Post*, November 8, 1952.
2. Richard Tanner Johnson, *Managing the White House: An Intimate Study of the Presidency* (New York: Harper & Row, 1974), 74–75; Drew Pearson, "Confessions of an S.O.B.: My Life in the White House Dog House," *Saturday Evening Post* 229 (November 10, 1956): 38; Pearson, notes for "More Confessions of an S.O.B." [c. 1961], Pearson to Tyler Abell, April 16, 1955, Pearson Papers; WMGR, *Washington Post*, October 21, 1954.
3. WMGR, *Washington Post*, July 9, 1945, March 29, 1969; 1946; Louis Galambos et al., eds., *The Papers of Dwight David Eisenhower: The Chief of Staff* (Baltimore: Johns Hopkins University Press, 1978), vol. 8: 1412–13.
4. "Drew Pearson Says Eisenhower Will Be Democratic Candidate," *Chester Times*, April 19, 1948; "Ike Deplores Boost for Presidency," *Washington Post*, May 28, 1948; Louis Galambos et al., eds., *The Papers of Dwight David Eisenhower: Columbia University* (Baltimore: Johns Hopkins University Press, 1984), vol. 10: 50, 64–65; Dwight Eisenhower to Pearson, May 13, 1948, Pearson Papers.
5. Louis Galambos et al., eds., *The Papers of Dwight David Eisenhower: NATO and the Campaign of 1952* (Baltimore: Johns Hopkins University Press, 1984), vol. 12: 123.
6. Pearson, notes from "More Confessions of an S.O.B." [c. 1961], Pearson to Dwight Eisenhower, February 23, 1952, Pearson Papers; Galambos et al., eds., *The Papers of Dwight David Eisenhower*, vol. 12: 846–47; Galambos et al., eds., *The Papers of Dwight David Eisenhower: NATO and the Campaign of 1952*, vol. 13: 1134–35.
7. Tyler Abell, ed., *Drew Pearson Diaries, 1949–1959* (New York: Holt, Rinehart and Winston, 1974), 190, 218.
8. Pearson, notes from "More Confessions of an S.O.B." [c. 1961], Pearson Papers; Abell, ed., *Drew Pearson Diaries*, 208–10.
9. Donald A. Ritchie, *Reporting from Washington: The History of the Washington Press Corps* (New York: Oxford University Press, 2005), 67–68; Abell, ed., *Drew Pearson Diaries*, 216.
10. WMGR, *Washington Post*, January 10, 1960; Roger Morris, *Richard Milhous Nixon: The Rise of an American Politician* (New York: Henry Holt and Company, 1990), 359; John A. Farrell, *Richard Nixon: The Life* (New York: Doubleday, 2017), 206–7.
11. Morris, *Richard Milhous Nixon*, 445–46; WMGR, *Washington Post*, December 10, 1948.
12. Pearson to Tyler Abell, September 25, 1952, Pearson Papers; Jack Anderson with James Boyd, *Confessions of a Muckraker: The Inside Story of Life in Washington during the Truman, Eisenhower, Kennedy and Johnson Years*

(New York: Random House, 1979), 325–26; WMGR, *Washington Post*, September 29, 1952; WMGR, September 23, 25, 1952, AU.

13. WMGR, *Washington Post*, June 18, 1954; for Eisenhower's hands-off approach, see David A. Nichols, *Ike and McCarthy: Dwight Eisenhower's Secret Campaign against Joseph McCarthy* (New York: Simon & Schuster, 2017).

14. Abell, ed., *Drew Pearson Diaries*, 228; Peter Hannaford, ed., *Washington Merry-Go-Round: The Drew Pearson Diaries, 1960–1969* (Lincoln, NE: Potomac Books, 2015), 240; Abell, ed., *Drew Pearson Diaries*, 228, 322; Pearson, notes from "More Confessions of an S.O.B." [c. 1961], Pearson to Tyler Abell, September 25, 1952, Pearson Papers.

15. Abell, ed., *Drew Pearson Diaries*, 229.

16. WMGR, *Washington Post*, April 22, 1952; Robert J. Donovan, *Boxing the Kangaroo: A Reporter's Memoir* (Columbia: University of Missouri Press, 2000), 55–56.

17. Arthur Krock, *In the Nation: 1932–1966* (New York: McGraw-Hill, 1966), 219–20.

18. Memorandum of Discussion at the 301st Meeting of the National Security Council, Washington, October 26, 1956, *Foreign Relations of the United States, 1955–1957, Foreign Aid and Economic Defense Policy* (Washington, DC: Government Printing Office, 1989), vol. 10: 124–25.

19. Sarah McClendon, *My Eight Presidents* (New York: Simon & Schuster, 1978), 42; Robert Pierpoint, *At the White House: Assignment to Six Presidents* (New York: Putnam, 1981), 123; Pearson, notes from "More Confessions of an S.O.B." [c. 1961], Pearson Papers; James Hagerty Oral History, 57–59, Drew Pearson Oral History, 21, Johnson Library.

20. Robert E. Clark oral history, 4, Dwight D. Eisenhower Library, Abilene, Kansas; Ben H. Bagdikian, *The Effete Conspiracy and Other Crimes by the Press* (New York: Harper & Row, 1972), 133; Jack Bell, *The Splendid Misery: The Story of the Presidency and Power Politics at Close Range* (Garden City, NY: Doubleday, 1960), 312; James C. Hagerty oral history, 23–24, Eisenhower Library; Patrick Anderson, *The President's Men: White House Assistants of Franklin D. Roosevelt, Harry S Truman, Dwight D. Eisenhower, John F. Kennedy and Lyndon B. Johnson* (Garden City, NY: Doubleday, 1968), 180–93.

21. Pearson, unpublished diary, April 1, 1954, Pearson Papers; Abell, ed., *Drew Pearson Diaries*, 407–8; Hannaford, ed., *Washington Merry-Go-Round*, 19.

22. Pearson, unpublished diary, February 23, 1953, August 14, 1969, Pearson Papers; Abell, ed., *Drew Pearson Diaries*, 237; Hannaford, ed., *Washington Merry-Go-Round*, 701–2; Pearson to Barbara Pearson Lange, July 5, 1948, Pearson Family Papers, American University; WMGR, *Washington Post*, November 10, 1952; Athan G. Theoharis and John Stuart Cox, *The Boss: J. Edgar Hoover and the Great American Inquisition* (Philadelphia: Temple University Press, 1988), 274.

23. Abell, ed., *Drew Pearson Diaries*, 48; Ezra Taft Benson, *Cross Fire: The Eight Years with Eisenhower* (Garden City, NY: Doubleday, 1962), 26, 565–66.

24. James C. Hagerty oral history, 8, Johnson Library; Richard M. Nixon, *RN: The Memoirs of Richard Nixon* (New York: Grosset & Dunlap, 1978), 378; Pearson on *The Mike Wallace Interview*, December 7, 1957, C-SPAN; Abell, ed., *Drew Pearson Diaries*, 269; see also William I. Hitchcock, *The Age of Eisenhower: America and the World in the 1950s* (New York: Simon & Schuster, 2018).

25. Abell, ed., *Drew Pearson Diaries*, 278–79.

26. WMGR, *Washington Post*, January 19, 1944, April 23, 1944; "Pearson Opens His Defense in $600,000 Suit," *Washington Post*, May 7, 1953.

27. Anderson with Boyd, *Confessions of a Muckraker*, 277; WMGR, *Washington Post*, May 20, 1953; Douglas A. Anderson, *A "Washington-Merry-Go-Round" of Libel Actions* (Chicago: Nelson-Hall, 1980), 143–48; Pearson to Joseph A. Millimet, June 1, 1967, Pearson Papers.

28. Williams was also Joe McCarthy's attorney. Evan Thomas, *The Man to See: Edward Bennett Williams: Ultimate Insider: Legendary Trial Lawyer* (New York: Simon & Schuster, 1991), 86.

29. Anderson, *A "Washington-Merry-Go-Round" of Libel Actions*, 169–79; Abell, ed., *Drew Pearson Diaries*, 334–35; *Gariepy v. Pearson et al.*, 207 F.2d 15 (D.C. Cir. 1953).

30. Pearson to Tyler Abell, June 20, 1955, Pearson Papers.

31. Abell, ed., *Drew Pearson Diaries*, 332; Philip Warden, "Drew Pearson Back Tax Case Set for Trial," *Chicago Tribune*, August 26, 1954; Warden, "Pearson Paid $7,592 on Back Income Taxes," *Chicago Tribune*, December 6, 1955.

32. Abell, ed., *Drew Pearson Diaries*, 218, 304, 416–17, 463.

33. Abell, ed., *Drew Pearson Diaries*, 361.

34. Abell, ed., *Drew Pearson Diaries*, 469–70.

35. Drew Pearson, "Confessions of an S.O.B.," *Saturday Evening Post* 229 (November 3, 1956): 91.

36. Anderson with Boyd, *Confessions of a Muckraker*, 325; Abell, ed., *Drew Pearson Diaries*, 379.

37. WMGR, October 27, 1956, AU.

38. WMGR, October 31, 1956, November 1, 1956, AU; "It Will Be Denied, But . . . ," *Time* 68 (November 5, 1956): 89; David A. Nichols, *Eisenhower 1956: The President's Year of Crisis: Suez and the Brink of War* (New York: Simon & Schuster, 2011), 192–95; William L. Rivers, *The Opinionmakers* (Westport, CT: Greenwood Press, 1965), 118–19.

39. WMGR, *Washington Post*, January 26, February 12, 1956; Gardner L. Bridge, "Hagerty Calls Pearson Story 'Scurrilous Lie,'" *Washington Post*, January 28, 1956; "Eisenhower Gets Pearson Apology," *New York Times*, February 12, 1956.

40. WMGR, *Washington Post*, January 1, 1956; Abell, ed., *Drew Pearson Diaries*, 366.

41. Laurence Laurent, "'Headline City' Telecast Gives Sketchy Picture," *Washington Post*, April 14, 1958; Hannaford, ed., *Washington Merry-Go-Round*, 585; Abell, ed., *Drew Pearson Diaries*, 318–19.

42. Sidney Blumenthal, "The Ruins of Georgetown," *New Yorker* 72 (October 21 & 28, 1996): 221–24; Abell, ed., *Drew Pearson Diaries*, 235; WMGR, August 22, 1951, AU; WMGR, *Washington Post*, February 22, 1967; see also Gregg Herken, *The Georgetown Set: Friends and Rivals in Cold War Washington* (New York: Alfred A. Knopf, 2014).

43. Herman Klurfeld, *Behind the Lines: The World of Drew Pearson* (Englewood Cliffs, NJ: Prentice-Hall, 1968), 202–3.

44. WMGR, *Washington Post*, June 27, 1954, December 6, 1955.

45. WMGR, *Washington Post*, June 30, 1955; see Adam Wildavsky, *A Study in Power Politics* (New Haven: Yale University Press, 1962).

46. Pearson, notes from "More Confessions of an S.O.B." [c. 1961], Pearson Papers; Johnson, *Managing the White House*, 90–91; Warren Unna, "Eisenhower Orders Dixon-Yates Power Contract Canceled," *Washington Post*, July 12, 1955.

47. Pearson, notes from "More Confessions of an S.O.B." [c. 1961], Pearson Papers; see Richard A. Baker, "A Slap at the 'Hidden-Hand Presidency': The Senate and the Lewis Strauss Affair," *Congress & the Presidency* 14 (Spring 1987): 1–16.

48. WMGR, *Washington Post*, April 12, 1959; Pearson, unpublished diary, June 11, 1954, Pearson Papers; Abell, ed., *Drew Pearson Diaries*, 305.

49. US Senate, Committee on Interstate and Foreign Commerce, *Nomination of Lewis L. Strauss*, 86th Cong, 1st sess. (Washington, DC: US Government Printing Office, 1959), 835–41.

50. Jack Anderson, manuscript for *Peace, War and Politics*, Anderson Papers; Jack Anderson with Daryl Gibson, *Peace, War, and Politics: An Eyewitness Account* (New York: Forge, 1999), 75–76; Timothy Mark Chambless, "Muckraker at Work: Columnist Jack Anderson and the Watergate Scandal, 1972–1974" (PhD diss., University of Utah, 1987), 45; Richard Harwood, "Two from the Old School," *Washington Post*, August 5, 1997; Robert G. Baker oral history, 75, Senate Historical Office; Abell, ed., *Drew Pearson Diaries*, 511, 523.

51. Anderson, *The President's Men*, 134–67.

52. Abell, ed., *Drew Pearson Diaries*, 324; WMGR, *Washington Post*, January 12, 1955.

53. WMGR, *Washington Post*, February 11, 12, 1958; see Bernard Schwartz, *The Professor and the Commissions* (New York: Alfred A. Knopf, 1959).

54. WMGR, *Washington Post*, February 4, 1958; Abell, ed., *Drew Pearson Diaries*, 427–30.

55. Pearson to Subscribing Editors, June 21, 1958, Pearson Papers; WMGR, *Washington Post*, May 13, June 16, 1958.

56. WMGR, *Washington Post*, June 16, 1958.

57. Pearson, "President Said to Have Sent Note of Thanks," *Washington Post*, June 17, 1958; "Hagerty News Conference and Drew Pearson's Statement," *New York Times*, June 18, 1958.

58. "Hagerty News Conference and Drew Pearson's Statement," *New York Times*, June 18, 1958; "Reply Made by Pearson," *Hartford Courant*, June 18, 1958.

59. Warren Unna, "Calls His Aide an 'Invaluable' Public Servant," *Washington Post*, June 19, 1958.

60. William M. Blair, "House Investigator Quits Inquiry; Admits Using Microphone in Hotel to Get New Evidence on Goldfine," *New York Times*, July 8, 1958; Robert C. Albright, "Textile Man Likens Acts to Gestapo," *Washington Post*, July 8, 1958; John Clayton, "Goldfine Room 'Bugging' Told," *Washington Post*, May 1, 1959; Anderson with Boyd, *Confessions of a Muckraker*, 306–7; Anderson with Gibson, *Peace, War, and Politics*, 85; Brit Hume, *The Inside Story* (Garden City, NY: Doubleday & Company, 1974), 32.

61. Mark Feldstein, *Poisoning the Press: Richard Nixon, Jack Anderson, and the Rise of Washington's Scandal Culture* (New York: Farrar, Straus & Giroux, 2010), 57–59; Susan Sheehan, "The Anderson Strategy: We Hit You— Pow! Then You Issue a Denial, and—Bam!—We Really Let You Have It," *New York Times Magazine* (August 13, 1972): 83.

62. Pearson, notes from "More Confessions of an S.O.B." [c. 1961]; Abell, ed., *Drew Pearson's Diaries*, 480; Jack Anderson, *Washington Expose* (Washington, DC: Public Affairs Press, 1967), 2–3; WMGR, *Washington Post*, June 20, 1958, September 17, 1958, February 10, 1960.

63. William Safire, "Abominable No-Man," *New York Times*, November 3, 1986; Michael J. Birkner, "Sherman Adams' Fall, and the Scandal Behind the Scandal," in *Scandal! An Interdisciplinary Approach to the Consequences, Outcomes, and Significance of Political Scandals*, eds. Alison Dagnes and Mark Sachleben (New York: Bloomsbury, 2013), 127–54.

64. "Bernard Goldfine Dies at 76; Went from Riches to Rags," *Washington Post*, September 23, 1967.

65. Pearson to Joseph B. Agnelli, January 24, 1958, Pearson Papers; Sam Lebovic, "The Forgotten 1957 Trial That Explains Our Country's Bizarre Whistleblower Laws," *Politico*, March 27, 2016.

66. Pearson to Agnelli, January 24, 1958, Pearson Papers; "Pentagon Tells Why It Kept Pearson's Data," *Washington Post*, March 12, 1957.

67. Abell, ed., *Drew Pearson Diaries*, 375–76; WMGR, *Washington Post*, March 27, 1957.

68. William Tucker, "Secrets Leak Guilt Pleaded by Nickerson," *Washington Post*, June 26, 1957; WMGR, *Washington Post*, June 27, 1957; Lebovic, "The Forgotten 1957 Trial That Explains Our Country's Bizarre Whistleblower Laws."

69. WMGR, *Washington Post*, June 27, 1957; Drew Pearson and Jack Anderson, *U.S.A.—A Second-Class Power?* (New York: Simon & Schuster, 1958), x; Craig Allen, *Eisenhower and the Mass Media: Peace, Prosperity, and Prime-Time TV* (Chapel Hill: University of North Carolina Press, 1993), 150–89; see also Edgar M. Bottome, *The Missile Gap: A Study of the Formulation*

of Military and Political Policy (Rutherford, NJ: Fairleigh Dickinson University Press, 1971).

70. Hannaford, ed, *Washington Merry-Go-Round*, 12–13.
71. WMGR, May 11, 1960, AU.
72. James Reston, *Sketches in the Sand* (New York: Alfred A. Knopf, 1967), 179–82; Michael R. Beschloss, *Mayday: Eisenhower, Khrushchev and the U-2 Affair* (New York: Harper & Row, 1986), 234; Harrison E. Salisbury, *Without Fear or Favor: The New York Times and Its Times* (New York: Ballantine, 1980), 512–13; Max Frankel, *The Times of My Life and My Life with the Times* (New York: Random House, 1999), 184, 207–8; Richard Reeves, "Why Presidents Lie," *George* 5 (May 2000): 54.
73. Jack Anderson, draft manuscript of *Peace, War and Victory*, Anderson Papers; Pearson, notes from "More Confessions of an S.O.B." [c. 1961], Pearson Papers.

Chapter 9

1. *The Mike Wallace Interview*, Guest, Drew Pearson, December 7, 1957, C-SPAN; WMGR, *Washington Post*, October 27, 1957.
2. Tyler Abell, ed., *Drew Pearson Diaries, 1949–1959* (New York: Holt, Rinehart and Winston, 1974), 407, 420; WMGR, *Washington Post*, February 16, 1958.
3. Donald A. Ritchie, *James M. Landis: Dean of the Regulators* (Cambridge, MA: Harvard University Press, 1980), 171–2; Theodore Sorensen, *Counselor: A Life at the Edge of History* (New York: HarperCollins, 2008), 151; Abell, ed., *Drew Pearson Diaries*, 407; Arthur Krock Memo [c. 1962]), Arthur Krock Papers, Princeton.
4. Pearson, unpublished diary, February 5, 1962, Pearson to Ellen Pearson Arnold, November 29, 1963, Pearson Papers; Kay Halle oral history, 3, John F. Kennedy Presidential Library.
5. Pearson to Ellen Pearson Arnold, November 29, 1963; Pearson, notes for a chapter "The Distrust Deepens" [c. 1969], Pearson Papers; WMGR, September 2, 3, 1937, April 22, 1938, AU.
6. Pearson to Walter Winchell, January 6, 1942, Pearson Papers.
7. WMGR, *Washington Post*, January 13, 1948, April 8, 1960; Abell, ed., *Drew Pearson Diaries*, 230, 248, 395, 421; Donald A. Ritchie, "Kennedy in Congress," in *A Companion to John F. Kennedy*, ed. Marc J. Silverstone (Malden, MA: Wiley Blackwell, 2014), 33–50; Michael Beschloss, ed., *Jacqueline Kennedy: Historic Conversations on Life with John F. Kennedy* (New York: Hyperion, 2011), 74–75; Robert D. McFadden, "John Kennedy 1954 Letter Brings $1,000," *New York Times*, May 26, 1972.
8. WMGR, *Washington Post*, August 26, 1956; Anderson to Robert F. Kennedy, April 26, 1957, Anderson Papers.
9. WMGR, *Washington Post*, October 27, 1957, April 5, 6, 1960.
10. WMGR, *Washington Post*, July 6, 1960.
11. WMGR, *Washington Post*, October 10, 1960.

12. Ritchie, *James M. Landis*, 172; Pearson, unpublished diary, September 30, 1960, Pearson Papers; David E. Koskoff, *Joseph P. Kennedy: A Life and Times* (Englewood Cliffs, NJ: Prentice-Hall, 1974), 433.

13. Pearson, unpublished diary, July 29, 1962, Pearson Papers; Peter Hannaford, ed., *Washington Merry-Go-Round: The Drew Pearson Diaries, 1960–1969* (Lincoln, NE: Potomac Books, 2015), 585; WMGR, *Washington Post*, July 7, 12, 1960, November 7, 1963; Jack Anderson with Daryl Gibson, *Peace, War, and Politics: An Eyewitness Account* (New York: Forge, 1999), 89–90.

14. Pearson to Karl A. Bickel, July 30, 1960, Pearson Papers.

15. Pearson, unpublished diary, August 3, 1960, September 15, 1960, Pearson Papers; WMGR, *Washington Post*, October 17, 1960; Hannaford, ed., *Washington Merry-Go-Round*, 43.

16. "Nixon's Loan Story Called a 'Smear,'" *Washington Post*, October 27, 1960; "Donald Nixon Admits He Got Hughes Loan," *Washington Post*, October 31, 1960; WMGR, *Washington Post*, November 1, 1960; Jack Anderson with James Boyd, *Confessions of a Muckraker: The Inside Story of Life in Washington during the Truman, Eisenhower, Kennedy and Johnson Years* (New York: Random House, 1979), 326–33; Jack Anderson and Michael Binstein, "Nixon's Paradoxical Nature," *Washington Post*, April 28, 1994.

17. "Pearson Denies Bid to Embarrass Nixon," *New York Times*, November 1, 1960; Drew Pearson and Jack Anderson, *U.S.A.—A Second Class Power?* (New York: Simon & Schuster, 1958), 286; Mark Feldstein, *Poisoning the Press: Richard Nixon, Jack Anderson, and the Rise of Washington's Scandal Culture* (New York: Farrar, Straus & Giroux, 2010), 59–69; Larry Tye, *Bobby Kennedy: The Making of a Liberal Icon* (New York: Random House, 2016), 123.

18. Drew Pearson to Merry-Go-Round Editors, February 10, 1964, Pearson, unpublished diary, October 29, 1960, Pearson Papers; Chalmers M. Roberts, *The Washington Post: The First 100 Years* (Boston: Houghton Mifflin, 1977), 341; "Nixon Side Accuses Pearson of 'Smear' in Loan Report," *Atlanta Constitution*, October 27, 1960; Hannaford, ed., *Washington Merry-Go-Round*, 44–45.

19. Hannaford, ed., *Washington Merry-Go-Round*, 46; Feldstein, *Poisoning the Press*, 70–74.

20. Pearson, unpublished diary, July 9, 1960, Pearson Papers; Hannaford, ed. *Washington Merry-Go-Round*, 30–31.

21. Pearson, unpublished diary, September 7, 1960, Pearson Papers; Douglas A. Anderson, *A "Washington Merry-Go-Round" of Libel Actions* (Chicago: Nelson-Hall, 1980), 192.

22. Pearson to Joseph A. Millimet, May 24, 1967, Pearson Papers.

23. Pearson to Joseph A. Millimet, June 1, 1967, Pearson Papers; Joseph A. Millimet to Tyler Abell, May 7, 1971, Abell Papers; Hannaford, ed., *Washington Merry-Go-Round*, 451.

24. *New York Times Co. v. Sullivan*, 376 U.S. 254 (1969); Anthony Lewis, *Make No Law: The Sullivan Case and the First Amendment* (New York: Random House, 1991), 9–14, 22–23, 45, 106, 143, 157.

25. *Monitor Patriot Co. v. Roy*, 401 U.S. 265 (1971).

26. Beschloss, ed., *Jacqueline Kennedy*, 322; Pearson, unpublished diary, April 20, 1964, Pearson Papers; WMGR, *Washington Post*, May 12, 1966.

27. WMGR, *Washington Post*, January 20, 1961; Hannaford, ed., *Washington Merry-Go-Round*, 58; "Remarks of Mr. Pearson," WTTG-TV, January 21, 1961, General CIA Records, www.cia.gov/library.

28. Edwin Guthman oral history interview #1, 34, Kennedy Library; Hannaford, ed., *Washington Merry-Go-Round*, 73, 78; WMGR, *Washington Post*, April 18, 1961.

29. Hannaford, ed., *Washington Merry-Go-Round*, 74; Pearson, notes [c. 1961], Pearson Papers; Paul B. Fay Jr., *The Pleasure of His Company* (New York: Harper & Row, 1966), 195.

30. WMGR, *Washington Post*, February 19, 1961, April 25, 1961; Hannaford, ed., *Washington Merry-Go-Round*, 69, 71.

31. Hannaford, ed., *Washington Merry-Go-Round*, 90; Pearson, unpublished diary, July 13, 1961, Pearson Papers; Ted Widmer, ed., *Listening In: The Secret White House Recordings of John F. Kennedy* (New York: Hyperion, 2012), 88–89.

32. Edwin Guthman oral history interview #1, 33, Kennedy Library.

33. Thomas J. Whalen, *Kennedy versus Lodge: The 1952 Massachusetts Senate Race* (Boston: Northeastern University Press, 2000), 21; Ben Bradlee, *A Good Life: Newspapering and Other Adventures* (New York: Simon & Schuster, 1995), 236; "Leon M. Pearson Dead; Reporter, Play Reviewer," *Washington Post*, April 30, 1963.

34. Jack Anderson, *Confessions of a Muckraker*, 312–13; Hannaford, ed., *Washington Merry-Go-Round*, 81; Sarah McClendon, *My Eight Presidents* (New York: Wyden Books, 1978), 51–52; Robert S. Allen and Paul Scott, "Press Sees 2 Sides of White House," *Los Angeles Times*, November 7, 1963; Chalmers Roberts, *First Rough Draft: A Journalist's Journal of Our Times* (New York: Praeger, 1973), 191.

35. WMGR, *Atlanta Constitution*, January 27, 1963; Hannaford, ed., *Washington Merry-Go-Round*, 191; Krock to Donald M. Ewing, March 7, 1963; David Brinkley to Krock, 1964, Krock Papers.

36. Pierre Salinger, *With Kennedy* (New York: Avon, 1967), 135–36, 296.

37. Hannaford, ed., *Washington Merry-Go-Round*, 170–71.

38. Drew Pearson, notes [c. 1962], Pearson Papers.

39. David Karr to Pearson, September 22, 1955, Pearson Papers.

40. WMGR, *Washington Post*, August 19, 1961; Luvie Moore Pearson, "My Thirty-Six Hours with Khrushchev," *Saturday Evening Post* 235 (April 7, 1962): 70–77; Herman Klurfeld, *Behind the Lines: The World of Drew Pearson* (Englewood Cliffs, NJ: Prentice-Hall, 1968), 221–36.

41. Drew Pearson, "K Asserts He's Ready for Talks on Berlin," *Washington Post*, August 28, 1961; Michael R. Beschloss, *Kennedy v. Khrushchev: The Crisis Years, 1960–1963* (New York: Edward Burlingame, 1991), 110–12, 289–90; Patrick Anderson, "The Truth about Drew Pearson," *Washingtonian* 3 (June 1968): 39; Anderson with Boyd, *Confessions of a Muckraker*, 137; Jack Anderson draft of article, "The Crimes of Khrushchev," for *Parade* [c. 1959], Anderson memo to Don Ludlow [c. 1962], Jack Anderson Papers.

42. WMGR, *Washington Post*, August 29, September 1, 2, 1961.

43. WMGR, *Washington Post*, September 1, 1961.

44. Hannaford, ed., *Washington Merry-Go-Round*, 96–99; Beschloss, *Kennedy v. Khrushchev*, 292–93; Robert Dallek, *An Unfinished Life: John F. Kennedy, 1917–1963* (Boston: Little, Brown and Company, 2003), 428.

45. Hannaford, ed., *Washington Merry-Go-Round*, 103.

46. Pierre Salinger, oral history interview #2, 178–81, Kennedy Library.

47. "Talk on Khrushchev," *Chicago Tribune*, October 29, 1961; Allison D. Boutros letter, September 6, 1961, Kendal Paul letter, September 11, 1961, Marilyn F. Humma letter, September 15, 1961, *Washington Post*; C. L. Sulzberger, "Foreign Affairs," *New York Times*, September 13, 1961; Joseph Alsop, "Matter of Fact," *Washington Post*, September 6, 1961.

48. Pearson to Washington Merry-Go-Round Editors, September 15, 1963, Pearson Papers.

49. Francis N. Connolly to Pearson, February 15, 1962, Pearson to Connolly, February 20, 1962, Pearson Papers.

50. "Goodbye Drew Pearson," *Wilmington Daily Press-Journal*, November 13, 1961; Pearson, unpublished diary, November 28, 1961, Pearson Papers.

51. *Long Beach, California, Press-Telegram*, August 8, 1962; *Wilmington Press-Journal*, December 21, 1961, clippings in Pearson Papers.

52. Two of Pearson's detractors devoted a chapter to what they called his "defending communist interests." See Frank Kluckhohn and Jay Franklin, *The Drew Pearson Story* (Chicago: Chas. Hallberg & Company, 1967), 121–38. Hannaford, ed., *Washington Merry-Go-Round*, 109; Drew Pearson, notes [c. 1962], Pearson Papers.

53. WMGR, *Washington Post*, October 17, 1961.

54. Hannaford, ed., *Washington Merry-Go-Round*, 143, 146; Immediate Release—Pearson Special—Attention Papers Interested in Pan American Problems, WMGR, September 6, September 7, 1962, AU.

55. Hannaford, ed., *Washington Merry-Go-Round*, 147–48; WMGR, October 26, 1962, AU.

56. J. Edgar Hoover to Joseph B. Agnelli, February 6, 1961, Louis B. Nichols to Pearson, January 15, 1957, Pearson to Charles E. Dierker, July 31, 1957, Pearson to J. Edgar Hoover, August 15, 1966, Pearson handwritten notes, Pearson Papers; WMGR, *Washington Post*, February 4, 1961; Natalie Robins, *Alien Ink: The FBI's War on Freedom of Expression* (New York: William Morrow and Company, 1992), 144, 149.

57. Horace Hall to Pearson, September 26, 1942, Pearson to Horace Hall, October 1, 1942, Pearson Papers; Drew Pearson, "How I Became Interested in Racial Justice," *Opportunity* 26 (April 1948): 62.

58. Paul Pearson, "My Family Letter," May 8, 1931, Paul Pearson to George Foster Peabody, April 18, 1933, Paul Pearson Papers; Paul Pearson to Drew Pearson, October 24, 1933, Pearson Papers; Hanson W. Baldwin, "Majority Opposes Pearson's Regime," *New York Times*, April 19, 1935.

59. Pearson to Leon Pearson, October 15, 1962, Pearson Papers; WMGR, *Washington Post*, May 8, 1946, July 20, 1946; Charles Delgadillo, *Crusader for Democracy: The Political Life of William Allen White* (Lawrence: University Press of Kansas, 2018), 168–76.

60. William Grimes, "Stetson Kennedy, Who Infiltrated and Exposed the Klan, Dies at 94," *New York Times*, August 30, 2011; Stetson Kennedy interview, *Talk of the Nation*, National Public Radio, May 23, 2005.

61. WMGR, *Washington Post*, June 3, 1946.

62. Pearson, unpublished diary, September 29, 1966, Pearson Papers; Drew Pearson, "Confessions of an S.O.B.: How to Make Enemies," *Saturday Evening Post* 229 (November 24, 1956): 37; WMGR, *Washington Post*, July 19, 20, 1946; Harold Paulk Henderson, *The Politics of Change in Georgia: A Political Biography of Ellis Arnall* (Athens: University of Georgia Press, 1991), 146; John Egerton, *Speak Now against the Day: The Generation before the Civil Rights Movement in the South* (New York: Alfred A. Knopf, 1994), 383–86.

63. WMGR, *Washington Post*, August 1, 1946; Jack Anderson, "Night in Alabama with Ku Klux Klan," *Washington Post*, August 26, 1979.

64. FBI wiretaps of Harry Dexter White's phones picked up the conversation between Karr and Pearson; D. M. Ladd memo to J. Edgar Hoover, December 31, 1946, FBI files, 94-HQ-8-350, Serials 283–374, RG65, NARA; WMGR, *Washington Post*, January 21, 1947, March 16, 1948, May 18, 1948, November 7, 1948.

65. Pearson to Tyler Abell, January 19, 1955, Pearson, unpublished diary, November 13, 1968, Pearson Papers; WMGR, *Washington Post*, February 1, 1955; Gil Klein, *Reliable Source: 100 Years at the National Press Club* (Nashville, TN: Turner, 2008), 62–68; Pearson, "Confessions of an S.O.B.: How to Make Enemies," 37.

66. WMGR, *Washington Post*, April 27, 1955.

67. "Reporter, Race Leaders Intimidated Says Pearson," *Chicago Defender*, March 26, 1955.

68. "Columnist Disputed," *New York Times*, April 29, 1955; "Hagerty Denies Probing Payne," *Chicago Defender*, May 7, 1955; Ethan Michaeli, *The Defender: How the Legendary Black Newspaper Changed America, from the Age of Pullman Porters to the Age of Obama* (Boston: Houghton Mifflin Harcourt, 2016), 314–18.

69. Drew Pearson, notes [c. 1962], Pearson Papers; WMGR, *Washington Post*, October 13, November 5, 1958, September 29, 1960.

70. WMGR, *Washington Post*, April 29, 30, 1961; Steven Levingston, *Kennedy and King: The President, the Pastor, and the Battle over Civil Rights* (New York: Hachette Books, 2017), 340–41; Taylor Branch, *Parting the Waters: America in the King Years, 1954–63* (New York: Simon & Schuster, 1988), 747–51.

71. WMGR, *Washington Post*, June 9, 1963.

72. WMGR, *Washington Post*, October 29, 1963.

73. WMGR, *Washington Post*, November 12, 1964; *Meridian Star*, November 12, 1964.

74. Pearson to Ellen Pearson Arnold, November 29, 1963, Pearson Papers; Hannaford, ed., *Washington Merry-Go-Round*, 208, 585.

75. Cartha D. DeLoach to Pearson, December 17, 1963, Pearson to DeLoach, December 23, 1963, Pearson to Abbott Washington, December 16, 1963, Pearson Papers; Natalie Robins, *Alien Ink: The FBI's War on Freedom of Expression* (New York: William Morrow and Company, 1992), 144–46.

76. Richard Helms memo to J. Lee Rankin, May 27, 1964, Assassinations Records Review Board, RG 233, NARA; Memorandum of Conversation between the President's Special Assistant for National Security Affairs (Bundy) and the Soviet Ambassador (Dobrynin), July 11, 1964, *Foreign Relations of the United States, 1964–1968, Soviet Union* (Washington, DC: US Government Printing Office, 2001), vol. 14: 97–98.

77. Lewis H. Lapham, "The King's Pleasure," *Harper's* 252 (March 1976): 12–18; Herbert J. Gans, *Deciding What's News: A Study of CBS Evening News, NBC Nightly News, Newsweek, and Time* (New York: Vintage Books, 1980), 245.

Chapter 10

1. Peter Hannaford, ed., *Washington Merry-Go-Round: The Drew Pearson Diaries, 1960–1969* (Lincoln, NE: Potomac Books, 2015), 208–9; William L. Rivers, *The Opinionmakers* (Westport, CT: Greenwood Press, 1965), 168.

2. Pearson notes, Pearson Papers; Lady Bird Johnson, *A White House Diary* (New York: Holt, Rinehart and Winston, 1970), 13–14; Drew Pearson oral history, 13, Johnson Library.

3. Pearson to Bess Abell, September 6, 1966, Pearson Papers.

4. Michael L. Gillette, *Lady Bird Johnson: An Oral History* (New York: Oxford University Press, 2012), 247; Johnson, *A White House Diary*, 354.

5. Pearson oral history, 10, Johnson Library; Herman Klurfeld, *Behind the Lines: The World of Drew Pearson* (Englewood Cliffs, NJ: Prentice-Hall, 1968), 248.

6. Charles Roberts oral history, 39–45, Johnson Library.

7. Chalmers Roberts oral history, 19–20, 32, Johnson Library.

8. WMGR, June 11, 1937, November 16, 1940, AU; WMGR, *Washington Post*, June 20, 1965; Robert A. Caro, *The Years of Lyndon Johnson: The Path to Power* (New York: Alfred A. Knopf, 1982), 606–26.

9. Robert A. Caro, *The Years of Lyndon Johnson: Means of Ascent* (New York: Alfred A. Knopf, 1990), 72, 270–75; Hannaford, ed., *Washington Merry-Go-Round*, 285; Drew Pearson oral history, 3, Johnson Library; WMGR, August 6, 1942, AU; WMGR, *Washington Post*, August 9, 1948.

10. Robert A. Caro, *The Years of Lyndon Johnson: Master of the Senate* (New York: Alfred A. Knopf, 2002), 481, 486; WMGR, *Washington Post*, November 10, 1960.

11. Pearson oral history, 5; WMGR, *Washington Post*, November 20, 1952, January 2, 1955, April 10, 1962.

12. Pearson oral history, 4; Klurfeld, *Behind the Lines*, 243–46; Tyler Abell, ed., *Drew Pearson Diaries, 1949–1959* (New York: Holt, Rinehart and Winston, 1974), 291; WMGR, *Washington Post*, December 1, 1963.

13. WMGR, *Washington Post*, January 10, 1961.

14. Pearson oral history, 6; WMGR, *Washington Post*, June 28, 1955, February 9, 1956; Pearson to William T. Evjue, February 17, 1956, Pearson Papers.

15. WMGR, *Washington Post*, March 27, 1956.

16. WMGR, March 27, 28, 1956, AU; Pearson, unpublished diary, December 27, 1963, March 31, 1965, August 24, 1968, Pearson Papers; Abell, ed, *Drew Pearson Diaries*, 358.

17. Jack Anderson memo to Pearson, May 1957, Pearson Papers; WMGR, *Washington Post*, August 24, 1958.

18. Pearson oral history, 7; Pearson to Fred Hartman, December 30, 1966, Anderson Papers.

19. Hannaford, ed., *Washington Merry-Go-Round*, 3; Pearson to Lyndon Johnson, February 1, 1960, Pearson Papers; WMGR, *Washington Post*, February 5, 1960, July 7, 1960, December 1, 1963.

20. Hannaford, ed., *Washington Merry-Go-Round*, 32; WMGR, *Washington Post*, July 15, 1960.

21. Hannaford, ed., *Washington Merry-Go-Round*, 34–35, 48; WMGR, *Washington Post*, October 7, 1960.

22. WMGR, *Washington Post*, July 27, 1961, December 1, 1963.

23. Hannaford, ed., *Washington Merry-Go-Round*, 135; WMGR, *Washington Post*, May 19, June 2, 1962; Randall B. Woods, *LBJ: Architect of American Ambition* (New York: Free Press, 2006), 412.

24. Bobby Baker with Larry L. King, *Wheeling and Dealing: Confessions of a Capitol Hill Operator* (New York: W. W. Norton, 1978), 82–83; Robert A. Caro, *The Years of Lyndon Johnson: The Passage of Power* (New York: Alfred A. Knopf, 2012), 282–87.

25. "Robert G. Baker Oral History Interviews," 51, Senate Historical Office; WMGR, *Washington Post*, November 15, 1963, December 26, 1963; Pearson, unpublished diary, November 22, 1963, Pearson Papers.

26. WMGR, *Washington Post*, December 1, 1963; Baker with King, *Wheeling and Dealing*, 154–71.

27. WMGR, *Washington Post*, February 5, 1964.

28. Pearson, unpublished diary, February 8, 1964, Pearson Papers; "Washington Wire," *Wall Street Journal*, February 7, 1964; Arthur Krock, "In the Nation," *New York Times*, February 7, 1964; Cabell Phillips, "White House Aides Seek to Impugn Baker Witness," *New York Times*, February 8, 1964; Douglas Kiker, "Johnson Honeymoon with Press Ending?" *Boston Globe*, February 9, 1964; Eric F. Goldman, *The Tragedy of Lyndon Johnson* (New York: Alfred A. Knopf, 1969), 82–83; Robert David Johnson, *All the Way with LBJ: The Presidential Election of 1964* (New York: Cambridge University Press, 2009), 52–53.

29. Pearson to Merry-Go-Round Editors, February 10, 1964, Pearson Papers; WMGR, *Washington Post*, July 5, 1953, February 12, 1964; Confidential Note to Editors, February 6, 1964, WMGR, February 7, 1964, AU; Hannaford, ed., *Washington Merry-Go-Round*, 231–32; Michael Beschloss, ed., *Taking Charge: The Johnson White House Tapes, 1963–1964* (New York: Simon & Schuster. 1997), 166–67, 232–33.

30. WMGR, *Washington Post*, November 27, 1963; Beschloss, ed., *Taking Charge*, 342; Hannaford, ed., *Washington Merry-Go-Round*, 228–29.

31. Pearson to Jack Anderson and Tom McNamara, December 8, 1963, Pearson Papers.

32. Pearson, unpublished diary, December 22, 23, 27, 1963, Pearson Papers.

33. Pearson, unpublished diary, January 28, 1964.

34. Pearson oral history, 17–18; Hannaford, ed., *Washington Merry-Go-Round*, 227, 237, 254–55; WMGR, *Washington Post*, February 18, 1964, May 6, 1965.

35. Goldman, *The Tragedy of Lyndon Johnson*, 191–92; Michael Beschloss, ed., *Reaching for Glory: Lyndon Johnson's Secret White House Tapes, 1964–1965* (New York: Simon & Schuster, 2001), 34; Jack Anderson, "Miller Offer Reported," *Washington Post*, September 13, 1964; Warren Weaver Jr., "Ex-Representative Says Miller Offered Him a Job," *New York Times,* September 15, 1964; Michael Posner, "Smith Gives His Version of Job Talk with Miller," *Washington Post*, September 15, 1964.

36. Beschloss, ed., *Reaching for Glory*, 95; Pearson, unpublished *diary*, October 17, 1964, Pearson Papers; Hannaford, ed., *Washington Merry-Go-Round*, 257, 266–67.

37. WMGR, *Gadsden Times*, October 19, 1964; Pearson, unpublished diary, October 16, 21, 1964, Pearson Papers; Hannaford, ed., *Washington-Merry-Go-Round*, 262.

38. Hannaford, ed., *Washington Merry-Go-Round*, 270; WMGR, *Washington Post*, September 26, 1964, November 1, 11, 1964.

39. WMGR, *Washington Post*, December 4, 1964.

40. Pearson, unpublished diary, March 18, 1965, Pearson Papers; Hannaford, ed., *Washington Merry-Go-Round*, 291, 297; WMGR, *Washington Post*,

December 3, 1964, February 27, 1965, March 6, 1965, March 8, 1965; WMGR, December 4, 1964, AU.

41. Conversation with Drew Pearson and office secretary, March 23, 1965, Secret White House Tapes, Lyndon B. Johnson Presidency, Miller Center, University of Virginia; Beschloss, ed., *Reaching for Glory*, 238–39; Hannaford, ed., *Washington Merry-Go-Round*, 297–98.

42. Pearson, unpublished diary, April 5, 1965, Pearson Papers; Hannaford, ed., *Washington Merry-Go-Round*, 307.

43. For the running debate between Alsop and Lippmann, see Donald A. Ritchie, *Reporting from Washington: The History of the Washington Press Corps* (New York: Oxford University Press, 2005), 148–58.

44. Jack Anderson with Daryl Gibson, *Peace, War, and Politics: An Eyewitness Account* (New York: Forge, 1999), 126; Jack Anderson interview with Tim Chambless, March 15, 1986, 33–34, Jack Anderson Papers; Hannaford, ed., *Washington Merry-Go-Round*, 624.

45. Pearson, unpublished diary, April 15, 1965, Pearson Papers; Hannaford, ed., *Washington Merry-Go-Round*, 325, 327; WMGR, *Washington Post*, April 12, 1965.

46. WMGR, *Washington Post*, May 3, 1965, May 7, 1965; Hannaford, ed., *Washington Merry-Go-Round*, 315; "Newsnight," WTOP-TV, May 9, 1965, General CIA Records, www.cia.gov/library.

47. Hannaford, ed., *Washington Merry-Go-Round*, 344–45.

48. Pearson, unpublished diary, May 26, 1965, July 18, 1965, Pearson to his grandchildren, December 25, 1965, Pearson Papers; Scottie Lanahan, "News to Me . . . March to Beat of Different Drums," *Washington Post*, April 17, 1967.

49. Katherine [Raley] Watkins oral history, Abell Papers.

50. Pearson, unpublished diary, June 1, 1966, Pearson Papers; Hannaford, ed., *Washington Merry-Go-Round*, 385.

51. Pearson to Evan Kemp, October 3, 1966, Pearson Papers.

52. David Karr to Pearson, November 9, 1967, Pearson Papers; Hannaford, ed., *Washington Merry-Go-Round*, 420.

53. Pearson, unpublished diary, November 20, 1967, April 1, 1969, Pearson Papers; Hannaford, ed., *Washington Merry-Go-Round*, 503.

54. Hannaford, ed., *Washington Merry-Go-Round*, 520; WMGR, *Washington Post*, November 13, 1967.

55. Patrick Anderson, "The Truth about Drew Pearson," *Washingtonian* 3 (June 1968): 40; Pearson memorandum for Herman Klurfeld, February 21, 1968, Pearson Papers; Klurfeld, *Behind the Lines*, 247.

56. Pearson to Lyndon B. Johnson, May 11, 1967, Pearson Papers; *David Susskind Show* Transcript, February 25, 1967, J. Edgar Hoover memo to Ramsey Clark, March 7, 1967, Jack Anderson FBI files, National Security Archives.

57. Pearson to Lyndon B. Johnson, March 11, 1968, Johnson to Pearson, March 13, 1968, Hannaford, ed., *Washington Merry-Go-Round*, 547–50.

58. Pearson oral history, 19.

59. Pearson, unpublished diary, January 18, 1963, Pearson Papers; David E. Koskoff, *The Senator from Central Casting: The Rise, Fall, and Resurrection of Thomas J. Dodd* (New Haven: New American Political Press, 2011), 89; "Francis R. Valeo, Secretary of the Senate, 1966–1977," 289–90, Oral History Interviews, Senate Historical Office; Jean M. White, "At 70, Pearson Hopes He's Still S.O.B.," *Washington Post*, December 17, 1967; WMGR, *Washington Post*, May 4, 1967.

60. Julius Klein believed that his closeness to Senator Joseph McCarthy and Roy Cohn "aroused some antagonisms in certain circles" and made him a "target of the radical left-wing groups." Julius Klein to J. Edgar Hoover, October 22, 1965, Gerald J. Zeiller memo to files, April 1, 1965, Anderson Papers; WMGR, *Washington Post*, January 26, 1966; Jack Anderson, *Washington Expose* (Washington: Public Affairs Press, 1967), 35–36; James Boyd, *Above the Law* (New York: New American Library, 1968), 111; Cartha DeLoach memo to A. Rosen, March 10, 1966, Jack Anderson FBI Files, National Security Archive.

61. Klurfeld, *Behind the Lines*, 255; Hannaford, ed., *Washington Merry-Go-Round*, 370; Pearson, unpublished diary, March 10, 1966, Pearson Papers.

62. Jack Zaiman, "Columnists Still Snipe at Dodd," *Hartford Courant*, March 9, 1966; Hannaford, ed., *Washington Merry-Go-Round*, 380; Anderson, *Washington Expose*, 32, 39.

63. Anderson, *Washington Expose*, 27–30.

64. Hannaford, ed., *Washington Merry-Go-Round*, 380–81; "Justice Dept. Denies Pearson Probe," *Washington Post*, April 2, 1966.

65. Richard Harwood, "Dodd's Image in Connecticut Unstained by Charges," *Washington Post*, April 3, 1966; "Congress: A Matter of Ethics," *Newsweek* 67 (April 11, 1966): 29; Jack Zaiman, "Pearson Continues His Attack on Dodd," *Washington Post*, March 15, 1966; Pearson, unpublished diary, April 3, 4, 1966, Pearson Papers.

66. James Boyd stayed connected with them, providing help for Pearson and Anderson's next book, *The Case against Congress*, and co-authoring Anderson's *Confessions of a Muckraker*. Boyd, *Above the Law*, 167, 170–73; Leonard Downie Jr., *The New Muckrakers* (Washington, DC: New Republic Book Company, 1976), 142; Hannaford, ed, *Washington Merry-Go-Round*, 411.

67. Hannaford, ed., *Washington Merry-Go-Round*, 394.

68. Jack Zaiman, "Dodd Censure Advocated," *Hartford Courant*, March 11, 1966; "Columnist to Continue Dodd Attack," *Hartford Courant*, April 28, 1967; Ben Franklin, "Senator Dodd's Ride on the 'Merry-Go-Round,'" *New York Times*, May 15, 1966; Koskoff, *The Senator from Central Casting*, 170–75, 199, 204.

69. Curt Heseltine, "Drew Pearson at the Brink of 70: Meet the Man Behind the Column," [c. December 1968], advertisement for Bell-McClure Syndicate, Anderson Papers; WMGR, *Washington Post*, May 12, 1966;

David A. Jewel, "Pearson Libel Counts Withdrawn by Dodd," *Washington Post*, December 13, 1967; Robert Waters, "Judge Decides in Dodd's Favor," *Hartford Courant*, January 17, 1968; "Drew Pearson to Ignore Ruling," *Hartford Courant*, January 19, 1968; "Appeals Court Rejects Last Dodd Complaint," *Washington Post*, February 25, 1969; Pearson, unpublished diary, May 21, 1969, Pearson Papers; Douglas A. Anderson, *A "Washington Merry-Go-Round" of Libel Actions* (Chicago: Nelson-Hall, 1980), 194–96; *Dodd v. Pearson*, 279 F. Supp. 101 (D.D.C. 1968).

70. WMGR, *Washington Post*, June 13, 1968; Robert Waters, "Sen. Dodd Strikes Back at Columnist," *Hartford Courant*, June 15, 1968; Pearson, unpublished diary, June 15, 1968, Pearson Papers.

71. "It Doesn't Take Much to Be Drew Pearson: Just Guts," *Editor & Publisher* (May 7, 1966); Robert Waters, "Anderson Gets Credit on Dodd," *Hartford Courant*, September 7, 1969; Neil A. Grauer, *Wits & Sages* (Baltimore: Johns Hopkins University Press, 1984), 19; Hannaford, ed, *Washington Merry-Go-Round*, 485; Pearson to Ben Bradlee, November 18, 1968, Pearson, unpublished diary, June 11, 1966, Pearson Papers; William F. Buckley Jr., *Cancel Your Own Goddam Subscription: Notes and Asides from National Review* (New York: Basic Books, 2007), 6–9.

72. Robert Yoakum, "The Dodd Case: Those Who Blinked," *Columbia Journalism Review* 6 (Spring 1967): 13–19; Yoakum, "Further Notes on Dodd," *Columbia Journalism Review* 6 (Summer 1967): 51–54.

73. Robert Waters, "Polls on Dodd Chances Puzzling," *Hartford Courant*, May 25, 1969; Joseph I. Lieberman, *The Legacy: Connecticut Politics, 1930–1980* (Hartford, CT: Spoonwood Press, 1981), 168–76; "Editor Tells of Pulitzer Controversy," *Washington Post*, May 9, 1967; Robert C. Jensen, "Heart Attack Ends Long Career of a Gadfly of Government," *Washington Post*, September 2, 1969; Anderson with Gibson, *Peace, War, and Politics*, 130; Maurice Carroll, "Jury Never Saw Pulitzer Winner," *New York Times*, May 9, 1967.

74. Hannaford, ed. *Washington Merry-Go-Round*, 558–59; Pearson, unpublished diary, March 31, 1968, Pearson Papers.

75. Hannaford, ed., *Washington Merry-Go-Round*, 583.

76. WMGR, *Washington Post*, February 14, 1961; Hannaford, ed., *Washington Merry-Go-Round*, 101, 551–52; Frank Mankiewicz oral history #9, 64, Robert Kennedy oral history project, Kennedy Library.

77. WMGR, March 3, 1967, AU; WMGR, *Washington Post*, March 7, 1967; Editorial Note, *Foreign Relations of the United States, 1964–1968, Dominican Republic; Cuba; Haiti; Guyana* (Washington, DC: Government Printing Office, 2005), vol. 32: 315; Jack Anderson, "Plot Disclosure Made CIA Squirm," *Washington Post*, May 2, 1979; Frank Mankiewicz oral history #5, 68–69, Kennedy Library.

78. WMGR, *Washington Post*, January 12, 1968, May 3, 1968, May 6, 1968; Gerry Robichaud to Jack Anderson, May 3, 1968, Anderson Papers; Roy Cohn oral history, 3, Kennedy Library.

79. Hannaford, ed., *Washington Merry-Go-Round*, 562, 578; C. D. DeLoach to Pearson, May 13, 1968, Pearson Papers; WMGR, *Washington Post*, April 9, 1968.

80. WMGR, *Washington Post*, March 24, 1968.

81. WMGR, *Washington Post*, March 24, 1968; Jack Anderson, "Senators Probe King Wiretapping," *Washington Post*, September 3, 1975; Mark Feldstein, *Poisoning the Press: Richard Nixon, Jack Anderson, and the Rise of Washington's Scandal Culture* (New York: Farrar, Straus & Giroux, 2010), 92.

82. Hannaford, ed., *Washington Merry-Go-Round*, 579–81.

83. Frank Mankiewicz oral history interview #9, 90, Kennedy Library; Jules Witcover, *85 Days: The Last Campaign of Robert Kennedy* (New York: William Morrow, 1988 [1969]), 176–77; WMGR, *Washington Post*, June 4, 1968; Hannaford, ed., *Washington Merry-Go-Round*, 582.

84. WMGR, *Washington Post*, June 6, 1969.

85. Hannaford, ed., *Washington Merry-Go-Round*, 584–88; WMGR, *Washington Post*, June 8, 1968; Pearson, unpublished diary, June 12, 1968.

86. WMGR, *Washington Post*, June 23, 1968, August 25, 26, 1968, September 2, 1968; Kyle Longley, *LBJ's 1968: Power, Politics, and the Presidency in America's Year of Upheaval* (New York: Cambridge University Press, 2018), 205–31.

87. WMGR, *Washington Post*, October 4, 1968, November 2, 1968.

88. Hannaford, ed., *Washington Merry-Go-Round*, 628–29; WMGR, *Washington Post*, November 23, 1968; Feldstein, *Poisoning the Press*, 95–101; Jack Anderson with James Boyd, *Confessions of a Muckraker: The Inside Story of Life in Washington during the Truman, Eisenhower, Kennedy and Johnson Years* (New York: Random House, 1979), 389.

89. Hannaford, ed., *Washington Merry-Go-Round*, 633–34; WMGR, *Washington Post*, November 20, 23, 1968; William M. Blair, "Psychiatric Aid to Nixon Denied," *New York Times*, November 14, 1968; "Vaporous Rumor," *Washington Post*, November 15, 1968; Anthony Summers with Robbyn Swan, *The Arrogance of Power: The Secret World of Richard Nixon* (New York: Viking, 2000), 318–20.

90. Hannaford, ed. *Washington Merry-Go-Round*, 639, 662.

Chapter 11

1. Bruce Oudes, ed., *From: The President: Richard Nixon's Secret Files* (New York: Harper & Row, 1989), 2–3. As his lawyer, William Rogers won a libel suit for Pearson brought by the attorney general of California, Frederick Napoleon Howser, in 1948, after the "Merry-Go-Round" accused him of taking a bribe from a bookie in Long Beach. A jury found that Pearson had told the truth and acted without malice.

2. Oudes, ed., *From: The President*, 30, 40; John A. Farrell, *Richard Nixon: The Life* (New York: Doubleday, 2017), 397.

3. Pearson to David Karr, January 28, 1969, Pearson Papers; Mark
    Feldstein, *Poisoning the Press: Richard Nixon, Jack Anderson, and the Rise
    of Washington's Scandal Culture* (New York: Farrar, Straus & Giroux,
    2010), 111.

4. WMGR, *Washington Post,* January 25, 1969.

5. Hannaford, ed., *Washington Merry-Go-Round,* 226, 490.

6. Jack Anderson with Daryl Gibson, *Peace, War, and Politics: An Eyewitness
    Account* (New York: Forge, 1999), 78; Timothy Mark Chambless,
    "Muckraker at Work: Columnist Jack Anderson and the Watergate
    Scandal, 1972–1974" (PhD diss., University of Utah, 1987), 42.

7. Pearson to Leon Pearson, October 15, 1962, Pearson Papers; "Smear
    Pushers Uncovered," *Liberty Letter* 99 (May 1969), Anderson Papers.

8. Pearson, unpublished diary, August 28, 1964, October 13, 1964, February
    11, 1965, "Drew Pearson—Biography," prospectus for a biography, Pearson
    Papers.

9. Drew Pearson to Joe and Georgie Arnold, August 1, 1966, Pearson Papers.

10. Hannaford, ed., *Washington Merry-Go-Round,* 315; Pearson, unpublished
    diary, May 26, 1965, May 20, 1966, February 26, 1969, Pearson Papers;
    "Drew's Heir," *Washington Observer Newsletter* 40 (June 15, 1967): 2,
    Anderson Papers.

11. Pearson, unpublished diary, January 25, 1965, February 3, 4, 1965, March
    5, 1965, Pearson Papers; Herman Klurfeld, *Behind the Lines: The World of
    Drew Pearson* (Englewood Cliffs, NJ: Prentice Hall, 1968), 233–34.

12. Pearson, unpublished diary, August 19, 1966, April 12, 1967, May 5, 1967,
    July 18, 1969, Pearson Papers.

13. Tyler Abell oral history #2, 13–14; Hannaford, ed., *Washington Merry-Go-
    Round,* 421; Stephen Green, "FCC Revokes WOOK License," *Washington
    Post,* September 13, 1975; Christopher Dickey, "WYCB: They're on the Air
    after 12 Years of Making Waves," *Washington Post,* August 15, 1978; "Drew
    Pearson on Elvis," The Pop History Dig, YouTube.

14. Tyler Abell oral history, interview #3: 5–6, 9, Abell Papers; Pearson notes on
    income breakdown [c. 1967], Pearson Papers.

15. William A. Roberts to Drew Pearson, December 28, 1950, Anderson
    Papers; Pearson to Ellen Arnold, April 19, 1963, Pearson Papers; Tyler Abell
    oral history, interview #4, 2–3, interview #5, 4, Katherine [Raley] Watkins
    oral history, Abell Papers.

16. Pearson to Joseph A. Millimet, May 24, 1967, Pearson Papers.

17. Pearson, unpublished diary, August 15, 1967, Pearson Papers; Ben Steelman,
    "Civil Rights Work Recounted in New Book; Later Battles Set Legal
    Precedents," *Wilmington,* North Carolina, *Star-News,* December 4, 2010.

18. Margaret Herring, "A Simple Question," in *Hands on the Freedom
    Plow: Personal Accounts by Women in SNCC,* eds. Faith S. Holsaert et al.
    (Urbana: University of Illinois Press, 2010), 399–402.

19. Margaret Herring McSurely, "Turning the Tables on Government Raiders,"
    in *It Did Happen Here: Recollections of Political Repression in America,* eds.

Budd Schultz and Ruth Schultz (Berkeley: University of California Press, 1989), 365–76; Steelman, "Civil Rights Work Recounted in New Book"; Catherine Fosl, *Subversive Southern: Anne Braden and the Struggle for Racial Justice in the Cold War South* (New York: Palgrave Macmillan, 2002), 306–9, 389.

20. WMGR, *Washington Post*, June 19, 1968, February 8, 1969; Hannaford, ed., *Washington Merry-Go-Round*, 687; "Ruth Young Watt, Chief Clerk, Permanent Subcommittee on Investigations, 1948–1979," oral history, 230–34, Senate Historical Office; "Activist Charges Legal Harassment," *New York Times*, November 25, 1982; US Court of Appeals for the District of Columbia Circuit, *Alan McSurely and Margaret McSurely v. John K. McClellan, et al., Thomas Ratliff, Individually and as Sometime Commonwealth Attorney for Pike County Kentucky*, 753 F.2d 88 (1985).

21. "Columnist Testifies Pearson Feared Blackmail," *New York Times*, December 7, 1982; Philip Smith, "Privacy Award Partly Upheld on Appeal," *Washington Post*, January 22, 1985; US Court of Appeals for the District of Columbia Circuit, *Alan McSurely and Margaret McSurely v. John J. McClellan et al.*, 521 F.2d 1024 (D.C. Cir. 1975); US Supreme Court, *McAdams v. McSurely*, 438 U.S. 189 (1978), 438 U.S. 189; Ruth Young Watt oral history, 230–34; Herring, "A Simple Question," 399–400.

22. Pearson, unpublished diary, May 16, 1966, Pearson Papers; Geoffrey Kabaservice, *Rule and Ruin: The Downfall of Moderation and the Destruction of the Republican Party, from Eisenhower to the Tea Party* (New York: Oxford University Press, 2012), 169–72.

23. Lawrence E. Davies, "Reagan Nominated in California; Brown Beats Yorty in Tight Race," *New York Times*, June 8, 1966; Seymour Korman, "Reagan Denies Aids [*sic*] Were Homosexuals," *Chicago Tribune*, November 1, 1967; WMGR, *Washington Post*, November 4, 1967; WMGR, special report for weekly papers, November 6, 1967, AU; Pearson, unpublished diary, October 12, October 31, 1967, November 1, 1967, Pearson Papers; Hannaford, ed., *Washington Merry-Go-Round*, 506–7, 509, 516.

24. Feldstein, *Poisoning the Press*, 109–10; Douglas M. Charles, *Hoover's War on Gays: Exposing the FBI's "Sex Deviates" Program* (Lawrence: University Press of Kansas, 2015), 294–95.

25. Pearson to J. Edgar Hoover, August 15, 1966, Pearson Papers; Natalie Robins, *Alien Ink: The FBI's War on Freedom of Expression* (New York: William Morrow and Company, 1992), 147.

26. Feldstein, *Poisoning the Press*, 109–101; H. R. Haldeman, *The Haldeman Diaries: Inside the Nixon White House* (New York: G. P. Putnam's Sons, 1994), 66; Anthony Summers, *Official and Confidential: The Secret Life of J. Edgar Hoover* (New York: G. P. Putnam's Sons, 1993), 375–76.

27. Pearson unpublished diary, December 25, 27, 28, 1967, February 14, 1968, Pearson Papers.

28. In addition to his fights with Dodd and Clark, the columnist had cited Corso as a "bush league" Joe McCarthy and helped defeat Representative

Pillion by mocking his conspiracy theories; Pearson, unpublished diary, December 18, 1967, April 10, 1969, "Drew Pearson—Biography," prospectus, Pearson Papers; Hannaford, ed., *Washington Merry-Go-Round*, 555–56.

29. Mitchel Levitas, "Will the Real Drew Pearson Please Stand Up?" *New York Times*, August 24, 1968; Scott Meredith to Pearson, January 17, 1969, Abell Papers; Pearson, unpublished diary, January 7, 1969.

30. Katherine [Raley] Watkins oral history.

31. Pilat, *Drew Pearson*, 297; Jack Eisen, "Robert S. Allen, Colorful Newsman in Washington," *Washington Post*, February 25, 1981; John M. Henshaw deposition, June 11, 1962, Anderson Papers; Ken Hoyt and Frances Spatz Leighton, *Drunk before Noon: The Behind-the-Scenes Story of the Washington Press Corps* (Englewood Cliffs, NJ: Prentice-Hall, 1979), 14.

32. Pearson, unpublished diary, March 22, 1969, Pearson Papers; Hannaford, ed., *Washington Merry-Go-Round*, 702–3.

33. Pearson to John N. Wheeler, November 28, 1944, Pearson Papers; Pearson, unpublished diary, June 24, 1969, Pearson Papers; Westbrook Pegler, "He's Not One to Turn the Other Cheek," *Atlanta Constitution*, June 8, 1949; Oliver Pilat, *Pegler: Angry Man of the Press* (Boston: Beacon Press, 1963), 235–39.

34. Pearson, unpublished diary, October 3, 1965, April 15, 20, 1967; Katherine [Raley] Watkins oral history.

35. Dan Tyler Moore to Tyler Abell, August 20, 1974, Abell Papers.

36. Pearson, unpublished diary, July 27, 1969, August 4, 21, 1969, Marian Canty to James R. Young, August 12, 1969, Pearson Papers; WMGR, *Washington Post*, September 2, 1969; "Drew Pearson, Columnist, Dies; Was Often a Center of Conflicts," *New York Times*, September 2, 1969; Robert C. Jensen, "Heart Attack Ends Long Career of a Gadfly of Government," *Washington Post*, September 2, 1969.

37. Tyler Abell to Peter McLaughlin, October 23, 1970, Abell Papers.

38. *Congressional Record*, 91 Cong., 1st sess. (1969), 26022–28; Louis Heren, "Son of a Bitch," *The Times*, January 16, 1975.

39. Tyler Abell to Peter McLaughlin, October 23, 1970, Tyler Abell to George Arnold [c. 1971], Abell Papers; William V. Shannon, "The Sol Hurok of the Washington Press Corps," *New York Times*, April 29, 1973; Evan Thomas, *The Man to See: Edward Bennett Williams: Ultimate Insider: Legendary Trial Lawyer* (New York: Simon & Schuster, 1991), 86.

40. Richard M. Cohen, "Drew Pearson's 7 Wills Untangled," *Washington Post*, January 19, 1975.

41. Richard M. Cohen, "Drew Pearson's 7 Wills Untangled," *Washington Post*, January 19, 1975; Katherine [Raley] Watkins oral history.

Epilogue
1. Pearson, unpublished diary, August 21, 1968, Pearson Papers.

2. Warren Woods to Tyler Abell, September 22, 1969, Abell Papers;
Natalie Robins, *Alien Ink: The FBI's War on Freedom of Expression*
(New York: William Morrow and Company, 1992), 146; Susan Sheehan,
"The Anderson Strategy: We Hit You—Pow! Then You Issue a Denial,
and—Bam!—We Really Let You Have It," *New York Times Sunday
Magazine* (August 13, 1972): 11; Jack Anderson with Daryl Gibson, *Peace,
War, and Politics: An Eyewitness Account* (New York: Forge, 1999), 126; Mark
Feldstein, *Poisoning the Press: Richard Nixon, Jack Anderson, and the Rise of
Washington's Scandal Culture* (New York: Farrar, Straus & Giroux, 2010),
112–14; Timothy Mark Chambless, "Muckraker at Work: Columnist Jack
Anderson and the Watergate Scandal, 1972–1974" (PhD diss., University of
Utah, 1987), 54–55.

3. Al Aronowitz, "A Talk with America's Number One Muckraker, Jack
Anderson," *Gallery* [undated], 35–36, Anderson Papers; *Q&A with Brit
Hume*, July 9, 2008, C-SPAN.

4. Chambless, "Muckraker at Work," 81–86; Jack Anderson interview by
Tim Chambless, March 15, 1986, 27, Anderson Papers; Jack Anderson, "An
Alternative Voice Never Stilled," *Washington Post*, April 2, 1985; Anderson
and Gibson, *Peace, War, and Politics*, 415.

5. Jack Anderson, "Pearson Foresaw U.N. Failures," *Washington Post*,
December 13, 1971; Feldstein, *Poisoning the Press*, 155–74, 200, 265–
66; see Jack Anderson with George Clifford, *The Anderson Papers*
(New York: Random House, 1973).

6. White House tape, December 22, 1971, cited in Feldstein, *Poisoning the
Press*, 182; Bob Woodward, "Hunt Told Associates of Orders to Kill Jack
Anderson," *Washington Post*, September 21, 1975; "Hunt: Plot Not to Kill,
Just Drug Anderson," *Washington Star*, September 29, 1975.

7. The Drew Pearson Foundation gave annual awards for investigative
reporting from 1971 to 1974 and was later dissolved. Feldstein, *Poisoning
the Press*, 291–312; Anderson with Clifford, *The Anderson Papers*, 128–30;
Tony Kornheiser, "Jack Anderson & His Crusading Crew," *Washington
Post*, August 7, 1983; Jack Anderson interview, May 23, 1979, Studs Terkel
Radio Archive; Chambless, "Muckraker at Work," 137, 149; Jack Anderson
interview by Tim Chambless, March 15, 1986, 12–15, Anderson Papers; "3 at
Post Get Prize for Probe," *Washington Post*, November 22, 1972.

8. Neil A. Gabler, *Wits & Sages* (Baltimore: Johns Hopkins University Press,
1984), 24; Douglas Martin, "Jack Anderson, Investigative Journalist Who
Angered the Powerful, Dies at 83," *New York Times*, December 18, 2005;
Howard Kurtz, "Jack Anderson, Gentleman with a Rake," *Washington Post*,
December 18, 2005.

9. William L. Claiborne, "Eagleton Says Story 'Damnable,'" *Washington Post*,
July 28, 1972; Maxine Cheshire, "Anderson on Eagleton: A Charge That
Didn't Stand Up," *Washington Post*, July 29, 1972; Sally Quinn, "William
True Davis: A Long Way from St. Joseph, Mo.," *Washington Post*, August 1,
1972; "Anderson Makes Full Retraction," *Washington Post*, August 2, 1972;

WMGR, *Washington Post*, August 5, 1973; Steve Weinberg, "What Modern Muckrakers Can Learn from an Old Pro's Triumphs and Blunders," *Columbia Journalism Review* (December 1989): 39; Herman C. Ahrens, "Jack Anderson: Washington's Watchdog," *Youth* (September 1973): 12.

10. David Corn, "Mellowing of a Muckraker," *The Nation* (November 14, 1987): 558; Walt Harrison, "The Making of a Muckraker," *Washington Post Magazine* (June 10, 1990): 44; Jack Anderson interview by Tim Chambless, 34; Howard Kurtz, "Jack Anderson Column in Jeopardy," *Washington Post*, October 15, 1991; Kurtz, "The Muckraker and the Oil Spill," *Washington Post*, December 22, 1992; Kurtz, "Jack Anderson, Gentleman with a Rake."

11. Anderson interview by Tim Chambless, March 15, 1986, 34, Anderson Papers; Richard Harwood, "Two from the Old School," *Washington Post*, August 5, 1997.

12. "Dear Readers," *Washington Post*, January 24, 1997; Mark Feldstein, "The Last Muckraker," *Washington Post*, July 28, 2004; Feldstein, *Poisoning the Press*, 353, 366–68. After Anderson's retirement, a diminished version of the "Washington Merry-Go-Round" continued under software executive Douglas Cohn and *Newsweek* reporter Eleanor Clift.

13. *Detroit Free Press v. Ashcroft* (6th Cir. 2002).

14. Kurt Wimmer and Stephen Kiehl, "Prosecution of Journalists under the Espionage Act? Not So Fast," *Communications Lawyer* 32 (Spring 2017): 24–29; Hadas Gold, "Donald Trump: We're Going to 'Open Up' Libel Laws," *Politico*, February 26, 2016; Sydney Embernov, "Can Libel Law Be Changed under Trump?" *New York Times*, November 13, 2016.

15. Eric Alterman, *What Liberal Media? The Truth about Bias and the News* (New York: Basic Books, 2003), 70–80; see also Victor Pickard, *America's Battle for Media Democracy: The Triumph of Corporate Liberalism and the Future of Media Reform* (New York: Cambridge University Press, 2014), 1; and Natalie Fenton, ed., *New Media, Old News: Journalism and Democracy in the Digital Age* (Thousand Oaks, CA: Sage, 2010).

16. WMGR, February 28, 1951, AU.

BIBLIOGRAPHY

———

MANUSCRIPT COLLECTIONS

Abell, Tyler. Papers. Potomac, Maryland
Alsop, Joseph and Stewart. Papers. Library of Congress
Anderson, Jack. Papers. George Washington University Library Special Collections
Federal Bureau of Investigations Record, National Archives and Records
    Administration
Krock, Arthur. Papers. Princeton University, Seeley Mudd Library
Pearson, Drew. Papers. Library of Congress [cited as Pearson Papers, LC]
Pearson, Drew. Papers. Lyndon B. Johnson Presidential Library [cited as Pearson
    Papers]
Pearson Family. Papers. American University Library Special Collections [cited as
    Pearson Family Papers]
Pearson, Paul M. Papers. Friends Historical Library, Swarthmore College [cited as
    Paul Pearson Papers]
Rosenblatt, Maurice. Papers. Library of Congress
Vassiliev, Alexander. Papers. Library of Congress

ONLINE ARCHIVES

American University Audio Visual Archives: https://www.american.edu/library/
    mediaservices/index.cfm
Churchill Archives Online: http://www.churchillarchive.com/
C-SPAN: https://www.c-span.org/
Drew Pearson's Washington Merry-Go-Round, American University Digital Research
    Archive (AU): https://auislandora.wrlc.org/islandora/object/pearson%3A1

General CIA Records: https://www.cia.gov/library/readingroom/collection/
    general-cia-records
National Public Radio (NPR): https://www.npr.org/series/4564213/historical-archives
National Security Archives: https://nsarchive.gwu.edu/
The Pop History Dig: https://www.pophistorydig.com/
ProQuest Historic Newspapers: https://www.proquest.com/products-services/pq-
    hist-news.html
Studs Terkel Radio Archive: https://studsterkel.wfmt.com/
Venona Documents, National Security Archive: https://www.nsa.gov/news-
    features/declassified-documents/venona/
White House Tapes, Lyndon B. Johnson Presidency, Miller Center, University of
    Virginia: https://prde.upress.virginia.edu/content/johnson

ORAL HISTORIES

Harry S. Truman Presidential Library
Jonathan Daniels, 1963
Ken Hechler, 1985
Cornelius J. Mara, 1971
Stephen J. Spingarn, 1967
Harry H. Vaughn, 1963

Dwight D. Eisenhower Presidential Library
Robert E. Clark, 1978
James C. Hagerty, 1973

John F. Kennedy Presidential Library
Edward R. Bayley, 1968
Roy Cohn, 1971
Edwin Guthman, 1968
Kay Halle, 1967
Frank Mankiewicz, 1969
Pierre Salinger, 1965

Lyndon B. Johnson Presidential Library
Robert S. Allen, 1969
James C. Hagerty 1971
Drew Pearson, 1969

Tyler Abell Family
Bess Abell, 2015
Tyler Abell, 2015–2017
Julie Hall, 2015
Matt Mitchell, 2016
Katherine Raley Watkins, 2017

US Senate Historical Office
Robert G. Baker, 2009
Scott I. Peek, 1992
George A. Smathers, 1989
Francis R. Valeo, 1985
Ruth Young Watt, 1979

NEWSPAPERS

Atlanta Constitution
Baltimore Sun
Boston Globe
Chicago Defender
Chicago Sun-Times
Chicago Tribune
Christian Science Monitor
Daily Mountain Eagle
Detroit Free Press
Hartford Courant
Los Angeles Times
Madison State-Journal
Meridian Star
New York Mirror
New York Times
Philadelphia Record
Pittsburgh Tribune-Review
Politico
Roanoke Times & World
Times of London
Wall Street Journal
Washington Evening Star
Washington Post
Washington Times-Herald
Wilmington Star-News

GOVERNMENT DOCUMENTS

Congressional Record. Washington, DC: Government Printing Office.
U.S. House of Representatives, Committee on Government Operations, *Government Contracts for Small Business*, 83rd Cong., 1st sess. Washington, DC: Government Printing Office, 1953.
U.S. Senate, Committee on Governmental Affairs, *Executive Sessions of the Senate Permanent Subcommittee on Investigations of the Committee on Government Operations, Eighty-Third Congress, First & Second Sessions, 1953–54.* Washington, DC: Government Printing Office, 2003.
U.S. Senate, Subcommittee of the Committee on Post Offices and Post Roads, *Investigation Concerning the Disclosure of Information Obtained Leaked through Censorship.* Washington, DC: Government Printing Office, 1944.

U.S. Senate Committee on Post Offices and Post Roads, *Censorship of Communications under Section 303 of the First War Powers Act*, 78th Cong., 2nd sess., Report 857. Washington, DC: Government Printing Office, 1944.

U.S. Senate Subcommittee of the Committee on Interstate and Foreign Commerce, *Hearings on the Nomination of Robert F. Jones to the Federal Communications Commission*, 80th Cong., 1st sess. Washington, DC: Government Printing Office, 1947.

U.S. Senate, Committee on Interstate and Foreign Commerce, *Nomination of Lewis L. Strauss*, 86th Cong, 1st sess. Washington, DC: Government Printing Office, 1959.

Public Papers of the Presidents of the United States, *Harry S. Truman, January 1 to December 31, 1949*. Washington, DC: Government Printing Office, 1964.

U.S. Department of State, *Foreign Relations of the United States*. Washington, DC: Government Printing Office, 1954, 1963, 1965.

COURT CASES

Detroit Free Press v. Ashcroft (6th Cir. 2002)

Dodd v. Pearson, 279 F. Supp. 101 (D.D.C. 1968)

Drew Pearson v. Joseph McCarthy, et al., Civil Action No 897-51, U.S. District Court for the District of Columbia.

Gariepy v. Pearson et al., 207 F.2d 15 (D.C. Cir. 1953).

McAdams v. McSurely, 438 U.S. 189 (1978), 438 U.S. 189.

Alan McSurely and Margaret McSurely v. John K. McClellan, et al., Thomas Ratliff, Individually and as Sometime Commonwealth Attorney for Pike County Kentucky, 753 F.2d 88 (1985), U.S. Court of Appeals for the District of Columbia Circuit.

Alan McSurely and Margaret McSurely v. John J. McClellan et al., 521 F.2d 1024 (D.C. Cir. 1975), U.S. Court of Appeals for the District of Columbia Circuit.

Monitor Patriot Co. v. Roy, 401 U.S. 265 (1971).

New York Times Co. v. Sullivan, 376 U.S. 254 (1964).

Powell v. McCormack, 395 U.S. 486 (1969).

THESES

Chambless, Timothy Mark. "Columnist Jack Anderson, the Secular Evangelist: Five Speeches in Utah between 1972 and 1975." Master's thesis in Speech Communication, University of Utah, 1977.

Chambless, Timothy Mark. "Muckraker at Work: Columnist Jack Anderson and the Watergate Scandal, 1972–1974." Ph.D. diss., University of Utah, 1987.

BOOKS

Abell, Tyler, ed. *Drew Pearson Diaries, 1949–1959*. New York: Holt, Rinehart & Winston, 1974.

Adams, John G. *Without Precedent: The Story of the Death of McCarthyism*. New York: W. W. Norton, 1983.

Allen, Craig, *Eisenhower and the Mass Media: Peace, Prosperity, and Prime-Time TV*. Chapel Hill: University of North Carolina Press, 1993.

Allen, Robert S. *Lucky Forward, The History of Patton's Third U.S. Army*. New York: Vanguard Press, 1947.

[Allen, Robert S., and Drew Pearson]. *More Washington Merry-Go-Round*. New York: Horace Liveright, 1932.

[Allen, Robert S., and Drew Pearson]. *Washington Merry-Go-Round*. New York: Horace Liveright, 1931.

Alsop, Joseph, with Adam Platt. *"I've Seen the Best of It": Memoirs*. New York: W. W. Norton, 1992.

Alsop, Stewart. *The Center: People and Power in Political Washington*. New York: Harper & Row, 1968.

Alterman, Eric. *What Liberal Media? The Truth about Bias and the News*. New York: Basic Books, 2003.

Anderson, Jack. *Washington Expose*. Washington, DC: Public Affairs Press, 1967.

Anderson, Jack, and James Boyd. *Confessions of a Muckraker: The Inside Story of Life in Washington during the Truman, Eisenhower, Kennedy and Johnson Years*. New York: Random House, 1979.

Anderson, Jack, with George Clifford. *The Anderson Papers*. New York: Random House, 1973.

Anderson, Jack, with Daryl Gibson. *Peace, War, and Politics: An Eyewitness Account*. New York: Forge, 1999.

Anderson, Jack, and Ronald W. May, *McCarthy: The Man, the Senator, the "Ism."* Boston: Beacon Press, 1952.

Anderson, Douglas A. *A "Washington Merry-Go-Round" of Libel Actions*. Chicago: Nelson-Hall, 1980.

Anderson, Patrick. *The President's Men: White House Assistants of Franklin D. Roosevelt, Harry S Truman, Dwight D. Eisenhower, John F. Kennedy and Lyndon B. Johnson*. Garden City, NY: Doubleday, 1968.

Anson, Robert Sam. *Exile: The Unquiet Oblivion of Richard M. Nixon*. New York: Simon & Schuster, 1984.

Bagdikian, Ben H. *The Effete Conspiracy and Other Crimes by the Press*. New York: Harper & Row, 1972.

Baime, A. J. *The Accidental President: Harry S. Truman and the Four Months That Changed the World*. New York: Houghton Mifflin Harcourt, 2017.

Baker, Bobby, with Larry L. King. *Wheeling and Dealing: Confessions of a Capitol Hill Operator*. New York: W. W. Norton, 1978.

Banner, James M., Jr., ed. *Presidential Misconduct: From George Washington to Today*. New York: The New Press, 2019.

Bayley, Edwin R. *Joe McCarthy and the Press*. New York: Pantheon Books, 1981.

Bealle, Morris A. *All America Louse: A Candid Biography of Drew A. Pearson*. Washington: Columbia Publishing Company, 1965.

Bell, Jack. *The Splendid Misery: The Story of the Presidency and Power Politics at Close Range*. Garden City, NY: Doubleday, 1960.

Bennett, Edward M. *Franklin D. Roosevelt and the Search for Victory: American-Soviet Relations, 1939–1945.* Wilmington, DE: Scholarly Resources, 1990.

Beschloss, Michael. *Kennedy v. Khrushchev: The Crisis Years, 1960–1963.* New York: Edward Burlingame, 1991.

Beschloss, Michael. *Mayday: Eisenhower, Khrushchev and the U-2 Affair.* New York: Harper & Row, 1986.

Beschloss, Michael. *Reaching for Glory: Lyndon Johnson's Secret White House Tapes, 1964–1965.* New York: Simon & Schuster, 2001.

Beschloss, Michael, ed. *Jacqueline Kennedy: Historic Conversations on Life with John F. Kennedy.* New York: Hyperion, 2011.

Beschloss, Michael, ed. *Taking Charge: The Johnson White House Tapes, 1963–1964.* New York: Simon & Schuster. 1997.

Best, Gary Dean. *The Critical Press and the New Deal: The Press Versus Presidential Power, 1933–1938.* Westport, CT: Praeger, 1993.

Bland, Larry I., ed. *The Papers of George Catlett Marshall.* Baltimore: Johns Hopkins University Press, 1986, vol. 2.

Bliss, Edward, Jr. *Now the News: The Story of Broadcast Journalism.* New York: Columbia University Press, 1991.

Boyd, James. *Above the Law.* New York: New American Library, 1968.

Bradlee, Ben. *A Good Life: Newspapering and Other Adventures.* New York: Simon & Schuster, 1995.

Branch, Taylor. *Parting the Waters: America in the King Years, 1954–63.* New York: Simon & Schuster, 1988.

Buckley, William F., Jr. *Cancel Your Own Goddam Subscription: Notes and Asides from National Review.* New York: Basic Books, 2007.

Bulman, David, ed. *Molders of Opinion.* Milwaukee: Bruce Publishing, 1945.

Burk, Robert F. *Dwight D. Eisenhower: Hero and Politician.* Boston: Twayne, 1986.

Campbell, Tracy. *Short of the Glory: The Fall and Redemption of Edward F. Prichard, Jr.* Lexington: University Press of Kentucky, 1998.

Caro, Robert A. *The Years of Lyndon Johnson: Master of the Senate.* New York: Alfred A. Knopf, 2002.

Caro, Robert A. *The Years of Lyndon Johnson: Means of Ascent.* New York: Alfred A. Knopf, 1990.

Caro, Robert A. *The Years of Lyndon Johnson: The Passage of Power.* New York: Alfred A. Knopf, 2012.

Caro, Robert A. *The Years of Lyndon Johnson: The Path to Power.* New York: Alfred A. Knopf, 1982.

Cecil, Matthew. *Branding Hoover's FBI: How the Boss's PR Men Sold the Bureau to America.* Lawrence: University Press of Kansas, 2016.

Cerf, Bennett. *At Random: The Reminiscences of Bennett Cerf.* New York: Random House, 2002.

Chaney, Lindsey, and Michael Cieply. *The Hearsts: Family and Empire—The Later Years.* New York: Simon & Schuster, 1981.

Charles, Douglas M. *Hoover's War on Gays: Exposing the FBI's "Sex Deviates"
Program.* Lawrence: University Press of Kansas, 2015.

Charns, Alexander. *Cloak and Gavel: FBI Wiretaps, Bugs, Information, and the
Supreme Court.* Urbana: University of Illinois Press, 1992.

Clague, Mark, ed. *The Memoirs of Alton Augustus Adams, Sr.: First Black
Bandmaster of the United States Navy.* Berkeley: University of California
Press, 2008.

Clymer, Kenton J. *Quest for Freedom: The United States and India's Independence.*
New York: Columbia University Press, 1995.

Cochran, Bert. *Harry Truman and the Crisis Presidency.* New York: Funk &
Wagnalls, 1973.

Cohn, Roy. *McCarthy.* New York: American Library, 1968.

Collins, Gail. *Scorpion Tongues: Gossip, Celebrity, and American Politics.* New York:
William Morrow, 1998.

Conant, Jennet. *The Irregulars: Roald Dahl and the British Spy Ring in Wartime
Washington.* New York: Simon & Schuster, 2008.

Costanzo, Michael B. *Author in Chief: The Presidents as Writers from Washington to
Trump.* Jefferson, NC: McFarland, 2019.

Craig, R. Bruce. *Treasonable Doubt: The Harry Dexter White Spy Case.* Lawrence:
University Press of Kansas, 2004.

Crispell, Brian Lewis. *Testing the Limits: George Armistead Smathers and Cold War
America.* Athens: University of Georgia Press, 1999.

Crosby, Donald F. *God, Church, and Flag: Senator Joseph R. McCarthy and
the Catholic Church, 1950–1957.* Chapel Hill: University of North Carolina
Press, 1978.

Dagnes, Alison, and Mark Sachleben, eds. *Scandal! An Interdisciplinary
Approach to the Consequences, Outcomes, and Significance of Political Scandals.*
New York: Bloomsbury, 2013.

Dallek, Robert. *An Unfinished Life: John F. Kennedy, 1917–1963.* Boston: Little,
Brown, 2003.

Deane, John R. *The Strange Alliance: The Story of Our Efforts at Wartime Co-
Operation with Russia.* New York: Viking, 1947.

Delgadillo, Charles. *Crusader for Democracy: The Political Life of William Allen
White.* Lawrence: University Press of Kansas, 2018.

Donovan, Robert J. *Boxing the Kangaroo: A Reporter's Memoir.* Columbia:
University of Missouri Press, 2000.

Downie, Leonard, Jr. *The New Muckrakers.* Washington, DC: New Republic Book
Company, 1976.

Drewry, John E., ed. *More Post Biographies: Articles of Enduring Interest about
Famous Journalists and Journals and Other Subjects Journalistic.* Athens:
University of Georgia Press, 1947.

Egerton, John. *Speak Now against the Day: The Generation before the Civil Rights
Movement in the South.* New York: Alfred A. Knopf, 1994.

Elliott, Carl, Sr., and Michael D'Orso. *The Cost of Courage: The Journey of an
American Congressman.* Tuscaloosa: University of Alabama Press, 2001.

Evans, M. Stanton. *Blacklisted by History: The Untold Story of Senator Joe McCarthy and His Fight against America's Enemies.* New York: Crown Forum, 2007.

Farber, Doris. *The Life of Lorena Hickok: E.R.'s Friend.* New York: William Morrow, 1980.

Fariello, Griffin. *Red Scare: Memories of the American Inquisition.* New York: Avon Books, 1995.

Farr, Finis. *Fair Enough: The Life of Westbrook Pegler.* New Rochelle, NY: Arlington House, 1975.

Farrell, John A. *Richard Nixon: The Life.* New York: Doubleday, 2017.

Fay, Paul B., Jr. *The Pleasure of His Company.* New York: Harper & Row, 1966.

Feeley, Kathleen A., and Jennifer Frost, eds. *When Private Talk Goes Public: Gossip in American History.* New York: Palgrave Macmillan, 2014.

Fehrman, Craig. *Author in Chief: The Untold Story of Our Presidents and the Books They Wrote.* New York: Avid Reader Press, 2020.

Feldstein, Mark. *Poisoning the Press: Richard Nixon, Jack Anderson, and the Rise of Washington's Scandal Culture.* New York: Farrar, Straus & Giroux, 2010.

Ferrell, Robert H., ed. *Dear Bess: The Letters from Harry to Bess Truman, 1910–1959.* New York: W. W. Norton, 1983.

Ferrell, Robert H., ed. *Off the Record: The Private Papers of Harry S. Truman.* New York: Harper & Row, 1980.

Fisher, Charles. *The Columnists.* New York: Howell, Soskin, 1944.

Frankel, Max. *The Times of My Life and My Life with the Times.* New York: Random House, 1999.

Freidin, Seymour K. *A Sense of the Senate.* New York: Dodd, Mead, 1972.

Gabler, Neil. *Winchell: Gossip, Power, and the Cult of Celebrity.* New York: Vintage, 1995.

Galambos, Louis, et al., eds. *The Papers of Dwight David Eisenhower.* Baltimore: Johns Hopkins University Press, 1978–2001, vols. 8–20.

Gans, Herbert J. *Deciding What's News: A Study of CBS Evening News, NBC Nightly News, Newsweek, and Time.* New York: Vintage Books, 1980.

Gellman, Irwin F. *Secret Affairs: Franklin Roosevelt, Cordell Hull, and Sumner Welles.* Baltimore: Johns Hopkins University Press, 1995.

Gillette, Michael L. *Lady Bird Johnson: An Oral History.* New York: Oxford University Press, 2012.

Glantz, Mary E. *FDR and the Soviet Union: The President's Battles over Foreign Policy.* Lawrence: University Press of Kansas, 2005.

Godfrey, Barbara Pearson Lange. *Man of Chautauqua and His Caravans of Culture: The Life of Paul M. Pearson.* Swarthmore, PA: privately printed, 2001.

Goldman, Eric F. *The Tragedy of Lyndon Johnson.* New York: Alfred A. Knopf, 1969.

Gould, Harold A. *Sikhs, Swamis, Students and Spies: The India Lobby in the United States, 1900–1946.* London: Sage, 2006.

Graff, Frank Warren. *Strategy of Involvement: A Diplomatic Biography of Sumner Welles.* New York: Garland, 1988.

Grauer, Neil A. *Wits & Sages.* Baltimore: Johns Hopkins University Press, 1984.

Hamby, Alonzo L. *Man of the People: A Life of Harry S. Truman.*
New York: Oxford University Press, 1995.

Hamilton, Charles V. *Adam Clayton Powell, Jr.: The Political Biography of an American Dilemma.* New York: Atheneum, 1991.

Hammond, William M. *Public Affairs: The Military and the Media, 1962–1968.* Washington, DC: Center of Military History, United States Army, 1988.

Hannaford, Peter, ed. *Washington Merry-Go-Round: The Drew Pearson Diaries, 1960–1969.* Lincoln, NE: Potomac Books, 2015.

Haynes, John Earl, and Harvey Klehr. *Venona: Decoding Soviet Espionage in America.* New Haven: Yale University Press, 1999.

Haynes, John Earl, Harvey Klehr, and Alexander Vassiliev. *Spies: The Rise and Fall of the KGB in America.* New Haven: Yale University Press, 2009.

Hechler, Ken. *Working with Truman: A Personal Memoir of the White House Years.* Columbia: University of Missouri Press, 1982.

Henderson, Harold Paulk. *The Politics of Change in Georgia: A Political Biography of Ellis Arnall.* Athens: University of Georgia Press, 1991.

Hersh, Seymour M. *Reporter: A Memoir.* New York: Random House, 2018.

Hiebert, Ray Eldon. *The Press in Washington: Sixteen Top Newsmen Tell How the News Is Collected, Witten, and Communicated from the World's Most Important Capital.* New York: Dodd, Mead, 1966.

Hochschild, Adam. *Spain in Our Hearts: Americans in the Spanish Civil War, 1936–1939.* Boston: Houghton Mifflin Harcourt, 2015.

Hollinger, David A. *Protestants Abroad: How Missionaries Tried to Change the World but Changed America.* Princeton: Princeton University Press, 2017.

Holsaert, Faith S., et al., eds. *Hands on the Freedom Plow: Personal Accounts by Women in SNCC.* Urbana: University of Illinois Press, 2010.

Hoyt, Ken, and Frances Spatz Leighton. *Drunk before Noon: The Behind-the-Scenes Story of the Washington Press Corps.* Englewood Cliffs, NJ: Prentice-Hall, 1979.

Hume, Brit. *Inside Story.* Garden City, NY: Doubleday, 1974.

Ickes, Harold L. *The Secret Diary of Harold L. Ickes.* New York: Simon & Schuster, 1953–1954, vols. 1–3.

Janeway, Michael. *The Fall of the House of Roosevelt: Brokers of Ideas and Power from FDR to LBJ.* New York: Columbia University Press, 2004.

Johnson, David K. *The Lavender Scare: The Cold War Prosecution of Gays and Lesbians in the Federal Government.* Chicago: University of Chicago Press, 2004.

Johnson, Haynes. *The Age of Anxiety: McCarthyism to Terrorism.* Orlando, FL: Harcourt, 2005.

Johnson, Lady Bird. *A White House Diary.* New York: Holt, Rinehart and Winston, 1970.

Johnson, Richard Tanner. *Managing the White House: An Intimate Study of the Presidency.* New York: Harper & Row, 1974.

Johnson, Robert David. *All the Way with LBJ: The Presidential Election of 1964.* New York: Cambridge University Press, 2009.

Kabaservice, Geoffrey. *Rule and Ruin: The Downfall of Moderation and the Destruction of the Republican Party, from Eisenhower to the Tea Party*. New York: Oxford University Press, 2012.

Keith, Caroline H. *"For Hell and a Brown Mule," The Biography of Senator Millard E. Tydings*. Lanham, MD: Madison Books, 1991.

Klehr, Harvey. *The Millionaire Was a Soviet Mole: The Twisted Life of David Karr*. New York: Encounter Books, 2019.

Klehr, Harvey, and Ronald Radosh. *The Amerasia Spy Case: Prelude to McCarthyism*. Chapel Hill: University of North Carolina Press, 1996.

Kline, Gil. *Reliable Source: 100 Years at the National Press Club*. Nashville, TN: Turner, 2008.

Kluckhohn, Frank L., and Jay Franklin. *The Drew Pearson Story*. Chicago: C. Hallberg, 1967.

Klurfeld, Herman. *Behind the Lines: The World of Drew Pearson*. Englewood Cliffs, NJ: Prentice-Hall, 1968.

Koskoff, David E. *Joseph P. Kennedy: A Life and Times*. Englewood Cliffs, NJ: Prentice-Hall, 1974.

Koskoff, David E. *The Senator from Central Casting: The Rise, Fall, and Resurrection of Thomas J. Dodd*. New Haven: New American Political Press, 2011.

Krock, Arthur. *In the Nation, 1932–1966*. New York: McGraw-Hill, 1966.

Krock, Arthur. *Memoirs: Sixty Years on the Firing Line*. New York: Funk & Wagnalls, 1968.

Kurtz-Phelan, Daniel. *The China Mission; George Marshall's Unfinished War, 1945–1947*. New York: W. W. Norton, 2018.

Lamphere, Ralph J., with Tim Shachterman. *The FBI-KGB War: A Special Agent's Story*. Macon, GA: Mercer University Press, 1995.

Leahy, William D. *I Was There: The Personal Story of the Chief of Staff to Presidents Roosevelt and Truman, Based on His Notes and Diaries Made at the Time*. New York: McGraw-Hill, 1950.

Levingston, Steven. *Kennedy and King: The President, the Pastor, and the Battle over Civil Rights*. New York: Hachette, 2017.

Lewis, Anthony. *Make No Law: The Sullivan Case and the First Amendment*. New York: Random House, 1991.

Lichtman, Robert M., and Ronald D. Cohen. *Deadly Farce: Harvey Matusow and the Informer System in the McCarthy Era*. Champaign: University of Illinois Press, 2004.

Longley, Kyle. *LBJ's 1968: Power, Politics, and the Presidency in America's Year of Upheaval*. New York: Cambridge University Press, 2018.

Mahl, Thomas E. *Desperate Deception: British Covert Operations in the United States, 1939–44*. Washington, DC: Brassey's, 1998.

Manchester, William. *American Caesar: Douglas MacArthur, 1880–1964*. Boston: Little, Brown, 1978.

Martin, George. *Madam Secretary, Frances Perkins*. Boston: Houghton Mifflin, 1976.

Martin, Ralph G. *Cissy*. New York: Simon & Schuster, 1979.

Marton, Kati. *True Believer: Stalin's Last American Spy*. New York: Simon & Schuster, 2016.

Matthews, Donald R. *U.S. Senators and Their World*. Chapel Hill: University of North Carolina Press, 1960.

Matusow, Harvey. *False Witness*. New York: Cameron & Kahn, 1955.

McClendon, Sarah. *My Eight Presidents*. New York: Wyden Books, 1978.

McDaniel, Rodger. *Dying for Joe McCarthy's Sins: The Suicide of Wyoming Senator Lester Hunt*. Cody, WY: WordsWorth, 2013.

Michaeli, Ethan. *The Defender: How the Legendary Black Newspaper Changed America, from the Age of Pullman Porters to the Age of Obama*. Boston: Houghton Mifflin Harcourt, 2016.

Mitchell, Franklin D. *Harry S. Truman and the News Media: Contentious Relations*. Columbia: University of Missouri Press, 1998.

Morris, Roger. *Richard Milhous Nixon: The Rise of an American Politician*. New York: Henry Holt, 1990.

Newman, Robert P. *Owen Lattimore and the "Loss" of China*. Berkeley: University of California Press, 1992.

Nichols, David A. *Eisenhower 1956: The President's Year of Crisis: Suez and the Brink of War*. New York: Simon & Schuster, 2011.

Nichols, David A. *Ike and McCarthy: Dwight Eisenhower's Secret Campaign against Joseph McCarthy*. New York: Simon & Schuster, 2017.

Nixon, Richard M. *RN: The Memoirs of Richard Nixon*. New York: Grosset & Dunlap, 1978.

Olson, James C. *Stuart Symington: A Life*. Columbia: University of Missouri Press, 2003.

Oshinsky. David M. *A Conspiracy So Immense: The World of Joe McCarthy*. New York: The Free Press, 1983.

Oudes, Bruce, ed. *From: The President: Richard Nixon's Secret Files*. New York: Harper & Row, 1989.

Patterson, James. *Mr. Republican: A Biography of Robert A. Taft*. Boston: Houghton Mifflin, 1972.

Pearson, Drew. *The President*. Garden City, NY: Doubleday, 1970.

Pearson, Drew. *The Senator*. Garden City, NY: Doubleday, 1968.

Pearson, Drew, with Jack Anderson. *The Case against Congress: A Compelling Indictment of Corruption on Capitol Hill*. New York: Simon & Schuster, 1968.

Pearson, Drew, with Jack Anderson, *U.S.A.: Second Class Power?* New York: Simon & Schuster, 1958.

Pearson, Drew, with Robert S. Allen. *The Nine Old Men*. Garden City, NY: Doubleday, Doran, 1936.

Pearson, Drew, with Constantine Brown. *The American Diplomatic Game*. New York: Doubleday, Doran, 1935.

Pierpoint, Robert. *At the White House: Assignment to Six Presidents*. New York: Putnam, 1981.

Pilat, Oliver Ramsay. *Drew Pearson: An Unauthorized Biography*. New York: Harper's Magazine Press, 1973.

Pilat, Oliver Ramsay. *Pegler: Angry Man of the Press.* Boston: Beacon Press, 1963.

Pleasants, Julian M. *Buncombe Bob: The Life and Times of Robert Rice Reynolds.* Chapel Hill: University of North Carolina Press, 2000.

Pogue, Forrest C. *George C. Marshall: Organizer of Victory.* New York: Viking, 1973.

Rauchway, Eric. *Winter War: Hoover, Roosevelt, and the First Clash over the New Deal.* New York: Basic Books, 2018.

Rees, David. *Harry Dexter White: A Study in Paradox.* New York: Coward, McCann & Geoghegan, 1973.

Reeves, Thomas C. *The Life and Times of Joe McCarthy.* New York: Stein and Day, 1982.

Reston, James. *Sketches in the Sand.* New York: Alfred A. Knopf, 1967.

Rickard, John Nelson, ed. *Forward with Patton: The World War II Diary of Colonel Robert S. Allen.* Lexington: University Press of Kentucky, 2017.

Ritchie, Donald A. *Electing FDR: The New Deal Campaign of 1932.* Lawrence: University Press of Kansas, 2007.

Ritchie, Donald A. *James M. Landis: Dean of the Regulators.* Cambridge, MA: Harvard University Press, 1980.

Ritchie, Donald A. *Press Gallery: Congress and the Washington Correspondents.* Cambridge, MA: Harvard University Press, 1991.

Ritchie, Donald A. *Reporting from Washington: The History of the Washington Press Corps.* New York: Oxford University Press, 2005.

Rivers, William L. *The Opinionmakers.* Westport, CT: Greenwood Press, 1965.

Roberts, Chalmers. *First Rough Draft: A Journalist's Journal of Our Times.* New York: Praeger, 1973.

Roberts, Chalmers. *The Washington Post: The First 100 Years.* Boston: Houghton Mifflin, 1977.

Robins, Natalie, *Alien Ink: The FBI's War on Freedom of Expression.* New York: William Morrow, 1992.

Romerstein, Herbert, and Eric Briendel. *The Venona Secrets: Exposing Soviet Espionage and America's Traitors.* Washington, DC: Regnery Publishing, 2000.

Ross, Ishbel. Ladies of the Press: *The Story of Women in Journalism by an Insider.* New York: Harper & Brothers, 1936.

Salinger, Pierre. *With Kennedy.* New York: Avon, 1967.

Salisbury, Harrison E. *Without Fear or Favor: The New York Times and Its Times.* New York: Times Books, 1980.

Schultz, Budd, and Ruth Schultz, eds. *It Did Happen Here: Recollections of Political Repression in America.* Berkeley: University of California Press, 1989.

Smith, Amanda. *Newspaper Titan: The Infamous Life and Monumental Times of Cissy Patterson.* New York: Alfred A. Knopf, 2011.

Sorenson, Theodore. *Counselor: A Life at the Edge of History.* New York: HarperCollins, 2008.

Steel, Ronald. *Walter Lippmann and the American Century.* Boston: Little, Brown, 1980.

Summers, Anthony. *Official and Confidential: The Secret Life of J. Edgar Hoover.* New York: G. P. Putnam's Sons, 1993.

Summers, Anthony, with Robbyn Swan. *The Arrogance of Power: The Secret World of Richard Nixon*. New York: Viking, 2000.

Sweeney, Michael S. *Secrets of Victory: The Office of Censorship and the American Press and Radio in World War II*. Chapel Hill: University of North Carolina Press, 2001.

Theoharis, Athan G., and John Stuart Cox. *The Boss: J. Edgar Hoover and the Great American Inquisition*. Philadelphia: Temple University Press, 1988.

Thomas, Evan. *The Man to See: Edward Bennett Williams: Ultimate Insider: Legendary Trial Lawyer*. New York: Simon & Schuster, 1991.

Trohan, Walter. *Political Animals: Memoirs of a Sentimental Cynic*. Garden City, NY: Doubleday, 1975.

Truman, Margaret. *Bess W. Truman*. New York: William Morrow, 1986.

Truman, Margaret. *Harry S. Truman*. New York: William Morrow, 1973.

Tye, Larry. *Bobby Kennedy: The Making of a Liberal Icon*. New York: Random House, 2016.

Tye, Larry. *Demagogue: The Life and Long Shadow of Senator Joe McCarthy*. Boston: Houghton Mifflin Harcourt, 2020.

Usdin, Steven T. *Bureau of Spies: The Secret Connections between Espionage and Journalism in Washington*. Amherst, NY: Prometheus Books, 2018.

Weil, Martin. *A Pretty Good Club: The Founding Fathers of the U.S. Foreign Service*. New York: W. W. Norton, 1978.

Welles, Benjamin. *Sumner Welles: FDR's Global Strategist, A Biography*. New York: St. Martin's Press, 1997.

West, Nigel, ed. *The Secret History of British Intelligence in the Americas, 1940–1945*. New York: Fromm International, 1999.

Whalen, Thomas J. *Kennedy versus Lodge: The 1952 Massachusetts Senate Race*. Boston: Northeastern University Press, 2000.

Widmer, Ted, ed. *Listening In: The Secret White House Recordings of John F. Kennedy*. New York: Hyperion, 2012.

Winchell, Walter. *Winchell Exclusive*. Englewood Cliffs, NJ: Prentice-Hall, 1975.

Witcover, Jules. *85 Days: The Last Campaign of Robert Kennedy*. New York: Quill, 1988 [1969].

Woods, Randall B. *LBJ: Architect of American Ambition*. New York: Free Press, 2006.

Wunderlin, Clarence W., Jr., et al., eds. *The Papers of Robert A. Taft*. Kent: Kent State University Press, 2003–2006, vols. 3–4.

ARTICLES AND BOOK CHAPTERS

Allen, Robert S. "My Pal, Drew Pearson." *Collier's* 124 (July 30, 1949): 14–16.

Anderson, Douglas A., and Dan Pingelton, "Examination of the Content of the 'Washington Merry-Go-Round.'" *Newspaper Research Journal* 3 (April 1982): 45–51.

Anderson, Patrick. "The Truth about Drew Pearson." *Washingtonian* 3 (June 1968): 37–41+.

Armour, Lawrence A. "Corporate Cinderella." *Barron's National Business and Financial Weekly* 43 (May 6, 1963): 5, 17–19.

Baker, Richard A. "A Slap at the 'Hidden-Hand Presidency': The Senate and the Lewis Strauss Affair." *Congress & The Presidency* 14 (Spring 1987): 1–16.

Bargeron, Carlisle. "Washington's Mighty Penmen." *Nation's Business* 34 (May 1, 1946): 58–60+.

Blumenthal, Sidney. "The Ruins of Georgetown." *New Yorker* 72 (October 21 & 28, 1996): 221–24.

Burtin, Oliver. "'A One-Woman Tea Party': Tax Resistance, Feminism, and Conservatism in the Life of Vivien Kellems." *Journal of Policy History* 28 (January 2016): 162–90.

Casey, Stephen. "The Campaign to Sell a Harsh Peace for Germany to the American Public, 1944–1948." *History* 90 (2005): 62–92.

Champagne, Anthony, and Reed Penny. "Margaret Fallon (Peggy) Palmer: A Portrait of Sam Rayburn's 'Lady Friend.'" *Southwestern Historical Quarterly* 120 (October 2016): 188–214.

"Chronic Liar." *Time* 42 (September 13, 1943): 18–20.

"Congress: A Matter of Ethics." *Newsweek* 67 (April 11, 1966): 29.

Corn, David. "Mellowing of a Muckraker." *The Nation* (November 14, 1987): 541+.

Crawford, Kenneth G. "He Refused to Be Smeared by Pearson." *Saturday Evening Post* 222 (November 16, 1949): 25+.

"Crusading Pays Lee . . . It Took Them from Sixth to *First!*" *Sponsor* 1 (February 1947): 9–14.

Dowling, Tom. "Who Knows What Evil Lurks in the Hearts of Men? Jack Anderson Knows." *Washingtonian* 6 (May 1971): 90–101.

Fried, Richard M. "The Idea of Conspiracy in McCarthy-Era Politics." *Prologue* 34 (Spring 2002): 45–47.

Gold, Victor. "Last of the Muckrakers." *Washingtonian* 32 (October 1997): 37.

"It Will Be Denied, but. . . ." *Time* 68 (November 5, 1956): 89.

Kiefer, L. K. "Drew Pearson's House in Historic Georgetown." *Better Homes & Gardens* 26 (December 1947): 44–45.

Klaw, Spencer. "Dave Karr in the President's Chair." *Fortune* 63 (June 1961): 154–57, 261–66.

Lange, Barbara Pearson. "Keep Your Suspenders Up!" *Swarthmore College Bulletin* (March 1966): 6–10.

Lapham, Lewis H. "The King's Pleasure." *Harper's* 252 (March 1976): 12–18.

Lovett, Christopher C. "On the Side of the Angels and the Fall of Joe McCarthy." *Emporia State Research Studies* 51 (2016): 8–29.

Molinaro, Dennis. "How the Cold War Began . . . with British Help: The Gouzenko Affair Revisited." *Labour* 79 (Spring 2017): 143–55.

"Pearson Smears Again." *National Review* 10 (January 14, 1961): 10–11.

Pearson, Drew. "Confessions of an S.O.B." *Saturday Evening Post* 229 (November 3, 1956): 23–25+; (November 10, 1956): 38–39+; (November 17, 1956): 44–45+; (November 24, 1956): 36+.

Pearson, Drew. "Growing Up in Swarthmore." In *Swarthmore Remembered*, edited by Maralyn Orbison Gillespie, 51–55. Swarthmore, PA: Swarthmore College, 1964.

Pearson, Drew. "How I Became Interested in Racial Justice." *Opportunity* 26 (April 1948): 62.

Pearson, Drew. "Paul Martin Pearson: 1871–1938." *Today's Speech* 7 (September 1959): 9–13.

Pearson, Drew. "The Senate." *Playboy* 16 (November 1969): 119–20+.

Pearson, Luvie Moore. "My Thirty-Six Hours with Khrushchev." *Saturday Evening Post* 235 (April 7, 1962): 70–72.

Pearson, Paul M. "The Chautauqua Movement." *Annals of the American Academy of Political and Social Sciences* 40 (March 1, 1912): 211–16.

Pearson, Paul M., and Barbara Pearson-Lange. "'Unorthodoxy Quakers' at Swarthmore." *Friends Journal* 12 (June 1, 1966): 284–85.

Pope, Dean. "The Senator from Tennessee." *The West Tennessee Historical Society Papers* 22 (1968): 102–22.

Pringle, Henry F. "SRL Washington Poll: Surveying the Capital Correspondents." *Saturday Review of Literature* 27 (October 14, 1944): 17–19.

"Querulous Quaker." *Time* 52 (December 13, 1948): 70–72, 75–76.

Reeves, Richard. "Why Presidents Lie." *George* 5 (May 2000): 54.

Ritchie, Donald A. "Kennedy in Congress." In *A Companion to John F. Kennedy*, edited by Marc J. Silverstone, 33–50. Malden, MA: Wiley Blackwell, 2014.

Ritchie, Donald A. "McCarthyism in Congress: Investigating Communism." In *The American Congress: The Building of Democracy*, edited by Julian Zelizer, 515–28. New York: Houghton Mifflin, 2004.

Rowan, Roy. "The Death of Dave Karr and Other Mysteries." *Fortune* 100 (December 1979): 94–96+.

Sherrill, Robert G. "Drew Pearson: An Interview." *Nation* 209 (July 7, 1969): 7–16.

Steele, Richard W. "News of the 'Good War': World War II News Management." *Journalism Quarterly* 62 (December 1985): 707–716, 783.

"Territories: Fight & Fantasy." *Time* 27 (July 22, 1935): 16–17.

White, William S. "Trying to Find the Shape—If Any—of the News in Washington." *Harper's* 217 (August 1958): 76–80.

Wimmer, Kurt, and Stephen Kiehl. "Prosecution of Journalists under the Espionage Act? Not So Fast." *Communications Lawyer* 32 (Spring 2017): 24–29.

Yoakum, Robert. "The Dodd Case: Those Who Blinked." *Columbia Journalism Review* 6 (Spring 1967): 13–19.

Yoakum, Robert. "Further Notes on Dodd." *Columbia Journalism Review* 6 (Summer 1967): 51–54.

INDEX